Abortion

Abortion

History, Politics, and Reproductive Justice after Morgentaler

Edited by Shannon Stettner,
Kristin Burnett, and Travis Hay

UBCPress · Vancouver · Toronto

26 25 24 23 22 21 20 19 18 17 5 4 3 2 1

Printed in Canada on FSC-certified ancient-forest-free paper (100% post-consumer recycled) that is processed chlorine- and acid-free.

Library and Archives Canada Cataloguing in Publication

Abortion : history, politics, and reproductive justice after Morgentaler / edited by Shannon Stettner, Kristin Burnett, and Travis Hay.

Includes bibliographical references and index.
Issued in print and electronic formats.
ISBN 978-0-7748-3573-2 (hardcover).–ISBN 978-0-7748-3575-6 (PDF).–
ISBN 978-0-7748-3576-3 (EPUB).–ISBN 978-0-7748-3577-0 (Kindle)

1. Abortion–Canada. 2. Abortion–Canada–History. 3. Abortion–Law and legislation–Canada. 4. Abortion–Political aspects–Canada. 5. Reproductive rights–Canada. 6. Women–Health and hygiene–Canada. 7. Women's health services–Canada. I. Stettner, Shannon, editor II. Burnett, Kristin, 1974-, editor III. Hay, Travis A., editor

HQ767.5.C2A245 2017   362.1988'80971   C2017-905918-1
C2017-905919-X

Canadä

UBC Press gratefully acknowledges the financial support for our publishing program of the Government of Canada (through the Canada Book Fund), the Canada Council for the Arts, and the British Columbia Arts Council.

This book has been published with the help of a grant from the Canadian Federation for the Humanities and Social Sciences, through the Awards to Scholarly Publications Program, using funds provided by the Social Sciences and Humanities Research Council of Canada.

Printed and bound in Canada by Friesens

Set in ITC Garamond Std by Marquis Interscipt
Copy editor: Caitlin Gordon-Walker
Proofreader: Kristy Lynn Hankewitz
Indexer: Noeline Bridge
Cover designer: TG Design

UBC Press
The University of British Columbia
2029 West Mall
Vancouver, BC V6T 1Z2
www.ubcpress.ca

Contents

Part 2: Experience

Part 3: Politics

Part 4: Discourse and Reproductive Justice

Acknowledgments

Many people are responsible for making this collection possible. First, we want to acknowledge Dr. Henry Morgentaler, whose life and passing inspired us to reflect on the state of abortion and abortion studies in Canada. His dedication and compassion were inspiring. We are equally indebted to and inspired by the countless activists who worked alongside Morgentaler and who were every bit as crucial as he was to the legal victories of the pro-choice movement. We remain grateful that they and others like them continue to advocate tirelessly to maintain, support, and further reproductive justice.

The activists, academics, and academic activists who contributed to this volume have been patient and supportive throughout a long process. We are thankful for their commitment to this collection. We are inspired by their work, which is vigorous, intelligent, and tremendously important. We are especially encouraged by the way in which their work serves as an exemplar of what activist academia can be. We extend a special thank you to Tracy Penny Light for her early involvement in, and enthusiasm for, the project. Tracy's strong belief in the importance of blending historical studies with examinations of contemporary politics informs the final structure of the book.

We are grateful to the anonymous reviewers who provided thoughtful feedback that made this collection stronger. And finally, we thank UBC Press and especially Darcy Cullen and Lesley Erickson for their support and guidance throughout the editorial process.

This book is dedicated to our human and (mostly) furry families: Adrian, Angie, Bob, Bons, Frankie, George, Kiera, Levon, Mary, Sam, Stevie, and Trigger.

Abortion

Introduction

Shannon Stettner, Kristin Burnett, and Travis Hay

THIS BOOK AROSE OUT of a desire to revisit the study of abortion history and politics, as well as to draw attention to the nascent but growing and dynamic scholarship on reproductive justice in Canada. In undertaking this exploration, we begin with the premise that abortion is about many histories and multiple and diverse voices and experiences occurring simultaneously.[1] Adopting an intersectional approach, this volume seeks to illuminate the complicated histories and politics of abortion in Canada; on that basis, a number of the chapters acknowledge and interrogate the inadequacies of the politics of "choice" and the limitations of concentrating on abortion as a single or one-dimensional issue. Indeed, what has become increasingly clear since the Supreme Court of Canada's decriminalization of abortion in 1988, referred to as the *Morgentaler* decision, is that we need to consider the past, present, and ongoing histories and experiences of abortion in Canada because they continue to shape and determine the reproductive lives of women, their families, and their communities.

The decriminalization of abortion following the *Morgentaler* decision has been referenced by many scholars and activists as a watershed moment for abortion rights in Canada, suggesting that the Supreme Court decision represented a more concrete and secure victory than is actually the case. As several works here address, the *Morgentaler* decision neither guaranteed a woman's right to an abortion nor signalled the end of anti-abortion efforts to recriminalize abortion. In the wake of the 2013 death of Canada's best-known abortion rights crusader, Dr. Henry Morgentaler, we felt it was an appropriate moment to reflect both on abortion politics in the generation that has passed since the *Morgentaler* decision and on the historical studies that are being undertaken in a post-*Morgentaler* era.

Sacrificed on the Altar of Compromise: The Politics of Abortion in Canada

On June 12, 1990, Torontonian Yvonne Jurewicz bled to death following a self-induced abortion. She was only twenty years old. The coroner estimated that it took Jurewicz twelve hours to die from the abortion that was likely performed with a coat hanger.[2] At the time, pro-choice[3] activists speculated that Jurewicz resorted to self-abortion following the recent efforts in the House of Commons to recriminalize abortion through Bill C-43.[4] On May 29, 1990, Bill C-43 passed in the House of Commons with 140 to 131 votes but ultimately did not gain Senate approval. The bill was Prime Minister Brian Mulroney's response to the 1988 Supreme Court decision that struck down Canada's 1969 abortion law, and it would have made abortion illegal and punishable by up to two years in prison, except when two physicians determined that the pregnant woman's physical, mental, or psychological health was in danger. The failure of the bill, it should be stated, was as much the result of anti-abortion advocates' objections to its perceived leniency as it was pro-choice advocates' opposition to the recriminalization of abortion except under limited circumstances.[5] The timing of Jurewicz's death was significant given that Canada's last officially recognized death from an illegal abortion took place in 1974.[6] However, it is difficult to determine what effect Jurewicz's death had on the legislation's failure. Writing about her death in an op-ed piece at the time, Allan Hutchinson and Lisa Fishbayn argued that Jurewicz had been "sacrificed on the altar of compromise."[7] It is clear that Bill C-43, like most legislation preceding it and subsequent efforts to recriminalize abortion, was concerned with the interests of physicians and ideas about fetal life, and not with the lives, maternal experiences, ambitions, hopes, or desires of women themselves. The following examination of the history of abortion regulations in Canada illustrates this point.

A number of factors have shaped, and continue to shape, access to abortion in Canada; these include (1) the federal–provincial division of powers that places health care under provincial jurisdiction; (2) activism both for and against the provision of abortion services; and (3) structural inequalities of abortion access that are informed by the social determinants of health, particularly race, class, ethnicity, and region/place of residence. These three areas, which are imbricated and intersecting, can be addressed through the adoption of a reproductive justice framework that expands the scope of reproductive rights beyond the "choice" of whether or not to have an abortion.[8] These areas are important to examine, moreover, because they form the backdrop against which all studies of abortion occur – even when they are not foregrounded.

Federal–Provincial Division of Powers

Until 1988, when Canada distinguished itself (albeit, not by design) as one of the only countries in the world not to have a federal law governing the availability of abortion, the nation's legislative history regarding abortion and access to contraceptives resembled that of other Western countries, especially the United Kingdom and the United States. In the late nineteenth century, the newly formed federal state consolidated laws against abortion and birth control in the new *Criminal Code*, making them offences punishable by imprisonment.[9] This state of affairs remained largely unchanged until May 1969 when Canada's abortion laws were amended under Bill C-150, the omnibus bill modifying Canada's *Criminal Code*. Under the new law, contraception was legalized, as was abortion, but the latter only under very particular circumstances. Specifically, abortion was allowed only when it was performed in an accredited hospital by a licensed physician after being approved by a Therapeutic Abortion Committee (TAC) comprised of at least three doctors who had determined that the pregnancy endangered either the life or the health of the pregnant woman.[10] What is important to note about the 1969 amendments is that much of the impetus behind the changes came from a desire to clarify the laws in relation to physicians. While there were a number of actors, including women themselves, who were invested in legal changes, the amendments did not necessarily improve access for women; rather, they served to clarify those circumstances under which physicians could legally and safely perform abortions, once again decentring the experiences of women in favour of focusing on the legal and bureaucratic aspect of abortion politics.[11] The liberalization of the abortion law did not end public discussion, however; if anything, the law was a turning point that witnessed the deepening polarization of those for and against legal abortion.

In Canada, the creation of TACs in 1969 compelled numerous women's organizations to condemn the new law as inadequate in addressing women's reproductive needs, with the most famous protest being the Abortion Caravan.[12] Following complaints about the difficulties women faced in gaining access to abortion services, the Committee on the Operation of the Abortion Law was established in 1975 to review the abortion law's implementation. The committee, known as the Badgley Committee (named after its chair, Robin Badgley), reported in January 1977 that the 1969 changes to the abortion law had not resulted in equitable treatment across the country. Rather, there were significant disparities in access, continued travel outside of Canada, delays in obtaining abortions inside the country, and discrepancies in how health was interpreted by TACs.[13] Women in rural parts of the country and the North were particularly impacted by these inequities.[14] Consequently, in addition to fighting for further decriminalization, abortion rights activists increasingly turned their attention to issues of access.

Several legislative developments have affected abortion access since 1969. In 1977, the same year that the Badgley Committee released its report, the *Federal-Provincial Fiscal Arrangements and Established Programs Financing Act* (EPFA) was created to help fund the provincially run health care programs through transfer payments, in the form of tax credits and cash grants, from the federal government to provincial governments on a per capita basis. In order to receive payments, provinces were expected to meet specific terms and conditions, although initially there was no mechanism whereby the federal government could withhold funds should any province fail to provide specific services. The funding arrangement initially established by the EPFA has evolved over the last four decades; both the program name and the funding formula have changed many times. What remains, however, is a relationship whereby the provinces provide health services toward which the federal government contributes funds under the assumption that the principles of the Canada Health Act (discussed below) are honoured and the federal government maintains the right, at least in theory, to challenge the provinces when they fail to provide adequate services.[15]

The *Canada Health Act* (CHA), which was passed in 1984, outlines five specific criteria that must be met by provincial health plans in order for them to be eligible for funding: public administration, comprehensiveness, universality, portability, and accessibility.[16] According to the CHA, every Canadian is to have "*timely* access to all medically necessary health services *regardless* of his or her ability to pay for those services."[17] Abortion rights advocates, as well as some politicians, argued (and still do argue) that abortion was (and is) a medically necessary procedure and that those provinces that fail to provide abortion services to women can and should be penalized by the federal government for this failure.[18] If one considers that "in 1984, abortions could legally be performed only in a hospital, after a Therapeutic Abortion Committee had certified that the procedure was necessary to preserve the life or health of the mother, [then] any legal abortion would, by definition, be medically necessary."[19] As yet, however, the federal government has failed to impose meaningful sanctions on those provinces withholding abortion services.[20]

In 1982, the passage of the *Canadian Charter of Rights and Freedoms* offered another avenue for abortion rights advocates to challenge existing legislation governing abortions. In 1983, Dr. Morgentaler, Dr. Robert Scott, and Dr. Leslie Frank Smoling opened a Toronto abortion clinic with the intention of challenging the abortion law in Ontario. Soon after the clinic opened, the Toronto police raided the clinic and charged the doctors with illegally providing abortions. In 1984, a jury acquitted the doctors, but the Ontario government appealed that decision. When the Ontario Court of Appeal overturned the 1984 acquittal and ordered a retrial, Morgentaler appealed that decision to the Supreme Court of Canada. Here, in 1988, some six years after its introduction, the *Charter of Rights and Freedoms* supported Morgentaler's challenge. According to section 7 of the Charter, "Everyone has the right to life, liberty and security of the person and the right not to be deprived thereof except in accordance with the principles of fundamental justice."[21] In January 1988, in *R v Morgentaler*, the Supreme Court of Canada declared that section 251 of the *Criminal Code* violated section 7 of the Charter, arguing that the law infringed upon a woman's right to security of the person and that the procedures whereby women were deprived of this right did not accord with fundamental justice.[22] The court further argued that the infringement of this right could not be justified under section 1 of the Charter, which guarantees that the rights laid out in the Charter will be "subject only to such reasonable limits prescribed by law as can be demonstrably justified in a free and democratic society."[23] Thus, abortion was no longer a criminal offence in Canada and, as legal scholar Joanna Erdman argues, "abortion services c[ould] legally be integrated into the health system and governed by the laws, regulations, and medical standards that apply to all health services."[24] The *Morgentaler* decision did not, however, guarantee any standard for how abortion would be integrated into existing health systems, and each province interpreted its responsibilities very differently.

The Supreme Court's decision created both a legislative vacuum and an opening for the introduction of new abortion regulations. The introduction of competing regulations and attempts to control access to abortion played out at both the federal and provincial levels. As discussed in the previous section, the first attempt to legislate on abortion following the 1988 Supreme Court decision, Bill C-43, resulted in one desperate young woman's attempted self-abortion and subsequent death. Since then, as several chapters in this book note, multiple attempts have been made to recriminalize abortion, primarily through bills originating with motions from individual backbenchers. Efforts to recriminalize abortion persist, in part, both because of the absence of a federal law and, as Johnstone argues in her chapter in this volume, because the Supreme Court decision stopped short of recognizing that women have a right to access abortion.[25] These two factors, combined with the unique interplay of federal and provincial powers, keeps the issue of abortion close to the surface of Canadian politics.

In the immediate aftermath of the 1988 decision, multiple provinces rushed to impose regulations on abortion.[26] The freedom of individual provinces to determine access has resulted in wide variations in services between provinces, as well as within provinces themselves.[27] Some provinces and territories only cover abortion up to twelve weeks, while others cover it up to twenty-four weeks after conception. Some allow clinic abortions, while others only fund hospital abortions. Until 2014, in New Brunswick, a woman required the referral of two physicians before she could obtain a fully-funded hospital abortion. In Prince Edward Island, clinical abortion services had never been available, although women could apply to be reimbursed for services obtained in Halifax, Nova Scotia, *if* they were able to secure a doctor's referral.[28] In 2016, PEI's provincial government conceded that it could no longer justify its stance and announced that abortion services would be made available on the island by the end of that year.[29]

Availability is affected not only by provincial regulations but also by the number and location of practitioners in each province or territory. For example, as of 2015, there were more abortion clinics in Quebec (thirty-six) than in all of the other provinces and territories combined (twenty-three).[30] The situation in Quebec is unique and the political terrain in the province has afforded women greater protection and support in guaranteeing access to abortion. In 2010, the Quebec National Assembly passed a unanimous motion that "reaffirms the right of women to free choice and to free and accessible abortion services," and called on the federal government, then under Stephen Harper's Conservative leadership, to do the same.[31] The motion was introduced in response to the Harper government's decision to preclude abortion funding from its G8 maternal health initiative. Parti Québécois member Carole Poirier went so far as to warn then Prime Minister Harper, "Don't try to reopen the debate. We're keeping an eye on you ... In Quebec, if you touch the right to abortion, it's explosive."[32] The relatively secure position of abortion access in Quebec in comparison to the rest of the country, argues Jill McCalla Vickers, stems directly from the nationalist movement and the "political dynamics of Canadian federalism," which require the federal and provincial governments to vie for the support of Quebec feminists, who are thus able to exercise greater influence within Quebec's provincial political system.[33] In contrast to Quebec, Ontario, the province with the second highest number of clinics, has only eleven clinics, and all but one are in the Greater Toronto Area or Ottawa. Meanwhile, there are twelve clinics spread throughout the remainder of the country. As we can see, abortion remains uneven and, outside of select locations, inaccessible or difficult to access for a great many Canadian women and these conditions continue to shape abortion politics, experiences, and activism.

Activism

Dr. Henry Morgentaler's court challenges had a significant impact on Canada's abortion laws. However, these court challenges formed only a part of a half-century long struggle against unjust laws; the court cases operated in tandem with national and provincial pro-choice organizations and individuals across Canada. While pro-choice organizations politically and financially worked to support Morgentaler's legal challenges, they also labored to galvanize public support for abortion access and to shift dominant attitudes regarding reproductive rights for women.

Morgentaler became visibly connected to abortion in 1967 when he testified in support of women's access to abortion services at the House of Commons Standing Committee on Health and Welfare on behalf of the Humanist Association of Canada. Following his return to Montreal, Morgentaler was inundated with requests from women seeking abortions.

Two years later, he quit his general practice to become a full-time abortion provider. By 1973, Morgentaler claimed to have provided five thousand abortions outside of a hospital setting, thus proving that a hospital setting was unnecessary for the provision of safe abortions. Because of his defiance, Morgentaler was tried three times for violating section 251 of the *Criminal Code* between 1973 and 1975, though he was acquitted each time.

Although Morgentaler's efforts often occupied centre stage in the media, it is important to remember that abortion rights groups formed across Canada to fight to have abortion fully legalized, often alongside Morgentaler. In 1974, the Canadian Association for the Repeal of the Abortion Law (CARAL) was established to protest Morgentaler's incarceration. Later, in 1980, CARAL changed its name to the Canadian Abortion Rights Action League/Association Canadienne pour le Droit d'Avortement, with a mandate to overturn the abortion law and provide political and financial support for Morgentaler's efforts. Provincial and local chapters of CARAL soon formed across the country. In 1982, CARAL's educational and research arm became a separate, non-political (and therefore eligible for charitable status) organization known as the Childbirth by Choice Trust. Other pro-choice groups were also organized; in Toronto, for example, the Ontario Coalition for Abortion Clinics (OCAC) was created in 1982 for the purpose of helping Morgentaler fight for legal abortion in the province.[34] Although a Toronto-based group, OCAC has often worked in concert with both national and other regionally based groups. As Beth Palmer outlines in this volume, OCAC organized a number of "abortion tribunals" throughout the 1970s and 1980s to highlight the law's unresponsiveness to women's needs.[35] Over time, groups like these have been supplemented (and sometimes replaced) by additional organizations. In 2004, CARAL officially disbanded but was replaced in 2005 by a new national organization titled the Abortion Rights Coalition of Canada.[36] While legal and political challenges to the law remained the primary agent of change, pro-choice organizations have played a significant role in advocating for the retention and expansion of women's reproductive rights.

Illustrative of the partial victory of the *Morgentaler* decision, since 1988 there have been at least "43 private members' bills introduced in the House of Commons containing anti-abortion implications."[37] Fortunately, none of these bills have passed. Nonetheless, and despite perceptions to the contrary, abortion remains highly regulated across Canada through the provincial colleges of physicians and surgeons, as well as on a provincial basis.[38]

Scholars, pundits, and activists are not alone in assessing the impact of Morgentaler and the *Morgentaler* decision. A poll conducted by Ipsos-Reid in 2004 found that 73 percent of young women between the ages of eighteen and twenty-four could not identify Dr. Morgentaler.[39] Some view this lack of recognition as an indication that women's right to access abortion services is seen as axiomatic by that generation; others fear that this ignorance puts women's hard-won reproductive rights at risk. In July 2014, just over a year after Morgentaler's death, the Morgentaler Clinic in Fredericton, New Brunswick was forced to close because the clinic could not continue to operate without Morgentaler's financial support.[40] Morgentaler's death and the subsequent clinic closure demonstrated the fragility of relying too much on one individual. In the aftermath, however, activists mounted a tremendous response to the vacuum created in New Brunswick. They quickly raised more than $100,000 towards reopening the clinic and rallied to make abortion access a deciding issue in the provincial election of September 2014. Clinic 554 opened at the old Morgentaler clinic location in January 2015. So, while Morgentaler was central to the movement(s) for bodily autonomy and leaves an important legacy, the New Brunswick response demonstrates that the movements for reproductive autonomy in the country are multi-faceted and dynamic, and that pro-choice sentiments remain strong.

Activism on the anti-abortion side was and remains opposed to any liberalization of abortion access in Canada. Numerous anti-abortion organizations have come into existence over the last five decades. The largest anti-abortion organizations in Canada include the Alliance for Life Canada (ALC), founded in 1968; Coalition for Life (CL), which is the political branch of ALC, formed in 1973; Toronto Right to Life Association (TRL), founded in 1971; Campaign Life Coalition (CLC), a splinter group from ALC/CL formed in 1978; Realistic, Equal, Active, for Life (REAL) Women of Canada, founded in 1983; and, more recently, the Canadian Centre for Bio-Ethical Reform, founded in 2001, which is discussed by Gordon and Saurette in this volume. Between 1973 and 1975, more than one million signatures were collected in protest of the 1969 reforms. Sociologist Michael Cuneo described the rather blasé reception of these petitions as "a watershed in the movement's history," which ultimately served to foment more "disillusionment, the growth of extremism, and heightened organizational panic" among activists and in the ranks of anti-abortion organizations.[41] In the following decade, Canadian anti-abortion activists successfully incorporated themselves into a broader, evangelical Christian "pro-family" movement, which emerged in tandem with a hostility towards and critique of feminist political agitation, sexual liberation and education, and LGBTQ rights.[42] To date, both sides remain entrenched in their perspectives and continue to advocate for state and public support.

Although it is necessary, as several of the essays in this volume demonstrate, to develop a fuller academic understanding of those opposed to abortion, it is equally important to appreciate how the popular media covers anti-abortion perspectives, groups, and organizations. The popular media insists on giving both sides of the abortion issue equal time, even though the majority of Canadians have historically (since the late 1960s) supported liberalized access to abortion. This disproportionate coverage contributes to the ongoing harassment of abortion advocates (health care providers and activists) as well as those women seeking abortion services. As academics continue to consider the resilience of anti-abortion advocates, even in the face of declining support, we must also hold the media accountable and interrogate the role they play in contributing to the nature of the ongoing debate.

The Social Determinants of Health and Reproductive Injustice in Canada

While women continue to feel the effects of anti-abortion activism through challenges to access and the continued shame and social stigma associated with the procedure, their reproductive health experiences continue to be shaped primarily by their living conditions, or social determinants of health.[43] These determinants affect reproductive experiences to varying degrees and include, but are not limited to, disability, early life experiences, education, employment and working conditions, food insecurity, health services, Indian status and/or Indigenous identity, gender, gender identity and/or expression, housing, income and income distribution, race, social exclusion, social safety net, and unemployment or job security. Women's abortion experiences are often mediated by more than one social determinant of health. For instance, the quality, type, and availability of health services differ dramatically both between provinces, and within them; income affects a woman's ability to travel to access services if they are not located nearby, while education can influence her ability to access and comprehend reproductive alternatives when abortion services are unavailable or undesirable.

It is important to acknowledge that women have experienced reproductive injustices throughout modern Canadian history. Prior to partial legalization in 1969, it was often only women who could afford to travel who could access safe abortions.[44] Even after decriminalization, the ability to travel remained important. In 1977, the Badgley Report indicated that more than fifty thousand Canadian women still travelled to the United States to access abortion services. These women reported travelling because they had either been denied an abortion by a therapeutic abortion committee or because they had chosen "not to submit to the humiliation and red tape" of such committees.[45] Geographic isolation could also have devastating consequences. In *An Act of Genocide* (2015), Karen Stote examines sterilization and abortion abuses against Indigenous women in northern Canada. Significantly, Stote recounts an investigation in the early 1990s that revealed that over one hundred Indigenous women in the North had reported receiving inadequate anesthesia while undergoing abortions. Shockingly, the Stanton Yellowknife Hospital, servicing primarily Inuit patients, was the only known hospital in Canada to use aspirin as the sole source of pain management during abortions.[46] While these examples represent some of the more extreme instances of reproductive injustices faced by women seeking abortions, it is clear that the 1988 Supreme Court decision did not end the violence or barriers to abortion access experienced by many women.

Social location, racialization, and class politics all function as social determinants of health in the context of reproductive justice. Multiple studies have recorded similar barriers that prohibit women's access to abortion services across the country. In 2012 and 2013, for example, Marion Doull and Christabelle Sethna mapped out the challenges that women living in the North, the Maritimes, and outside major urban centres faced when seeking access to abortion services.[47] Their work notes that 25 percent of the women studied reported paying more than $300 out of pocket for abortion procedures that were not covered by their home province – a fee that would make abortion inaccessible to women without the necessary financial means.[48] Other barriers included factors such as age: for example, women under thirty were more likely to have travelled over one hundred kilometres to access abortion services.[49] In 2014, Colleen MacQuarrie and her research team exposed the repercussions that the lack of local abortion services had had on women in PEI.[50] Women in PEI were regularly forced to leave the province (and sometimes country) to access abortion, a development that has reportedly contributed to attempts to self-abort as well as to unwanted pregnancies being carried to term.[51] Angel M. Foster and colleagues found in 2017 that even after abortion access was theoretically liberalized in New Brunswick, women continued to face barriers, including the cost of travel, physicians' resistance to the procedure, and extremely long wait times that threatened to interfere with their ability to have an abortion.[52] These studies underscore that reproductive injustices continue to occur even when there are no federal or provincial laws that expressly prohibit abortion.

Although they receive far less media attention and public outrage, the obstacles to abortion services that women in northern Canada face are every bit as alarming as those confronting women in the Maritimes. In particular, the regimes of reproductive surveillance to which Indigenous women have been subjected add another layer to the already intersectional issue of reproductive health and abortion in Canada and demonstrate that public health data collection is experienced differently by different communities.[53] The lack of medical facilities in many Indigenous communities in Canada, combined with a lack of mobility and financial resources, poses a serious impediment to accessing reproductive justice. Sethna and Doull found that women who self-identified as First Nations or Métis were three times more likely than white women to report that they had to travel more than one hundred kilometres to obtain abortion services.[54] Jennifer K. Cano and Angel M. Foster similarly found in 2016 that women in the Yukon experienced difficulty accessing abortion services since there was only one facility in the territory providing abortions (and only twice per month, at particular times). Limited availability, which resulted in long wait times and travel outside of the territory for services, was compounded by financial costs such as transportation (e.g., public transportation, hotel, and gas), IUDs, and medication as well as personal costs (such as maintaining privacy and navigating anti-abortion physicians who were reluctant to refer patients to abortion providers).[55]

If we consider class politics as well as the racial stratification of mobility in the context of Canadian reproductive justice, we can begin to appreciate the extent to which racialization, location or geography (particularly on or off reserve), access to funds for travel, and the socio-legal ability to leave the country have all functioned in fundamental ways to restrict reproductive justice. The history of abortion, access, and reproductive injustice in

Canada, then, needs to be understood as an ongoing narrative of struggle marked by small successes and a constant vigilance against efforts to roll back the hard-won gains that have been made with respect to women's reproductive rights.

Moving Forward: The Promise of Reproductive Justice

In both Canada and the United States, hard-won victories of reproductive health advocates – whether at the federal, state, or provincial levels – have constantly been met with growing opposition and the unrelenting mobilization of anti-abortion forces. Indeed, women's right to abortion access rests on the continued tenure of sympathetic elected representatives, judicial appointments, and physicians. This is a major problem, since the rights of women to control their reproductive lives cannot be subject to the whims of politics and religion if reproductive justice is to become a sustainable and attainable social goal. Marlene Gerber Fried, in her closing address at the Abortion: The Unfinished Revolution conference held in Charlottetown, PEI, in August 2014, keenly observed that the pro-choice movement has allowed the 1974 *Roe v Wade* decision (the American counterpart to the 1988 *Morgentaler* decision) to set the standard of access that the pro-choice movement struggles endlessly to secure, defend, and maintain. In part, this is a function of the constant attacks and the shape-shifting tactics employed by anti-abortion movements; however, it also reflects the shortcomings of pro-choice movements to fully adopt a reproductive justice framework that is suited to the Canadian context. As such, real access – that is, access that is guaranteed, unrestricted, and immune to the vagaries of politicians in power – can only be achieved through an epistemological revolution that fundamentally transforms how society perceives the subjectivity of women and the ownership of their reproductive lives and choices. When people secure control over their own rights "to have children, not to have children, and to parent the children [they] have in safe and healthy environments," they are able to exercise the "human right to make personal decisions about [their lives]."[56] A movement pursuing such an approach has grown and evolved in the United States and is increasingly gaining supporters across Canada.

SisterSong, a grassroots organization started by women of colour, adopted the term "reproductive justice" over "choice" because its members believed this term captured the structural and social changes that are required in order to bring about the transformation of society that would truly put women in control of their reproductive lives. Loretta Ross, one of the founders and a long-time national coordinator of SisterSong, defines "reproductive justice" as the

> complete physical, mental, spiritual, political, social and economic well-being of women and girls, based on the full achievement and protection of women's human rights. It offers a new perspective on reproductive issue advocacy, pointing out that for Indigenous women and women of color it is important to fight equally for (1) the right to have a child; (2) the right not to have a child; and (3) the right to parent the children we have, as well as to control our birthing options, such as midwifery. We also fight for the necessary enabling conditions to realize these rights. This is in contrast to the singular focus on abortion by the pro-choice movement.[57]

Reproductive justice advocates believe that, by focusing solely on abortion, pro-choice organizations are constantly in a crisis management situation that limits the range of their responses and the breadth of their choices, especially for racialized and marginalized women. Conversely, advocating for reproductive justice obligates the state and the broader society to ensure that the social, political, economic, and cultural conditions that are necessary for implementing and living one's choices exist for everyone. The reproductive health issues that women experience across their life span cannot be understood in isolation from larger social and economic contexts. Reproductive justice and choice requires the "transform[ation of] power inequalities and [the] creat[ion of] long-term systemic change ... and recognizes that all individuals are part of families and communities and that our strategies must lift up entire communities in order to support individuals."[58] Without this acknowledgment, how can we ensure that women, regardless of their identity and location, have the right to control their lives, which includes but is not limited to the right to access a safe legal abortion within their own communities? These kinds of epistemological and conceptual questions – and their histories – need to be explored further.

Contextualizing the Collection

How historians have approached abortion can be categorized into several distinct phases. Early works that examine women's reproductive lives focus on the criminalization of abortion in the nineteenth century as part of physicians' efforts to professionalize. Such studies draw attention to the efforts of individual physicians who provided abortions in spite of the law and larger efforts to capture abortionists through women's "dying declarations."[59] Another phase of abortion historiography investigates the decade of reform that led up to the 1969 omnibus bill.[60] A third phase, which emerged during and in the aftermath of the 1988 Supreme Court decision, looks at the heated exchanges that occurred between pro-choice and anti-abortion factions during those decades.[61] Constituting a new phase is a growing and dynamic field of scholarship that has turned its focus upon women's abortion experiences in the mid- to late twentieth century, led in large part by the work of historian Christabelle Sethna.[62]

Overwhelmingly, the literature on abortion in Canada remains dominated by articles and essays, both scholarly and popular. While there are several good monographs on the issue, they are not abundant.[63] To date, the two foundational works on Canadian abortion history and politics are *The Bedroom and the State: The Changing Practices and Politics of Contraception and Abortion in Canada, 1880–1997* (1986, 1997) by Angus McLaren and Arlene Tigar McLaren, and *The Politics of Abortion* (1992) by Janine Brodie, Shelley A.M. Gavigan, and Jane Jenson. The former studies abortion alongside contraception, recognizing that historically and experientially the two practices were intimately connected; the latter analyzes the legal and political developments in Canada from the mid- to late twentieth century, dissecting the dominant discourses and value systems that advocate on both sides of the issue.[64] To date, most of the literature on abortion in Canada has focused on the experiences of white and frequently middle-class women. Studies that have looked at the experiences of racialized and marginalized women tend to concentrate on how these women's reproductive lives are subject to disproportionate scrutiny and regulation. Such works typically do not focus solely on abortion history but instead address abortion in the context of looking at how medical and political regulatory histories gave rise to eugenics. State eugenics policies had disparate impacts on Indigenous, immigrant, and disabled women in Alberta, British Columbia, and northern Canada.[65] Closely tied to works examining the regulation of Indigenous and racialized women's reproductive lives are those that seek to understand the ways in which Indigenous and racialized women are disproportionately affected by environmental contaminants. Few studies try to illuminate how Indigenous people have controlled their reproductive lives for generations.

Perhaps this oversight is a function of the overwhelming focus on ill health within Indigenous communities in Canada, where people are struggling not just to have children but also to keep the children they do have from being forcibly removed through the residential school system and so-called child welfare policies.[66] Several works within this collection seek to provide more nuanced accounts of the regulation of Indigenous and racialized women's reproductive lives – not to suggest that such regulation did or does not exist or constitute a powerful force within communities but rather to propose that these histories are far more complicated than they are often represented to be.

The methodologies employed by the authors within this collection are eclectic and varied, and strategically so. Focusing on federal policies, provincial particularities, legal frameworks, and medical regimes is essential to understanding the power relations operating within the Canadian context; however, these strategies of understanding top-down reproductive politics have the tendency to erase, elide, or displace the lived experiences of women within medical, legal, and statist structures. Thus, while important to understanding the broader picture, such approaches do not access, communicate, or deal with the fact that abortion is not an abstract concept, but always a lived experience constituted by social relations. Nevertheless, although centring the experiences of women is important, it is also essential to understand the human element of power relations involved in the provision of and access to abortion. We must also acknowledge the many ways in which knowledge produced about the histories of reproductive justice and oppression differs fundamentally from other areas of inquiry that are less politicized and personal.

This volume was organized in a collaborative and interdisciplinary fashion: it brings together scholars of history, women's studies, Indigenous studies, sociology, environmental studies, law and society, ethnography, cultural theory, and others. By approaching reproductive justice in this way, the editors strive to produce a collection that minimizes blind spots, centres ethical concerns, and resists the reproduction of problematic power relations related to gender, race, class, ability, sexuality, and other categories of identity that have been wielded as weapons by regimes of reproductive oppression. It is impossible to put together a collection free from any and all problems. We did not, for instance, address the issues that transgender and non-binary people face in regard to reproductive health and justice. These are extremely important and pressing issues and need to be addressed properly and not as an aside. We hope that the organization of the volume will centre many other issues of inequality for the reader's consideration rather than manage these problems in a way that ignores concerns central to determining whose choice matters, whose voices are heard, and whose experiences shape our understanding of abortion. To that end, we have grouped the essays into four themes: History, Experience, Politics, and Discourse and Reproductive Justice.

History

The chapters in the section on history identify different threads of the abortion experience in the geographical area that came to be known as Canada prior to the 1988 *Morgentaler* decision. Accordingly, the contributions in this section focus on colonialism, Christianity, Crown authority, regional particularities, and women's struggles against the state and society to speak to personal reproductive concerns with an authoritative voice. The first chapter, "Different Histories: Reproduction, Colonialism, and Treaty 7 Communities in Southern Alberta, 1880–1940" by Kristin Burnett, helps situate this collection in its proper settler colonial context. By reviewing the histories and struggles associated with the reproductive practices of the Niitsítapi Nation, this chapter offers an important historical foundation to the essays that follow by foregrounding colonialism and racism as key constitutive factors in Canadian iterations of reproductive oppression. Burnett's chapter helps to dislodge common understandings of reproductive freedom and choice as merely the decision to terminate a pregnancy or not. In expanding this model to include the ability to have and raise children in a physically and culturally safe environment, Burnett helps readers think about reproductive justice in a more multidimensional way.

Rebecca Beausaert's "Not Guilty but Guilty? Race, Rumour, and Respectability in the 1882 Abortion Trial of Letitia Munson" investigates Victorian sensibilities towards abortion through the intersections of race, gender, and justice. Importantly, this chapter provides an analysis of the social feelings, orthodoxies, and normative conceptions of abortion in the late nineteenth century and offers a striking example of why racial power relations must always be understood as co-constituted with gendered orders of reproductive oppression. In doing so, it centres racial politics in Victorian regimes of reproductive control – a category of inquiry that has rarely occupied a prominent position in discussions of nineteenth-century histories of abortion. Instead, such conversations have typically focused on nursing, midwifery, and the professionalization of medical regimes.

Jumping ahead a century, Erika Dyck's "Abortion and Birth Control on the Canadian Prairies: Feminists, Catholics, and Family Values in the 1970s" challenges what we think we know about the relationship between feminism, the Catholic Church, birth control, and notions of family in the 1970s by examining discourses surrounding the idea of the modern family in a Saskatchewan-based Catholic newspaper called *The Prairie Messenger*. Dyck argues that Catholic women who wanted to limit the size of their families drew strong connections between reducing fertility, familial responsibility, and well-being. She suggests that any examination of reproductive history needs to move beyond simplistic categories of for or against and instead look to the day-to-day choices made by families and women. By doing so, Dyck's contribution stresses the in-between spaces and grey areas in public dialogue on birth control and abortion that allow us to see the nuances and complexities of the reproductive choices women make.

Experience

Over the last decade, several new scholars of women's reproductive health have contributed to our understandings of women's abortion experiences and uncovered new voices in discussions of abortion. Drawing on this rich field of scholarly literature, the essays in this section investigate reproductive health as a lived struggle and social experience within Canadian history. In "He Is Still Unwanted: Women's Assertions of Authority over Abortion in Letters to the Royal Commission on the Status of Women in Canada," Shannon Stettner shows how Canadian women in the 1960s sought to actively shape the terrain of their reproductive lives by investigating the ways in which they contested the authoritative basis of twentieth-century legal discourses on abortion. Drawing on the submissions of women to the Royal Commission on the Status of Women, Stettner elucidates that, contrary to previously held assumptions, women were very willing to speak publicly about abortion and contraception, and regularly refused to occupy the position of the passive and silent woman. Her work speaks to the broader contestation of voice, authority, and representation in the spaces of abortion law reform. The letters she examines are rich sources that suggest women from a broad range of religious and socio-economic backgrounds used their authority to speak about their lives, the importance of access to abortion on request, and how "kitchen table feminism" was an important part of the push for abortion law reform in the 1960s.

Continuing with a focus on experience as a site of struggle in Canadian histories of abortion activism is Beth Palmer's "Abortion on Trial: Abortion Tribunals in the 1970s and 1980s." Palmer analyzes the role that mock tribunals played in late twentieth-century abortion activism in Canada. This essay underscores how the use of feminist organization, public performance, and social spectacle entered into and shaped the terrain on which battles for abortion access were fought. Importantly, Palmer helps us to think more dynamically about how factors come to constitute the politics of reproductive choice in Canada.

In the next chapter, Katrina Ackerman employs a methodology that helps readers engage historically with experiences of abortion in the Maritimes in the 1970s and 1980s. Titled "The Dark, Well-Kept Secret: Abortion Experiences in the Maritime Provinces," the chapter draws on oral histories and government documents to trace the history of a particular regime of reproductive oppression that emerged in the Maritimes following the 1969 amendments. Complementing previous chapters, this contribution illuminates how cultural coercion and social networks of meaning negotiated the backlash that rendered the "*a*-word" unspeakable in Canada's eastern provinces. Ackerman's chapter dovetails both geographically and historically with Stettner's and Palmer's discussions on abortion activism and social organizing for abortion access in the 1960s, '70s, and '80s.

By focusing on process instead of historical inquiry, the next chapter opens up a critical space to discuss the politics of abortion research. "When Research Is Personal and Political: Researchers Reflect on the Study of Abortion" by Marion Doull, Christabelle Sethna, Evelyne Morrissette, and Caitlin Scott reflects on the consequences of studying abortion and the ethnographic pitfalls associated with the pursuit of testimony. The authors suggest that more attention needs to be paid to the experiences of researchers who opt to tackle sensitive topics and that observing the need for self-care should always be incorporated into the research design. Typically, concern over potential research harms focuses on those being studied, but this chapter instead scrutinizes the personal and professional detriments that studying abortion can have on the lives of female academics.

Politics

The third section in this collection focuses on the implications of the *Morgentaler* decision and its impact on abortion access and a generation of women in Canada. At the time, the 1988 Supreme Court decision was heralded as a huge victory for women and reproductive choice; however, this "victory" is much more complicated than it initially seemed and its implications are still being weighed and studied as women's "right to choose" is simultaneously eroded, operationalized, challenged, and celebrated as a sign of social progress. In Frances E. Chapman and Tracy Penny Light's "Functionally Inaccessible: Historical Conflicts in Legal and Medical Access to Abortion," the authors review the ways in which anti-abortion movements in Canada have been successful in recruiting the rhetoric of medicalization to limit women's access to abortion. Chapman and Penny Light explore how medicalized discourses of abortion encourage the conception of reproductive choice as having nothing to do with other forms of social, legal, and economic justice. The authors underscore that addressing the structural impediments to abortion is not as simple as providing medical access and legalization, as histories of backlash disclose the uncomfortable truth that such state-centred "victories" are provisional and vulnerable to reactionary violence. By unpacking medicalization as a discursive strategy of reproductive oppression, the authors lay the groundwork for a deeper analysis of the legal and medical right to abortion explored in subsequent chapters.

In her chapter, "*Morgentaler* and the Technological Production of Embodiment," Jen Rinaldi critically examines the politics of grounding women's right to access abortion in section 7 of the *Charter of Rights and Freedoms* (the right to the security of the person). Although this was a strategic and necessary move at a particular period in Canadian history, Rinaldi argues that the positioning of women's access to abortion as a health care issue that is between a woman and her doctor tends to produce an imbalance of power between health care providers and women seeking abortion. Rinaldi adds to this collection's discussion on the politics of reproductive justice by demonstrating, like the other chapters in this section, that sites of victory or liberal progress can just as quickly become sites of oppression and surveillance.

Rachael Johnstone, in "Between a Woman and Her Doctor? The Medicalization of Abortion Politics in Canada," examines how, in the decades following *Morgentaler*, an increasing reliance on medical narratives has depoliticized health in general and women's access to abortion in particular. Significantly, Johnstone demonstrates that discourses of medicalization and health care have been employed by both anti-abortion and pro-choice advocates in a fashion that disassociates women and the reproductive choices they make from the social, economic, and political contexts in which they must make reproductive decisions. In exploring these tensions, Johnstone affirms that abortion access is most appropriately viewed through a lens of reproductive justice and social equity rather than through the categories of health care and access to medical intervention.

Lori Brown, J. Shoshanna Ehrlich, and Colleen MacQuarrie's chapter, "Subverting the Constitution: Anti-abortion Policies and Activism in the United States and Canada," looks at how jurisdictional boundaries and politics between national and subnational actors have served to erode women's access to abortion. Using a comparative framework, the authors look at Mississippi and PEI, comparing the destabilization of women's reproductive rights through the "well-coordinated and funded attacks by anti-choice groups" at the provincial and state levels. The United States and Canada have similar histories regarding the recognition of women's right to privacy and safety of person in the Supreme Court (*Roe v Wade* in 1973 and *Morgentaler* in 1988, respectively). Indeed, comparing the two locales reveals that, despite what Canadians may think, there are remarkable similarities between Mississippi and PEI and political actors in both milieus have vowed to make their state or province an "abortion-free zone." This chapter reminds us of the benefits of conceiving of abortion politics using a transnational lens to complicate our understandings of anti-abortion activism.

Discourse and Reproductive Justice

The final section of this collection moves debates about, and studies of, abortion in new and important directions, illuminating the opportunities posed by the adoption of a reproductive justice framework. Kelly Gordon and Paul Saurette, in "The Future of Pro-choice Discourse in Canada," focus on the changing nature of anti-abortion activism as a means of exploring the discursive and rhetorical arenas used to challenge abortion access in Canada. Of particular significance is the authors' exploration of how the anti-abortion movement has appropriated feminist ideals and pro-woman language so that it can construct itself as sensible, secular, progressive, and liberal. This was a key discursive shift for the anti-choice movement, the authors insist, as the legal landscape had evolved as a site of struggle for abortion access largely because of feminist organizing; accordingly, anti-choice movements appropriated feminist rhetoric in a backlash effort to roll back these feminist victories and recast the terrain on which struggles for abortion access are fought.

In "Reproductive Justice in Canada: Exploring Immigrant Women's Experiences," Laura Salamanca examines the stories of women who were, and are, underserved by the Morgentaler paradigm of abortion access in Canada (characterized by the 1988 Supreme Court decision, which held that restricting access to abortion was a violation of women's Charter rights). Looking specifically at racialized, impoverished, and/or immigrant women, Salamanca's ethnographic project shows that it is difficult to construct a clean and ordered narrative of feminist progress in the context of Canadian abortion services. Centring more marginalized social positions in her analysis, Salamanca articulates how the intersecting politics of citizenship, race, gender, and class have barred access to abortion in extra-legal ways since 1988.

Finally, in "Toxic Matters: Vital and Material Struggles for Environmental Reproductive Justice," Sarah Wiebe investigates the poisoning of the Aamjiwnaang First Nation through industrial pollution in the region known as Canada's Chemical Valley. This chapter brings together different threads of reproductive justice and oppression: colonialism, racism, and the need to acknowledge how reproductive oppression is not a practice that is limited to the boundaries of women's biological bodies. Environmental contamination acts in concert with the Canadian state to fundamentally attack the very reproductive capacities of Indigenous communities. Her work promotes the necessity of theorizing reproductive justice in an expansive fashion that resists ignoring those marginalized by multiple constituted regimes of reproductive oppression. Wiebe creates conceptual linkages with issues raised by Burnett in the first essay of this collection by centring the politics of settler colonialism as formative in the ways in which reproductive justice is understood in a Canadian context. Significantly, Wiebe points out that limitations to women's reproductive autonomy are imposed not only through anti-abortion legislation but also through less obvious and visible factors that work to undermine women's choices and reproductive freedoms in enormously problematic and violent ways.

ooo

Although several of the chapters in this volume include Quebec in their analyses, no chapter focuses solely on Quebec or the question of access to abortion for French-speaking women in Canada. While this omission may elicit criticism of the collection that is certainly warranted, we believe the absence reflects the comparative ease with which women in the province can access abortion, which serves as a testament both to the effectiveness of feminist organizing and the responsiveness of successive provincial governments. Consider the previously mentioned avowals of public support made by mainstream political figures in Quebec in response to Harper's 2010 decision to curtail funding to international aid organizations that offered abortion as part of their spectrum of reproductive health services. It is also noteworthy that when a call for papers for this collection was issued, we did not receive a single submission that focused entirely on French-speaking women in Canada or on Quebec. However, we received an overwhelming number of non-Canadian submissions which we used to put together a second edited collection on transnational abortion history.[67]

The essays in this volume that focus on particular regions or spaces do so in order to centre those women and areas that face the greatest challenges to women's reproductive freedoms. Questions of coloniality, race, and federalism figure prominently in the scholarship included here. As readers can see in chapters like Sarah Wiebe's, the ongoing settler colonial project continues to subject particular racialized and marginalized bodies and communities to reproductive violence and oppression in ways that demand urgent critiques and more expansive analyses of the many factors that structure reproductive choices. What is more, as readers will see in Katrina Ackerman's contribution, the regional and provincial politics of abortion in Canada are such that PEI "proudly" remained an "abortion-free province" until 2016. Such a state of affairs necessitates clarification and greater scholarly consideration than other provinces. For these reasons, our collection reflects the regional and topical urgencies associated with reproductive oppressions in the Canadian context.

Read holistically, the chapters affirm the need to think about abortion in a reproductive justice framework that resists totalizing narratives, the privileging of certain women's experiences of abortion over others, and the construction of abortion access through a legal or medical lens that removes other socio-economic and historical factors. This collection serves as a call to encourage dialogue and intellectual and political engagement with reproduction as a multiply constituted and inherently relational category of social life that has embodied in its history the problematics of colonialism, race, gender, and class that are central to the development of social justice frameworks in Canada. To this end, the arrangement of the chapters in this collection is meant to foreground the importance and necessity of reproductive justice in a Canadian context while continuing to take very seriously the fraught social relations that establish Canada as a country that disproportionately withholds access to abortion from women occupying various identities and social locations. We seek to enhance historical understandings of Canadian regimes of reproductive control and oppression and engage with the various struggles, and the different forms they have taken, to transgress these violent limitations and secure abortion services with or without the support of the state, provincial authorities, or the medical establishment.

Notes

1 Here, we draw on Lesley Biggs's call for historians to rethink midwifery, given the many different voices and experiences occurring simultaneously across the country. Lesley Biggs, "Rethinking the History of Midwifery in Canada," in *Reconceiving Midwifery*, ed. Ivy Lynn Bourgeault, Cecilia Benoit, and Robbie Davis Floyd (Montreal and Kingston: McGill-Queen's University Press, 2004), 17–45.

2 Jane Armstrong and Paula Todd, "Call Could Have Saved Woman, Coroner Says," *Toronto Star*, June 15, 1990, 2; "Botched Abortion Attempt Kills Toronto Woman, 20," *Globe and Mail*, June 13, 1990, A10; Rudy Platiel, "Coalition Says Abortion Bill Must Go in Wake of Death," *Globe and Mail*, June 14, 1990, A12.

3 We use "pro-choice," "abortion rights advocates," and "reproductive justice advocates" to reference those in favour of abortion access. We use "anti-abortion" to indicate those opposed. The authors in subsequent chapters use the terminology they feel most accurately describes their subjects.

4 Andrew Duffy, "Pro-choice Groups Say Abortion Bill Will Lead Women to Risk Their Lives," *Toronto Star*, June 14, 1990, 2. Jurewicz was not the only woman who performed an illegal abortion in the midst of talks of recriminalization. On June 2, 1990, a sixteen-year-old Kitchener, Ontario, man was charged with attempting to perform an illegal abortion on his pregnant girlfriend. See "Illegal Abortion," *Globe and Mail*, June 2, 1990, A12.

5 On discussion and ultimate defeat of Bill C-43, see Janine Brodie, "Choice and No Choice," in *The Politics of Abortion*, ed. Janine Brodie, Shelley A.M. Gavigan, and Jane Jenson (Toronto: Oxford University Press, 1992), 58–116.

6 Michael Valpy, "Just Coincidence ... or a Sad Reminder," *Globe and Mail*, June 15, 1990, A08. On July 31, 1991, Bill C-43 died in the Senate following a tied vote. Despite the media and activist attention directed to Jurewicz's death, scholars attribute the defeat of the bill to anti-abortion activism; Conservative politicians and anti-abortion, pro-family organizations viewed Bill C-43 as too lenient.

7 Allan Hutchinson and Lisa Fishbayn, "Sacrificed on the Altar of Compromise," *Globe and Mail*, June 15, 1990, A15.

8 We produce the word "choice" in quotation marks to acknowledge that although abortion is legally accessible, many factors (e.g., socio-cultural, economic, place of residence, and so on) make actually accessing such services difficult or impossible for many. For a discussion on the problematic nature of the choice paradigm, see Shannon Stettner, *Without Apology: Writings on Abortion in Canada* (Edmonton: Athabasca University Press, 2016), 7–9.

9 Criminalization of abortion and birth control began early in the nineteenth century but was codified in the first *Criminal Code* of Canada in 1892, following Confederation in

1867. See Janine Brodie, Shelley A.M. Gavigan, and Jane Jenson, *The Politics of Abortion* (Toronto: Oxford University Press, 1992); Shelley A.M. Gavigan, "On 'Bringing on the Menses': The Criminal Liability of Women and the Therapeutic Exception in Canadian Abortion Law," *Canadian Journal of Women and the Law* 1, 2 (1986): 279–312.

10 On reform of the 1969 law, see Alphonse de Valk, *Morality and Law in Canadian Politics: The Abortion Controversy* (Dorval, QC: Palm Publishers, 1974); Larry Collins, "The Politics of Abortion: Trends in Canadian Fertility Policy," *Atlantis* 7, 2 (1982): 2–20; Angus McLaren and Arlene Tigar McLaren, *The Bedroom and the State: The Changing Practices and Politics of Contraception and Abortion in Canada, 1880–1997,* 2nd ed. (Toronto: Oxford University Press, 1997); Gavigan, "On 'Bringing on the Menses'"; F.L. Morton, *Morgentaler v. Borowski: Abortion, the Charter, and the Courts* (Toronto: McClelland and Stewart, 1992); Brodie, Gavigan, and Jenson, *The Politics of Abortion*; Anne A. McLellan, "Abortion Law in Canada," in *Abortion, Medicine and the Law,* ed. J. Douglas Butler and David F. Walbert (New York: Facts on File, 1992), 333–36; Melissa Haussman, *Abortion Politics in North America* (Boulder, CO: Lynne Rienner, 2005); Brenda Margaret Appleby, *Responsible Parenthood: Decriminalizing Contraception in Canada* (Toronto: University of Toronto Press, 1999), 87–197.

11 See Shannon Stettner, "Women and Abortion in English Canada: Public Debates and Political Participation, 1959–1970" (PhD diss., York University, 2012).

12 See, for example, Christabelle Sethna and Stephen Hewitt, "Clandestine Operations: The Vancouver Women's Caucus, the Abortion Caravan, and the RCMP," *Canadian Historical Review* 90, 3 (2009): 463–96; Shannon Stettner, "'We Are Forced to Declare War': Linkages between Women's Anti-war Protests and the 1970 Abortion Caravan," *Social History/Histoire sociale* 46, 92 (2013): 159–78.

13 Canada, Committee on the Operation of the Abortion Law, *Report of the Committee on the Operation of the Abortion Law* (Ottawa: Minister of Supply and Services, 1977), 17–26.

14 Committee on the Operation of the Abortion Law, *Report of the Committee,* 446–49.

15 In 1995, the federal government announced that provincial payments issued under the mandate of the EPFA were to be combined with the Canada Assistance Plan into a single funding structure: the Canada Health and Social Transfer (CHST). In an apparent effort to increase transparency and to retouch provincial-federal relations, payments for health and social services were separated following the *First Ministers' Accord on Health Care Renewal* in 2003; from this point forward, Canada Health Transfers (CHT) and Canada Social Transfers (CST) were to be two separate payment blocks. More recent changes have seen cash transfer payments without tax credits. See Kenneth F.T. Cust, *A Just Minimum of Health Care* (New York: University Press of America, 1997), 22–25; Terry Boychuk, "After Medicare: Regionalization and Canadian Healthcare Reform," *Canadian Bulletin of Medical History* 26, 2 (2009): 353–78; and Department of Finance Canada, "History of Health and Social Transfers," December 15, 2014, https://www.fin.gc.ca/fedprov/his-eng.asp.

16 *Canada Health Act,* RSC 1985, c C-6, http://www.parl.gc.ca/content/sen/committee/372/soci/rep/repoct02vol6part7-e.htm.

17 Shannon Stettner, "When Is an Abortion 'Medically Necessary'?" *Impact Ethics,* April 30, 2014, http://impactethics.ca/2014/04/30/when-is-an-abortion-medically-necessary/.

18 See, for example, Abortion Rights Coalition of Canada "Position Paper # 1: Abortion Is a Medically Required Service and Cannot Be Delisted," January 2011, http://www.arcc-cdac.ca/postionpapers/01-Abortion-Medically-Required.pdf; Howard A. Palley, "Canadian Abortion Policy: National Policy and the Impact of Federalism and Political Implementation on Access to Services," *Publius: The Journal of Federalism* 36, 4 (2006): 566.

19 Shannon Stettner, "A Brief History of Abortion in Canada," in *Without Apology: Writings on Abortion in Canada,* ed. Shannon Stettner (Athabasca, AB: Athabasca University Press, 2016), 47.

20 For example, Nova Scotia was fined for refusing to fully fund abortion clinics, but the federal government collected only $200,000 in penalties between 1995 and 2000 despite yearly potential penalties of $130,000. See Haussman, *Abortion Politics in North America,* 95–96; Palley, "Canadian Abortion Policy," 565–86.

21 *Canadian Charter of Rights and Freedoms,* s 2, Part I of the *Constitution Act, 1982,* being Schedule B to the Canada Act 1982 (UK), 1982, c 11 [*Charter*] .

22 *R v Morgentaler,* [1988] 1 SCR 30.

23 *Charter,* s 1.

24 Joanna Erdman, "In the Back Alleys of Health Care: Abortion, Equality, and Community in Canada," *Emory Law Journal* 56 (2007): 1093.

25 Note that we are not advocating for a federal abortion law, unless it is one that shores up a woman's right to abortion without reservation.

26 Shelley A.M. Gavigan discusses the provincial responses in depth. See Shelley A.M. Gavigan, "Morgentaler and Beyond: The Legal Regulation of Reproduction," in *The Politics of Abortion,* 140–45.

27 Unless stated otherwise, the following statistics are from "Abortion Coverage by Region," National Abortion Federation (NAF) Canada, accessed July 26, 2015, http://www.nafcanada.org/access-region.html.

28 Women could obtain prescriptions for medical abortions but had to find a pharmacy willing to prescribe both of the necessary pills together.

29 Kevin Bissett, "PEI Announced Location of Clinic Offering Abortions," *Toronto Star,* September 16, 2016, https://www.thestar.com/news/canada/2016/09/16/pei-announces-plans-to-build-clinic-offering-abortions.html.

30 See Michelle Siobhan Reid, "Access by Province," The Morgentaler Decisions: A Twenty-Fifth Anniversary Celebration, accessed July 26, 2015, http://www.morgentaler25years.ca/the-struggle-for-abortion-rights/access-by-province/.

31 Ingrid Peritz and Rhéal Séguin, "Quebec MNAs Challenge Harper's Abortion Stance," *Globe and Mail,* May 19, 2010, http://www.theglobeandmail.com/news/politics/quebec-mnas-challenge-harpers-abortion-stance/article1211328/.

32 Ibid.

33 Jill McCalla Vickers, "Quebec and English-Canadian Feminists 40 Years after the Bird Commission," *Equity Matters* (blog), May 26, 2010, http://www.ideas-idees.ca/blog/quebec-and-english-canadian-feminists-40-years-after-bird-commission.

34 Catherine Dunphy's biography of Morgentaler provides a comprehensive look at the campaigns surrounding Morgentaler's efforts. Catherine Dunphy, *Morgentaler: A Difficult Hero* (Toronto: Random House, 1996).

35 See Beth Palmer, "Choices and Compromises: The Abortion Movement in Canada, 1969–1988" (PhD diss., York University, December 2012), 218–29.

36 On the emergence of ARCC, see Lianne McTavish, "Virtual Activism and the Pro-choice Movement in Canada," *Canadian Woman Studies* 25, 3–4 (2006): 121–26.

37 Paul Saurette and Kelly Gordon, "Arguing Abortion: The New Anti-abortion Discourse in Canada," *Canadian Journal of Political Science* 46, 1 (2013): 158.

38 For contemporary access issues, see Christabelle Sethna and Marion Doull, "Accidental Tourists: Canadian Women, Abortion Tourism and Travel," *Women's Studies: An Interdisciplinary Journal* 41, 4 (2012): 457–75.

39 "Who Is Dr. Henry Morgentaler?" Ipsos, December 4, 2004, http://www.ipsos-na.com/news-polls/pressrelease.aspx?id=2483.

40 See Craig Takeuchi, "Fredericton's Morgentaler Clinic Closing after 20 Year Fight," *The Straight,* April 11, 2014, http://www.straight.com/blogra/624911/frederictons-morgentaler-abortion-clinic-closing-after-20-year-fight.

41 Michael W. Cuneo, *Catholics against the Church: Anti-abortion Protest in Toronto 1969–1985* (Toronto: University of Toronto Press, 1989), 12.

42 For more information, see Margrit Eichler, *The Profamily Movement: Are They For or Against Families?* (Ottawa: Canadian Research Institute for the Advancement of Women, 1986); Lorna Erwin, "What Feminists Should Know About the Pro-family Movement in Canada: A Report on a Recent Survey of Rank-and-File Members," in *Feminist Research: Prospect and Retrospect,* ed. Peta Tancred-Sheriff (Canadian Research Institute for the Advancement of Women, 1998), 266–278; and Donna Gill, "REAL Women and the Press: An Ideological Alliance of Convenience," *Canadian Journal of Communication* 14, 3 (1989): 1–16.

43 Juha Mikkonen and Dennis Raphael, *Social Determinants of Health: The Canadian Facts* (Toronto: York University School of Health Policy and Management, 2010), http://www.thecanadianfacts.org/The_Canadian_Facts.pdf.

44 Christabelle Sethna, "All Aboard? Canadian Women's Abortion Tourism, 1960–1980," in *Gender, Health, and Popular Culture: Historical Perspectives,* ed. Cheryl Krasnick Warsh (Waterloo: Wilfrid Laurier University Press, 2011), 95.

45 *Report of the Committee on the Operation of the Abortion Law,* 160.

46 Karen Stote, *An Act of Genocide: Colonialism and the Sterilization of Aboriginal Women* (Fernwood Publishing, 2015), 77.

47 Sethna and Doull, "Accidental Tourists"; Christabelle Sethna and Marion Doull, "Spatial Disparities and Travel to Freestanding Abortion Clinics in Canada," *Women's Studies International Forum* 38 (2013): 52–62. For a similar discussion on the disparity between rural and urban access to abortion services, see Wendy V. Norman, Judith A. Soon, Nanamma Maughn, and Jennifer Dressler, "Barriers to Rural Induced Abortion Services in Canada: Findings of the British Columbia Abortion Providers Survey (BCAPS)," *PLoS One* 8, 6 (2013): https://doi.org/10.1371/journal.pone.0067023.

48 Sethna and Doull, "Spatial Disparities," 55.

49 Ibid., 56.

50 Colleen MacQuarrie, Jo-Ann MacDonald, and Cathrine Chambers, "Trials and Trails of Accessing Abortion in PEI: Reporting on the Impact of PEI's Abortion Policies on Women," Collen MacQuarrie Blog, January 2014, http://colleenmacquarrie.blogspot.com/2014/01/research-report-understanding-for.html [accessed 29 June 2017].

51 Ibid.

52 Angel M. Foster, Kathryn J. LaRoche, Julie El-Haddad, Lauren DeGroot, and Ieman M. El-Mowafi, "'If I Ever Did Have a Daughter, I Wouldn't Raise Her in New Brunswick': Exploring Women's Experiences Obtaining Abortion Care before and after Policy Reform," *Contraception* 95, 5 (2017): 477–84.

53 Randi Cull, "Aboriginal Mothering under the State's Gaze," in *Until Our Hearts Are on the Ground: Aboriginal Mothering, Oppression, Resistance and Rebirth,* ed. D. Memee Lavell-Harvard and Jeanette Corbiere Lavell (Toronto: Demeter Press, 2006).

54 Sethna and Doull, "Spatial Disparities," 56–57.

55 Kristina I. Vogel, Kathryn J. LaRoche, Julie El-Haddad, Andréanne Chaumont, and Angel M. Foster, "Exploring Canadian Women's Knowledge of and Interest in Mifepristone: Results from a National Qualitative Study with Abortion Patients," *Contraception* 94, 2 (2016): 137–42.

56 SisterSong, "Why Is Reproductive Justice Important for Women of Color?" accessed April 10, 2015, http://www.sistersong.net/index.php?option=com_content&view=article&id=141&Itemid=81.

57 Loretta Ross, "Understanding Reproductive Justice: Transforming the Pro-choice Movement," *Off Our Backs* 36, 4 (2006): 14.

58 Asian Communities for Reproductive Justice, "What Is Reproductive Justice?" accessed April 10, 2015, http://strongfamiliesmovement.org/what-is-reproductive-justice.

59 On abortion in the nineteenth century see, for example, Gavigan, "On 'Bringing on the Menses'"; Constance Backhouse, *Petticoats and Prejudice: Women and Law in Nineteenth-Century Canada* (Toronto: Women's Press, 1992); Susanne Klausen, "Doctors and Dying Declarations: The Role of the State in Abortion Regulation in British Columbia, 1917–37," *Canadian Bulletin of Medical History* 13, 1 (1996): 53–81; Michael McCulloch, "'Dr. Tumblety, the Indian Herb Doctor': Politics, Professionalism, and Abortion in Mid-Nineteenth-Century Montreal," *Canadian Bulletin of Medical History* 10 (1993): 49–66; Angus McLaren, "Illegal Operations: Women, Doctors and Abortion, 1886–1939," *Journal of Social History* 26, 4 (1993): 797–816.

60 On the 1960s decade of reform, see Appleby, *Responsible Parenthood,* and de Valk, *Morality and Law in Canadian Politics.*

61 On later twentieth-century abortion politics, see Gail Kellough, *Aborting Law: An Exploration of the Politics of Motherhood and Medicine* (Toronto: University of Toronto Press, 1996); McLellan, "Abortion Law in Canada"; Morton, *Morgentaler v. Borowski*; and Brodie, Gavigan, and Jenson, *The Politics of Abortion.*

62 On women's abortion experiences, see Childbirth by Choice Trust, *No Choice: Canadian Women Tell Their Stories of Illegal Abortion* (Toronto: Childbirth by Choice Trust, 1998); Beth Palmer, "'Lonely, Tragic, but Legally Necessary Pilgrimages': Transnational Abortion Travel in the 1970s," *Canadian Historical Review* 92, 4 (2011): 637–64; Christabelle Sethna, "All Aboard? Canadian Women's Abortion Tourism, 1960–1980," in *Gender, Health and Popular Culture,* ed. Cheryl Krasnick Warsh (Waterloo, ON: Wilfred Laurier University Press, 2011), 89–108; Christabelle Sethna, Beth Palmer, Katrina Ackerman, and Nancy Janovicek, "Choice, Interrupted: Travel and Inequality of Access to Abortion Services since the 1960s," *Labour/Le Travail* 71 (2013): 29–48; Catherine Haney, "Towards Legitimate Nursing Work? Historical Discursive Constructions of Abortion in *The Canadian Nurse,* 1950–1965," *Canadian Bulletin of Medical History* 31, 2 (2014): 93–115.

63 For unpublished dissertations and theses, see Frances Wasserlein, "'An Arrow Aimed at the Heart': The Vancouver Women's Caucus and the Abortion Campaign, 1969–1971" (master's thesis, Simon Fraser University, 1990); Tracy Penny, "'Getting Rid of My Trouble': A Social History of Abortion in Ontario, 1880–1929" (master's thesis, Laurentian University, 1995); Tracy Penny Light, "Shifting Interests: The Medical Discourse on Abortion in English Canada, 1850–1969" (PhD diss., University of Waterloo, 2003); Stettner, "Women and Abortion in English Canada"; and Beth Palmer, "Choices and Compromises: The Abortion Rights Movement in Canada 1969–1988" (PhD diss., York University, 2012).

64 Other important political and legal analyses of abortion in Canada include Haussman, *Abortion Politics in North America,* and Erdman, "In the Back Alleys of Health Care." See also Palley, "Canadian Abortion Policy"; Jessica Shaw, "Abortion as a Social Justice Issue in Contemporary Canada," *Critical Social Work* 14, 2 (2013), http://www1.uwindsor.ca/critical socialwork/abortion_in_canada#Top; Stephanie Paterson, Francesca Scala, and Marlene K. Sokolon, *Fertile Ground: Exploring Reproduction in Canada* (Montreal and Kingston: McGill-Queen's Press, 2014); Paul Saurette and Kelly Gordon, *The Changing Voice of the Anti-abortion Movement: The Rise of "Pro-woman" Rhetoric in Canada and the United States* (Toronto: University of Toronto Press, 2016).

65 On eugenics and sterilization generally, see Angus McLaren, *Our Own Master Race: Eugenics in Canada, 1885–1945* (Toronto: McClelland and Stewart, 1990); Linda Revie, "More Than Just Boots! The Eugenic and Commercial Concerns behind A.R. Kaufman's Birth Control Activities," *Canadian Bulletin of Medical History* 23, 1 (2006): 119–43; Sheila Gibbons, "'Our Power to Remodel Civilization': The Development of Eugenic Feminism in Alberta, 1909–1921," *Canadian Bulletin of Medical History* 31, 1 (2014): 123–42; Amy Samson, "Eugenics in the Community: Gendered Professions and Eugenic Sterilization in Alberta, 1928–1972,"

Canadian Bulletin of Medical History 31, 1 (2014): 143–463; Erika Dyck, *Facing Eugenics: Reproduction, Sterilization, and the Politics of Choice* (Toronto: University of Toronto Press, 2013); and Karen Stote, *An Act of Genocide: Colonialism and the Sterilization of Aboriginal Women* (Halifax, NS: Fernwood, 2015).

66 On Indigenous motherhood, see D. Memee Lavell-Harvard and Jeanette Corbiere Lavell, eds., "*Until Our Hearts Are on the Ground": Aboriginal Mothering, Oppression, Resistance, and Rebirth* (Toronto: Demeter Press, 2006) and D. Memee Lavell-Harvard and Kim Anderson, *Mothers of the Nations: Indigenous Mothering as Global Resistance, Reclaiming and Recovery* (Toronto: Demeter Press, 2015). For examples of the Canadian child welfare system, see Vandha Sinha and Anna Kozlowski, "The Structure of Aboriginal Child Welfare in Canada," *International Indigenous Policy Journal* 4, 2 (2013): 1–21, and Brittany Baker, Alfred Taiaiake, and Thomas Kerr, "An Uncaring State? The Overrepresentation of First Nations Children in the Canadian Child Welfare System," *Canadian Medical Association Journal* 186, 14 (2014): E533–35. There is a wealth of literature on residential schooling in Canada; for example, see *Honouring the Truth, Reconciling for the Future: Summary of the Final Report of the Truth and Reconciliation Commission of Canada* (Winnipeg: Truth and Reconciliation Commission, 2015).

67 See Shannon Stettner, Katrina Ackerman, Kristin Burnett, and Travis Hay, *Transcending Borders: Abortion in the Past and Present* (London: Palgrave MacMillan, 2017).

Part 1
History

1
Different Histories
Reproduction, Colonialism, and Treaty 7 Communities in Southern Alberta, 1880–1940

Kristin Burnett

> I hate how the people out there are clapping their hands at the non-Native pro-choice movement, and totally ignoring our long-standing and well documented history of self control over reproductive choices. It's disrespectful to pretend like RJ [Reproductive Justice] wasn't alive in our communities ... their indoctrination/colonization has manipulated things so that we weren't allowed to follow the way we always did things. Our RJ was made illegal on purpose, but that's never mentioned anywhere. The other thing that makes me mad about these organizations ignoring and dismissing our history is if they do finally admit there are "some cases" of Native people practicing autonomy over our own bodies, the argument then turns to, "Well it's not modern pharmacology" or "Well ok, Natives had an idea but they didn't scientifically understand what biological effects those herbs were having."
>
> – Theresa Lightfoot[1]

This quotation communicates some important points and themes central to this chapter and its examination of Indigenous modes of birth control. Affirming the reproductive practices of Indigenous peoples as knowledge-centred systems that helped women manage their fertility and reproductive lives, Lightfoot's passage is also critical of the insidious ways in which settler colonialism has elided and constructed Indigenous reproductive technologies and the peoples who practised them. Her words point to the fact that non-Indigenous scholars have rarely seen Indigenous reproductive knowledges *as knowledge,* and in this way have often failed to see these practices as sites of learning and areas fit for scholarly inquiry.[2] It is in this manner that Indigenous modes of birth control and reproductive practices are constituted as subjugated knowledges, and the pro-choice movement, as articulated by mainstream feminists, often reproduces settler colonialism and discourses of violence that affect Indigenous peoples in general and Indigenous women in particular.[3]

Taking Lightfoot's formulation as a starting point, this chapter revisits the reproductive practices of Indigenous communities and focuses specifically on the Niitsítapi or Blackfoot Nation (located in present-day southern Alberta and northern Montana). The Niitsítapi observed a tried and trusted system of beliefs and practices about contraception that included but were not limited to abortion. Settler colonialism and racism have reshaped the landscape of Treaty 7 communities and altered cultural beliefs and practices related to birth control and reproduction. This chapter looks at the changing history of reproductive practices in Treaty 7 communities during the twentieth century in order to chart what we can know about Niitsítapi birth control and abortion practices and illuminate how colonialism has reframed understandings of reproductive knowledge among the Niitsítapi.

Before exploring what can be known about Niitsítapi reproductive practices, consideration must be paid to how their erasure is a reflection of "colonial relationships [that] are themselves gendered and sexualized."[4] The destruction of Indigenous reproductive practices and beliefs is a double-fronted assault that targets both Indigenous bodies of knowledge and Indigenous bodies. First, the knowledge of Indigenous peoples is debased and delegitimized in order to produce narratives about Indigenous peoples that characterize them as nations and cultures without real knowledge, especially of healing or curative practices.[5] Indigenous peoples must be made to appear as if they are out of place, irrelevant, or in need of saving – as so-called primitive remnants that are either dying or chaotic bodies without rational thought or knowledge and thus in need of salvation and state intervention. Within this process, Frantz Fanon describes colonialism as unsatisfied with merely

> holding a people in its grip and emptying the native's brain of all form and content. By a kind of perverted logic, it turns to the past of the

> oppressed people, and distorts, disfigures, and destroys it ... the total result looked for by colonial domination was indeed to convince the natives that colonialism came to lighten their darkness.[6]

Second, working in concert with this assault on Indigenous bodies of knowledge is the embodied violence of settler colonialism on the colonized. Thus, the other prong of the attack on reproductive practices comes in the form of settler colonial policies, regulatory projects, exercises of governance, and carceral regimes that use medical, state, police, military, and even academic institutions to take control of Indigenous bodies.[7] This settler colonial assault is one of the most intimate of bodily violences and is central to the sustained operation of settler colonialism. When you control the right of people "to have children, not to have children, and to parent the children [they] have in safe and healthy environments" you steal the "human right [for people] to make personal decisions about one's life."[8] To borrow the words of Andrea Smith, once again, such "gender[ed] violence operates to not only destroy [I]ndigenous peoples, but to destroy their sense of being a people."[9]

Over the past century, the Canadian state has systematically and discursively produced the conditions necessary to destroy and undermine Indigenous reproductive practices that are deeply embedded in community cohesion and well-being.[10] The imposition of Euro-Canadian norms and beliefs on Indigenous peoples through the assimilative enterprises of the church and the state, embodied in institutions like the residential school system, interrupted the intergenerational transmission of knowledge and characterized the traditional practices of Indigenous peoples, especially women, as harmful to their communities.[11] Residential schools interred tens of thousands of children and prevented them from participating in and learning from their communities. The criminalization of Indigenous beliefs and practices and the imposition of Western public health regimes and medicine has served the interests of the state and not Indigenous communities.[12]

To date, Canadian historiography has been woefully inadequate in terms of addressing those silences surrounding the reproductive practices of Indigenous peoples living on Turtle Island and connecting their erasure to larger settler colonial processes.[13] In part, this myopia could be a function of the culture of death that has dominated many historical explorations of health among Indigenous peoples and their communities in the claimed boundaries of the Canadian state.[14] The disproportionate attention that has been paid in the historical literature to high rates of morbidity and mortality in Indigenous communities has masked the survival of reproductive practices, as well as their importance and centrality, particularly in the current environment where Indigenous communities are fighting to keep and raise their children in the face of ongoing threats of state theft. It is troubling to recall in this context that Indigenous peoples in Canada comprise only 3 percent of the population yet make up more than 40 percent of the children in foster care.[15] The federal government and churches and their missionary organizations have long sought to force Indigenous peoples into adopting Euro-Canadian child rearing practices. The stereotype of Indigenous women "as unfit parents in need of state observation, guidance, and intervention" has a long and powerful history in Canada.[16] There is an enormous body of literature on efforts of the state to destroy Indigenous family and child-rearing practices.[17] However, less work has been undertaken that looks at how Indigenous women controlled their reproductive lives.

In Canada, the focus on abortion and the struggle for legalization and access has overshadowed an examination of other reproductive practices and knowledges, as well as confirmed and reified the supremacy of biomedicine. The growth of colonial/settler colonial, critical race, and disability studies in the last several decades challenges these oversights. Indigenous scholars on Turtle Island have established a rich body of literature that details the centrality of women to their communities, the importance of social and community cohesion, and Indigenous epistemologies regarding health and well-being. Kim Anderson records the importance of women in an interview with Mosôm Danny: "Women were the centre and core of our community and our nation. No nation ever existed without the fortitude of our grandmothers, and all of those teachings have to be somehow recovered."[18]

It is important to move beyond the focus on abortion to a reproductive justice framework because the right of women to control their bodies is not solely about the "unyok[ing of] sexual intercourse from procreation" but rather the "right to the social, economic, political, legal, and cultural circumstances that foster voluntary reproductive choices"[19] for women and their communities. Andrea Smith notes that the mainstream pro-choice movement, which focuses primarily on access to abortion and birth control, is limiting for racialized groups because it "promotes the structures of oppression which prevent women of colour from having real choices or healthy lives."[20] Reproductive justice and choice also seeks to identify and "transform power inequalities and create long-term systemic change ... and recognizes that all individuals are part of families and communities and that our strategies must lift up entire communities in order to support individuals."[21] In women's pursuit of safe and effective birth control, however, alternative cultural understandings of birth control methods have not been well studied. Historian Angus McLaren criticizes the failure of scholars to examine birth control practices that do not conform to biomedical definitions of contraception.[22] For instance, historians have almost entirely overlooked the history of contraception practices in Niitsítapi communities, especially during the late nineteenth and early twentieth centuries. Childbirth in Indigenous communities was, and still is, a topic of interest, especially in recent decades, as midwives and their supporters search for an example of a less medicalized and female-centred birth culture.[23] Historians have thus largely disregarded the fact that Indigenous people employed their own means of contraception that were effective, reliable, and appropriate within their cultural context. In order to investigate the reproductive practices of the Blackfoot this chapter draws on a variety of records from oral histories, the unpublished field notes of anthropologists who worked among the Niitsítapi during the late 1930s as part of a field school run by anthropologist Ruth Benedict, and interviews conducted by ethnobotanists with Niitsítapi Elders about plant use during the 1960s and 1970s.

What follows is an overview of the economic, social, and political landscapes of western Canada, a brief discussion of the state's assault on midwives among the Niitsítapi, a description of the birth control practices of the Niitsítapi, and an examination of how the same period can be interpreted to produce very different understandings and histories regarding reproductive beliefs and understandings.

The Economic, Social, and Political Landscapes of Western Canada

The Niitsítapi Nation, meaning original people, is comprised of three tribes: the Siksika (Blackfoot), Kainai (Blood), and Piikani (Peigan). The Piikani are further divided into the North and South Peigan tribes. Currently, the Siksika, Kainai, and North Peigan live in present-day southern Alberta while the South Peigan live in Montana and are referred to as the Blackfeet. These current divisions reflect the drawing of national boundaries in the nineteenth century and not internal tribal divisions.[24] During the late nineteenth and twentieth centuries, the Niitsítapi witnessed dramatic political, economic, and social transformations. The numbered treaties were negotiated in the 1870s, with Treaty 7 signed in 1877. Throughout the 1880s and 1890s Indigenous peoples in this area were increasingly confined to reserves, which limited their ability to pursue land-based activities in order to feed their families and ensure individual and community health and well-being.[25] The buffalo, a staple in the diet of the Niitsítapi, were nearly wiped out by 1883 and local resources were further burdened by the growth of non-Indigenous settlement.[26] Movement was further circumscribed after the Northwest Rebellion of 1885 created unfounded concern among Euro-Canadians for the vulnerability of white women and resulted in the imposition of the pass system.[27] The pass system prohibited Indigenous people from leaving the boundaries of their reserves without the permission of the local Indian agent.

Simultaneously, the federal government increased its social, cultural, political, and economic assault on Indigenous peoples in the Prairie West. These decades witnessed the dramatic expansion of the residential school system and the internment of tens of thousands of Indigenous children. Residential schools, in combination with state policy, were designed to destroy Indigenous cultures by separating children from their families and communities and interrupting the intergenerational transmission of knowledge. Further, amendments to the *Indian Act* limited the ability of Indigenous people to participate in the Western economy, to practise Indigenous forms of governance, and to pursue those Indigenous healing and curative practices which had long kept their communities healthy. It is in this context that Indigenous peoples began to experience an assault on their reproductive practices.

The Assault on Indigenous Midwifery and Childbirth

In southern Alberta, it was not until after the First World War that the Department of Indian Affairs (DIA) undertook concerted efforts to control where childbirth took place in Treaty 7 communities.[28] Prior to the First World War, the midwifery practices of Indigenous peoples remained largely ignored. A series of interviews conducted in the 1990s with Treaty 7 Elders born between 1905 and 1935 revealed that the formidable reservoir of obstetrical knowledge Indigenous women possessed and had passed on from generation to generation continued to be important for community health and well-being. Out of 200 interviewees, 142 Elders provided details about the circumstances surrounding their birth. Not surprisingly, the interviews show that before 1920 only 6 people were born at the reserve hospital while, of the 94 Elders born after 1920, 45 were born in the hospital and 43 at home.[29] Most women before 1920 and many women after 1920 continued to have their children at home where they were attended by experienced midwives, who provided pre- and postnatal care with the support of female family members.[30] Meanwhile, the role of the midwife did not end when women gave birth and felt capable of taking care of the baby themselves; instead, long-term associations developed wherein midwives formed an important relational connection to the individuals and families they helped bring into the world.[31] Further evidence of the pervasiveness and efficacy of Indigenous midwifery lies in the fact that non-Indigenous women drew on their expertise across the Prairie West as well.[32]

Efforts in reserve communities in the Treaty 7 area to monitor expectant mothers, alter the locations of birth, and intervene in delivery were not significant until the 1920s for several reasons. First, long-held and enduring racist stereotypes that characterized the childbirth experience of Indigenous women as animal-like and painless made biomedical intervention by the state appear pointless, especially when the state did not want to become involved in health care provision for Indigenous people in the first place.[33] Second, the relative success of Indigenous midwives made the involvement of nurses and physicians unnecessary for Indigenous women. Indeed, it was only after structural changes took place in reserve hospitals that women chose to stay in the hospitals for birth. For example, nurses began to permit children to remain with their mothers in the hospital and advances in asepsis and surgical techniques dramatically improved women's chances of survival. Further, women regularly used the hospitals on a seasonal basis, choosing to be in the hospital during the winter months and give birth in camps or houses during the summer.[34]

According to Pamela White, the First World War served as a watershed moment in the federal government's struggle to refashion Indigenous motherhood and this included changing where and how women gave birth.[35] State efforts to "modernize" Indigenous motherhood were further compounded by the growing belief among the Euro-Canadian medical community that women required professional medical personnel to deliver babies: if not doctors, then at least nurses with obstetrical training.[36] For

Indigenous women, this belief regarding the necessity for medical intervention and standardization of childbirth and motherhood was even stronger. The DIA and churches regularly blamed Indigenous women for the failure of their communities to assimilate and for the high rates of infant mortality, despite evidence that poverty and chronic illnesses associated with poverty were the biggest problem. [37]

Those women who died on reserve in childbirth while being attended by midwives were labelled irresponsible because they did not give birth in the hospital attended by a physician.[38] For instance, Dr. Alan Kennedy censured an Indigenous woman who died from postpartum complications in 1926. Kennedy located the reason for this woman's death in her failure to go to the reserve hospital, despite the fact that, once it was clear the woman needed help and Kennedy was called, he steadfastly refused to attend to her while she remained at home. In a letter explaining the event, Kennedy expressed his hope that this incident would serve as an exemplar to other Kainai women about the dangers of giving birth at home. However, since most Euro-Canadian women continued to give birth at home during this period, it is clear that Kennedy referred in particular to the danger "posed by Indigenous homes."[39] Indigenous women were, and continue to be, identified as a high-risk group despite the presence of significant familial support. The DIA most likely knew that many Indigenous women chose to be attended by Indigenous midwives and believed that altering the location of the birth – that is, from home to hospital – would help end this practice. The pathologization of Indigenous women as bad mothers can be seen clearly in this transfer of birthing spaces; of course, this setter colonial process that targeted reproduction as a new frontier occurred in a post–First World War paradigm that saw all births in First Nations communities as high-risk.[40] This history signals the fact that assaults on midwifery emerged in tandem with the broader assault on reproductive practices of Indigenous communities.

Birth Control

It is noteworthy that the one facet of Indigenous women's therapeutic practices that the Department of Indian Affairs and its medical and educational institutions did not try to take control of or eradicate during this period was contraception.[41] The unpublished field notes of the anthropologists who studied the Niitsítapi during the 1930s contain brief glimpses of contraceptive practices. Esther Goldfrank was told by one of her informants, Violet, that a woman who no longer wanted to have children would visit a medicine woman who would "tie her up."[42] Children, according to Violet, came from the power of the snake. Thus, a medicine woman would prevent conception by tying a snakeskin around the woman's waist.[43] Besides this, medicine women would often counsel menstruating women to paint their stomachs with yellow paint as a preventative measure.[44]

Claude Schaeffer, who worked in southern Alberta during the 1930s with Goldfrank, documented a wealth of information about Niitsítapi birth control practices but never published it. Schaeffer was the only man among the group of anthropologists in the 1930s to record evidence of contraceptive practices among the Niitsítapi. He interviewed Mrs. Victor Chief Coward and noted that, after having three children, she sought out Mrs. Mountain Sheep Woman to prevent further pregnancies. Mrs. Mountain Sheep Woman, whose ability to prevent conception came from the rattlesnake and the otter, instructed Mrs. Victor Chief Coward to bathe in a creek, stand over a smudge, and paint her face with yellow earth paint during the first new moon every month (i.e., the time of ovulation).[45] Smudging is a cleansing ceremony where an individual burns sweetgrass (or sometimes sage or cedar) and, using their hands, brushes or rubs the smoke over their body. Mrs. Victor Chief Coward followed these instructions for eighteen months before she stopped, "knowing [there was] no chance for further pregnancies."[46] In addition, the medicine woman gave Mrs. Victor Chief Coward a bracelet made of otter skin with a figure of a snake drawn on the inside to wear during the new moon.[47] Schaeffer also interviewed Jappy Takes Gun On Top, the only man he encountered who practised birth control medicine. Takes Gun On Top was not interviewed by Goldfrank. His ability to prevent conception was derived from the snake in the form of a beaded necklace.[48] Takes Gun On Top also helped women who miscarried, but what form that help took is not indicated in the field notes.

The prescriptions outlined by Violet, Mrs. Victory Chief Coward, and Jappy Takes Gun On Top were similar in terms of contraceptive practices: every month during the full moon, women were to bathe in a creek, stand over a smudge of sweetgrass, paint their faces or stomachs yellow, and wear a token, possibly made of otter skin, with the symbol of a snake or butterfly inscribed on it. Also, they were never to lend an article of clothing to another person. If these interdictions were followed, pregnancy could be prevented. Schaeffer made notes about a woman who failed to follow the instructions given to her. Mrs. Phillip Arrowtop, after an extremely difficult delivery of twins, had approached Mrs. Mountain Sheep Woman, who instructed her to paint her face and smudge her shawl and warned her never to lend an article of personal clothing to anyone.[49] Mrs. Phillip Arrowtop broke these injunctions and as a result had two more children. Mrs. Mountain Sheep Woman treated her again, and this time she did not transgress the prohibitions. She did not conceive again.[50]

These examples, though limited, point to a shared belief in the efficacy of non-biomedical methods of contraception among the Niitsítapi; Indigenous people relied on them because they worked. McLaren criticizes scholars for failing to discuss the ability of the sacred to influence fertility. Instead, historians have regarded such methods as evidence that a culture does not possess contraceptive knowledge.[51] This ignores the psychological impact these methods had and have on people. Birth control does not necessarily apply solely to the biological process of conception (the sperm meeting the egg); it can refer to a whole range of methods. Schaeffer, for example, noted that the Niitsítapi used late weaning as a means of regulating and spacing births. Old Lady Bull Calf told him that "a mother would instruct her married daughter to let [her] body nurse until [the baby] stops of its own accord."[52] According to her, a woman should "nurse [her] baby as long as she desires, whenever the child wants another sibling she will cease."[53] Western science now acknowledges that nursing babies reduce a woman's fertility[54] and historians know that early-modern Europeans too used this method of birth control.[55]

Years later, as part of a community project to record the knowledge of Niitsítapi Elders before it was lost, Beverly Hungry Wolf related a story told to her by her grandmothers regarding the spiritual powers that helped prevent childbirth:

> The ones who had these powers would make up symbols of snakes or butterflies, which were considered powerful in childbirth. These were given to women who wanted no children. They had to wear them all the time, next to their bodies. For instance, snakes were made from buckskin, stuffed, and worn like a belt. The stuffings were made of special materials, and the snake bodies were specially covered with beadwork and sacred paints. Often the women were instructed to stand over a smudge of special incense, so that the smoke could rise up to their bodies. They had to do this every night for as long as they wanted no more children.[56]

The use of visible markers to indicate a desire to limit fertility suggests that the onus or expectation for birth control did not fall solely on the shoulders of women; those markers informed *both* sexes. Perhaps because birth control practices were relatively common knowledge in the community, there was a sense of shared responsibility among female and male sexual partners. In a hunting and gathering community where mobility was of paramount importance and resources were limited, responsibility for limiting the size of the community was shared by all and essential to societal well-being. This lies in stark contrast to Euro-American cultures, which firmly place the onus on the individual couple, and more often than not, on just the woman.[57] Indeed, the discourses of the birth control movement, eugenics, and scientific motherhood have all reinforced the notion that women are doubly responsible for both conception and contraception. While women remain "*in charge*" of these processes they have not necessarily been empowered by them. Women can obtain birth control in clinics and pharmacies but the professionalization of the birth control movement has ensured that contraceptive knowledge lies under the purview of a select few.[58] In contrast, in Niitsítapi communities, although there were experts who counselled women about controlling fertility, the knowledge was diffuse.

Sacred and ceremonial forms of birth control were not the only methods practised by the Niitsítapi. In the 1930s, Goldfrank's informant Hilda told her:

> Women take medicine to keep from having children. Many get it from a medicine woman. She knew of one woman who, when her period did not come, took a strong drink of pepper tea so as not to have kids – knows of no other kind of abortion. Women will go to a medicine woman for a brew when they are pregnant.[59]

An informant provided Schaeffer with evidence that women used certain types of roots for abortion. This person also told him that abortifacients (substances that induce abortion) were considered a bad thing and equivalent to murder and that such practitioners were not highly regarded.[60] Schaeffer recorded only two women as knowing how to induce miscarriages in this way. A woman named Mrs. Pete Home Gun gave this information to Schaeffer and she made it clear that she had refused any aid offered by these women.[61] Given that abortion was generally illegal or unobtainable in Canada until 1988, and in the United States until 1974, the evidence provided by Schaeffer's informants about such practices was mediated by contemporary debates surrounding abortion and birth control. It is also quite possible that these women were graduates of the residential school system and their testimony reflected the worldviews of Christian churches and not their own. Indeed, Mrs. Pete Home Gun's awareness of these services suggests that abortifacients may have been widely used.

Goldfrank and Schaeffer's unpublished field notes are unusual for their accounts of Niitsítapi's contraceptive practices. That Jane Richardson Hanks, the only other woman who participated in the field school, did not record such customs may suggest that gender was not the principal factor in determining whether or not such material was recorded. However, it is possible that Lucien Hanks, Richardson's research partner and husband, affected her access to, and interest in, such information. Their fieldwork and subsequent publications on the Niitsítapi were all collaborative. Nevertheless, the picture is more complicated. Schaeffer is an unusual figure. Given his gender, one might assume a lack of interest in the topic of contraception or access to potential informants, yet Schaeffer took extensive notes on contraception and, interestingly, spoke to the only male informant regarding birth control practices. Perhaps, in this last instance, Schaeffer's gender gave him access to information that Goldfrank's did not give her. Schaeffer was also one of the first professional anthropologists to write about two-spirited people among Indigenous Nations. Indeed, in a career that witnessed few publications, his 1965 article "The Kutenai Female Berdache: Courier, Guide, Prophetess, and Warrior" stands out. It suggests Schaeffer was inclined to look beyond those areas of inquiry considered conventional within the heteronormative discipline of anthropology.

There is also evidence to suggest that the contraceptive knowledge recorded by anthropologists in the late 1930s persisted into the post–Second World War period. In 1969, as part of an oral history project, Niitsítapi Elder George First Rider revealed that a woman who did not want to get pregnant could drink a combination of three herbs: cut-leaf anemone, crooked stem, and wild liquorice.[62] Similarly, several years later when ethnobotanists John Hellson and Morgan Gadd performed fieldwork with Niitsítapi Elders regarding plant use, they learned that knowledge about traditional contraceptive practices had persisted in the community and was still being applied. Hellson and Gadd noted that the Niitsítapi practised two methods of birth control in particular. One involved a special ceremonial bundle, which, according to Hellson and Gadd, was the property of a specific practitioner whose services could be purchased. The second method involved drinking a herbal mixture containing abortifacients. This was notably different from the bundle in that it was a contraceptive technique a woman could employ independently.[63]

Hellson and Gadd's informants recounted information consistent with that related by Schaeffer and Goldfrank in the 1930s. The researchers' field notes offered evidence regarding the objects and materials that prevented conception. These items were otter skin wristlets with the design of a snake, yellow ochre, and some plant material[64] – all of which resembled items that Goldfrank and Schaeffer's informants had described decades earlier. However, unlike Goldfrank and Schaeffer, Hellson and Gadd sought out more detailed information regarding which plants were used, how they were prepared, and for what purposes. For instance, Hellson and Gadd's informants indicated that the plant materials were the flowers and leaves of the new birch sucker, which were ingested if the bundle failed to prevent conception. The informants also identified two other plants as abortifacients: crooked stem and Yellowstone draba.[65] The researchers' field notes discussed here, in conjunction with oral histories and ethnobotanical studies, reveal that Indigenous people relied on both spiritual methods and medicinal plants to prevent conception and continued to do so long before and well after anthropologists arrived in the 1930s.

A Window into Settler Society in the 1930s

The observations made by non-Indigenous peoples (and primarily men) of Indigenous birth control practices reflected Euro-Canadian culture and beliefs during the late nineteenth and early twentieth centuries. Indeed, the unpublished field notes of these anthropologists are particularly interesting and deserving of further examination for what they can reveal about contemporary non-Indigenous beliefs about birth control. While there is a wealth of information in the field notes regarding Indigenous reproductive knowledge, it is absent from the published works of the anthropologists. The anthropologists' omission from their published work of information on contraceptive practices in Niitsítapi communities, as well as Euro-American society, can be placed at the intersection of debates taking place around birth control that were deeply rooted in contemporary anxieties about immigration and cultural understandings about who was responsible for birth control. The anthropological interviews can be read as texts upon which non-Indigenous peoples projected anxieties, interests, and ambiguities about reproduction and its relationship to racial politics during the interwar period. It is no coincidence that the harshly xenophobic anti-immigration rhetoric in North America reached a high point during the 1920s and 1930s, fuelled as it was by economic crises and growing nativist movements. The withdrawal of Canada and the United States from international politics and the passing of legislation like Canada's 1923 *Chinese Exclusion Act,* which banned the entry of all Chinese people, also reflected these fears. By the 1930s, Canada had dramatically reduced the number of non-white immigrants it accepted from outside the United States and Britain.

Increasing numbers of non-white and non-British immigrants and falling birth rates among middle-class Euro-Canadian women during this period lent credence to popular fears regarding racial degeneration and "race suicide." Efforts were undertaken to limit the ability of groups that were seen as unfit to reproduce.[66] Social reformers lobbied for the criminalization of abortion and birth control under the 1892 *Criminal Code*, making the dissemination and procurement of related information indictable offences.[67] Intimately intertwined with anti–birth control and abortion legislation was the rise of eugenics, which reflected the medicalization of social problems and the belief that a heartier "race" could be ensured through better breeding and child rearing practices.[68] Thus, birth control was not about women gaining control over their own bodies and the right to voluntary reproduction but rather about ensuring only certain women reproduced. In the United States, almost thirty states passed eugenics-based laws during the early twentieth century and chose to perform sterilizations on populations labelled as undesirable.[69] In Canada, Alberta and British Columbia passed sterilization acts in 1928 and 1933, respectively.[70] Indigenous people in both countries were disproportionately targeted by the state for sterilization.[71] State authorities would only have become concerned about Indigenous people's continued use of birth control if Euro-Canadian women had also begun to draw on such knowledges to limit their fecundity.

o o o

Reproductive justice needs to be understood in an expansive fashion that is not limited to reproductive rights or the revocation of access to Western medicine and modern hospitals. As this study shows, embedding Niitsítapi communities within the architecture of the settler state for the purposes of "modernizing" Indigenous motherhood was an act of disruption that prevented reproductive justice rather than facilitated it, and it is only through attending to the various vectors of colonial control and violence that we can begin to understand those factors that prevent the realization of reproductive justice in the geographic area now known as Canada. For example, efforts to reclaim reproductive cultures and knowledges continue in the face of high rates of child apprehension, the evacuation of Indigenous women living in northern and rural First Nations to southern urban centres for birth, the persistent denigration of Indigenous motherhood, and the ongoing epidemic of disappeared and murdered Indigenous women. The Niitsítapi possessed a tried and trusted system of reproductive practices that were effective and were passed from generation to generation through apprenticeship processes and knowledge transmission practices that were shared for the well-being of the community. The failure of historians and other academics to examine these practices is a reflection of ongoing colonial processes that seek to erase or compartmentalize Indigenous knowledges and traditions. The effort to deny cultures their knowledge and traditions forms part of a boarder system of colonial violence and erasure that works to construct Indigenous peoples as having no past, present, or future.

Currently, there is a revitalized and powerful movement to reclaim and assert Indigenous reproductive knowledges as a part of an ongoing "political act that inspires the continued assertion of Indigenous identities and sovereignty."[72] By reading the oral histories, field notes, and testimonies of historical actors involved in the transmission of Indigenous birth control technologies (or in their attempted disruption), we can begin to understand the ways in which the present historical moment is embedded or even trapped within a settler colonial history wherein Indigenous knowledges are devalued, obscured, or even targeted for destruction. This colonial process has not been successful, but (as the above examples demonstrate) it has been continually reproduced and reconstituted within multiple sites of health care, medicine, and other areas of governance. Thus, while these histories bear the imprint of settler colonial violence and power relations, they also speak to the resilience of oral traditions, the knowledge transmission techniques of Elders, and the productive capacity of the intergenerational relationships that were formed and continue to form between Indigenous women.

Notes

1 Theresa Lightfoot, quoted in Jessica Danforth, "Reproductive Justice – For Real, For Me, For You, For Now," Battered Women's Support Services: The Violence Stops Here, http://www.nativeyouthsexualhealth.com/reproductivejustice.pdf.

2 For discussions of epistemological violence or "suppressed knowledges," see Emma LaRocque, *When the Other Is Me: Native Resistance Discourse, 1850–1990* (Winnipeg: University of Manitoba Press, 2010); Audra Simpson, *Mohawk Interruptus: Political Life across the Borders of Settler States* (Durham, NC: Duke University Press, 2014); and Glen Sean Coulthard, *Red Skin, White Masks: Rejecting the Colonial Politics of Recognition* (Minneapolis: University of Minnesota Press, 2014).

3 For examples, see Andrea Smith, *Conquest: Sexual Violence and American Indian Genocide* (Cambridge, MA: South End Press, 2005); Barbara Gurr, *Reproductive Justice: The Politics of Health Care for Native American Women* (New Jersey: Rutgers University Press, 2015); and Karen Stote, *An Act of Genocide: Colonialism and the Sterilization of Aboriginal Women* (Halifax, NS: Fernwood Publishing, 2015).

4 Smith, *Conquest*, 1.

5 Jodi Byrd, *The Transit of Empire: Indigenous Critiques of Colonialism* (Minneapolis: University of Minnesota Press, 2011); Paulette Regan, *Unsettling the Settler Within: Indian Residential Schools, Truth Telling, and Reconciliation* (Vancouver: UBC Press, 2010); and Sherene Razack, *Looking White People in the Eye: Gender, Race, Class, and Culture in Courtrooms and Classrooms* (Toronto: University of Toronto Press, 1998).

6 Frantz Fanon, *Wretched of the Earth*, trans. Constance Farrington (New York: Grove Press, 1966), 210–11.

7 Devon Abbot Mihesuah and Angela Cavender Wilson, eds., *Indigenizing the Academy: Transforming Scholarship and Empowering Communities* (Lincoln, NB: University of Nebraska Press, 2004) and Ruth Wilson Gilmore, *Golden Gulag: Prisons, Surplus, Crisis, and Opposition in Globalizing California* (Berkeley, CA: University of California Press, 2007). For an elaboration on the "carceral state" in a Canadian historical context, see Mona Oikawa, *Cartographies of Violence: Japanese Canadian Women, Memory, and the Subjects of Internment* (Toronto: University of Toronto Press, 2012).

8 SisterSong, "Why Is Reproductive Justice Important for Women of Color?" http://www.sistersong.net/index.php?option=com_content&view=article&id=141&Itemid=81.

9 Andrea Smith, "Against the Law: Indigenous Feminism and the Nation-State," *Affinities: A Journal of Radical Theory, Culture, and Action* 5, 1 (2011): 65.

10 Leanne Simpson, *Dancing on Our Turtle's Back: Stories of Nishnaabeg Re-Creation, Resurgence, and a New Emergence* (Winnipeg, MB: Arbeiter Ring Publishing, 2011).

11 For examples of this discursive violence, in no particular order, see Sarah Carter, *Capturing Women: The Manipulation of Cultural Imagery in Canada's Prairie West* (Montreal and Kingston: McGill-Queen's University Press, 1997); Carol Higham, *Noble, Wretched, and Redeemable: Protestant Missionaries to the Indians in Canada and the United States, 1820–1900* (Albuquerque, NM: University of New Mexico Press, 2000); Sheila McManus, *The Line Which Separates: Race, Gender, and the Making of the Alberta-Montana Borderlands* (Lincoln, NB: University of Nebraska Press, 2005); Adele Perry, *Beyond the Edge of Empire: Gender, Race, and the Making of British Columbia, 1849–1871* (Toronto: University of Toronto Press, 2001); and Anne McClintock, *Imperial Leather: Race, Gender, and Sexuality in the Colonial Context* (New York: Routledge, 1995).

12 For examples of this, see Maureen Lux, "We Demand Unconditional Surrender: Making and Unmaking the Blackfoot Hospital, 1890s to 1950s," *Social History of Medicine* 25, 3 (2012): 665–84; Maureen Lux, "Care for the Racially Careless: Indian Hospitals in the

Canadian West, 1920–1950s," *Canadian Historical Review* 91, 3 (2010): 407–34; and Mary-Ellen Kelm, "Diagnosing the Discursive Indian: Medicine, Gender, and the Dying Race," *Ethnohistory* 52, 2 (2005): 371–406.

13 "Turtle Island" is the term used by the Original Peoples and nations to refer to the continent now called North America.

14 The term "culture of death" is borrowed from Maureen Lux's work *Medicine That Walks: Disease, Medicine, and Canadian Plains Native People, 1880–1940* (Toronto: University of Toronto Press, 2001).

15 Randi Cull, "Aboriginal Mothering under the State's Gaze," in *"Until Our Hearts Are on the Ground": Aboriginal Mothering, Oppression, Resistance, and Rebirth*, ed. D. Memmee Lavell-Harvard, and Jeanette Corbiere Lavell (Toronto: Demeter Press, 2006), 149.

16 Cull, "Aboriginal Mothering under the State's Gaze," 141.

17 There is a wealth of literature on residential schooling in Canada. For example, see Truth and Reconciliation Commission of Canada, *They Came for the Children: Canada, Aboriginal Peoples, and Residential Schools* (Winnipeg, MB: Canadian Truth and Reconciliation Commission, 2012); John Milloy, *A National Crime: The Canadian Government and the Residential School System, 1879 to 1986* (Winnipeg: University of Manitoba Press, 1999); and Roland Chrisjohn and Sherri Young, *The Circle Game: Shadows and Substance in the Indian Residential School Experience* (Penticton First Nation, BC: Theytus Books, 1997). For examples of the Canadian child welfare system, see Vandha Sinha and Anna Kozlowski, "The Structure of Aboriginal Child Welfare in Canada," *International Indigenous Policy Journal* 4, 2 (2013): 1–21; Brittany Baker, Alfred Taiaiake, and Thomas Kerr, "An Uncaring State? The Overrepresentation of First Nations Children in the Canadian Child Welfare System," *Canadian Medical Association Journal* 186, 14 (2014): E533–35; and Allyson Stevenson, "Vibrations across a Continent: The 1978 Indian Child Welfare Act and the Politicization of First Nations Leaders in Saskatchewan," *American Indian Quarterly* 37, 1 (2013): 218–36.

18 Kim Anderson, *Life Stages and Native Women: Memory, Teachings, and Story Medicine* (Winnipeg, MB: University of Manitoba Press, 2011), 162.

19 Joyce Berkman, "The Fertility of Scholarship on the History of Reproductive Rights in the United States," *History Compass* 9, 5 (2004): 433.

20 Andrea Smith, "Beyond Pro-choice versus Pro-life: Women of Color and Reproductive Justice," *Feminist Formations* 17, 1 (2005): 135. For discussions about the limits of second-wave feminism for racialized women, see Sam Grey, "Decolonising Feminism: Aboriginal Women and the 'Global Sisterhood,'" *enweyin*, 8 (2003–04): 9–23; Ruth Frankenberg, *White Women, Race Matters: The Social Construction of Whiteness* (Minneapolis: University of Minnesota Press, 1993); Aileen Moreton-Robinson, *Talkin' Up to the White Woman: Indigenous Women and Feminism* (St. Lucia, AU: University of Queensland Press, 2002); and Benita Roth, *Separate Roads to Feminism: Black, Chicana, and White Feminist Movements in America's Second Wave* (New York: Cambridge University Press, 2003).

21 Asian Communities for Reproductive Justice, "What Is Reproductive Justice?" http://strongfamiliesmovement.org/what-is-reproductive-justice.

22 Angus McLaren, *Reproductive Rituals: The Perception of Fertility in England from the Sixteenth to the Nineteenth Century* (Don Mills, UK: Oxford University Press, 1984), 5.

23 Margaret MacDonald, "Tradition as Political Symbol in the New Midwifery in Canada," in *Reconceiving Midwifery*, ed. Ivy Lynn Bourgeault, Cecilia Benoit, and Robbie Davis-Floyd (Montreal and Kingston: McGill-Queen's University Press, 2004), 46–66.

24 David G. McCrady, *Living with Strangers: The Nineteenth-Century Sioux and the Canadian-American Borderlands* (Toronto: University of Toronto Press, 2009).

25 Sarah Carter, *Aboriginal People and Colonizers of Western Canada* (Toronto: University of Toronto Press, 1999), 95–96; Treaty 7 Elders and Tribal Council, with Walter Hildebrandt,

Sarah Carter, and Dorothy First Rider, *The True Spirit and Original Intent of Treaty 7* (Montreal and Kingston: McGill-Queen's University Press, 1996).

26 Andrew Isenberg, *The Destruction of the Bison* (Cambridge, MA: Cambridge University Press, 2000), 159.

27 Carter, *Capturing Women*.

28 Kristin Burnett, *Taking Medicine: Women's Healing Work and Colonial Contact in Southern Alberta, 1880–1930* (Vancouver: UBC Press, 2010), 153–68.

29 Flora Zaharia and Leo Fox, eds., *Kitomahkitapiiminnooniksi: Stories from Our Elders*, volumes 1–3 (Edmonton, AB: Donahue House, 1995).

30 Wendy Mitchinson, *Giving Birth in Canada, 1900–1950* (Toronto: University of Toronto Press, 2001), 173–78.

31 Kristin Burnett, "Obscured Obstetrics: Indigenous Midwives in Western Canada," in *Recollecting: Lives of Aboriginal Women of the Canadian Northwest and Borderlands*, ed. Sarah Carter and Patricia McCormack (Edmonton, AB: Athabasca University Press, 2011), 169; Dena Caroll and Cecilia Benoit "Aboriginal Midwifery in Canada: Merging Traditional Practices and Modern Science," in *Reconceiving Midwifery*, ed. Ivy Lynn Bourgeault, Cecilia Benoit, and Robbie Davis-Floyd (Montreal and Kingston: McGill-Queen's University Press, 2004), 265–71.

32 For an example, see Burnett, *Taking Medicine*, 47–66.

33 Patricia Jasen, "Race, Culture, and the Colonization of Childbirth in Northern Canada," *Social History of Medicine* 10, 3 (1997): 384–89.

34 Library and Archives Canada (LAC), RG1/1540, Blood Hospital Monthly Reports, October 1923 to November 1924; Glenbow Archives (GA), Lucien M. and Jane Richardson Hanks fonds, M8458, box 3, file 64, 1.

35 High enlistment rejection rates during the First World War led to increasingly broader concern regarding the health of Canadians. Thus, women and mothers were held responsible for the ill health of the Canadian population. Pamela White, "Restructuring the Domestic Sphere: Prairie Indian Women on Reserves – Image, Ideology, and State Policy, 1880–1930" (PhD diss., McGill University, 1987), 237–39.

In addition, a study performed by the federal government in the early 1920s revealed that Alberta had the highest maternal mortality rate in the country and that complications from pregnancy and childbirth were the second leading cause of death among women in Canada. Sharon Richardson, "Frontier Health Care: Alberta's District and Municipal Nursing Services, 1919–1976," *Alberta History* 46, 1 (1998): 2–3.

36 Cynthia Comacchio, *Nations Are Built of Babies: Saving Ontario's Mothers and Children, 1900–1940* (Montreal and Kingston: McGill-Queen's University Press, 1993). See also Gwenith Siobhan Cross, "'A Midwife at Every Confinement': Midwifery and Medicalized Childbirth in Ontario and Britain, 1920–1950," *Canadian Bulletin of Medical History* 31, 1 (2014): 139–59.

37 Richardson, "Frontier Health Care," 2–3.

38 Burnett, *Taking Medicine*, 157–58; Comacchio, *Nations Are Built of Babies*; Mitchinson, *Giving Birth in Canada*, 173–78.

39 Grey Nuns Archives, Montreal (GNAM), Hôpital Notre-Dame-des-Sept-Douleurs/Stand Off, Blood Reserve, Alberta L049 (hereafter HNDSD), Doc. 170, Dr. Kennedy to Blood Agent Faunt, January 25, 1926.

40 Carol Couchie and Sheila Sanderson, "A Report on Best Practices for Returning Birth to Rural and Remote Aboriginal Communities," *Society of Obstetricians and Gynaecologists of Canada* 188 (2007): 250–56; Janet Smylie, Sue Crengle, Jane Freemantle, and Maile Taualii, "Indigenous Birth Outcomes in Australia, Canada, New Zealand, and the United States – An Overview," *The Open Women's Health Journal* 4 (2010): 7–17; Jessica Shaw, "The

Medicalization of Birth and Midwifery as Resistance," *Health Care for Women International* 34 (2013): 522–36.

41 Burnett, *Taking Medicine*, 153–68.

42 GA, Esther Goldfrank, M243, field notes (hereafter Goldfrank, field notes).

43 Ibid.

44 Ibid.

45 GA, Claude Schaeffer, M1100/137, field notes (hereafter Schaeffer, field notes).

46 Ibid.

47 Ibid.

48 Ibid.

49 Ibid.

50 Ibid.

51 McLaren, *Reproductive Rituals*, 5.

52 Schaeffer, field notes.

53 Ibid.

54 R.V. Short, M.B. Renfree, G. Shaw, and P.R. Lewis, "Contraceptive Effects of Extended Lactational Amenorrhea: Beyond the Bellagio Consensus," *Lancet* 337, 8743 (1991): 715–17.

55 Angus McLaren, *Sexuality and Social Order: The Debate over Fertility of Women and Workers in France, 1770–1920* (New York: Holmes and Meier, 1983), 11–13.

56 Beverley Hungry Wolf, *The Ways of My Grandmothers* (New York: William Morrow and Co., 1980), 203.

57 Linda Gordon, *Woman's Body, Woman's Right: A Social History of Birth Control in America* (New York: Viking Penguin, 1976), 407–9.

58 Ibid., 252–56.

59 Goldfrank, field notes.

60 Schaeffer, field notes.

61 Ibid.

62 First Nations University of Canada, Indian History Film Project, IH AA079, interview, George First Rider, Kainai Elder, n.d.

63 John Hellson and Morgan Gadd, *Ethnobotany of the Blackfoot Indians* (Ottawa: National Museums of Canada, 1974), 57.

64 Ibid.

65 Ibid., 58.

66 Jana Grekul, Harvey Krahn, and Dave Odynak, "Sterilizing the 'Feeble-Minded': Eugenics in Alberta, Canada, 1929–1972," *Journal of Historical Sociology* 17, 4 (2004): 358–59.

67 Mariana Valverde, "When the Mother of the Race Is Free?": Race, Reproduction, and Sexuality in First-Wave Feminism," in *Gender Conflicts: New Essays in Women's History*, ed. Franca Iacovetta and Mariana Valverde (Toronto: University of Toronto Press, 1992), 16–17.

68 See, for example, Johanna Schoen, *Choice and Coercion: Birth Control, Sterilization, and Abortion in Public Health and Welfare* (London: University of North Carolina Press, 2005) and Comacchio, *Nations Are Built of Babies*.

69 Philip Reilly, *The Surgical Solution: A History of Involuntary Sterilization in the United States* (Baltimore, MD: Johns Hopkins University Press, 1991); Edwin Black, *War against the Weak: Eugenics and America's Campaign to Create a Master Race* (Morrisville, NC: Dialog Press, 2008).

70 Grekul, Kahn, and Odynak, "Sterilizing the 'Feeble-Minded,'" 362–63.

71 Jane Lawrence, "The Indian Health Service and the Sterilization of Native American Women," *American Indian Quarterly* 24, 3 (2000): 400–19; Erika Dyck, *Facing the History of Eugenics: Reproduction, Sterilization, and the Politics of Choice in 20th-Century Alberta* (Toronto: University of Toronto Press, 2013).

72 Rebeka Tabobondung, Sara Wolfe, Janet Smylie, Laura Senese, and Genevieve Blais, "Indigenous Midwifery as an Expression of Sovereignty," in *Mothers of the Nations: Indigenous Mothering as Global Resistance, Reclaiming, and Recovery*, ed. D. Memee Lavell-Harvard and Kim Anderson (Toronto: Demeter Press, 2014), 71. See, for example, the Rankin Inlet Birthing Centre in Nunavut, http://www.aboriginalmidwives.ca/toolkit/rankin; Tsi Non:we Ionnakeratstha' Six Nations Maternal and Child Centre, http://www.aboriginalmidwives.ca/toolkit/six-nations; and Seventh Generation Midwives Toronto, http://www.sgmt.ca/.

2

Not Guilty but Guilty?

Race, Rumour, and Respectability in the 1882 Abortion Trial of Letitia Munson

Rebecca Beausaert

In the early morning of September 16, 1882, thirty-five-year-old white hotel waitress Ellen Weingardner was found dead in her home in the township of Oxford West, just outside the town limits of Woodstock, Ontario. Letitia Munson, an older black empiric in the community, discovered the remains in the temporary home that she had provided to Weingardner in the spring of 1882. At the time of her death, medical officials estimated that Weingardner was seven to eight months pregnant.[1] The deceased was found in bed surrounded by a large quantity of blood; in a post-mortem examination of the body, doctors also discovered puncture wounds in Weingardner's uterus. Suspicion soon fell on Munson, a suspected abortionist with "a very bad reputation"[2] around town. At Munson's home, authorities discovered instruments and pharmacopeia often used to induce abortions. At the fall session of the assize court that year, Munson was charged with "procuring a miscarriage," but much to the surprise of Woodstock's citizenry, the jury rendered a verdict of "not guilty" and the case was dismissed.[3]

In a town chiefly populated by Anglo-Celtic Protestants, the trial of Letitia Munson raises important questions about how race, gender, justice, rumour, and respectability were socially constructed in small communities. That the case made headlines in at least nine different newspapers across southern Ontario speaks to both the story's compelling nature and the moral outrage that it provoked throughout Woodstock and the surrounding area.[4] Reporters repeatedly condemned Munson's supposedly dissolute character and her suspect knowledge of obstetrical medicine. By stripping Ellen Weingardner of any agency over her own body and placing her as the victim of a distrustful black "doctress," the press attempted to sway the public's opinion of Munson by implying that her medical services should be controlled and regulated. Such a response illustrates sociologist Clayton James Mosher's claim that "Black offender/White victim crimes represented the greatest threat to the prevailing white structure of authority."[5]

Though Munson insisted that her ability to treat illness should be considered a valuable community asset, the press condemned her as a "terrible bane."[6] Her character was further maligned when the press claimed that she had been flagrantly performing abortions for some time, despite efforts by local authorities to impede her. Indeed, even after the acquittal, she was still forced to face the accusations reporters meted out in the press in their attempts to reinforce the white moral and social order of the community.

Of the abortion cases tried in Oxford County prior to Munson's in 1882, none provoked the same sort of sensationalized response from the media due to the racial dynamics at play. Through a careful discursive reading of various newspaper accounts, this essay examines how the ramifications of Letitia Munson's case "extended beyond the courtroom [and] into the realm of popular discourse."[7] It addresses the struggle and slanderous accusations that an elderly black widow faced when she circumvented white legal and moral authority. Munson's experience reveals how members of Woodstock's small black population were marginalized by the print media and, by extension, the public readership.

From newspaper accounts, it is clear that Munson played an important role in Woodstock by disbursing health care to disadvantaged individuals, yet she remains an obscure figure in African Canadian women's history. At a time when Woodstock's medical community was wholly male, Munson offered critical attention and refuge to black and white females in need at the expense of her reputation. The ways that the trial was sensationalized and the press's estimation of her character, however, undeniably hindered Munson's ability to continue providing medical services to the community.

A Brief History of Black Settlement in Oxford County

The history of race relations in Oxford County, described by historian Joyce Pettigrew as one of mutual assistance and affection, was far more complicated and wrought with interracial conflict than has previously been acknowledged. Located approximately 140 kilometers southwest of Toronto, Oxford County's residents in the nineteenth century were largely of English, Scottish, and Irish descent. By 1881, the county seat of Woodstock boasted a population of 5,373.[8] However, just prior to this, Oxford County was home to the fifth largest concentration of blacks in the province.[9] According to 1881 census figures, forty-two men, women, and children of "African origin" were living in the town of Woodstock alone.[10]

After the abolition of slavery within the British Empire in 1833 and the passage of the 1850 Fugitive Slave Act in the United States, Oxford County became the destination for a number of freed and escaped slaves travelling north largely via the waterways of the Great Lakes. Blacks were recorded living in the area as early as 1829, situated principally in the township of South Norwich and the towns of Ingersoll and Woodstock. A large community of abolitionist Quakers in the Norwich area and employment opportunities in Ingersoll and Woodstock account for these settlement clusters.[11] Jobs dried up in the 1850s and 1860s, however, when competition developed with Irish immigrants.[12] Subsequently, many blacks left and moved on to other communities in search of work while others returned to the United States to reunite with family after the Civil War.

Racial Discrimination and the Law

Recently, in their critiques of the first generation of black historical scholarship in Canada, historians have acknowledged the problem of characterizing regions that received large waves of black migrants (like Upper Canada/Canada West) as welcoming havens devoid of racial prejudice. In these first studies, authors described incidences of racism as occurring within a vacuum; such conflicts were rarely pinpointed as long-term factors which negatively shaped the experiences of blacks living in biracial communities. In *A Safe Haven,* Joyce Pettigrew contends that blacks prospered in Oxford County because whites, such as the sizable community of Quakers, felt a responsibility to help provide them with jobs, homes, and religious and educational institutions.[13] Similar to the studies of earlier African Canadian historians such as Fred Landon and Daniel Hill, Pettigrew's account characterizes blacks in Oxford as voiceless freedom-seekers.[14] Pettigrew states that "stories of discrimination are few" in Oxford County because "the black settlers were ... a progressive group of people."[15] However, she merely mentions in passing the presence of the Ku Klux Klan and segregated schools.[16] Such depictions mask the complicated relationships that developed between black migrants and white Canadians, as well as the endemic hardships and extreme racism that racial minorities faced.[17] Indeed, as Owen Thomas contends, discrimination did not cease once the forty-ninth parallel was crossed.[18] Though Canada was not a "perfect refuge," it was, as Sharon Hepburn notes, "better than the United States."[19] However, according to Barrington Walker, "blacks [still] faced a daunting number of barriers to full inclusion in Canadian society" and were usually "restricted to the lowest forms of menial wage labour."[20] As the Munson trial reveals, when blacks in Oxford County became entangled with the law, entrenched attitudes about race and gender reached far beyond the walls of the courthouse.[21] For visible minorities within the court system, ultimately their "race was on trial too."[22] Historically, racialized women had a notably complex and tenuous relationship with the law. In the 1911 case of accused murderess Angelina Napolitano, her Italian heritage and ethnically motivated stereotypes unquestionably influenced how victims and villains were identified and treated in public discourse.[23] When seamstress Clara Ford, who was identified as mulatto, was tried for the murder of a prominent white Toronto man in 1894, suspicions based on her "African blood" became a point of contention, though she, like Munson, was acquitted.[24]

When fleshing out popular attitudes towards blacks, particularly in communities with sizable populations of white citizens, legal sources such as judges' bench books and court transcripts can "shed critical light on how 'blackness' [was] articulated, constructed, deployed, contested, imagined, and re-imagined in juridical discourse."[25] The local media disseminated these meanings to its readership, especially when the black villain/white victim paradigm was indirectly at the heart of a criminal case, thus resulting in greater interest in the proceedings. For instance, in 1895 when a "young colored man" was charged with seducing a "prepossessing mulatto" girl under the *Charlton Seduction Act*, the *Woodstock Sentinel Review* reported that the court room was "crowded with spectators."[26]

Except for an entry in the *Dictionary of Canadian Biography* and a brief mention in an assize court minute book,[27] Letitia Munson's story has survived solely through newspaper headlines. Though crime stories in newspapers were often "glib" and "formulaic," veiled articulations of race, class, and gender can be gleaned from these reports.[28] Beyond providing the purported facts of a case, reporters also spoke to and shaped the attitudes of the dominant social groups in the community, particularly regarding the moral standing of the victim and purported villain within the community and whether justice was served or denied.

The Death, Inquest, and Trial

On September 22, 1882, the inquest into Ellen Weingardner's death began, less than a week after her remains were found. Letitia Munson told the court that she had known Weingardner, a former hotel waitress, for five years. Around 1877, Weingardner took up "intimate relations" with a male hotel employee; after this liaison resulted in a pregnancy, Weingardner sought out Munson for support.[29] It is unclear how or why she came to consult the older black woman, but the press claimed that women often went to Munson to get rid of their "incumberances."[30] Weingardner eventually gave birth to a baby girl at Munson's home, then left town shortly thereafter. In the late spring of 1882, Weingardner returned to Woodstock, accompanied by her four-year-old daughter and husband, John Camp.[31] Weingardner was pregnant once again and sought out Munson for "assistance and advice."[32] A week later, Camp disappeared, so Munson offered Weingardner her second home, on an adjoining lot, where Weingardner remained for the duration of her pregnancy.[33]

On the night of Friday, September 15, 1882, Weingardner walked uptown to Stark's Drug Store where she sought out local physician George L. Beard. A clerk agreed to send Dr. Beard out to see her, but no visit was ever made.[34] At the inquest and trial, neighbours testified that they saw Weingardner on the night in question and she appeared ill. Munson stated at the inquest that Weingardner had been suffering from ague, but that she refused to treat her for fear of making the ailment worse or causing death.[35] Munson claimed to have left Weingardner at ten o'clock in the evening, and when she went to check on her at six o'clock the next morning, found the woman deceased in her bed. Witnesses corroborated Munson's story and agreed that she had been seen visiting Weingardner during the night in question. Upon discovery of Weingardner's body, Munson asked her son Frederick to alert neighbours Catharine and Barbara McGinnis that Weingardner had died in the night.

Coroner Archibald McLay testified that Weingardner was seven or eight months enceinte when he examined her the afternoon following her death.[36] Munson informed the coroner that Weingardner had gone into labour the previous evening, but that she did not attend because "she was an old woman and could not stay up."[37] According to medical reports, however, Weingardner had not attempted to deliver the child before her death.

In his testimony, Woodstock Police Chief Constable Thomas McKee described bloody footprints near Weingardner's bed, as well as a blood-stained tub and ashes sprinkled over blood marks on a path to her home. The *Guelph Weekly Herald* reported that the bed where Weingardner lay was in a "dreadful condition," soaked in blood and surrounded by blood-stained clothing. McKee then explained that he had searched Munson's home and found several instruments, particularly one that was long and curved wrapped in cloth in a trunk under a bed. He claimed to have found other evidence, including "five sets of instruments, such as would be used in cases of abortion," letters asking for advice "about getting rid of ... indiscretions," and capsules of balsam copaiba, a medicine used for a variety of ailments.[38] The *Globe* reported that one of the instruments was marked with blood and there were also recipes for medicines, at least one of which "was for use in the fiendish commerce with infant life."[39]

Dr. Levi H. Swan and Dr. Albert B. Welford performed a post-mortem examination of Weingardner's body and testified that "instrumental violence" was the cause of death. Their inspection uncovered a punctured membrane in her uterus, believed to have been caused by the insertion of a round wire or knitting needle.[40] A second examination was performed by Dr. Beard and Dr. Hugh M. McKay who could not accurately conclude how Weingardner died; they believed natural causes of a rupture or placenta praevia, while rare, may have caused death.

When the inquest into Weingardner's death closed at the end of September 1882, the jury stated that it was clear Weingardner had died as the result of premature labour, most likely caused by Munson's interference. At this point, Munson was arrested and held in the county jail until November 16, when her trial commenced. In the court room, it was reported that she presented a "very respectable appearance," wearing her "best dress and shawl and a silk quilted hood." She "listened attentively ... wearing a shrewd expression, and evidently following the line of the argument closely."[41] In his opening remarks, prosecutor F.R. Ball pronounced that Munson either performed Weingardner's abortion alone or assisted the deceased in the crime. He questioned Munson's son Frederick and a black man named Joseph Anderson who was boarding with the Munsons about their knowledge of her actions on the night of September 15. Anderson stated that he had seen Weingardner walking to town, but knew nothing else. Frederick was described as "wearing his usual, stolid, imperturbable look" and "doling out his never-failing 'I don't know' and 'I don't remember,'" to the examiner's questions. His only knowledge of Munson's actions was seeing her speak to Weingardner in their yard earlier in the evening.[42]

Neighbours Catharine and Barbara McGinnis were then called as witnesses. Catharine remembered that there were indeed bloody clothes near the deceased's bed and that Weingardner had been ill in the days prior, the result of an injury she sustained while doing some laundry. Barbara added that bloody marks near the door of Weingardner's home had been covered over with ashes by Munson who told them she did so to protect their dress hems. Another neighbour, Harriette Packer, who also saw Weingardner's remains the morning after her death, offered a different perspective, echoing others' sentiments that Munson did not "bear a good character among the neighbors."[43]

When called to the witness stand, Chief Constable McKee reiterated his initial observation of Weingardner's body and home and corroborated Barbara McGinnis's testimony that bloody marks near the door had been covered with ashes by Munson. However, he acknowledged that during his search of Munson's home, upon his discovering ten or fifteen locked trunks, Munson readily handed the keys over and did not object to his search of their contents.[44]

Munson's defence attorney, J.W. Nesbitt, called upon Dr. Beard and Dr. McKay who repeated their initial assessment that Weingardner's death may have been triggered by natural causes.[45] Nesbitt then called a character witness, Charlotte Ross, who testified that she was an acquaintance of Weingardner and that the deceased had been very weak lately. Ross called the court's attention to Weingardner's "great destitution" and to the fact that she had in the past "begged assistance" from Ross.[46]

Following his examination of these witnesses, Nesbitt addressed presiding Justice Osler and the jury, emphasizing that, even if Weingardner had died because of instrumental violence, there was no way of determining whether Munson had assisted. He asked the jury to consider Weingardner's motives for procuring the abortion, particularly the fact that "the deceased was a poor miserable outcast, without a dollar in the world."[47] Nesbitt concluded by reminding the jury that "this was one of those cases in which Dame Rumour was busy, and about which untrue statements were made in the press." He pleaded with them "to disabuse their minds of anything of the kind," referring specifically to those rumours being spread about Munson's character.

After the defence presented its concluding remarks, prosecutor Ball began his address to the court by reiterating that he "felt sure that prejudice of colour would not affect [the jurors'] minds in any way."[48] He went on to question why Munson moved Weingardner to a separate home and why she did not alert authorities as soon as she discovered Weingardner's remains. Ball argued that, as a mother herself, Munson surely did not leave Weingardner alone when she was in difficulty; therefore, Munson must have been present when she died. He stated that such cases were becoming "too common" and so, "in the interests of law and justice, and for the protection of society they were bound to find a verdict of guilty."[49] It is clear that Ball felt the jury should make an example of Munson.

Before the final verdict was read, Osler remarked to the court that the Crown had a good case against the accused, particularly regarding the evidence found in Munson's home and the inconsistency of her statements concerning the state of Weingardner's health. However, the jury rendered a verdict of "not guilty" and Munson was discharged.[50] In its concluding remarks on the trial, the *Woodstock Sentinel-Review* declared that while the "jurors were morally certain of the prisoner's guilt," they could not "conscientiously convict" her since "the case against [Munson] did not prove to be even as strong as anticipated, and the anticipation fell short of any hope of conviction."[51] Though, legally, Munson was absolved of any responsibility for Weingardner's death, the journalist's expression of hope for, and anticipation of, guilt demonstrates disagreement with the acquittal.

Reporting the Crime

In late nineteenth-century towns like Woodstock, weekly newspapers (or "weeklies") were important sources of information, education, and entertainment for the literate public. However, they rarely contained fresh news because smaller population densities meant that citizens often knew of the local newsworthy stories before they ever made it to print.[52] Not surprisingly, scandalous crime stories typically occupied the front pages because of their controversial nature; sensationalized headlines, especially for violent and sexual crimes, often accompanied the stories. Sometimes the sordid details of these affairs hit too close to home in smaller communities because of locals' familiarity with the victim or the accused. Such stories also served as cautionary tales aimed at defending the defined social order of a community, as evidenced by the number of trials that were well-documented by local and far-reaching news media outlets alike.[53]

Munson's defence attorney argued in his concluding address that the jury must take into consideration the press's treatment of both the case *and* Munson's character because many statements that he claimed were untrue had recently been published. In various newspaper accounts of the alleged crime, the more heinous-sounding *murder* was often used interchangeably with *abortion*. In the assize court minute book, Munson's official charge is "procuring a miscarriage," but late nineteenth-century legal constructions of miscarriage and abortion were ambiguous at best.[54] For example, though the term "murder" was never used in the courtroom, the *Toronto Globe*'s headline on September 26, 1882, read "Committed for Murder" when describing Munson's supposed complicity in Weingardner's death.

Despite inferences by defence attorney J.W. Nesbitt and witness Harriette Packer that socio-economic status may have influenced Weingardner to abort her pregnancy, the press did not question Weingardner's finances or character. At the inquest, when one of Weingardner's former employers was called as a character witness, she testified that Weingardner "appeared to be respectable" because she had told her that she was married and a mother.[55] As such, a certain level of respectability was conferred upon her. In media accounts, Weingardner was frequently portrayed as the naive victim of not only men's sexual desires but also Munson's purportedly cunning and suspect knowledge. In cases of abortion where the mother survived, some women *were* denigrated by the press for seeking an abortionist's services, but at the Munson trial the press remained mute on this aspect of the case, simply stating that Weingardner "appears to have suffered much hardship during her life."[56] According to Constance Backhouse, "abortion trials typically focused on the abortionist, not the immediate desperation of an unwilling pregnant woman."[57] Munson, then, was forced to face the full brunt of the alleged crime and its aftermath.

An "Interesting Family"

During the inquest, a reporter from the *Toronto Globe* travelled to Woodstock to record the proceedings and view the scene of the alleged crime. In an interview with the "old doctress and her interesting family," the reporter observed that Munson "came slowly along, leaning heavily on a short stick," but willingly shared her side of the story.[58] She told the reporter that she was 110 years old, born a slave on a plantation in North Carolina. Her master sent her to accredited physicians and nearby Indigenous people to learn the "healing art" so that she may be useful around the plantation. According to the reporter, Munson surprisingly "show[ed] great facility in conversation, using language quite above the reach even of one educated with the masses."[59]

The reporter also described Munson's physical appearance at length, that of "a well preserved old negro woman, with a look of great intelligence and rather pleasant face with a red bandana handkerchief in turban shape on her head. Her eyes gleaming over her spectacles, and her benevolent repetition of the appellation 'chile' to whomever she addresses."[60] Munson's son Frederick, "a heavy built, ungainly youth" with a "threatening gleam in the great black eyes," was also mentioned. During the reporter's survey of the alleged crime scene, he found in the family's "little cottage" a "treasury of articles of considerable value" including numerous quilts and more expensive metal items like jewellery and cutlery. The reporter concluded that these items must be "stolen goods" or that they were sent to Munson "as pay for her services."[61]

According to Munson's own account of her origins, she settled in Oxford County in the early 1860s. A marriage register confirms that Commedess Munson and Letitia (née Leeney) were married in Woodstock on January 22, 1862.[62] They purchased two frame houses in the Gore of Oxford West Township, just southwest of Woodstock's town limits. The marriage register lists Munson as twenty-two at the time of her marriage, which conflicts with her own account of her age; the *Globe* reporter judged her to be no more than seventy-three years of age.[63] The Munson household, according to data from the 1881 census, consisted of Letitia and her husband Commedess (age sixty-four), as well as five children, ranging from one to eighteen years of age.[64] In the 1871 census, only a four-year-old child, Frederick, resided with the couple. During the trial, reporters noted that both Commedess and a daughter died sometime in 1881. Based on their ages, locations of birth, and Letitia's advancing age, it is likely that most of the children noted in the 1881 census were adopted. Taking in children, both temporarily and through a formalized system of adoption, was a widespread custom in many African Canadian households.[65]

Midwife and Healer or Abortionist and Murderess?

In addition to providing vivid descriptions and assumptions about her family, the press also questioned Munson's experience as a healer; in some accounts, she is classified as an "abortionist" or "old doctress" while in others she is described as the more maternal-sounding "granny." Historically, the idiom *doctress* was loaded with negative connotations about unacceptable feminine behaviour. Suspicion surrounded doctresses because they offered more general medical services, leaving childbirth to midwives and crossing the gender line by practising like men.[66] When asked if she performed abortions, Munson stated that pregnant women often approached her, but she never performed the requested procedures, instead offering to help send them to a poorhouse in the United States where they could give birth discreetly. Munson recalled one time when a father brought his pregnant daughter to her and offered a cow in exchange for killing and disposing of the infant upon birth. Munson claimed she refused the dreadful request, but did act as midwife during the delivery. When the infant died a week later, local authorities advised Munson not to "make trouble about it" and to hastily burn the corpse in her garden.[67]

The press argued Munson had long been a menace to local police and neighbours alike. However, research failed to uncover much evidence to support this claim, with the exception of a notation in the gaol register from August 1882 when Munson was incarcerated for five days for "procuring an abortion."[68] Nonetheless, the media emphasized that Weingardner's death was just one in a long list of alleged crimes of which Munson was guilty but for which she was never prosecuted. According to the *Globe,* the Weingardner case conjured up memories of all the "alleged horrors connected with the Munson family" and demonstrated that "this old negress must be the incarnation of untold villainy."[69]

When asked how she generated income, Munson told reporters that she took in boarders and told fortunes, but primarily worked as a midwife and healer.[70] The *Globe* suggested that Munson offered unlicenced medical services "avoided by regular practitioners," though she told the *Globe* reporter that her old age prevented her from practising medicine very often.[71] She admits that some women approached her for medical advice, but she chiefly performed common procedures like lancing boils, doing so not only for financial gain, but also "out of charity."[72] As a healer and obstetrical consultant, Munson testified that she was working "for the good of the public" and ought to receive praise for her benevolence. She cited Weingardner as an example, noting that she had given the woman a home rent-free and "otherwise assisted her" when "all others had cast her out."[73]

Midwifery, according to historian J.T.H. Connor, "constitutes the oldest, most traditional, and culturally widespread health care activity."[74] In the antebellum South, it was not uncommon for enslaved women like Munson to receive midwifery training on plantations. They were highly valued and respected in both black and white populations during this period, often being entrusted with the medical care of the white master's family as well.[75] Elderly enslaved women, because of intellectual and maternal connotations associated with age and gender, were thought to possess specialized knowledge of female anatomy, childbirth, and child rearing.[76] Though abortion was considered a heinous crime in both free and enslaved societies in the South, female healers would perform the procedure if a mother's death was imminent. On plantations, abortions presented a conundrum because, while it might save the mother's life, an aborted fetus represented financial loss for the master. However, Tanfer Emin Tunc argues that performing abortions and ingesting abortifacients were common within the relative privacy of the slave quarters as ways to control fertility.[77]

It is impossible, however, to calculate how many female healers and midwives practised in Ontario communities because this sort of occasional employment was rarely listed in the census.[78] Midwifery generally consisted of networks of "'neighbor midwives' who aided each other in their travails."[79] Education often derived from women's own experiences in the birthing room as mothers, observers, and helpers. If they displayed "'good character' and experience,"[80] midwives and female healers were usually left alone by the medical profession. Some male physicians, especially in rural areas and smaller communities, welcomed the services of midwives because of their breadth of experience. For physicians it was the so-called "dirty, ignorant and dangerous" midwives who posed a threat.[81] Because they charged less and could offer expectant mothers companionship and compassion, many women preferred the services of the local midwife.[82]

Abortion, Morality, and Respectability

Given that Weingardner was deceased and could not respond to the charge of unlawfully seeking an abortion, prosecutors and the press concentrated on Munson's role in the alleged crime. Most cases that went to trial involved such a dynamic. In the Dominion of Canada, abortion was illegal with a maximum sentence of life imprisonment.[83] Throughout the nineteenth century, increasing attention was paid to the passage of such fertility control laws because declining birth rates in an increasingly secularized society posed serious moral concerns. At the same time, medical standards were rising, placing a wedge between the "regulars" (i.e., educated doctors) and the "irregulars" or "quacks" (i.e., uneducated doctors or doctors of colour).[84] Many regular doctors refused to perform abortions for legal, moral, or religious reasons, and those who did often became implicated in high-profile scandals and malpractice suits. However, in normal circumstances, most licensed physicians did have the legal authority to perform abortions. Dr. Hugh McKay, a licensed obstetrician and witness for the defence during the Munson trial, indicates in his record books that he performed abortions after diagnosing potentially fatal conditions like uterine and dysmenorrheal hemorrhaging.[85]

When women wished to rid themselves of unwanted pregnancies, they could ably find irregular abortionists, though regular physicians saw such practice as "socially destructive" and as the "solvent of sexual morality and the antithesis of the Christian family."[86] Some abortionists advertised their services in local newspapers, albeit in carefully shrouded medical jargon. When female midwives were found guilty of performing abortions, male medical professionals used the opportunity to assert their own moral authority and to thwart women's power to control reproduction.[87] Because of their illicitness, however, it is impossible to conclude how many abortions were performed, and by whom, and how many resulted in death.

Given that Letitia Munson was a recent widow and raising four children, it is not surprising that she used her medical skills to provide for her family. This was a common practice among older women living in smaller communities where physicians were scarce.[88] Like Munson, other black women in Oxford County were forced to work to subsist. According to the 1881 census, common occupations for black women included domestic service, laundering, millinery work, and being a "workwoman."[89] A number of black women also used their homes as boarding houses.[90] While Oxford County contained a relatively sizable population of blacks in the 1870s and 1880s, they did not benefit from the same structures of social and collective assistance found in communities with higher densities of black residents such as Raleigh and Buxton in Kent County. In predominantly white communities like Woodstock, blacks survived solely through a strict adherence to specific codes and norms of respectability as defined by the white social order. Black women were further marginalized based on gender; few options for what was seen as suitable female employment meant that black women were often forced to perform hard, physical labour that did not conform to white constructions of genteel womanhood.[91]

Munson's choice of occupation meant that local authorities monitored her actions and home life more closely. They were especially concerned with the number of visitors arriving at the Munson household well into the night. Local children reported seeing "white faces peering out" of the windows and citizens whispered that "Granny Munson was engaged in some nefarious trade." Frightened neighbours were convinced that "dark unmentioned crimes" were occurring at Munson's "dark little house where the blinds were always closed, and the door, apparently, never."[92] Employing the adjective "dark" to describe the Munson household and juxtaposing it with the "white" faces was a means of fear-mongering by the press; the white population was warned that they would be "blackened" or "darkened" if they visited her dark home.[93] Such carefully selected diction about race was common in stories about alleged deviance and criminal behaviour. When the *Globe* reporter interviewed Munson, for instance, he stated that she "might easily be taken for the original of Uncle Tom's faithful wife Chloe."[94] Likening Munson to such a popular and beloved literary figure suggested the existence of a "racially harmonious world in which mutual trust and caring existed for the benefit of all involved."[95] Munson, however, posed a risk to Woodstock because of her seemingly cunning ways and a fear that "even if guilty [she] would be able to cover her tracks so well that it would be almost impossible to trace her course."[96] Her skill and intelligence, as the *Globe* reporter indicated, was surprising, but also unnatural and therefore suspect, dangerous, and in need of regulation.

The hardships Munson faced, such as her precarious income and the deaths of her husband and daughter, were dubbed "suspicious" and "strangely sudden" by the media.[97] Such events, and other alleged horrors, propelled a witch hunt of sorts by the Woodstock police. The *Globe* noted that authorities had been long been trying to find a reason to incarcerate Munson. This particularly damning piece declared that "everybody was prepared to give instances of Mrs. Munson's depravity, and though not even charged with any crime ... by the popular mind [she] was guilty of all that was suspected of her, and much more."[98]

Newspaper accounts of the case provide few positive reflections of Munson's character and standing within the community, though, by all accounts, she met socially acceptable standards of respectability. At some point in her past, Munson had rid herself of the slave name of "Lucretia," adopting the similarly sounding "Letitia."[99] Disposing of slave names in favour of more popular white, and often biblically inspired, ones was a marker of being amenable to white society.[100] Respectability was also measured by property ownership, and the Munsons owned not one but two homes.[101] Finally, Munson aided the community by taking young black children into her home, as well as desperate women like Ellen Weingardner. When Weingardner's husband "left her without any money," Munson said she did not wish to see the woman homeless. As repayment, Weingardner did household chores.[102] Despite such acts of generosity, particularly towards young, unmarried girls in the community, Munson was still judged for circumventing white norms of respectability.

o o o

Little is known about Letitia Munson and her family following the conclusion of the trial in November 1882, apart from Frederick Munson's marriage to Feemie Curtis of Chatham, Ontario, in 1885.[103] After this, Munson and her family virtually disappear from the historical record. Her notoriety and advancing age likely meant Munson had difficulty securing work and, without a means to provide for her family, was forced to leave Woodstock.

While Letitia Munson was not the first or only accused abortionist to stand trial in Oxford County, her case was certainly unique in terms of how racialized and gendered ideologies swayed the press's opinion of her character. Though some reporters sympathetically noted Munson's garrulity and high level of intelligence, to most, her role as an arbiter of immoral practices posed a distinct threat to the community's well-being. Unlike juries, who based their decisions on reliable evidence in a court room, the local media carried out its own form of unsubstantiated justice through exaggerated, sensationalized, and inconsistent reports of Munson's role in the alleged crime.

In her attempts to carve a niche for herself in the community, Munson became implicated in Weingardner's death because she was a member of a marginalized racial minority. Though she offered much-needed advice and attended women in need, she circumvented norms of white respectability and the moral principles of regular physicians by supposedly performing unlawful abortions. Though lack of evidence resulted in her acquittal, the community at large, including the press, clearly felt an injustice had been done. Instead of acknowledging her education and benevolence, reporters crafted a story of an elderly black doctress performing suspicious and illegal medical procedures in a community of unsuspecting white men and women.

Notes

This chapter first appeared in the Autumn 2014 edition of *Ontario History* 107, 2: 165–90. It has been modified from its original format.

1 "Found Dead," *Woodstock Sentinel-Review*, September 22, 1882, 1.
2 Ibid.
3 Archives of Ontario (AO), RG 22–3906–0-8, Oxford County Supreme Court assize minute book, "The Queen v. Letitia Munson" (hereafter "The Queen v. Letitia Munson").
4 Reports and reprints about the trial were found in newspapers such as the *Toronto Globe, Dumfries Reformer, Hamilton Spectator, London Free Press, Toronto Mail, Woodstock Sentinel-Review, Ingersoll Chronicle, Toronto World,* and *Guelph Weekly Herald.*
5 Clayton James Mosher, *Discrimination and Denial: Systemic Racism in Ontario's Legal and Criminal Justice Systems, 1892–1961* (Toronto: University of Toronto Press, 1998), 195.
6 "Letitia Munson," *The Globe*, November 17, 1882, 1.
7 Barrington Walker, *Race on Trial: Black Defendants in Ontario's Criminal Courts, 1858–1958* (Toronto: University of Toronto Press, 2010), 12.
8 Canada, *Census of Canada, 1881 – Population* (Ottawa: Dominion Bureau of Statistics, 1881), 83.
9 Michael Wayne, "The Black Population of Canada West on the Eve of the American Civil War: A Reassessment Based on the Manuscript Census of 1861," in *A Nation of Immigrants: Women, Workers, and Communities in Canadian History*, ed. Franca Iacovetta (Toronto: University of Toronto Press, 1998), 71–76.
10 Canada, *Census of Canada, 1881*, 286.
11 Joyce A. Pettigrew, *A Safe Haven: The Story of the Black Settlers of Oxford County* (Otterville, ON: South Norwich Historical Society, 2006), 59.
12 Pettigrew, *A Safe Haven*; Mosher, *Discrimination and Denial*, 83.
13 Pettigrew, *A Safe Haven*, 40.
14 For a collection of Landon's writings, see *Ontario's African-Canadian Heritage: Collected Writings by Fred Landon, 1918–1967*, ed. Karolyn Smardz Frost, Bryan Walls, Hilary Bates Neary, and Frederick H. Armstrong (Toronto: Natural Heritage Books, 2009) and Daniel G. Hill, *The Freedom-Seekers: Blacks in Early Canada* (Agincourt, ON: Book Society of Canada, 1981).
15 Pettigrew, *A Safe Haven*, 40.
16 Ibid., 40–41.
17 See Jason H. Silverman, *Unwelcome Guests: Canada West's Response to American Fugitive Slaves, 1800–1865* (Millwood, NY: Associated Faculty Press, 1985); James W. St.G. Walker, *"Race," Rights, and the Law in the Supreme Court of Canada: Historical Case Studies* (Toronto: The Osgoode Society for Canadian Legal History and Wilfrid Laurier University Press, 1997); Clayton James Mosher, *Crime and Colour, Cops and Courts: Systemic Racism in the Ontario Criminal Justice System in Social and Historical Context, 1892–1961* (Toronto: Commission on Systemic Racism in the Ontario Criminal Justice System, 1993).

18 Owen Thomas, "Cultural Tourism, Commemorative Plaques, and African-Canadian Historiography: Challenging Historical Marginality," *Histoire sociale/Social History* 29, 58 (1996): 431–39.
19 Sharon A. Roger Hepburn, "Following the North Star: Canada as a Haven for Nineteenth-Century American Blacks," *Michigan Historical Review* 25, 2 (1999): 93.
20 Walker, *Race on Trial*, 3.
21 See Constance Backhouse, *Colour-Coded: A Legal History of Racism in Canada, 1900–1950* (Toronto: Osgoode Society for Canadian Legal History by University of Toronto Press, 1999); Robin Winks, *The Blacks in Canada: A History* (New Haven, CT: Yale University Press, 1971).
22 Walker, *Race on Trial*, 183
23 See Karen Dubinsky and Franca Iacovetta, "Murder, Womanly Virtue, and Motherhood: The Case of Angelina Napolitano, 1911–1922," *Canadian Historical Review* 72, 4 (1991): 505–31.
24 Carolyn Strange, "Wounded Womanhood and Dead Men: Chivalry and the Trials of Clara Ford and Carrie Davies," in *Gender Conflicts: New Essays in Women's History*, ed. Franca Iacovetta and Mariana Valverde (Toronto: University of Toronto Press, 1992), 159.
25 Barrington Walker, "The Tale of Ida Jane and George: Murder, Miscegenation, and Bastardy in 1893 Raleigh, Ontario," *Canadian Review of American Studies* 30, 2 (2000): 212.
26 "A Young Couple of Color," *Woodstock Sentinel-Review*, January 10, 1895, 8.
27 Gus Richardson, "Mrs. Letitia (Lecitia) Munson," *Dictionary of Canadian Biography Online 1881–1890,* vol. 11, http://www.biographi.ca/en/bio.php?id_nbr=5728.
28 Amanda Glasbeek, *Feminized Justice: The Toronto Women's Court, 1913–34* (Vancouver: UBC Press, 2009), 22.
29 Description by reporters in "Oxford Assizes," *Woodstock Sentinel-Review,* November 24, 1882, 4.
30 "Abortion at Woodstock," *Toronto World,* September 23, 1882, 1
31 The name is "Camp" or "Kemp," depending on the newspaper consulted.
32 "Oxford Assizes," *Woodstock Sentinel-Review,* 4.
33 The home is referred to as a "shanty."
34 "Found Dead," *Woodstock Sentinel-Review,* 1.
35 "Ague" was a nineteenth-century term for malaria or prevalent fever.
36 "Enceinte" is a synonym for pregnancy. "Oxford Assizes," *Woodstock Sentinel-Review,* 4.
37 "Oxford Assizes," *Woodstock Sentinel-Review,* 4.
38 "A Horrible Crime," *Guelph Weekly Herald,* September 28, 1882, 3.
39 "Letitia Munson," *Toronto Globe,* 1.
40 "Found Dead," *Woodstock Sentinel-Review,* 1.
41 "Oxford Assizes," *Woodstock Sentinel-Review,* 4.
42 Ibid.
43 "Found Dead," *Woodstock Sentinel-Review*, 1.
44 "Oxford Assizes," *Woodstock Sentinel-Review,* 4.
45 *Placenta praevia* is when the placenta is attached to the uterine wall close to or covering the cervix.
46 "Oxford Assizes," Woodstock Sentinel-Review, 4.
47 Ibid.
48 Ibid.
49 Ibid.
50 Through research into the identities of jury members using the 1881 census, it appears that all jury members were white males.
51 "Oxford Assizes," *Woodstock Sentinel-Review,* 4.

52 Paul Voisey, *High River and the Times: An Alberta Community and Its Weekly Newspaper, 1905–1966* (Edmonton, AB: University of Alberta Press, 2004), xviii–xxiii.
53 Ibid., 56.
54 "The Queen v. Letitia Munson."
55 "Found Dead," *Woodstock Sentinel-Review,* 1.
56 "Committed for Murder," *Toronto Globe,* September 26, 1882, 2.
57 Backhouse, *Petticoats and Prejudice,* 163.
58 "Committed for Murder," *Toronto Globe,* 2.
59 Ibid.
60 Ibid.
61 Ibid.
62 He is identified as "Commadess" in the 1881 census, "Comegyss" in the 1871 census and 1885 record of his son Frederick's marriage, "Comegs" in the 1861 census, and "Cummings" in the Oxford County Marriage Register. "Commadess" has been used throughout this chapter because at the time of the trial it was the most recent mention of his name. Available sources contain variances of Letitia Munson's name including "Latitia," "Letrita," "Lucretia," and "Lecitia." The more-widely cited "Letitia" has been used here. AO, MS 248 Reel 12, County Marriage Registers of Ontario Canada, 1858–1869, Volume 26, Oxford County.
63 In the census, Munson is listed as forty-three years old in 1871 and sixty-three years old in 1881. See LAC, Census of Canada, 1871, Schedule 1 – Nominal Return of the Living, Ontario, South Oxford, http://www.bac-lac.gc.ca/eng/census/1871/Pages/about-census.aspx; LAC, Census of Canada, 1881, Schedule 1 – Nominal Return of the Living, Ontario, Oxford South, http://www.bac-lac.gc.ca/eng/census/1881/Pages/about-census.aspx (hereafter Census of Canada 1881, Oxford South).
64 Census of Canada 1881, Oxford South. In the 1861 census, only "Comegs" Munson is listed as living in Oxford County.
65 Sharon A. Hepburn, *Crossing the Border: A Free Black Community in Canada* (Urbana: University of Illinois Press, 2007), 100–2.
66 Rebecca J. Tannenbaum, *The Healer's Calling: Women and Medicine in Early New England* (Ithaca and London: Cornell University Press, 2002), 118.
67 "Committed for Murder," *Toronto Globe,* 2.
68 County of Oxford Archives, RG2, Series 6, Treasurer Box 1, Subseries A, Administration of Justice 1850–1887, Return of Prisoners Confined in the Gaol of the County of Oxford, dated at Woodstock.
69 "Committed for Murder," *Toronto Globe,* 2.
70 "Abortion at Woodstock," *Toronto World,* 1.
71 Ibid.
72 "Committed for Murder," *Toronto Globe,* 2.
73 Ibid.
74 J.T.H. Connor, "'Larger Fish to Catch Here Than Midwives': Midwifery and the Medical Profession in Nineteenth-Century Ontario," in *Caring and Curing: Historical Perspectives on Women and Healing in Canada*, ed. Dianne Dodd and Deborah Gorham (Ottawa: University of Ottawa Press, 1994), 103.
75 Tanfer Emin-Tunc, "The Mistress, the Midwife, and the Medical Doctor: Pregnancy and Childbirth on the Plantations of the Antebellum American South, 1800–1860," *Women's History Review* 19, 3 (2010): 399. See also Rebecca Fraser, *Courtship and Love among the Enslaved in North Carolina* (Jackson: University Press of Mississippi, 2007).
76 For more on black midwives on plantations, see V. Lynn Kennedy, *Born Southern: Childbirth, Motherhood, and Social Networks in the Old South* (Baltimore, MD: Johns Hopkins University Press, 2010).

77 Emin-Tunc, "The Mistress, the Midwife, and the Medical Doctor," 397.
78 Suzanne Morton, "Separate Spheres in a Separate World: African-Nova Scotian Women in Late-19th-Century Halifax County," in *Separate Spheres: Women's Worlds in the 19th-Century Maritimes*, ed. Janet Guildford and Suzanne Morton (Fredericton, NB: Acadiensis Press, 1994), 193.
79 See Charlotte G. Borst, *Catching Babies: The Professionalization of Childbirth, 1870–1920* (Cambridge, MA: Harvard University Press, 1995).
80 Connor, "Larger Fish Here to Catch Than Midwives," 109.
81 C. Lesley Biggs, "The Case of the Missing Midwives: A History of Midwifery in Ontario from 1795–1900," *Ontario History* 75, 1 (1983): 31.
82 Ibid., 29.
83 Mollie Dunsmuir, "Abortion: Constitutional and Legal Developments," Government of Canada Depository Services Program, last modified May 6, 2004, http://dsp-psd.pwgsc.gc.ca/Collection-R/LoPBdP/CIR/8910-e.htm.
84 Backhouse, *Petticoats and Prejudice*, 143.
85 AO, F 775, MU2118 F 2189, Hugh M. McKay fonds, "Record of Midwifery Case."
86 Michael McCulloch, "'Dr. Tumblety, the Indian Herb Doctor': Politics, Professionalism, and Abortion in Mid-Nineteenth-Century Montreal," *Canadian Bulletin of Medical History* 10 (1993): 52.
87 Leslie J. Reagan, "Linking Midwives and Abortion in the Progressive Era," *Bulletin of the History of Medicine* 69, 4 (1995): 573, 589.
88 See Cecilia Benoit, "Mothering in a Newfoundland Community: 1900–1940," in *Delivering Motherhood: Maternal Ideologies and Practices in the 19th and 20th Centuries,* ed. Katherine Arnup, Andrée Lévesque, and Ruth Roach Pierson (London and New York: Routledge, 1990), 185.
89 "Workwoman" refers to a female who performed all manner of work, or one especially gifted in needlework.
90 For more on black women and the labour market, see Peggy Bristow, "'Whatever You Raise in the Ground You Can Sell It in Chatham': Black Women in Buxton and Chatham, 1850–65," in *"We're Rooted Here and They Can't Pull Us Up": Essays in African Canadian Women's History,* ed. Peggy Bristow et al. (Toronto: University of Toronto Press, 1994), 69–142.
91 Morton, "Separate Spheres in a Separate World," 200–1.
92 "Letitia Munson," *Toronto Globe,* 1.
93 Barrington Walker, "The Gavel and the Veil of Race: 'Blackness' in Ontario's Criminal Courts, 1858–1958" (PhD diss., University of Toronto, 2003), 84.
94 "Committed for Murder," *Toronto Globe,* 2.
95 Kennedy, *Born Southern,* 104. See also Fraser, *Courtship and Love among the Enslaved in North Carolina,* 25.
96 "Committed for Murder," *Toronto Globe,* 2.
97 Ibid.
98 Ibid.
99 "Found Dead," *Woodstock Sentinel-Review,* 1.
100 Hepburn, *Crossing the Border,* 111.
101 Ibid., 45.
102 "Found Dead," *Woodstock Sentinel-Review,* 1.
103 AO, RG 80–7, MS 934 Reel 5, Indexes to Marriages 1873–1929. At the time, Munson was working as a cabinet maker. According to the 1891 census, a four-year-old child (also named Frederick Munson) is listed as living with Curtis's parents in Chatham, but he is referred to as a "nephew." See Census of Canada online, 1891, accessed February 20, 2010, http://www.bac-lac.gc.ca/eng/census/1891/Pages/1891.aspx.

3

Abortion and Birth Control on the Canadian Prairies

Feminists, Catholics, and Family Values in the 1970s

Erika Dyck

> "Bless me, Father, for I have sinned, I ... " With these words, I open my confession to my priest. I then proceed to tell him all my sins – all except one, that is. That one I cannot tell him for if I did, he would be unable to give me absolution for my sins; unless, of course, I can promise him that I will never break that law of the church again, and that I cannot do. For you see, I know I will commit that sin over and over again and I will go right on committing it year after year. I can't help it. I just cannot go on having one pregnancy after another.
>
> – Joan O'Donnell, "A Catholic Mother Answers the Pope: Husbands and Wives Are Flesh-and-Blood People, Not Holy Saints"

Using a pseudonym to protect her family, a Catholic woman wrote the article cited above for *Chatelaine* magazine in 1968, following a statement issued by the Pope that all forms of contraception and abortion were strictly prohibited. The author explained to *Chatelaine* readers that she was a married mother of four and devoutly Catholic. She admitted that her third and fourth pregnancies had been unwanted and riddled with medical problems, including an ulcer that her doctor warned was exacerbated by her anxiety over insufficient family finances. She realized that if she remained strictly faithful to the teachings of her Church, she could continue to have children until menopause, and this prospect terrified her.

She then reflected on her Catholic upbringing and the family values it had instilled in her:

> the sun shone on the mother of a large family. She was the finest example of Catholic motherhood. I wonder, now that I am older, however, if their respect was based on the actual personal worth of the mother herself, or if it was based solely on the number of children she had brought into the world, proving her devoutness as a Catholic.[1]

After recalling stories from her friends and neighbours, and even her own mother's untimely death during childbirth, the author concluded that her Church was out of step with the realities faced by modern North American families. This short article expressed the personal feelings of one conflicted Canadian Catholic mother, but her comments touched upon a much broader set of sentiments that resonated throughout Canadian homes in the late 1960s and 1970s.[2]

Abortion politics had reached a fever pitch by the early 1970s, and conflicting perspectives on the issue clashed with contemporaneous cultural and political movements, including the women's movement; the so-called sexual revolution; the expansion of the welfare state, which included provisions for publicly funded health care; and the repositioning of the Catholic Church within Canada. Abortion debates, however, took centre stage within broader discussions over reproductive rights that had been brewing throughout the century. Second-wave feminism gained momentum throughout the 1960s and altered the language of choice when it came to women's rights, including women's stated right to sexual expression and control over their fertility. The introduction of new medical technologies, in particular, the birth control pill, reinforced women's new social position. The "pill" promised to release women from their biological fates and ushered in new possibilities for describing equality. The power and promise of this chemical innovation had far-reaching consequences, not only for women as mothers and individuals, but for the cultural discourse surrounding the morality of reproduction and the sanctity of the modern family.[3] In this essay, I argue that Canadian Catholics began articulating their own responses to these changing dynamics about the modern family. In particular, some western Canadian bishops offered a more liberal interpretation of papal doctrine in an attempt to retain the full support of women, such as the one who wrote to

Chatelaine cited above, who were struggling to balance the demands of family, work, and faith.

The decriminalization of abortion emerged within this highly charged atmosphere of reproductive politics. For some, abortion represented the next logical progression in a series of steps taken to secure reproductive autonomy. For others, abortion represented a serious affront to the natural laws of humanity and the moral code of civilized society. By exploring Catholic reactions to abortion and focusing on responses from one particular Catholic news outlet centred in Saskatchewan, I seek to trace the way that English Canadians participated in contemporary debates about modern family values.[4] Debates about abortion arose as part of a longer set of discussions over contraception, but in many ways abortion was set apart. Canadian Catholic bishops seized upon the distinction between preventing reproduction and ending it as one way of appealing to Canadian laity. Saskatchewan Catholics reacted strongly to the issue and many provided firm support for launching pro-life campaigns. Others, however, especially Catholic women in Saskatchewan, began articulating a feminist view that prioritized family rights over individual rights, but did so while critiquing the way the Church continued to restrict women's roles within the Catholic hierarchy. By examining these various reactions, from those of the Pope to those of Catholic feminists in Saskatchewan, it becomes clear that the issue of abortion helped to crystalize social divisions, but also produced new alliances.

Decriminalizing Abortion

The changing legal status of abortion in Canada came as part of a series of amendments to the Canadian *Criminal Code* in a federal omnibus bill initiated under Prime Minister Pierre Elliott Trudeau in 1969, who publicly stated in a somewhat flippant remark that "the state has no business in the bedrooms of the nation."[5] The original Canadian *Criminal Code* of 1892 had prohibited abortions, alongside abortifacients and any devices or advice leading to abortions.[6] The law had not been significantly revisited for over seventy-five years, until Trudeau's government tackled the issue alongside contraception, homosexuality, and other sexual acts, thus representing changing cultural attitudes towards sex and individual freedoms.[7] The law substantially changed the legality of abortions by permitting qualified physicians to perform the operation without risk of criminal offence and allowing women to legally seek and procure abortions, assuming they could find willing practitioners.

The change in law indicated that a woman could obtain an abortion if she had the approval of a Therapeutic Abortion Committee demonstrating in writing its "opinion [that] the continuation of the pregnancy of such female person would or would be likely to endanger her life or health."[8] Historian Christabelle Sethna has argued that this legal change did very little to improve access to abortions, as many physicians felt that the risk of criminal liability remained a serious concern. As Sethna has pointed out, Canadian women had long sought abortions; the amended law, it seemed, merely gave more people a rallying point from which they could articulate a series of grievances.[9]

Opposition to the omnibus bill's changes to the laws concerning abortion came from all sides. Some feminists felt that the new law did not go far enough towards securing women's autonomy over reproductive health decisions. They resented the way that the bill empowered an abortion committee to decide whether or not a surgery could be performed, and decried the idea that the law insisted that a woman's health be endangered before abortion could be recommended. Others directly opposed the decriminalization altogether and were unsatisfied with the vague application of the notion of health as a deciding factor in these cases; they worried that health concerns would balloon out of control to include all manner of excuses, from economic to political, and that claims about health risks would stray far from mortality, where they presumably belonged. Catholic pro-life campaigns arose and referred to the recent encyclical issued by the Pope, *Humanae Vitae,* which denounced abortion as an open contravention of Catholic doctrine, a direct assault on families, and an aggressive policy of feticide. Bouyed by the encyclical, several outspoken Catholics organized to protect the rights of the unborn. However, not all Catholics adopted the view articulated by the Pope, even when it came to abortion. Catholic feminists displayed consternation over the tension between women's and children's rights and began developing their own interpretations.

Several months after the omnibus bill passed, dissatisfied women's liberation activists initiated a movement they referred to as an "abortion caravan," beginning in Vancouver. Reproducing the model of the 1935 On to Ottawa Trek by unemployed men during the Depression, the women gathered supporters as they travelled east to Ottawa. These women surpassed their historical counterparts, however, whose progress en masse was halted in Regina; in contrast, the women took their march all the way to Ottawa, carrying a coffin adorned with coat hangers and placards denouncing the government's resolution to keep abortion decisions in the hands of hospital committees. Historians Christabelle Sethna and Steve Hewitt have explored this campaign, including the failed attempts of the Royal Canadian Mounted Police (RCMP) to control it. According to Sethna and Hewitt, the women ultimately gathered in front of 24 Sussex Drive because the RCMP had not taken the women activists seriously and had no training in dealing with female protesters.[10] However, these women were not the only ones marching in Ottawa protesting the new abortion laws. Approximately one hundred anti-abortion activists countered the abortion caravan that day, and other, larger groups later employed the same tactics as part of a burgeoning Canadian pro-life lobby.[11]

Canadian Catholics Respond to *Humanae Vitae*

Even before the change in abortion and contraception laws in Canada, the issue of reproductive rights attracted considerable attention internationally, and one particularly key component of that debate came from the Catholic Church.[12] The birth control pill had been introduced in North America in the mid-1960s to much controversy. The scientists behind the pill included biologist Gregory Pincus and obstetrician John Rock, both of whom were urged along and funded by feminists and family planning advocates Margaret Sanger and Katherine McCormack. While Sanger and McCormack had deep roots in the eugenics movement and were implicated with the Malthusian League for population control, Rock, the physician, was sympathetic, despite being deeply Catholic.[13] As the science of the pill improved and the results from patients stabilized, Rock grew increasingly confident that medical science had developed a solution to global population pressures and that even the Catholic Church should accept the logic of a chemical solution to the burden of fertility, particularly among poor regions and families. Catholic teaching, he reasoned, allowed for sexual relations during a woman's "safe period," even with the express intention of avoiding conception.[14] He further reasoned that the birth control pill merely ensured a consistent and prolonged safe period through the aid of synthetic hormones. Rock believed the pill reinforced what the Church espoused as natural methods, but simply provided scientific security. Rock's biographers put it this way: "In 1964, John Rock expressed confidence that within a few years the pill would change the mind of the Catholic Church about the intrinsic evil of contraception, easing anxieties about unwanted pregnancies for millions of couples around the world. Once the Church liberalized its attitude toward birth control, he believed, the problem of global overpopulation could be addressed."[15] Birth control also reduced or eliminated a reliance on abortions, which the Church and the Catholic laity regarded as well beyond natural law. Rock was correct that the Church took the issue of contraception under serious consideration, but like many others within the Catholic fold he was dismayed by the Pope's reaction.

Pope Paul VI's response to the introduction of the pill was encapsulated in the 1968 papal encyclical *Humanae Vitae,* where he explicitly condemned all contraceptive measures in strict and unwavering terms. He expressly condemned anything that contributed to the "direct interruption of the generative process already begun" and went on to specify abortion and sterilization of either women or men. [16] For many Catholics, this definitive statement espousing a conservative attitude towards reproduction signalled the ossification of the Church and its waning grip on the realities faced by modern families. The statement attracted dissenters and splinters within the organization, and Canadian Catholics became part of that larger trend.

Following the announcement from Rome, Canadian bishops gathered in St. Boniface in Winnipeg, Manitoba, and issued their own response, known as the Winnipeg Statement, which stated that they permitted Catholic couples to practise contraception "in good conscience" and remain upstanding members of the faith.[17] The Canadian bishops' declaration promised a more flexible interpretation of the sanctity of human life and church doctrine, at times allowing even for a more liberal discussion of abortion, especially among Catholic women.[18] The Winnipeg Statement aroused controversy among Catholics, especially the laity, and pitted groups against one another as it deepened the divide between Catholic interpretations of feminism, reproduction, and family values.

Christian Authority in Twentieth-Century Canada

Canadian historians have debated the degree to which secular ideals stimulated cultural shifts in moral authority. David Marshall has argued that Christianity bowed to a more secular agenda dominated by materialism and leisure.[19] Marshall's work tracks the decline in church membership following the First and Second World Wars, suggesting that the welfare state assumed many of the responsibilities once held by the church. Michael Gauvreau and Nancy Christie disagree and instead argue that religion in Canada reoriented itself in the first half of the twentieth century to face challenges of modern social welfare in new ways, especially through a renewed institutional commitment to social work and health care.[20] Abortion politics put the new moral compass to a test, and the Catholic Church staked out its position in the debates in an effort to regain its own cultural position within a changing, even modernizing, society.

According to historian Brenda Appleby, the cumulative changes to contraception triggered reactions from religious quarters throughout Canada. In her appraisal of their reactions, she found that Catholics tended to distinguish between civil law and moral law, the latter being an arena over which they still retained significant authority.[21] By the 1960s, it appeared that Roman Catholics anticipated a more relaxed attitude that would allow for moderation of the menstrual cycle to ensure a "safe period" as part of the discourse on responsible parenthood, both to appease parishioners and to bring about ecumenical consensus.[22]

Historian and Jesuit priest Terence Fay provided a sweeping history of Catholics in Canada, including a short section on the issue of contraception. He describes how Canadian bishops split from papal tradition in their reaction to *Humanae Vitae.*[23] As Fay explains, the reaction represented two growing factions within Catholicism in Canada, one evolving into the pro-life camp and the other organizing around social justice principles and taking cues from social gospel and women's liberation movements. Catholic women were especially caught up in this division, but as Fay demonstrates, the laity in Canada remained polarized and "it happened that not many clergy were involved in pro-life activities."[24] In other words, the Catholic hierarchy and the Catholic laity began moving in different directions, in a manner that was exacerbated by contests over how to interpret and practise the morals of contraception. Appleby supports this view, but also shows that Canadian bishops, while comparatively lenient on the issue of contraception, remained fundamentally opposed to abortion. This demarcation further distinguished their response from other Christian reactions throughout Canada, who continued to see the issues as interconnected, whether they supported or denounced the practices.[25]

Fay shows that this division deepened throughout the 1970s, particularly among Catholic women, some of whom chose to dissent from the

Church openly, and others who formed pro-life organizations and instead remained focused on the sanctity of the family rather than defining the issue as one specific to women. Abortion arose in these debates as a key concern, crystalizing the issue for some who tolerated contraception but refused to place abortion on the same spectrum. Interpreting these matters became a defining feature of Catholic feminism.

The Winnipeg Statement

The Catholic Church in western Canada faced specific challenges throughout the early and mid-twentieth century. In particular, it confronted the growing popularity of the social gospel movement and the charismatic political leadership of Protestant ministers who fused religion and politics to evangelize the West under the banner of progress. James Shaver Woodsworth (1874–1942) in Manitoba and Tommy Douglas (1904–86) in Saskatchewan accomplished this directly through connections with the social gospel movement as they led the Cooperative Commonwealth Federation. In Alberta, the social gospel fed the Social Credit Party with William Aberhart and then Ernest Manning at the political helm. These populist Protestant Prairie politicians used religious principles and tactics to connect with the electorate and consequently challenged the Catholic Church to maintain and expand its community connections. Reflecting on this matter, William F. Ryan, an insider and long-time senior executive and adviser to the Canadian Council of Catholic Bishops, suggested that western Canadian Catholics had already shown a willingness to adopt new social and policy initiatives on the path towards modernizing and accepting a new relationship between Church and State. The primary evidence for this acceptance came from the overwhelming support for medicare in the mid-1960s, in which Catholics participated fully and enthusiastically. Indeed, Justice Emmett Hall, the lead commissioner on the 1964 Royal Commission on Health Services, was "a distinguished Catholic layman."[26] Such factors may have helped to pave the way towards a greater acceptance of medical science and modern technology as it pertained to family planning.

Considering the perspectives of the Catholic laity, Ryan critiqued the conservatism of the Church, stating:

> [T]he publishing of the *Humanae vitae* with its unexpected rejection of artificial contraception proved a supreme test for the solidarity of the

> Canadian bishops ... They stood with Paul VI in his pastoral teaching, but they also stood with those faithful laity who could not, even with an informed conscience, accept this teaching on artificial contraception – advising them that this should not keep them away from the sacraments.[27]

In the Winnipeg Statement, the Canadian bishops agreed that the family remained a sacred and fundamental unit, but could not abide by the lack of attention to new medical knowledge that provided reproductive solutions. They addressed this point directly in their response to the *Humanae Vitae*: "the argumentation and rational foundation of the encyclical, which are only briefly indicated, have failed in some cases to win the assent of men of science, or indeed of some men of culture and education who share in the contemporary empirical and scientific mode of thought."[28] Finally, they expressed their own support for medical science in the field of contraception: "We earnestly solicit the help of medical scientists and biologists in their research into human fertility. While it would be an illusion to hope for the solution of all human problems through scientific technology, such research can bring effective help to the alleviation and solution of problems of conscience in this area."[29]

The Canadian bishops sparked controversy by invoking the language of science and by allowing Catholics to act "in good conscience" on the matter of birth control. Some Canadians felt that this more liberal interpretation was irresponsible and had disastrous consequences. Vincent Foy, priest of the Archdiocese of Toronto, who during the 1960s was director of the Archdiocesan Catechetical Office, regularly lamented the Winnipeg Statement and the deleterious effects it had on Canadian Catholicism. In 1998, on the thirtieth anniversary of *Humanae Vitae,* he complained that

> about 90% of married Canadian Catholics believe that they can contracept [sic] without sin and that contraceptive practice is not an obstacle to the reception of Holy Communion. In Canada Catholics abort, contracept, are sterilized, and are divorced at about the same rate as non-Catholics. Could there be a more ominous omen of what the future holds in store for the Church in Canada?"[30]

Others similarly associated the Winnipeg Statement's loosening of morals and break from the Vatican with corruption in modern culture, and, in particular, with a waning faith in family values. However, the Canadian

Council of Catholic Bishops remained collectively supportive of the Winnipeg Statement in spite of individual dissent among some of the high-ranking bishops.

Canadian Catholic Feminists Respond

The 1970s language of feminism blended with new, more empowering connotations associated with reproduction as a matter of choice. Choice, in the eyes of supporters, did not contradict morality. Women recognized that access to abortion surgeries or birth control technologies might help ensure that they took the path of morality and grew up to be suburban wives and mothers. Post–Second World War ideals of affluence and a nuclear family became more attainable when coupled with the possibility of planning a family with reasonable assurances.[31]

Catholic women were tangled up in these broader trends. Some found stronger allegiances with mainstream feminism and moved away from the Church. Others stood steadfastly behind the Church and rallied in opposition to the language of choice, which they associated with corrupting values such as materialism, selfishness, and secularity. Others still attempted to find a middle position: one that was both feminist and Catholic.[32]

For example, La Leche League, developed in the United States, articulated a perspective that celebrated motherhood, feminism, and Catholicism. Historically, according to historian Jule DeJager Ward, La Leche League "was born of Catholic moral discourse on family life and nurtured by the scientific convictions of a sociobiological ethic. The League has very strong convictions about the needs of families."[33] DeJager Ward described La Leche League as self-consciously both feminist and Catholic, and an organization that formed in the post–Second World War period in an attempt to articulate a middle way for Catholic women in the context of escalating concerns over the politics of motherhood. Like the Canadian bishops, the League "made a conscious decision to engage in an ongoing conversation with scientific research and to keep their organization pluralist in constituency and secular in ethos."[34] Put simply, women felt caught in a moral quandary and found their position within the Church troubling: "Catholicism encompasses a complex and often confusing understanding of women: it perceives them as subordinate to men in human relationships yet equal with men before God."[35] DeJager Ward explains that La Leche League women see themselves as feminist but not necessarily part of second-wave feminism, which they reject as a denial or resistance of motherhood as a defining feature of feminism. Instead they position themselves within a longer tradition of feminism that places infants at the centre and as the highest priority – even above women themselves.[36] La Leche League moved away from its Catholic origins over time, but continued to contribute to discussions on the relationship between motherhood and feminism. Returning to early twentieth-century principles of feminism rooted in maternal precepts, La Leche League women reaffirmed their status as mothers as the defining feature of their feminism. Founded as a Catholic organization, the League also furnished women with a discourse that found common ground between mainstream feminism and Catholic doctrine in the 1960s.

La Leche League spread into Canada during the 1960s, but Canadian women – both Catholic and non-Catholic – had also begun formulating a similar response to combat the contemporary liberal feminist movement with opposing perspectives from women who maintained more traditional views on femininity and family. One important player within this historical context was the Saskatchewan-based Catholic newspaper *The Prairie Messenger*. This weekly newspaper connected Prairie Catholics to world events, travelling lectures, papal encyclicals, and local current events from its base at St. Peter's College in Muenster, Saskatchewan. Benedictine monks of St. Peter's Abbey had established Muenster at the turn of the twentieth century and set up St. Peter's College as an affiliate of the University of Saskatchewan in 1921. The college became a centre for Catholic education and boasted one of the largest libraries in the region. Located in an area with a high proportion of German Catholics, St. Peter's College and its *Prairie Messenger* became an important institution for distributing Catholic literature throughout the Prairies during this period.

Throughout the early 1970s, the *Prairie Messenger* featured articles related to contraception and abortion, most of which reaffirmed the official Catholic position on the issues. It often relied on women's views and responses as a way to bolster the credibility of the perspectives it published and, consequently, to foster a sense of Catholic feminism in the Prairies. In an article in the *Prairie Messenger*, journalist Edna Hudson found that Gloria V. Heffernan, a Chicago physician, had "called abortion 'the final insult,'" and stated that 'the strange compulsion for abortion is in reality the ultimate exploitation of women by immature men: technocrats, generally imbued with a myopic sense of social awareness and unable to interpret or control their own sexuality.'"[37] Heffernan, according to Hudson, fit the profile of a modern woman, this time a physician, who expressed her disgust simultaneously for patriarchal sexual relations and for the response by women who saw abortion as a solution to these social imbalances. Drawing on elements of second-wave feminism, Heffernan fused maternal and professional feminist perspectives into a coherent defence against abortion.

Other articles in the *Prairie Messenger* suggested that, while abortion campaigns revolved in part around issues of access and social justice for impoverished women that Catholics should be concerned about, the statistics indicated that it was more often middle-class women who took advantage of abortion services, reinforcing the notion that contraception was a ruse for selfishness and anti-family views. A report from Member of Parliament Douglas Roche explained to *Prairie Messenger* readers that the number of abortions in Canada had risen steadily since the change in the abortion law, and that, in fact, it had quadrupled in the early 1970s. Roche was particularly concerned with the rates of increase in British Columbia, Ontario, and Alberta, which he identified as the wealthiest provinces. He suggested that "these figures support the argument that abortions are being permitted for reasons far beyond health; to argue otherwise is to suggest that it is more dangerous to a mother's health to be pregnant in a rich, instead of a poor, province."[38]

Some women continued to support the Vatican's teachings on reproduction and organized pro-life and family alliance committees to counsel women against contraception and abortion, but women's activism within the Church remained constrained. A statement from the Vatican in 1975, reprinted in the *Prairie Messenger,* suggested that "women may be disappointed" after learning that the "church wants women to have a fitting role in church life and decision-making, but women's liberation groups ... are harboring 'impossible expectations.'"[39] It appeared that while women played an important role in activating certain discussions and carrying out the day-to-day work of the church, the notion of "liberation" or equality, concepts espoused by the women's liberation movement, went too far. Women were still not in a position to take on higher roles within the Church administration or advance women's perspectives within the hierarchy. Although the newspaper did not elaborate on this issue, it appeared that, in spite of advances in some areas, women within the Church remained on the margins of authority.

The *Prairie Messenger* did not publish women's reactions to the Vatican's statement, though women may have chosen other publishing outlets or simply found other ways to exercise their perspectives if they were not aligned with the Pope's. For example, the *Chatelaine* article cited at the beginning of this chapter indicates that some Catholic women openly questioned what they recognized as a clash between modern feminism, modern families, and Catholic prescriptions for each; some such women added their voices to mainstream women's organizations and articulated their concerns in those more receptive environments. The physician John Rock, who helped to develop and later market the birth control pill, also grew disillusioned with a Church that he felt failed to confront the realities of modern medicine and society. As early as the 1950s, medical reports in the United Kingdom demonstrated that the numbers of Catholic women seeking birth control, sterilization, and abortion were climbing, representing already 30 percent of the cases in the 1950s while those activities remained illegal.[40] Edmonton hospital administrators feared that the rising demand for sexual sterilization operations was creating an untenable strain on hospital resources. Catholic hospitals refused to provide abortions, which left the remaining hospitals to take on the extra demand.[41] Yet reports in Alberta indicated that increasing numbers of Catholic women were demanding contraception and abortion services.[42] Catholic families had begun making their own decisions, whether in "good conscience" as the Canadian bishops encouraged, as a personal decision to step away from the Church, or within some delicate and often invisible mixture of faith, feminism, and family values.

Chatelaine magazine took the idea of contraception to a global level in an attempt to shatter the myth of Catholicism and birth control. An editorial in 1968 claimed that "the average annual birthrate in the eleven Roman Catholic countries of Europe, is eighteen per thousand and in the fifteen non-Roman Catholic countries, exactly the same."[43] The editor pointed out the hypocrisy of dividing the issue along religious lines and went on to suggest that "the tragedy, then, is not that populations will automatically boom because of the Pope's announcement. The tragedy is that individual devout Catholics may feel in conscience that they have to go against the highest authority of the church."[44]

By 1975 there was a growing anti-abortion lobby in Canada, fuelled in part by the Catholic opposition to birth control and abortion. Lobbyists collected signatures on a petition to revoke the abortion laws and initiated a march that attracted nearly three thousand people to the gates of Parliament, compared with the meager hundreds who had occupied the ground outside the prime minister's house as part of the abortion caravan five years earlier. One Regina woman involved in the march told the *Prairie Messenger* that "for the first time the cloud lifted and I realized that it was the unborn child that brought the East and West together putting political prejudices aside."[45] She remarked on the mixture of cultures, languages, and religious denominations that seemed to be represented in the assembly of protesters. The marchers submitted a petition with over a million signatures, thirty-three thousand of which came from Saskatchewan alone, demanding that the prime minister reverse his decision to decriminalize abortions, claiming that hospital abortion committees were "not accountable to anyone for their actions."[46] The march, called the Alliance for Life, claimed that 43,201 legal abortions had taken place in 1973 alone, which implied that abortions on demand were indeed taking place in Canadian hospitals in spite of the provisions spelled out in the law that abortions could only occur when health risks were at stake. One of the chief critiques of the law was that the language of health remained vague and open to abuse. Instead, the Alliance for Life insisted that abortions should only be legal when the woman's life was in grave danger.

The *Prairie Messenger* maintained its pro-life position in these debates, but demonstrated that even within the pro-life campaign perspectives varied. The paper suggested that women dominated pro-life marches, which illustrated that women's views did not fit neatly into a single camp. Catholic feminists tried to carve out their own position in the debates, and at this time formed a new organization called Feminists for Life, which first took root in the Midwestern United States. Feminists for Life vehemently claimed in their statement of purpose that "we demand an end to all legal, social and economic discrimination against women," but "we believe it is inconsistent to demand rights for ourselves and deny them to unborn babies." They went on to criticize other feminist organizations for taking a pro-abortion stance, suggesting that "by diverting time and energy into abortion legislation feminist organizations have deemphasized the struggle for legal and social equality."[47] The root of the abortion issue for these Catholic feminists was the struggle for women to help promote social equality such that women did not need to resort to abortion, and to increase the flow of information about birth control so that women had greater control over their own bodies. This position represented an open break from the official Church doctrine, as spelled out in *Humanae Vitae*, but continued to uphold the rights of the unborn child, language that was being taken up with increased frequency. In particular, Feminists for Life targeted the

National Organization for Women (NOW) for its liberal views on abortion and worked to expel members from within its chapters who tolerated abortions. They maintained: "We are concerned that many sections of the women's movement regard women's liberation as inseparable from a policy of abortion on demand. We might fight for social justice and real support for pregnant women in difficulties, rather than the negative and reactionary policy of destroying human life in the womb."[48] Moreover, Feminists for Life argued that "the abortion movement is not a true part of the women's movement," believing that it denigrated women and mothers.[49]

By the mid- to late 1970s, the lines became more entrenched, dividing Catholic feminists from women's liberationists, and birth control or contraceptives from abortion. Although women continued to spill outside of these categories and cross boundaries, the politics of abortion had served to realign moral authority over modern family values. Feminist voices arose throughout, embracing, resisting, and compromising on the issues of contraception. Contraception itself became subject to multiple interpretations as to what constituted a contraceptive practice, ranging from surgical sterilization, to birth control pills, and ultimately to abortion. Different acts invited different supporters and detractors, and each new alliance grafted itself onto a moral map for interpreting family values.

Women, Conservatives, and Abortion Politics in the Twenty-First Century

In 2012, then prime minister Stephen Harper came under attack from opposition members as well as from within the ranks of his own Conservative Party for not effectively managing abortion legislation. Fellow Conservative officials publicly demanded that the prime minister reopen the debates surrounding abortion laws. Stephen Woodworth, Member of Parliament for Kitchener Centre, introduced a private member's bill in 2012 asking that a special committee of the House of Parliament be struck to revisit the *Criminal Code* on the issue of when a "child becomes a human being."[50] Woodworth called for a medical investigation to bring forth evidence surrounding the definition of life at the time of conception, which by implication defines abortion as murder, subject to criminal consequences.

The vote on this bill was held on September 26, 2012, and the motion was defeated by a vote of 203 to 91. Among the ninety-one Members of

Parliament who supported the bill was the Minister for the Status of Women, Rona Ambrose, representing Edmonton-Spruce Grove, a self-professed libertarian and fan of Ayn Rand, according to her Wikipedia entry.[51] The public responded to her vote by creating a petition demanding that Ambrose resign as minister, claiming that she could not fairly represent and promote the status of women while holding such decidedly anti-women and anti-choice views.[52] Ambrose defended her actions, claiming that she voted in support of the bill on account of the discrimination against girls in sex-selection abortions, but pro-choice and organizations for the advancement of women denigrated the minister for adopting what they regarded as a clear anti-women and anti-autonomy position.

Canadian Catholic bishops are also still invested in these questions. In 2013, as Pope Benedict XVI decided to step down from the papacy, Canadian bishop Marc Ouellet emerged as one of the front-runners in the quest for the next pope. In an interview with Canadian Broadcasting Corporation's Peter Mansbridge, Ouellet spoke about several major social issues facing the world today, including: "the role of women in the church, gay marriage, and abortion."[53] The interview revealed that women had been organizing for equality within the Catholic hierarchy, but were officially considered "unclean during menstruation; inferior in every way; and the source of original sin."[54] Ouellet indicated that the issue of women in the church, as with gay marriage and abortion, was of less concern than the pressing issues of the modern day, claiming that "we have to go, you know, with the time – and it's not easy to move forward."[55]

Forty-four years after the decriminalization of abortion, the issue continues to divide Canadians. The most recent public expressions of these divisions have taken place among right-wing politicians and Catholic officials whose claims over family values are woven into their own moral discourses. This historical examination of the debates in the 1970s suggests, however, that the politics of abortion, whether as part of contraception or as a stand-alone issue, have not galvanized Canadians into simplistic categories of those who are for and those who are against the practice. Instead, they have stimulated more nuanced responses from Canadian families themselves who, in spite of challenges from powerful moral authorities, have changed the landscape for defining families through their actions rather than waiting for legal, political, or moral authorities to advise them on how to design a modern family.

Notes

Special thanks to Rachel Malena and Blaine Wickham for their research assistance; funding for this project was provided by SSHRC. Thanks also to graduate students and faculty from the Department of History, University of Saskatchewan, who provided feedback on an earlier draft of this chapter.

1 Joan O'Donnell, "A Catholic Mother Answers the Pope: Husbands and Wives Are Flesh-and-Blood People, Not Holy Saints," *Chatelaine,* November 1968, 96.

2 For a much fuller discussion of *Chatelaine* magazine, how women perceived it, and the extent to which it promoted critical feminist views, see Valerie Korinek, *Roughing It in the Suburbs: Reading Chatelaine Magazine in the Fifties and Sixties* (Toronto: University of Toronto Press, 2000).

3 For literature on the birth control pill, see, for example, Elizabeth Watkins, *On the Pill: A Social History of Oral Contraceptives, 1950–1970* (Baltimore, MD: Johns Hopkins University Press, 1998); Christabelle Sethna, "The University of Toronto Health Service, Oral Contraception and Student Demand for Birth Control, 1960–1970," *Historical Studies in Education/Revue d'histoire de l'éducation,* 17, 2 (2005), 265–92; and Lara Marks, *Sexual Chemistry: A History of the Contraceptive Pill* (New Haven, CT: Yale University Press, 2001).

4 The French Canadian part of this history is quite different and has been well told by Denyse Baillargeon. She explains first that support for eugenics, which had been widespread in English Canada, found almost no support in Quebec, as it was almost always associated with restricting births, which was anathema to Catholic doctrine. However, already by the 1940s, the Catholic Church's parish clinics "had come to be considered a favourable environment for the communication of Catholic teachings about contraception and the family." Denyse Baillargeon, *Babies for the Nation: The Medicalization of Motherhood in Quebec, 1910–1970,* trans. W. Donald Wilson (Waterloo, ON: Wilfrid Laurier University Press, 2009), 81, 189. Given the dominant influence of the Catholic Church, combined with its own changing authoritative status during the Quiet Revolution in Quebec, this issue falls well beyond the scope of the current essay. For more on the topic, however, see Baillargeon, *Babies for the Nation.*

5 Quoted in Angus McLaren and Arlene Tigar McLaren, *The Bedroom and the State: The Changing Practices and Politics of Contraception and Abortion in Canada, 1880–1980* (Toronto: McClelland and Stewart, 1986), 9.

6 Calgary Health Services Archives, Foothills Hospital H-037, "Section 237 of the Criminal Code Prior to the Amendment," document used by the Foothills Hospital, received February 18, 1970, 1.

7 Ibid., 2.

8 Ibid.

9 Christabelle Sethna, "All Aboard? Canadian Women's Abortion Tourism, 1960–1980," in *Gender, Health and Popular Culture: Historical Perspectives,* ed. Cheryl Krasnick Warsh (Waterloo, ON: Wilfrid Laurier University Press, 2011), 90–91.

10 Christabelle Sethna and Steve Hewitt, "Clandestine Operations: The Vancouver Women's Caucus, the Abortion Caravan, and the RCMP," *Canadian Historical Review* 90, 3 (2009): 491.

11 Sethna and Hewitt, "Clandestine Operations," 488.

12 The Catholic Church had weighed into these debates many times, including, during the 1920s, on matters more specifically related to eugenics. According to historian Sharon Leon, American Catholics had even "embraced the goals of positive eugenics, which promoted marriage and reproduction of 'superior' types," though "they disagreed with

eugenicists' methods of distinguishing between superior and inferior persons." Sharon Leon, "'Hopelessly Entangled in Nordic Pre-suppositions': Catholic Participation in the American Eugenics Society," *Journal of the History of Medicine and Allied Sciences* 59, 1 (2004): 5.

13 Margaret Marsh and Wanda Ronner, *The Fertility Doctor: John Rock and the Reproductive Revolution* (Baltimore, MD: Johns Hopkins University Press, 2008). Marsh and Ronner directly explore John Rock's personal campaign to convince the Catholic Church of the value of the birth control pill, and his personal disillusionment that followed the *Humanae Vitae.*

14 This point is confirmed also in Denyse Baillargeon's study of Catholic marriage classes in Quebec. Baillargeon, *Babies for the Nation*, 189.

15 Marsh and Ronner, *The Fertility Doctor,* 247.

16 Encyclical Letter *Humanae Vitae,* Supreme Pontiff Paul VI (1968), ss 14, 15, 16, "Unlawful Birth Control Methods."

17 Canadian Council of Catholic Bishops, "Canadian Bishops' Statement on the Encyclical *Humanae Vitae,*" Saint Boniface, Manitoba, September 27, 1968 (hereafter Winnipeg Statement).

18 Ibid.

19 David Marshall, *Secularizing the Faith: Canadian Protestant Clergy and the Crisis of Belief, 1850–1940* (Toronto: University of Toronto Press, 1992).

20 See Michael Gauvreau and Nancy Christie, *A Full-Orbed Christianity: The Protestant Churches and Social Welfare in Canada, 1900–1940* (Montreal and Kingston: McGill-Queen's University Press, 2001).

21 Brenda Margaret Appleby, *Responsible Parenthood: Decriminalizing Contraception in Canada* (Toronto: University of Toronto Press, 1999), 8.

22 Ibid., 8.

23 Terence Fay, *A History of Canadian Catholics: Gallicianism, Romanism and* Canadianism (Montreal and Kingston: McGill-Queen's University Press, 2002), 314.

24 Ibid., 314.

25 Appleby, *Responsible Parenthood,* 78.

26 William F. Ryan, "Personal Recollections and Reflections on the Implementation of the Second Vatican Council by the Canadian Conference of Catholic Bishops (1964–1990)," *Historical Studies* 73 (2008): 3.

27 Ibid., 5.

28 Winnipeg Statement, s 17.

29 Winnipeg Statement, s 27.

30 Vincent Foy, "Humanae Vitae – 30 Years: The Effects of the Winnipeg Statement," *Catholic Insight* 6, 6 (1998): 15.

31 For examples of literature on this topic, see Elaine Tyler May, *Homeward Bound: American Families in the Cold War Era* (New York: Basic Books, 1988); Valerie Korinek, *Roughing It in the Suburbs: Reading Chatelaine Magazine in the 1950s and 1960s* (Toronto: University of Toronto Press, 2000); and Veronica Strong-Boag, "Home Dreams: Women and the Suburban Experiment in Canada, 1945–60," *Canadian Historical Review* 72, 4 (1991): 471–504.

32 For more on the complicated dynamics faced by Catholic women on this issue, see Baillergeon, *Babies for the Nation.* For a set of intimate reflections on being Catholic and seeking birth control, see Chana Gazit and David Stewart, dirs., *The Pill,* PBS documentary, "The American Experience."

33 Jule DeJager Ward, *La Leche League: At the Crossroads of Medicine, Feminism, and Religion* (Chapel Hill, NC: University of North Carolina Press, 2000), 4.

34 Ibid., 5.

35 Ibid.
36 Ibid., 67, 73.
37 Elizabeth Hudson, "Abortionists Betray Feminists," *Prairie Messenger,* August 24, 1975, 50.
38 "Tighten the Abortion Law," *Prairie Messenger,* March 16, 1975, 14.
39 "Women May Be Disappointed," *Prairie Messenger,* September 21, 1975, 2.
40 Based on details provided in J.M.A. Ansari and H.H. Francis, "A Study of 49 Sterilized Females," *Acta Psychiatrica Scandinavica* 54, 5 (1976): 316.
41 Walter Nagel, "Sterilization Conditions Spelled Out for Trustees," *Calgary Herald,* April 18, 1970, 55.
42 Calgary Health Services Archives, Foothills Hospital, H-037, Brief relating to "Sexual Sterilization and Therapeutic Abortions in the Royal Alexandra Hospital [Edmonton]," presented to the Executive Director, Mr. Nye, and the Board of Governors of the Royal Alexandra Hospital, [no date, but likely 1970], 2.
43 "The Pope and the Pill," *Chatelaine,* November 1968, 1.
44 Ibid.
45 Patricia Poston (Regina), "Pro-life March on Ottawa an Unforgettable Experience," *Prairie Messenger,* July 15, 1975, 4.
46 Peter Novecosky, "Abortion Law Will Change," *Prairie Messenger,* February 23, 1975, 1, 53.
47 Ibid., 53.
48 Ibid.
49 Ibid.
50 Stephen Woodworth, M-312, House of Commons, 16th Report, 41st Parliament, 1st Session, http://www.parl.gc.ca/HousePublications/Publication.aspx?DocId=5437818.
51 http://en.wikipedia.org/wiki/Rona_Ambrose, accessed March 6, 2013. Even on her Wikipedia page – publicly accessible, and likely written by her staff – she self-identifies this way.
52 See, for example, "Rona Ambrose Resignation Petition Hits 6,100 Signatures after Abortion Vote," *National Post,* September 28, 2012, http://news.nationalpost.com/2012/09/28/petition-calling-for-status-of-women-ministers-job-after-abortion-vote-garners-6100-signatures/.
53 CBC News, "Papal Contender Says Issue of Women in Church 'Secondary,'" March 6, 2013, http://www.cbc.ca/news/canada/story/2013/03/05/pope-election-women.html.
54 CBC News, "Papal Contender Says Issue of Women in Church 'Secondary.'"
55 Ibid.

Part 2
Experience

4

He Is Still Unwanted

Women's Assertions of Authority over Abortion in Letters to the Royal Commission on the Status of Women in Canada

Shannon Stettner

In 1968, when abortion was illegal in Canada, R.H. of Windsor, Ontario,[1] wrote to the Royal Commission on the Status of Women in Canada (RCSW) arguing passionately for the legalization of abortion on request, stating unequivocally that the decision to have an abortion should rest solely with the pregnant woman:

> I speak from experience – experience that has caused not only myself, but my three children a lot of pain. I had an unwanted child eight years ago – he is still unwanted – no matter how wrong or guilty I may feel in feeling this way. This child ... has changed the course of five lives drastically. No child! And I repeat – no child should be brought into the world unwanted.[2]

Her letter is startling to read. At a time when motherhood was venerated as a benchmark of womanhood, it was unusual for a mother to admit that her living child was and remained unwanted. The frankness in this letter stems, in part, from the nature of the commission, which was a uniquely female space. It speaks also to my argument that women used their personal experiences, speaking as experts on their own lives, to assert authority over the issue of abortion. They saw the commission as a legitimate avenue for seeking to change or maintain aspects of laws that touched their personal lives – and by extension those of other women. Women's letters reveal strong positions on abortion, including voices resolutely against any liberalization of the abortion law, offering a glimpse into anti-abortion sentiments before the proliferation of organized pro-life groups.[3] More frequently, women's letters advocated for a compassionate, responsive, liberalized abortion law. Submissions to the commission provide a unique glimpse into the lives of Canadian women, illuminating the widespread and diverse nature of second-wave feminism in Canada.

Although *Chatelaine,* a women's magazine, is often credited with opening public discussion of abortion in Canada through its 1959 article "Should Canada Change Its Abortion Law?" subsequent public debate highlighted the place of physicians, represented by the Canadian Medical Association (CMA); lawyers, represented through the Canadian Bar Association (CBA); churches; and politicians. An indication of the successful medicalization of abortion, public dialogue in the 1960s focused on the CMA's push to clarify the abortion law to protect its members against prosecution.[4] By 1966, both the CMA and the CBA overcame internal divisions to adopt statements calling for the reform of the law to allow for abortion under certain circumstances. Early that same year, four Members of Parliament introduced legislation addressing the place of abortion and contraception in the *Criminal Code* of Canada. These proposed bills were referred to the House of Common's Standing Committee on Health and Welfare, which held hearings at different points between 1966 and 1968 on abortion and contraception. A 1967 Gallup poll reported that 71 percent of Canadians supported the liberalization of the abortion law.[5] Although dissenting voices remained, there was a discernable general agreement among key actors about the need to modify the abortion law. This was accomplished through Bill C-150, which became the *Criminal Law Amendment Act, 1968–69*. Introduced in 1967, Bill C-150 was delayed by the 1968 federal election campaign, but was passed in May 1969 under the Liberal Government of Prime Minister Pierre Trudeau. It enabled a woman to obtain an abortion when a Therapeutic Abortion Committee of no less than three physicians determined her pregnancy threatened her life or health. While the law protected doctors and partially legalized abortion, access remained restricted and many women's groups responded negatively to the new law.[6] The RCSW hearings, held throughout 1968, coincided with ongoing public discussion, but the *Report of the Royal Commission on the Status of Women in Canada* (1970) was not tabled in Parliament until December 1970, after the new abortion law was already in effect. Women's submissions to the commission, and even the commission's recommendations, were more liberal than the new abortion law, indicating that the law did not reflect the views of the majority of women who presented to the commission, but rather satisfied the concerns of other actors.

Early feminist writing about the RCSW cited it as a key event in the course of Canadian second-wave feminism. Initiated by Prime Minister Lester B. Pearson in 1967 after a memorable campaign by a coalition of women's groups, it was designed to assess the quality of life of Canadian women, including the impact of the *Criminal Code*.[7] Through 1967 and 1968, research reports were commissioned, submissions were sought, and public hearings were held. The RCSW has been called a consciousness-raising exercise, the "first success" of second-wave feminism, and "an idea whose time had come."[8] Political scientist Sue Findlay elaborates on the importance of the RCSW, noting, "It was through the very participation of thousands of women nationwide that the Commission ultimately won legitimacy in the eyes of Canadian women."[9] Several articles about the RCSW take the form of reflection pieces or assessments of the commission's successes and failures at various points after the release of its final report.[10] Less attention has been directed towards the content of Canadian women's participation, with three noteworthy exceptions. Annis May Timpson analyzes what women said about strategies for child care in their briefs to the commission, Barbara Freeman reveals important, often controversial themes in the media's reporting of women's testimony, and Joan Sangster uses women's submissions to reveal their work experiences, especially in relation to the increased workforce participation of mothers.[11] To contribute to this understanding of Canadian women's concerns in the transformative decade of the 1960s, I analyze here the content of letters and briefs to the RCSW as they pertain to abortion.

This article also adds to the growing body of literature on Canadian women's abortion experiences. Recent works by Christabelle Sethna and Beth Palmer analyze women's exhausting efforts to obtain abortions outside of Canada in the 1960s and 1970s when access to abortion in the country was either illegal or unreliable.[12] Prior to these works, most of the literature concentrated on efforts of major actors – especially physicians, clergymen, lawyers, and politicians – to liberalize the abortion law throughout the 1960s.[13] This literature paid little attention to the place of women in the reform decade. Political scientist Jane Jenson's observation of the public abortion debate in the 1960s is that women never "gained recognition as major actors in the debate."[14] Jenson argues that "women in the mid-sixties did not have the political resources to press their positions *or even a language* in which they could express them [my italics]."[15] She also argues that during the reform era, "women's voices were diffused and weak" because "women had not yet developed the powerful collective identity with which they could name themselves and act on a gender-based solidarity."[16] For her, then, the absence of strong, woman-defined or women-organized groups meant that, for much of the decade, women were relatively ineffectual political actors. Jenson's interpretation remains important because new research has not overturned this narrative of abortion law reform; the relative absence of women from the 1960s abortion debate is generally unquestioned. And yet the allegedly diffused and weak nature of women's voices needs to be interrogated. By understanding the personal as political and accepting that individual voices can be powerful in shifting dominant understandings of the place of abortion in a modernizing society, we can suggest that women's voices in this decade were central to placing the abortion debate in the public sphere and contributing to change. In her spatial history of second-wave feminism in America, Anne Enke looks for examples of the women's movement "*outside* and *alongside* as well as within the institutions and actors bearing the name 'feminist,'" demonstrating that the women's movement was indeed widespread and diverse.[17] Enke's encouragement to look for the women's movement in sites not usually considered political allows us to see the domestic setting as a political space, such that the act of a woman writing to the RSCW while sitting alone at her kitchen table is evidence of feminist activism. This chapter, then, contributes to our growing understanding of Canadian women's feminism through an analysis of women's thoughts on and experiences with abortion in the 1960s, understanding even individual voices as politically powerful. Diffused they may have been, but weak they were not.

The RCSW was a complex forum that was at once very public, as royal commissions are designed to be, and yet oddly private in the sense that, because it was run primarily by women about women's issues, it was interpreted by many Canadian women as an opportunity for them to share their personal feelings and intimate experiences. Freeman relates that the RCSW was initially mocked or derided by the mainstream press because of its focus and make-up.[18] Such marginalization would have reinforced the idea that the commission was a woman's space. This unique aspect of the RCSW, combined with the sensitive subject matters addressed, was compounded by the fact that many everyday women were not used to expressing themselves or being heard publicly on matters like abortion. Yet in the letters to the RCSW, women's voices can be heard both individually and through group submissions. According to Deborah P. Britzman, "Voice ... suggests the individual's struggle to create and fashion meaning, assert standpoints, and negotiate with others. Voice permits participation in the social world."[19] Carefully hearing women's voices expressed in submissions to the RCSW shows women indeed held positions on abortion and were able – and eager – to share them.

Many submissions to the RCSW took the form of autobiographical letters, which is not surprising given women's long history as letter writers. While some women requested that their names be kept private, they nevertheless wanted their personal experiences and opinions taken into consideration in the hope of facilitating or preventing change. For some women, the RCSW was a site of knowledge construction, a sort of consciousness-raising exercise that engendered reflection, discussion, and sharing. For others, the commission provided an opportunity to share already strongly held beliefs. In their submissions, women constructed their authority to speak on the issue in a variety of ways. Most commonly, they drew from their own lives, including their experiences with pregnancy, childbirth, and motherhood, and their experiences as children. Other women highlighted their professional experiences and education, as well as social characteristics like age, as the basis of their authority. Still other women represented their authority as being based in their rejection or acceptance of religious and moral dictates, often reiterating positions they learned from external authorities. Finally, some women argued that their authority over the issue stemmed from their identities as women. As the people most directly affected by unwanted pregnancies, they sought, at the very least, the greater involvement of women in the public arena or, more forcefully, women's total control over the abortion decision. The range of strategies used in women's submissions to the commission suggests that these ordinary women had a myriad of positions on abortion and an ability and willingness to be heard on the issue when presented with a forum in which they felt comfortable or invested. Examining women's constructions of authority allows their voices to be heard by highlighting either what women believed was important or what they perceived would be most important or credible to their audience. Before analyzing women's submissions to the RCSW, it is illuminating to look at some of the mechanics of the commission in relation to the reception and use of those contributions.

Setting the Stage for Women's Voices

Some 468 numbered briefs and around one thousand letters of opinion were submitted to the RCSW.[20] For this research, I reviewed all briefs and letters of opinion contained in the RCSW archives, separating out the nearly two hundred documents that reference abortion. The resulting evidence of women's opinions on abortion was abundant, and I narrowed it down by highlighting submissions written by, or including the signatures of, individual women whenever possible, because they were more likely to reference personal experiences with reproductive concerns. Also, signing an individual name to a brief or letter, especially knowing it could become public, seems like a political act worthy of attention, particularly when one considers the small towns represented in the following pages. Still, it is important to note that the briefs written by organizations or groups were generally written following group discussion and consensus building and also importantly reveal women's thoughts on, and constructions of, authority over abortion. Among the numbered briefs, there are both lengthy submissions from groups or associations and submissions from individual women that are essentially letters of opinion. In the archived files of the RCSW, there are many other such letters of opinion that were not assigned a brief number, but were grouped with similar letters and divided by province of origin. There are fewer submissions from the Maritime provinces and northern Territories, but the other regions of the country are well represented, with no discernable positions on abortion being characteristic of specific regions. In reviewing the files, it seems as though, in the classification process, later submissions from individuals were treated as letters of opinion while earlier ones were designated as briefs, suggesting a lack of uniformity in how letters from individuals were labelled. It is not clear how or if this inconsistency affected interpretation by commissioners or commission analysts. The majority of the letters and briefs addressed a variety of themes, although a few addressed abortion solely. In their letters, women often included identifying information, but this information was inconsistently provided, making generalizations about demographic characteristics difficult.

Joan Sangster argues that women's letters of opinion "assumed a low priority" because they were "more subjective and particularistic" than the briefs and further argues that the commissioners "favoured submissions that provided 'hard' evidence, with statistics (presumed not to lie), and concrete, pragmatic, realistic policy suggestions."[21] My research, however, found several indications that the commissioners acknowledged the importance of women's contributions in all forms.[22] Both the chair of the commission, Florence Bird, and one commissioner, Elsie Gregory MacGill, were quoted in the press advising women that letters of opinion would be given the same consideration as formal briefs.[23] Although I disagree with Sangster's characterization of the commission's treatment of letters, whether or not personal letters were valued as much as more report-like submissions is not as important as the fact that the public assertion of the commissioners' willingness to treat letters of opinion on an equal footing with briefs may well have encouraged submissions from women who otherwise might have been uncomfortable writing to the RCSW. On this point, Monique Bégin, executive secretary of the RCSW, has strenuously argued that the commission's final report reflects the will of those who participated. On the subject of collecting data, she recalls, "We granted maximum importance to the process – the public's movement through public hearings, briefs, and recommendations – that distinguishes royal commissions from 'expert' studies and research."[24] She further contends that "because of the absence of a general [theoretical framework], the commission remained as close as possible to the *women of Canada whose voices we wanted to amplify* [my italics]."[25] Moreover, it is important to remember that the Commission was not a static entity, but rather that it, and those associated with it, changed during the course of its mandate. Bird and others later reported being changed personally and politically by the testimonies they heard, suggesting, as Bégin asserts, that testimonies were important to the commission in multiple ways.[26] Finally, in the RCSW's report, the commissioners called for a liberalization of the abortion law that was in line with the majority of sentiments presented through the letters and briefs, indicating they had listened to, and heard, the women of Canada who participated in the process.[27]

Asserting Authority over Abortion

Many women expressing opinions on abortion shared motherhood as a common experience. In her study of motherhood issues in the first half of the twentieth century in Canada, Cynthia Comacchio argues that "reproduction is more than procreation: it encompasses the socialization, physical maintenance, and emotional nurture of family members."[28] Historically, women have used abortion for fertility control and it was not unusual for them to cite their roles and identities as mothers to argue for the well-being of existing children when justifying the termination or prevention of a pregnancy.[29] In submissions to the RCSW, some women drew their authority from their experiences as mothers and presented arguments for pregnant women's well-being that referenced their existing children, and sometimes raised concerns for the well-being of unborn children. One such woman wrote passionately of the need for legal sterilization and abortion, stating:

> If I collapse with a mental breakdown, the five children and my husband suffer ... Who would care for them? I *am* needed here! I don't feel I am alone in this particular problem. There must be many many mothers who feel just as strongly as I do ... There are many who's [sic] only form of birth control is to abstain. This is the end of a good marriage.[30]

The reference to the health of her marriage, in a society that valorized heterosexual marriage, is also noteworthy. Concern for the pregnant woman was also expressed by G.O. of Willowdale, Ontario, who thought abortion laws should be abolished and the decision left to the pregnant woman: "After all, she is the one who has by far the major responsibility for looking after and rearing the child, which is one of the most difficult tasks that can be undertaken by an individual and which calls for the utmost patience, self-sacrifice, devotion and love. These are all characteristics that cannot be forced."[31] G.O. continued, expressing concern for the unborn: "I feel in this day and age that much the greater crime is perpetrated against humanity in bringing into the world a child who is unwanted and will therefore be unloved and rejected, thus setting on the road of life a warped and stunted human being with all its attendant misery and unhappiness."[32] The authors of these submissions, then, saw voluntary motherhood as in the best interest of both women and children.

Others similarly wrote expressing concern for the unwanted children. Diana C. Louis of Montreal supported abortion on request by arguing:

> There are those who object to abortion as they feel it is the destruction of life ... But, how about the more subtle destruction of life or personality ... The "battered children" ... The rejected children ... Many of these are illegitimate children who are kept by their mothers, but who are

always the butt of her displeasure even if she subsequently marries and has other children. This is the history of many of our delinquents.[33]

F.R. of Manitoba referenced personal experiences when she wrote to the RCSW stating her unequivocal belief in a pregnant woman's autonomy. She explained: "I am writing this letter on behalf of the present and future unborn and unwanted children. I am speaking from bitter experience. I am nearing 80 years of age and am still cursing the day I was born." She continued, "Oh! yes, my parents were properly married ... But I was not wanted, so was raised in an iceberg home – as are all unwanted children. The effect on a child of such loneliness and bitterness can never be removed."[34] Written from the perspective of an unwanted child, this letter was a powerful indictment against involuntary motherhood and for the right of all children to be born wanted. Given increased attention directed towards human rights in post–Second World War Canada, expressing concern for the welfare of the unborn makes sense; for some women, this concern meant legalizing abortion to protect unwanted children from future neglect or abuse.

Motherhood legitimated an expertise drawn from personal experience. Knowledge gained from unplanned and unwanted pregnancies also prompted women to address abortion in their letters to commissioners. When A.R. from Bassana, Alberta, wrote to the RCSW, she signed her letter "Desperate" instead of with her proper name. Her letter was an emotional argument for accessible, legal, elective sterilization, in which she touched powerfully on abortion. Although sterilization was not mentioned in the *Criminal Code*, Linda Revie reports that in the early twentieth century, professional associations "advised doctors that the operation was illegal, except as a medical necessity," and Angus McLaren and Arlene Tigar McLaren note that it was not until the late 1970s that vasectomies and tubal ligations became increasingly popular strategies for limiting additional births.[35] The letter by "Desperate" demonstrates the difficulty some women had accessing voluntary sterilization: "I asked my doctor for an operation and he treated me like I had asked for an abortion! I did not! ... I was ... *terrified* that I would have another baby. I only wanted to be sterilized ... Isn't that a better solution than *the wish for an abortion* and the *pressure* that comes with *too many children*."[36] The author of this letter related that her desire to avoid another pregnancy and child was so strong that she was willing to ignore her moral and religious feelings in order to end a pregnancy through abortion, signalling to the commissioners that the status quo not only was untenable, but also pushed women to contravene regulations – legal, social, and religious. Her experience with her doctor, moreover, demonstrated that conferring authority for the decision on the medical profession was an insufficient solution. Her rejection of medical authority also underlined the legitimacy of her own ideas on the matter.

Among the other ways women attempted to demonstrate their authority – or expertise – on the abortion question was to draw from their work experiences. K.T.C. of North Bay, Ontario, established her qualifications at the beginning of her brief, asserting, "This is not a brief. Only my views as a wife, mother of 5 children and a teacher of 28 kindergarten children."[37] She continued, despairing, "To think that a mother-to-be is willing to murder her innocent unborn child is just too incomprehensible. Isn't it the duty of our government to protect *all* its people, particularly the innocent children, even those yet unborn?"[38] K.T.C.'s self-identification as a wife, mother, and teacher underscored her authority as a woman whose identity – both personal and professional – involved caring for others, particularly children. P.D. from Dorval, Quebec, also began her letter with identifying characteristics: "I am 41 years of age, happily married with 6 children aged 17-7 years ... I have been associated over several years with social work ... and with voluntary service ... I am at college aiming for an Arts degree in Communication Arts."[39] P.D.'s careful construction of her identity is notable. While she did not elaborate as to the reasons for her opinions, two paragraphs later she listed the words "Abortion, Starvation, War" and beside them wrote, "are all legal but each is illicit." All of her identities (wife, mother, social worker, volunteer, student) added layers to her authority – such that, for her at least, they either negated the need to explain why she held the position on abortion that she did or suggested that, to her, the wrongness of abortion was axiomatic. Overall, these letters demonstrate, as Kathy Davis suggests, that women's identities are "ongoingly negotiated."[40] Lessons learned from one identity were translated through lessons learned from another, such that no one identity functioned alone at any given time but rather worked in tandem to reinforce authority claims.

When presenting their opinions, women did not rely solely on their own experiences or credentials, but also looked to external sources to bolster the legitimacy of their claims. One such tactic involved referencing organized religion, which, after the medical profession, was perhaps the actor most jockeying for a say in the abortion debate. Throughout the 1960s, Canadian churches involved themselves in public dialogues on abortion and also discussed the matter in their governing bodies and memberships.[41] In letters to the RCSW, however, there was no consensus about the extent to which women adhered to religious dictates and several women condemned religion or religious leaders' involvement in the abortion debate. Much of the criticism was directed at the Roman Catholic Church in particular. Marielle Demorest of Richmond, British Columbia, wrote: "The Catholic Church, to which I belong, has of course a strong objection [to abortion] ... How can a house ful [sic] of celibate bishops and male politicians decide what is the course to take in such a personal matter?"[42] M.M. of Ottawa pointed to the preponderance of religious male voices in the debate, as well as those of male politicians: "The voices most often heard on this subject are those of church men or government men who have an interest in maintaining the status quo and who obviously don't have to worry over thoughts of getting an abortion."[43] These letters were frank indictments against the Church and male religious authorities.

Conversely, women also used religion to argue against abortion, defending organized religions or denying that the churches were major actors opposing legal abortions. Mildred Moir of Halifax, Nova Scotia, contended that "contrary to popular belief, those who are opposed to abortion are not opposed on the grounds of faith," and argued rather that abortion "properly comes under the Department of Justice" since "abortion is a violation of justice."[44] G.G. of Cornwall, Ontario, vehemently opposed to abortion "except to save the mother's life," similarly wrote: "I am not a Roman Catholic, a point which I personally consider quite irrelevant, but which is raised by those who favour abortion with astounding frequency."[45] In contrast, Rita M. Moran of Edmonton, Alberta, unabashedly referenced her religious beliefs in her brief: "We who have been enriched by Christian teaching look on abortion as the evil it is ... The soul is present at the time of conception and any interference with the products of conception is interfering with a living soul."[46] H.B. of Manning, Alberta, looked to religious persons to solve the problem of abortion when she appealed "to the C.W.L. [Catholic Women's League], K of C. [Knights of Columbus], all religious and conscientious orders, and all interested organizations, to support the cause of our mothers in defense of our children, who may, one day, very well be our defense; had they not been snuffed out of existence."[47] Reflecting the heterogeneity of religious beliefs, these excerpts show a range of feeling over the place of religion in relation to the abortion issue.

Strategies designed to demonstrate the authority of a position or belief are related to, yet different from, efforts to determine *who* should have authority over the abortion decision. Many women argued forcefully that women, as those who get pregnant, should be at least centrally if not solely responsible for the decision to terminate a pregnancy. Their frustration at their perceived lack of a voice in the public debate and their desire to alter that silence were forcefully and frequently articulated in their submissions to the commission. B.H. of Sudbury, Ontario, wrote:

> If a woman wants an abortion, its no one else's business at all, least of all should it concern M.P.s (mostly men) and Priests, Bishops etc., who know nothing about these subjects anyway ... A woman, no matter who, and no matter how much money she has should be allowed to have an abortion. It concerns no one else whatever.[48]

Dorothy E. Stogre of Penticton, British Columbia, eloquently argued that a pregnant woman alone is aware of her circumstances and limitations, and reasoned, "If a woman is considered intelligent enough to be entrusted with the care and upbringing of a family, surely she must be intelligent enough to make this most vital decision."[49] M.T. of Chilliwack, British Columbia, a mother of five children, supported abortion on request, noting: "I think the only person that is affected is the woman with the problem. It is *her* problem only, and she is the one who should decide what she is going to do with her body, a simple matter of – the womans [sic] body, her problem, her decision, her life."[50] With a touch of humour, she added that "statistics prove that most accidents happen in the home, let us be realistic and admit the fact, the bedroom is no exception."[51] Whether expressing themselves through rational thought, frustration, anger, humour, or other emotions, many women who wrote to the commission claimed that the authority over the abortion decision belonged solely to the pregnant woman in question.

Similar to submissions addressing who should make the abortion decision, some women lamented the relative lack of women's voices in public debates and policy decisions. R.G. of Haney, British Columbia, wrote: "Laws that directly affect us as women should be decided on by women. Abortion, birth control and divorce concern us all, yet no one asked my opinions before changing these laws."[52] One of the most emotionally argued letters came from W.E. D'Altroy of Burnaby, British Columbia, who pleaded powerfully against letting men decide women's fate:

> I ... am appauled [sic] to find that in this enlightened supposedly free era that right now at this moment we have a number of old and middle aged men mauling [sic] over the abortion law – still trying to make up THEIR minds whether they should allow females the freedom of controling [sic] their bodies – a freedom men have always taken. How come, that body of individuals is not entirely women (the only sex the problem afflicts) and made up of women doctors, social workers, mothers and *just* women. How do men, regardless of their training, ever think they fully understand a thing that can never happen to them?... There should be *no* law on abortion – it should be the decision of each female whether she wants a child or an abortion.[53]

Women's desire for the greater involvement of both professional and pregnant women in the making of abortion laws and decisions stemmed from the fact that they were the ones experiencing the fears and realities of unplanned and unwanted pregnancies and illegal abortions, and from their anger that their opinions were not solicited, their voices not heard. To this end, the commission provided an important corrective since it functioned as a vehicle through which women's voices could be heard or to which, in the case of letters of opinion and briefs, women could voice their fears, frustrations, and desires.

Indeed, women linked the question of who should have authority over the abortion decision to questions of equality. Of women in the 1960s, Jenson argues that "few as yet had a critique of the system of gender relations which subordinated women to men and silenced female voices in public debates."[54] Sangster disagrees, arguing that many working women who wrote to the commission "identified ideological barriers and structural inequalities in society," and her findings also extend to reproductive freedom.[55] Inez Baker of Willowdale, Ontario, for example, wrote, "As long as woman is treated like an animal to be bred – with the master (government, church, etc.) exercising the controls – her position in society can never be considered one of equality – she is enslaved!"[56] Norma F. Bricknell of Edmonton, Alberta, wrote emphatically on the issue: "At the moment ... I, a woman – mother of four children – I, am an accessory to crimes against this law. I buy birth control pills! to prevent conception! ... The doctor who prescribes the pills; the druggist who stocks and sells the pills are all criminal under this law ... IT WOULD CERTAINLY IMPROVE MY STATUS IF SECTION 150 was thrown out."[57] These letters indicate that many women perceived a link between control over their reproductive choices and their status within Canadian society more generally, indicating an awareness that surely predated the RCSW.

Yet some women did not want equality as it was envisioned by second-wave feminism or women's liberation movements. Mary Cooper of Ottawa wrote a memorable brief against abortion in which she attacked the women's movement. Specifically, she was critical of "super feminists whose zeal is untempered by a broader human concern."[58] She continued: "These self-styled liberals talk glibly about a woman's 'absolute right to her own body' – unmindful that abortion destroys the body of another human being ... This push for easy abortion is the cancer of the women's movement – a misdirected liberalism run wild and out of control." Similarly, G.B.S. of Burnaby, British Columbia, believed the women's movement was out of touch with the general public, reporting that after lengthy discussion with other women, she believed that "mostly women wish to get married and bear children. God intended it this way, creating us in a manner that we might become a wife and mother."[59] In opposition to the previous group of letters, these women rejected changes to their roles that they feared would sacrifice the protection they felt inherent in the status quo and their understandings of what women were both created for and wanted to do. Notably, there is a perception among these women that motherhood was a defining role to which women should aspire and which, for them, encompassed certain natural or instinctual beliefs.

Diffused but Not Weak: Women's Voices in the RCSW

It is noteworthy that, in the RCSW's final report, the recommendation that abortion be made available to any woman on request during the first twelve weeks of pregnancy appears in a chapter called "Women and the Family" and not under the "Criminal Law" chapter. The commissioners recognized abortion as "one of the oldest forms of birth control," and reported that most women who sought abortions were married with two or three existing children.[60] The report referenced public hearing testimony, noting that while women spoke eloquently from both sides of the issue, the statement that "a woman should have control of her own body" was a popular construction.[61] Although the commissioners had endeavoured to produce a unanimous report, abortion was one of the key issues preventing consensus.[62] Commissioners Jacques Henripin, Doris Ogilvie, and Elsie Gregory MacGill all issued separate statements on abortion, which appear at the back of the report. Both Henripin and Ogilvie were against liberalizing the law. Although the Catholic Henripin admitted that the "trend of a large section of public opinion" favoured liberalization, he believed that the value of fetal life outweighed the convenience a liberalized abortion law would supposedly afford the woman in question.[63] Conversely, MacGill asserted that the commission's recommendations did not go far enough and prophetically claimed that, unless the 1969 law was immediately repealed, "prohibitions and penalties" would "linger on for a decade or two more to harass and punish women."[64] For her, the issue was "a private medical matter between patient and doctor."[65] This dissent within the commission is a good reflection of the complex nature of abortion politics and the diversity of opinion witnessed in submissions to the commission. It also illuminates abortion as one of those topics on which it is almost impossible to find compromise: despite admitting that majority opinion supported a liberalized abortion law, for example, Henripin could not betray his personal feelings.

Of letters written to the RCSW, Sangster argues that "they were more likely to be letters of complaint, critique, or calls for change: the very satisfied and unconcerned would have been less likely to write."[66] Certainly, women seeking to change Canada's abortion law seem to have written most often; these were women who were invested in changing the status quo. Yet a fair number of women raised their voices against change; these were women either invested in maintaining the status quo or concerned about the lives of the unborn. The presence of these voices in a forum designed to investigate and further women's status illuminates the contested nature of the meaning(s) of feminism. When women wrote to the commission, they did so because they wanted to be heard and used many strategies in their efforts to construct their authority over the issue of abortion. Many women shared personal experiences and private thoughts that are surprisingly intimate, bravely giving voice to almost unimaginable statements like "*He is still unwanted*." In these examples, women claimed authority by virtue of their experiences or identities as mothers or as women who had dealt with unplanned or unwanted pregnancies. Others drew on work or educational training and experience to ground their opinions. Women also argued that women, whether as professionals or as pregnant women, should have a (greater) say in abortion decisions. In doing so, they were addressing authority differently – in this instance answering the question of who has the authority to decide whether a woman should have an abortion, and arguing forcefully for the place of women in that decision. Ultimately, through the act of writing to the commission, women had the occasion not only to verbalize what they (already) thought about unplanned pregnancies and abortion, but also to share their expertise born through their own personal experiences and layered identities. These letters, regardless of stance or strategy, demonstrate that women were not silent, without positions, or uncritical of women's status. Their letters – thoughtful, fretful, and angry – reveal many of their passionately held beliefs about abortion. The RCSW is but one venue in which women's voices can be found during this decade of abortion law reform. It is hard to imagine that these voices did not contribute to the wider public dialogue, even if only as the undercurrent shifting dominant understandings of unplanned and unwanted pregnancies. As importantly, this analysis suggests Canadian second-wave feminism was widespread and occurring in places that were outside and alongside sites we normally recognize as feminist.

Notes

A longer version of this chapter was first published as "'He Is Still Unwanted': Women's Assertions of Authority over Abortion in Letters to the Royal Commission on the Status of Women in Canada," *Canadian Bulletin of Medical History* 29, 1 (2012): 151–71.

1 In this chapter, I reproduce women's names when they were included in the appendix of the *Report of the Royal Commission* and use initials when quoting from letters of opinion, which were never publicized.

2 "Letters of Opinion Ontario," Library and Archives Canada (LAC), RG 33/89, RCSW, vol. 9.

3 For a history of anti-abortion activism in Canada, see Michael W. Cuneo, *Catholics against the Church: Anti-abortion Protest in Toronto 1969–1985* (Toronto: University of Toronto Press, 1989).

4 See, for example, Tracy Penny Light, "Shifting Interests: The Medical Discourse on Abortion in English Canada, 1850–1969" (PhD diss., University of Waterloo, 2003); Larry Collins, "The Politics of Abortion: Trends in Canadian Fertility Policy," *Atlantis* 7, 2 (1982): 2–5; and Brenda Margaret Appleby, *Responsible Parenthood: Decriminalizing Contraception in Canada* (Toronto: University of Toronto Press, 1999), 29–36.

5 Barbara M. Freeman, *The Satellite Sex: The Media and Women's Issues in English Canada, 1966–1971* (Waterloo, ON: Wilfred Laurier University Press, 2001), 168.

6 Jane Jenson, "Getting to *Morgentaler,*" in *The Politics of Abortion,* ed. Janine Brodie, Shelley A.M. Gavigan, and Jane Jenson (Toronto: Oxford University Press, 1992), 44.

7 Cerise Morris, "'Determination and Thoroughness': The Movement for a Royal Commission on the Status of Women in Canada," *Atlantis* 5, 2 (1980): 1–21; Freeman, *The Satellite Sex,* 25–27.

8 Penny Kome, *Women of Influence: Canadian Women and Politics* (Toronto: Doubleday, 1985), 85; Naomi Black, "The Canadian Women's Movement: The Second Wave," in *Changing Patterns: Women in Canada,* ed. Sandra Burt , Lorraine Code, and Lindsay Dorney (1988; repr., Toronto: McClelland and Stewart, 1990), 83–84; Morris, "Determination and Thoroughness," 16.

9 Sue Findlay, "Facing the State: The Politics of the Women's Movement Reconsidered," in *Feminism and Political Economy: Women's Work, Women's Struggles,* ed. Heather Jon Maroney and Meg Luxton (Toronto: Methuen, 1987), 35.

10 Florence Bird, *Anne Francis: An Autobiography* (Toronto: Clark Irwin, 1976); Dawn Black, *20 Years Later: An Assessment of the Implementation of the Recommendations of the Royal Commission on the Status of Women,* ed. Marika Morris (Ottawa: Office of Dawn Black, MP: 1990); Monique Bégin, "The Canadian Government and the Commission's Report," in *Women and the Canadian State,* ed. Caroline Andrew and Sandra Rogers (Montreal and Kingston: McGill-Queen's University Press, 1997), 21–38.

11 Annis May Timpson, "Royal Commissions as Sites of Resistance: Women's Challenges on Child Care in the Royal Commission on the Status of Women," *International Journal of Canadian Studies* 20 (1999): 123–48; Joan Sangster, "Invoking Experience as Evidence," *Canadian Historical Review* 92, 1 (2011): 135–61.

12 Beth Palmer, "'Lonely, Tragic, but Legally Necessary Pilgrimages': Transnational Abortion Travel in the 1970s," *Canadian Historical Review* 92, 4 (2011): 637–64; Christabelle Sethna, "All Aboard? Canadian Women's Abortion Tourism, 1960–1980," in *Gender, Health, and Popular Culture: Historical Perspectives,* ed. Cheryl Krasnick Warsh (Waterloo, ON: Wilfrid Laurier University Press, 2011): 89–108.

13 Larry Collins, "The Politics of Abortion: Trends in Canadian Fertility Policy," *Atlantis* 7, 2 (1982): 2–20; Janine Brodie, Shelley A.M. Gavigan, and Jane Jenson, eds., *The Politics of Abortion* (Toronto: Oxford University Press, 1992); Melissa Haussman, *Abortion Politics in North America* (Boulder, CO: Lynne Rienner, 2005).

14 Jenson, "Getting to *Morgentaler,*" 25–26, 31.

15 Ibid., 25–26.

16 Ibid., 21.

17 Anne Enke, *Finding the Movement: Sexuality, Contested Space, and Feminist Activism* (Durham, NC: Duke University Press, 2007), 4–5.

18 Freeman, *The Satellite Sex,* 29–33.

19 Deborah P. Britzman, *Practice Makes Practice: A Critical Study of Learning to Teach* (Albany, NY: SUNY Press, 2003), 34.

20 Canada, *Report of the Royal Commission on the Status of Women* (Ottawa: Queen's Printer, 1971). There are also organizational and classification ambiguities. It is not clear that all one thousand letters of opinion were actually archived. Sangster believes that this number does not reflect the archived collections. See Joan Sangster, *Transforming Labour: Women and Work in Post-war Canada* (Toronto: University of Toronto Press, 2010), 344–45n87.

21 Sangster, "Invoking Experience as Evidence," 136–37.

22 Many studies commissioned by the RCSW were not statistical in nature. See "Relations with Participants – Miscellaneous," LAC, RG 33/89, RCSW, vol. 36.

23 Anne Bond, "They Search for Definition Answers to Women's Status," "Scrapbook No. 1," LAC, RG 33/89, RCSW, vol. 40; "A Letter May Be a 'Brief' to Status Commission," *Toronto Star*, February 9, 1968, "Scrapbook No. 1," LAC, RG 33/89, RCSW, vol. 40.

24 See Bégin, "The Royal Commission," 29, 33; and Bégin, "The Canadian Government and the Commission's Report," 14.

25 Bégin, "The Royal Commission," 31.

26 Monique Bégin asserts that while MacGill came to the Commission already a feminist, Bird, Lange, Lapointe, and Ogilvie "became feminists in their own right. This politicization occurred through a process of group education: the reading of essays and existing research material, followed by the shared experience of the public hearings." See "Public Relations – Reports," LAC, RG 33/89, RCSW, vol. 35; and Bégin, "The Royal Commission," 28.

27 *Report of the Royal Commission on the Status of Women in Canada,* 286.

28 Cynthia Comacchio, *Nations Are Built of Babies: Educating Ontario's Mothers and Children, 1900–1940* (Montreal and Kingston: McGill-Queen's University Press, 1993), 6. See also Wendy Mitchinson, *Giving Birth in Canada, 1900–1950* (Toronto: University of Toronto Press, 2002), 13.

29 See Angus McLaren and Arlene Tigar McLaren, *The Bedroom and the State: The Changing Practices and Politics of Contraception and Abortion in Canada, 1880–1997* (Toronto: Oxford University Press, 1997), 32–51; and Stephen Brooke, "'A New World for Women?' Abortion Law Reform in Britain during the 1930s," *American Historical Review* 106, 2 (2001): 431–59.

30 "Letters of Opinion – Alberta," LAC, RG 33/89, RCSW, vol. 8.

31 "Letters of Opinion – Ontario," LAC, RG 33/89, RCSW, vol. 8, 5–136.

32 Ibid., 5–136.

33 File 364, LAC, RG 33/89, RCSW, vol. 17.

34 "Letters of Opinion – Manitoba," LAC, RG 33/89, RCSW, vol. 8.

35 Linda Revie, "More Than Just Boots! The Eugenic and Commercial Concerns behind A.R. Kaufman's Birth Controlling Activities" *Canadian Bulletin of Medical History* 23, 1 (2006): 135; McLaren and McLaren, *The Bedroom and the State,* 134.

36 "Letters of Opinion – Alberta," LAC, RG 33/89, RCSW, vol. 8.

37 "Letters of Opinion – Ontario," LAC, RG 33/89, RCSW, vol. 8.

38 Ibid.

39 "Letters of Opinion – Quebec," LAC, RG 33/89, RCSW, vol. 9.

40 Kathy Davis, "What's in a Voice? Methods and Metaphors," *Feminism and Psychology* 4, 3 (1994): 357.

41 See, for example, Appleby, *Responsible Parenthood*, 62–82, 87–197.

42 File 281, LAC, RG 33/89, RCSW, vol. 15.

43 "Letters of Opinion – Ontario," LAC, RG 33/89, RCSW, vol. 9.

44 File 431, LAC, RG 33/89, RCSW, vol. 18.

45 "Letters of Opinion – Ontario," LAC, RG 33/89, RCSW, vol. 9.

46 File 117, RG 33/89, LAC, RCSW, vol. 12.

47 "Letters of Opinion – Alberta," LAC, RG 33/89, RCSW, vol. 8.

48 "Letters of Opinion – Ontario," LAC, RG 33/89, RCSW, vol. 9.

49 File 250, LAC, RG 33/89, RCSW, vol. 14.

50 "Letters of Opinion – British Columbia," LAC, RG 33/89, RCSW, vol. 7.

51 Ibid.

52 "Letters of Opinion – British Columbia," LAC, RG 33/89, RCSW, vol. 17.

53 File 258, LAC, RG 33/89, RCSW, vol. 14.

54 Jenson, "Getting to *Morgentaler,*" 25–26.

55 Sangster, "Invoking Experience as Evidence," 143.

56 File 254, LAC, RG 33/89, RCSW, vol. 14.

57 File 388, LAC, RG 33/89, RCSW, vol. 17.
58 File 438, LAC, RG 33/89, RCSW, vol. 18.
59 "Letters of Opinion – British Columbia," LAC, RG 33/89, RCSW, vol. 7.
60 *Report of the Royal Commission on the Status of Women in Canada*, 280, 282.
61 Ibid., 285.
62 Freeman, *The Satellite Sex*, 36–38.
63 *Report of the Royal Commission on the Status of Women in Canada*, 422–23.
64 Ibid., 4329.
65 Ibid.
66 Sangster, "Invoking Experience as Evidence," 144.

5

Abortion on Trial

Abortion Tribunals in the 1970s and 1980s

Beth Palmer

On February 15, 1973, activists at the University of British Columbia (UBC) held an event called Women's Tribunal on Abortion, Contraception, and Sterilization as part of Women's Studies Week. At the tribunal, twenty-six women recounted their personal experiences with reproductive issues, highlighting the shortcomings of abortion services prior to and following the amendments to the *Criminal Code* in 1969 that legalized abortion in certain circumstances. According to UBC organizers, the tribunal, and similar ones held across the country, had "mobilizing power" and were "a major step forward for ... the abortion law repeal campaign."[1] These tribunals were a particularly effective pro-choice strategy in the 1970s because they highlighted several key pro-choice arguments. First, they highlighted the unjust abortion laws in Canada at the time. Second, they gave women a forum to discuss their own experiences safely, and to contextualize them within a wider framework, clearly elucidating the connections between the personal and the political. Furthermore, they were able to draw female and male pro-choice activists together, galvanizing a movement across the country while also serving an educational purpose. Lastly, they helped to break down the stigma often associated with abortion by creating a space for people to speak publicly about abortion and personal experiences.

By the 1970s, Canadian pro-choice activists were confident that they were supported by a "silent majority." It was crucial to mobilize this support in a public way, in order to counter the vocal anti-choice movement. One of the main strategies used in the pro-choice movement in Canada in the

1970s and 1980s was to define the debate and harness mainstream support by engaging with the public and public space in non-threatening ways. As abortion activism on both sides of the debate became an increasingly publicized social issue in Canada in the 1970s, the idea of the spectacle became a valuable activist tool. Abortion is at once a highly charged social issue, a simple medical procedure, and a personal choice. Both pro-choice and anti-abortion activists used – as they continue to do today – public spaces to attract supporters, drawing on public demonstrations featuring buttons and placards to publicize the issue. Spectacle, in a range of forms, serves to push an inherently private, medicalized issue into the public realm. Beyond bringing visibility to the issue, spectacle helps to disseminate a range of information in a non-threatening way and to engage the audience in a more interactive, thought-provoking discussion. This chapter will explore the ways that the pro-choice movement in Canada has historically used spectacle to reach out to potential supporters, specifically through the use of mock abortion tribunals, which used theatre and public space to draw attention to the need for safe and accessible abortion services.

Setting the Stage for Tribunals

Immediately following the 1969 omnibus bill that decriminalized abortions, provided they were approved by a Therapeutic Abortion Committee (TAC), activists realized that the new laws effected many barriers that continued to restrict access to abortion services. As hospitals lacked the means or the willingness to establish TACs, abortion services were unevenly available to women, with ease of access depending on many socio-economic factors, most notably women's geographic and social location. Some activists continued to help women to access services through referrals, while others fought to further liberalize the laws. In order to draw attention to the persistent limitations imposed on abortion services in Canada following the 1969 omnibus bill, activists across the country used mock tribunals to put the laws on trial and hold the criminal system accountable. These tribunals allowed women seeking abortions and service providers to give their own accounts of their experiences while also highlighting the shortcomings of the law. As such, they provide an important snapshot into both the legal issues and the activist mentality of the early 1970s.

Mock tribunals were one way to bring abortion into the public realm. In the 1970s, these theatrical presentations would allow members of the public to pretend to testify against the discriminatory nature of the abortion laws. Tribunals were a combination of political chastisement, legal challenge, personal narrative, and theatre. In a typical tribunal, a mock judge would preside over a simulated court, charging section 251 of the *Criminal Code* with discrimination against women. Women who had sought abortions, medical practitioners, and others would testify, recounting their personal experiences or, in order to preserve anonymity, the experiences of others. The tribunals at once challenged the TAC system while also allowing individuals to share their experiences. Rather than promoting the idea of an oversimplified standard abortion client, the pro-choice movement sought to tease out individual experiences with the TACs.

Abortion tribunals likely originated with the New York City radical feminist group Redstockings. Founded in 1968, Redstockings took up abortion rights as a central issue, calling for the repeal of abortion laws in 1969. When the New York State Legislature's Joint Legislative Committee on the Problems of Public Health discussed a bill to repeal the state's abortion laws, the 1969 hearings drew on thirteen expert testimonies provided by twelve men, who were doctors, psychiatrists, attorneys, politicians, and a former judge, and one woman, a nun. Many members of Redstockings attended the hearings, waiting until the final address to verbally challenge the so-called expert witnesses, shouting out, "what better experts are there on abortion than women?"[2] The Redstockings demanded a public hearing to allow for women's expert testimony to be heard and, when this demand was denied, they organized one of their own. On March 21, 1969, the Redstockings staged a public hearing at Washington Square Methodist Church in Manhattan, where a dozen women testified before an audience of three hundred people, including the press.[3] The Redstockings maintained that publicly testifying helped women to link consciousness-raising strategies to the feminist project of recognizing that the personal is political.

The Personal Is Political

Tribunals drew on mass mobilization strategies typically associated with in-the-streets demonstrations. A closer examination of abortion tribunals illustrates the ways that the movement embodied the feminist idea that the personal is political. These tribunals, held across Canada, were built on the premise that disclosing a history of abortion could be an empowering experience. Throughout the 1970s, pro-choice activists saw abortion as an intensely personal choice that was profoundly shaped by political issues. Carol Hanisch's 1969 essay "The Personal Is Political" outlined the defence of consciousness-raising as a tool of political action rather than personal therapy. Hanisch maintained that "personal problems are political problems. There are no personal solutions at this time. There is only collective action for a collective solution."[4] Mock tribunals were an extension of this consciousness-raising. By offering a public venue for women to share their own experiences with abortion, to connect their personal accounts to those of other women, and to place these collective experiences within a wider framework, mock tribunals provided a public site where the personal and the political explicitly overlapped.

Using the Language of the Law

Tribunals were able to forge connections across a broad audience, from the more radical early pro-choice activists to more mainstream organizations and institutions, in part by drawing on legal discourses to frame the abortion debate. In particular, the format of the tribunal appealed to doctors, nurses, social workers, teachers, and nurses: professional groups "whose work brings them into contact with the need for abortion law repeal."[5] Beyond this connection, these professionals were also potential donors.[6] Abortion tribunals gave voice to women seeking abortions, but also created a space where all experiences with abortion services could be brought forward and validated. Tribunal organizers in Vancouver clearly explained that because tribunals gave "an open public expression to women's situation, [they became] a pole of attraction around which many different women's groups may unite."[7] Attracting a wider support base was critically important for the pro-choice movement during the 1970s as activists worked to organize a mass social movement.

Tribunal organizers highlighted the key objectives of holding tribunals. First, and perhaps most importantly, tribunals gave women a voice in an otherwise disempowering situation. They sought "to make known the intense suffering caused to women by the present archaic laws" and "to give voice to some of the millions of women whose experiences corroborate these charges."[8] In this sense, tribunals helped to identify a seemingly silent pro-choice majority centred around women's personal experiences, while also acknowledging that women shared similar, unspoken experiences. Building on this notion, the tribunals also sought to challenge the dominant view that the 1969 omnibus bill had effectively liberalized the abortion law and improved accessibility. Tribunal organizers and participants decried this myth by underlining the many ways in which women continued to lack control over their reproductive capacities. Because barriers persisted, and were even reinforced by the 1969 amendments, tribunals also worked to challenge the misguided belief that women were somehow to blame for their reproductive needs, that their sexual choices, rather than systemic barriers, were the key issue. Lastly, in the words of organizers, tribunals provided an effective platform "to make it clear that, although the struggle is not yet won for women's right to control our own bodies, consciousness of the depth and range of women's suffering is mounting and more and more women are entering the fight."[9] To be sure, these differing aims were all intertwined: tribunals highlighted the shortcomings of the legal changes by using legal language and presentation. Doing so effectively served to entice a wider spectrum of supporters ranging from women seeking a space to tell their own stories to those more comfortable with a detached professional discourse.

The Effects/Outcomes/Impact of Tribunals?

Earlier tribunals were an effective pro-choice action and, in 1986, the Ontario Coalition for Abortion Clinics (OCAC) organized concurrent tribunals in Ontario,[10] British Columbia,[11] Alberta,[12] and Manitoba.[13] Testimonials at the OCAC tribunals highlighted both the diversity of those seeking and providing abortions and the different experiences of abortion clients. These tribunals were a combination of public talks, guerrilla theatre, and consciousness-raising. They were effective at garnering the public's attention; they were also, in the words of one participant, "a lot of fun."[14] In this sense, organized tribunals not only drew in supporters but also served to bolster activists' enthusiasm. Mock tribunals attended to the gravity of the situation arising from lack of abortion access while also undermining the legal and medical regulatory bodies that imposed barriers on women's access to reproductive control. The tribunals acted out and visually represented, in a concrete setting, activists' belief that the TAC system essentially put women on trial, forcing them to plead their cases in front of a panel of doctors acting as judges. Holding tribunals challenged the legitimacy of the TAC structure by giving women "a chance ... to turn the tables around. Instead of [women] being on trial, we are going to unite together in communities across Canada and Quebec, and we are going to put section 251 on trial."[15] Holding tribunals across the country helped to illustrate the commonalities of inaccessible abortion across the country while also highlighting the regional specificities of situations that arose for women facing unwanted pregnancies.

While there were benefits for women speaking out about their abortions, organizers also recognized that some women might have been more willing to share their experiences anonymously. To prepare for the tribunals, activists advertised at birth control information centres, community health clinics, women's centres, and women's organizations, as well as asking counselors to present the tribunals as a possibility to their clients.[16] Organizers believed that having women tell their own stories was the most effective way of conveying the implications, both material and emotional, of inaccessible abortion. While they maintained that anonymous testimonies were also important contributions, they acknowledged that they were "probably not as dramatic" as first-hand accounts.[17] That said, the fact that women were contributing to these tribunals anonymously was persuasive evidence that reproductive rights and abortion in particular remained highly stigmatized issues. In some instances, photography was prohibited and the media was asked to refrain from releasing any identifying information about those women who testified.[18]

Beyond providing a venue to speak publicly, tribunals also provided some women with a sense of closure by objectively assessing access to abortion in Canada and concluding that the problems of the current system were structural. Reflecting on the February 1973 "Woman's Tribunal on Abortion, Contraception and Sterilization" at the University of British Columbia, organizers commented that "every testimony verified the charges that women do not control our bodies, that the current laws and practices disrupt and cripple countless lives, and that the Canadian government must be indicted for its role in denying women the right to choose."[19] Beyond challenging the current system, these abortion tribunals also gave women a voice, reminded the public that abortion was not something for which women should be blamed, educated the public, fostered a pro-choice community that could engage an array of groups, raised funds, and drew attention to the need for birth control and abortion services and the government's responsibility to improve these services.[20]

Tribunals also provided a way to reframe debates on abortion. Typically, discussions about abortion access were framed by discourses of medicalization and liberalization, as Jane Jenson has shown.[21] As a result, women's voices and experiences tended to be absent from many official discussions about abortion access. Tribunals were a way to rectify this omission. As doctors, nurses, and patients offered their testimonials, the potential for these narratives to help effect change became increasingly apparent. Beyond being an educational tool, these personal stories could also be used to integrate the personal side of abortion, which was otherwise absent, into medical and legal discussions. Tribunal tactics of sharing personal stories and situating them within a broader context were integrated into other pro-choice projects. A brief presented by the Canadian Association for the Repeal of the Abortion Law (CARAL) to the Minister of Health in 1981 included a woman's personal story and charted the barriers she faced at every step when trying to obtain an abortion in 1980.[22] Under the heading "One Woman's Story," CARAL shared the experience of a twenty-four-year-old woman who was directed by a doctor to an anti-abortion group for counselling. After finding a doctor in a nearby city willing to perform the abortion, the anonymous patient learned that the physician did not accept payment through the Ontario Health Insurance Plan, and that the procedure would cost $200. After finding a doctor at a greater distance, the woman rented a car, booked a trip, and travelled to obtain the abortion. Unable to stay in the city for her post-operative checkup, the woman returned to her community, where her original doctor chastised her for having the procedure, suggested she should practice abstinence, and hesitated to perform the checkup. The patient was unequivocal in her assessment that "the process is humiliating," explaining that she had been treated as though she were "'sleezy,' 'irresponsible,' 'cheap,' 'unfeeling,' and 'selfish.'"[23] CARAL submitted its brief to the Minister of Health with this personal anecdote to give a face to the issue of abortion access and also to demonstrate the widespread implications of inaccessibility that could not be measured with typical statistics.

Social Position and Diverse Experiences of Abortion

Typically, women's testimonials highlighted key issues for the pro-choice movement as women reflected candidly about their difficulties and successes accessing abortions across the country. While testifying, women assessed the benefits or hindrances of their age, marital status, location, class, and other markers that impacted their ability to navigate the health care system in order to obtain an abortion. The Kitchener-Waterloo Women's

Place presented an interesting juxtaposition of experiences in its July 1975 newsletter and demonstrated the different services women received depending on various social markers. One woman, who identified as a married, middle-class professional, explained that she had "no difficulty" obtaining an abortion in Regina, Saskatchewan, in 1972. However, though she described her experience with the doctor, nurses, and hospital as "excellent," she recounted her confusion over payment. Because her abortion was performed in a hospital, the bill was directed to medicare. While this followed standard protocol, the doctor later asked for further payment, sending a second bill to the patient. This extra billing was a common practice for abortion procedures in the 1970s.[24] The woman refused to pay the bill and the issue ended there, but the implication is clearly that women who were trying to keep their abortion from friends or family, or who had limited experience with the health care system, might be compelled to pay these extra fees despite the fact that the doctors had no legitimate reason for charging them. In contrast to the married professional, a twenty-two-year-old woman in Swift Current, Saskatchewan, provided a testimonial detailing her difficulty obtaining an abortion. The patient reported having to "prove her instability," and saw three doctors before one would refer her case to a TAC. One doctor interrogated her about her relationship and sexual experience, another provided her with contact information for the anti-choice group Birthright, and only the third helped her obtain the procedure. This patient described her experience as fraught with "unnecessary hardship and anxiety," a situation that was exacerbated by the fact that, as a young rural woman, she had few advocates in the health care system or elsewhere.[25]

Medical Professionals at the Abortion Tribunals

Pro-choice medical professionals also testified in the tribunals. Many doctors and nurses publicly attributed their pro-choice stance to a particular moment when they did not perform an abortion upon request, only to learn later that the woman sought a back-alley abortion and subsequently required serious medical attention.[26] Dr. Henry Morgentaler drew upon this trope, describing a patient who committed suicide after he refused to perform an abortion. Morgentaler later acknowledged that this story was an exaggeration, explaining: "I wanted to make my point. I don't think I ever had a patient who committed suicide, although I had lots of women who threatened to commit suicide if they didn't get help."[27] In a 1967 article, "Abortion: The Law that Kills," Morgentaler was unequivocal in his assessment that the laws criminalizing abortion were profoundly dangerous for women as a whole, but also on a very personal, individual level. He explained:

> In my 12 years of general practice, I have been confronted many times by women who implored me to give them an abortion, who were desperate. I had to refuse. I had to watch them drift away in mental agony, usually to find some abortionist and end up in a hospital bleeding or barely alive, to resign themselves to having a baby they did not want.[28]

Morgentaler's depiction of his patients as "desperate" in no way suggests that he considered their responses unwarranted, but rather that he understood that their desperation could easily be tempered by allowing doctors to perform the relatively easy medical procedures.

Providing testimony at a 1986 tribunal in Edmonton, Karen, a registered nurse, provided an account with her first experience with the dangers of abortion, which occurred in 1969. Her testimony was both performative and informative, intended to convey the authority of personal experience within a safe space. Karen's account touches on the connections between class, ethnicity, and accessibility while highlighting the needlessness of denying women necessary abortion services:

> The nurse in charge came away from the phone very upset. She said, "Set up the room for isolation. We have one of those bloody back-street coat-hangers coming up. Probably another one who can't speak English is going to die and we can't even talk to her ... " I was stunned. All I could do was listen to what the other nurses had to say. As the other RNs discussed past cases I became frightened especially by their unanswered questions: How many more? Why can't they get proper medical help before rather than after coming here like this? After all, medical technology is available. Who are we to judge what people need? If a woman needs an abortion she'll find someone to do it. They all could tell you so many stories about the ones who found it. Why couldn't it be safe? There's enough pain in choosing abortion. They didn't deserve this. Both nurses were very angry that Canadian women had to go to New York or Sweden. That is, only those who could afford it get safe medical care to deal with unwanted pregnancies.[29]

Following Karen's testimony, the mock tribunal judge declared that the abortion law was discriminatory on the basis of class, while also ruling that it denied women equal protection and benefit of the law and the right of life, liberty, and security of person as per the *Canadian Charter of Rights and Freedoms*. The judge concluded by mandating free-standing clinics, which would provide abortions for women "under the best medical conditions with the most modern and safest techniques in an atmosphere of caring and compassion."[30] The mock tribunals provided an ideal forum to challenge the law and posit clinics as the solution. Testimonies from women who had sought illegal abortions in free-standing clinics furthered this defence of clinics, as one woman's statement ended with the assertion that, following her abortion, she was "thanking God for abortion clinics."[31] Particularly when contrasted with gruesome tales from medical professionals about botched abortions, or with personal testimonies detailing the fears and dangers arising from back-alley abortions or the degrading nature of TACs and doctors who abuse their authority, clinics emerged in these mock tribunals as a humane, safe, and efficient alternative to TACs and the abortion law.

Building a Mass Movement

These tribunals held across the country, often in tandem with one another, were a particularly effective tool in building a mass movement. As public spectacles, the tribunals garnered attention for the pro-choice movement, while clearly highlighting the diverse issues affecting women in need of abortions. Furthermore, the tribunals posited clinics as a (temporary) solution to the problems facing women needing abortions. Given the magnitude of issues arising from the inaccessibility of abortion services and the vague – though legitimate – calls for "free abortion on demand," this objective helped to encourage new activists as they joined the movement. Reflecting on their experiences of organizing tribunals, the organizers of the February 1973 tribunal at UBC maintained that the action was critical to building a mass action, a "major step forward for the Coalition and for the abortion law repeal campaign."[32] These tribunals helped to foster a new focus within the pro-choice movement on women's individual experiences, helping to situate them within a broader context of inaccessibility, women's rights, women's liberation, and various social markers such as race, class, age, and location. These tribunals represented a shift away from focusing on a radical reorganization of society, instead allowing for an individual narrative that could ultimately be used for collective good.[33]

Building on the idea of giving voice to individual women, the mock tribunals also took the law, a tool that was often disempowering and even threatening, and reframed legal intervention. These mock tribunals emphasized the ways that the legal system, the political system, and society in general failed to protect women's safety and women's rights. By giving women an opportunity to voice their own experiences with abortion, tribunals were a means of flipping the traditional legal narrative to reveal the shortcomings of the law. Rather than charging individuals with legal violations, these tribunals put the system on trial. The 1973 UBC tribunal laid the following charges:

> 1. The Canadian government has denied women the right to control our reproductive lives;
> 2. The Canadian abortion laws force women to become criminals in the eyes of the state;
> 3. Under the aegis of these laws, women are sterilized against their wills;
> 4. Under the aegis of these laws, women are kept in ignorance of our bodies and the process of reproduction is mystified;
> 5. Abortion laws and contraception laws result in unwanted children;
> 6. Restrictions such as hospital committees, psychiatric approval, and accredited hospitals are unconstitutional, in that they are not required for any other medical procedure;
> 7. Abortion laws cause unnecessary delay, inconvenience, and expense for women seeking what should be a simple medical procedure;
> 8. Abortion services are unevenly available and non-existent in certain parts of BC and Canada;
> 9. The abortion laws force women to degrade, humiliate, and incriminate themselves by declaring themselves mentally ill;
> 10. All abortion laws are unconstitutional;
> 11. Abortion laws deny women life and liberty, in that we are forced to expose ourselves to the mental and physical dangers of unsafe, back-street abortionists, in order to terminate unwanted pregnancies;
> 12. If the so-called right-to-life groups are successful in their attempts to make Canadian laws more restrictive, women will continue to die from illegal abortions, and the quality of human life for women, men, and children will continue to be retarded, distorted, and oppressive.[34]

The organizers of the Vancouver tribunal went on to propose several recommendations, including repealing various sections of the *Criminal Code* of Canada to improve access to birth control information, technologies, and sexual education.[35]

But the tribunals also provided another advantage for the pro-choice movement. Organizers were surprised to discover that tribunals were less vulnerable to anti-choice attacks than in-the-street demonstrations. British Columbian organizers expected an anti-abortion counter-demonstration or disruption, but none occurred. The organizers credited this lack of anti-abortion presence to the fact that tribunals were places where testimony was provided in a "serious atmosphere."[36] Because women took ownership of their own experiences while highlighting the individual decisions that shaped these experiences, the anti-abortion movement had limited means to challenge these highly personal narratives.

Building on the testimonials from tribunals, the pro-choice movement drew on another public tactic, that of women's personal declarations of abortions. Recognizing the benefits of these individual voices joined to form a persuasive collective argument, the pro-choice movement continued to solicit personal experiences with abortion. "Coming out" as an abortion client became a political strategy in and of itself. Publicly identifying yourself as a woman who had obtained an abortion served many purposes. Describing abortion experiences publicly has a rich international history. In 1971, a French manifesto signed by 343 women, including Simone de Beauvoir, declared that they had had abortions. Building on this strategy, the inaugural issue of *Ms.* magazine featured a petition signed by fifty-three well-known American women, including Gloria Steinem, Nora Ephron, and Lillian Hellman, declaring that they had had illegal abortions. Towards the end of the 1970s and into the 1980s and '90s, this tactic was employed by Canadian groups. Pro-choice organizations across the country organized different campaigns, including CARAL's 1982 Stand Up and Be Counted petition directed at the federal government.

Campaigns encouraging women to share their experiences with abortion sought stories about the entire spectrum of experiences, including experiences of both illegal and TAC-approved abortions, abortions offered on a pay-what-you-can basis and those that were prohibitively expensive, abortions performed in clinics, hospitals, and other sites, and abortions that required women to obtain referrals, make use of shuttle services, or undertake significant travel and those that required no referral and barely any travel. Sharing personal experiences of abortion at once helped to highlight the need for free abortion on demand while also demonstrating the highly personal implications of inaccessibility. Asking women to share these personal experiences helped to politicize abortion inaccessibility, simultaneously destigmatizing the procedure and identifying barriers that might otherwise go unnoticed. In a 1982 letter to CARAL supporters, Catherine Daw described her own experience, publicly discussing her abortion:

> We are asking all women who have had an abortion to stand up and be counted. As someone who has had an abortion, I know how difficult this can be. For a couple of years afterward I felt as if I had a secret burden, even though I knew I had made the right decision for me at the time. When I finally did talk about the abortion, it was a great relief to find that the people I cared about understood and supported my choice ... I was fortunate when I had my abortion – it was post 1969, I was knowledgeable and in a major centre where it was relatively accessible. But I have spoken to women with experiences drastically different from mine and it makes me want to fight even harder for safe, legal abortions.[37]

CARAL thus framed its Stand Up and Be Counted petition as both an effective educational and lobbying too land a source of empowerment for women caught in otherwise disempowering situations.

Publicly discussing personal experiences of abortion empowered women by challenging the notion that there was a particular type of woman likely to seek out the procedure. Too often, women seeking TACs, illegal abortions in clinics, or illegal abortions in non-clinic settings were portrayed in the media and in public discussions as marginalized women, often teenagers or young single women, from non-urban centres, with less education and lower incomes, and with little support.[38] Providing first-person narratives thus helped to show the different experiences women had trying to obtain abortions, effectively demonstrating the differential treatment available to Canadian women, as highlighted by the Kitchener-Waterloo newsletter discussed earlier. Individuals' stories also served to demonstrate the universal need for abortion. Women seeking abortion were rich and poor, urban and rural, married and single, and young and old, and they were able to draw on support networks to a varying degree. As these patients shared their stories, it became increasingly difficult for politicians, the media, and the public to dismiss women seeking abortions as radical, irresponsible women undeserving of this medical procedure. This pervasive narrative shamed and oppressed women, and was contested by women who publicly shared their experiences that offered an alternative to this stereotype.

These personal stories helped, too, to contextualize statistics. The implications of declarations that "more than 30% of women in Ontario live in communities where hospitals do not perform abortions" were made manifest in descriptions such as the plight of a young woman, Louise, forced to travel from northern Ontario to Toronto for an abortion, an undue burden compounded by the fact that her husband had recently been laid off.[39] The strategy of including personal experiences in various materials and actions helped to highlight the extent to which abortion was at once an individual and a collective issue. First-person narratives illustrated the inextricable links between the personal and the political.

This movement was further advanced by sheer numbers. Recognizing that some women would not feel comfortable sharing their personal experiences, CARAL amended its Stand Up and Be Counted campaign to include a less personal standardized statement. The form letter simply stated: "I have had an abortion. I publicly join thousands of Canadian women in demanding repeal of all laws that restrict our reproductive freedom." Publicity material included a tear-away portion that included space for a name and signature, as well as a disclosure that this information would be used in CARAL's federal and provincial lobbying efforts and in its advertising.[40]

Sharing personal experiences remains a pro-choice strategy, effective because it is empowering and destigmatizing. In 1998, Childbirth by Choice published *No Choice: Canadian Women Tell Their Stories of Illegal Abortion.*[41] These first-hand accounts were a particularly valuable evidence base – irrefutable because they referred only to personal experiences but, taken together, forming a more complete picture of the state of abortion access and the importance of reproductive choice. More recently, groups have begun using the Internet to collect personal stories, notably Arts 4 Choice,[42] which used its website to solicit personal stories via questionnaire and email, and Canadians for Choice, which solicited personal experiences "for the purpose of public awareness."[43]

These tactics have also been embraced by the anti-choice movement – most notably with its Silent No More campaign. At anti-abortion protests in both Canada and the United States, women bear signs proclaiming "I Regret My Abortion" and both men and women hold placards announcing "Men Regret Lost Fatherhood." At anti-abortion rallies, women and men are also invited to share their "personal testimonies of hurt and healing to help others avoid the pain of abortion."[44] As was the case in the 1970s and 1980s, political opponents – this time pro-choice advocates – still find themselves ill-equipped to challenge these personal narratives. The pro-choice movement, so rooted in the adage that the personal is political, is particularly attuned to the reality that women respond to their experiences differently.

Approaches advocating for women's reproductive choice and access have evolved from the tribunals of the 1970s and 1980s, but publicly sharing abortion experiences remains an effective pro-choice strategy, embracing new tools, particularly social media, to unite activists across vast distances. In 2015, American writer Lindy West started #ShoutYour Abortion, an Internet-based campaign encouraging women to come forward and share their experiences "from the harrowing to the mundane."[45] West recounts seeing a Facebook post responding to Congressional attempts to defund Planned Parenthood in the United States, in which activist Amelia Bonow wrote about having an abortion at a Planned Parenthood clinic and then explained: "I am telling you this today because the narrative of those working to defund Planned Parenthood relies on the assumption that abortion is still something to be whispered about. Plenty of people still believe that on some level – if you are a good woman – abortion is a choice which should be accompanied by some level of sadness, shame or regret."[46] In only a few days, the hashtag #ShoutYourAbortion garnered over 250,000 posts on Twitter, with women from around the world sharing their own experiences with abortion. Contributing to this forum created an online community of support for women, including abortion providers, women who had had abortions, and pro-choice women.[47]

Building on the momentum from #ShoutYourAbortion, Bonow and others have initiated #TogetherForAbortion, with events coinciding in fifty states to commemorate the forty-third anniversary of the *Roe v Wade* ruling in the United States. The #TogetherForAbortion campaign describes itself as central to "a critical shift in the way our culture talks about abortion."[48] This event is part of a longer tradition of women defining their own experiences in a way that appropriately reflects them both personally and politically.

There was a decided shift in the narrative on abortion in Canada in 2014. For the first time, all three federal leaders of the officially-recognized political parties publicly stated their intention to support abortion services, albeit to different degrees and to different ends.[49] In New Brunswick, a provincial law ensured that abortions are only funded if they are performed in one of two hospitals after being declared medically necessary by two physicians – harkening back to the TACs of the 1970s. New Brunswick was the only province in Canada where a private abortion clinic, the Morgentaler Clinic, did not receive public funding for providing the medical service of abortion, which cost between $700 and $850 depending on the length of gestation. Many women paid out-of-pocket and the clinic estimated that it had waived approximately $10,000 per year in fees for women who could not afford the cost.[50] When the clinic announced that it would close its doors, activists organized public protests and an online crowdfunding campaign that raised over $130,000. Sustained social and political pressure also led then recently elected Premier Brian Gallant to announce in November that his government would be overturning the two-doctor rule, effective January 15, 2015, which means that abortion is now classified as any other insured medical procedure by the provincial government.[51] Abortion access remains uneven across the country, and there is still no abortion provider on Prince Edward Island (PEI) (see Brown, Ehrlich, and MacQuarrie, this volume). However, providing further evidence of the shift in narrative with regards to abortion in Canada, PEI Premier Robert Ghiz publicly declared that he was pro-choice for the first time during his year-end interview with the *Charlottetown Guardian*.[52] In 2015, less than two weeks after being appointed Minister of Health, Jane Philpott announced that equalizing access to abortion across Canada was a priority: "We know that abortion services remain patchy in parts of the country, and that rural women in particular face barriers to access. Our government will examine ways to better equalize access for all Canadian women."[53] These political shifts did not happen in a vacuum: they are certainly the result of decades of work from pro-choice activists across the country.

In the 1970s, tribunals were a particularly effective strategy because they created a specific and persuasive type of public space in which to share personal experiences, while also locating these personal stories within a broader political context. Today's pro-choice movement has built on this history, normalizing discussions about reproductive justice and access. The struggle to ensure that all women have access to safe and accessible contraception and abortion procedures continues, but today's activists are building on a tradition of activism and reframing it in such a way that pro-choice sentiment becomes associated with mainstream opinion. These attempts to locate a pro-choice discourse within a dominant social and political narrative, however, comes at the risk of obscuring the diverse challenges facing Canadian women whose experiences are defined by region, class, race, ethnicity, and other social markers. Exploring the history of pro-choice activism and the role of mock tribunals offers one potential tool for situating individual experiences within a universal narrative of choice.

Notes

1 The BC Chapter, "A Tribunal in B.C. March 17, 1973," City of Vancouver Archives (CVA), Pro-choice Records, Add. MSS 1486, 576-D-3, file 2, "Birth Control + Abortion" (hereafter "Birth Control + Abortion"), 4.
2 Jennifer Nelson, *Women of Color and the Reproductive Rights Movement* (New York: New York University Press, 2003), 28–31.
3 Ibid., 36.
4 Carol Hanisch, "The Personal Is Political," in *Radical Feminism: A Documentary Reader*, ed. Barbara A. Crow (New York: New York University Press, 2000), 114.
5 "Birth Control + Abortion," 1.
6 Ibid.
7 Ibid.
8 Ibid.
9 Ibid., 2.
10 Patricia Antonyshyn, B. Lee, and Alex Merrill, "Marching for Women's Lives: The Campaign for Free-Standing Abortion Clinics in Ontario," in *Social Movements, Social Change: The Politics and Practice of Organizing*, ed. Frank Cunningham, Sue Findlay, Marlene Kadar, Alan Lennon, and Ed Silva (Toronto: Between the Lines, 1988), 129–56, 145.
11 "Program: Women's Tribunal on Abortion, Contraception and Sterilization, a Part of Women's Week, Thursday, February 15, 1973," CVA, Pro-choice Records, Add. MSS 1486, 576-E-6, file 5: "Abortion and BCCRAL (BC Coalition to Repeal the Abortion Laws) – Tribunal at UBC" (hereafter "Abortion and BCCRAL Tribunal at UBC").
12 Alberta Status of Women Action Committee (ASWAC), "Abortion Tribunals: The Canadian Abortion Law on Trial," Provincial Archives of Alberta (PAA), ASWAC fonds, acc. 1997.0305, box 25, file 276.
13 "Program: Women's Tribunal on Abortion, Contraception and Sterilization, a Part of Women's Week, Thursday, February 15, 1973," Canadian Women's Movement Archives (CWMA), National Action Committee on the Status of Women (NAC) fonds, X10–24–4, series 2 (New Campaign, no box or files, Ontario Coalition for Abortion Clinics [OCAC]).
14 Donna Liberman, interview with author, August 12, 2010, Burnaby, British Columbia.
15 OCAC, "What Are Tribunals, and Why Have Them?," CWMA, CWMA fonds, X10–1, box 79, "Ontario Coalition for Abortion Clinics (Toronto, On): Posters, Leaflets and Other Material, 1981–1991 (1 of 3)," July 1985, 1.

16 Ibid., 2.
17 Ibid.
18 ASWAC, "Edmonton Abortion Tribunal Script," PAA, ASWAC fonds, accession number: 1997.0305, box 25, file 276 (hereafter "Edmonton Abortion Tribunal Script"), 3.
19 "Birth Control + Abortion," 4.
20 Ibid., 2.
21 Jane Jenson, "Getting to *Morgentaler*: From One Representation to Another," in *The Politics of Abortion,* ed. Janine Brodie, Shelley A.M. Gavigan, and Jane Jenson (Toronto: Oxford University Press, 1992), 15–55.
22 Canadian Abortion Action Rights League (CARAL), "A Brief to the Minister of Health, the Honourable Dennis R. Timbrell, September 22, 1981," CWMA, CWMA fonds, X10–1, box 7, "CARAL/ACDA (Toronto, On.): Briefs, 1972–1972," appendix 2, 10.
23 Ibid., 10–12.
24 Woman's Place, K-W Woman's Place Newsletter, vol. 2, no. 7, July 1975, SFUA, WBC, fonds 00111, container 00005, "Ontario Women's Centres – Kitchener/Waterloo, 'Woman's Place' 1974–1975" F-111-6-0-16.
25 Ibid.
26 "Speak Out for Choice: The Abortion Law on Trial," 6.
27 Quoted in Catherine Dunphy, *Morgentaler: A Difficult Hero* (Toronto: Random House, 1996), 79.
28 Henry Morgentaler, "Abortion: The Law that Kills," Library and Archives Canada (LAC), Association for the Review of Canadian Abortion Laws (ARCAL) fonds, MG 28 I 350 vol. 2, "Morgentaler, Henry, N.D., 1967–1975," 6.
29 "Edmonton Abortion Tribunal Script," 6.
30 Ibid., 48.
31 "Speak Out For Choice: The Abortion Law on Trial," 9.
32 "Birth Control + Abortion," 4.
33 For a detailed examination of the socialist movement's early impact on the pro-choice movement in Canada, see Ann Thomson, *Winning Choice on Abortion: How British Columbian and Canadian Feminists Won the Battle of the 1970s and 1980s* (Victoria, BC: Trafford Publishing, 2004), particularly Chapter 1, "Feminism Arrives at Simon Fraser University," 1–9.
34 "Abortion and BCCRAL Tribunal at UBC," 3.
35 Ibid., 3.
36 "Birth Control + Abortion," 4.
37 Catherine Daw, "Dear Friend, 1982," CWMA, CWMA fonds, X10–1, box 7, "CARAL/ACDA (Toronto, On.): Correspondence, Donation Cards and Other Material Re: Lobbying and Fundraising, 1975–1992 (2 of 2)," 1.
38 Leslie Reagan reveals the minor changes in the ways the media depicted women who had had abortions, from the turn-of-the-century "image of the victimized single woman" to the socially stigmatized single woman in need. Leslie J. Reagan, *When Abortion Was a Crime: Women, Medicine, and Law in the United States, 1867–1973* (Berkeley, CA: University of California Press, 1997), 23, 189.
39 OCAC, "Draft of Leaflet (Jan. 1983) Legalize Free-Standing Abortion Clinics," CWMA, CWMA fonds, X10–1, box 79, "Ontario Coalition for Abortion Clinics (Toronto, On): Minutes and Related Material, 1982–1983," 1.
40 CARAL, "Freedom of Choice," CWMA, CWMA fonds, X10–1, box 79, "Ontario Coalition for Abortion Clinics (Toronto, On): Minutes and Related Material, 1982–1983," 1.
41 Childbirth by Choice Trust, *No Choice: Canadian Women Tell Their Stories of Illegal Abortion* (Toronto: Childbirth by Choice Trust, 1998).
42 Arts4Choice, "Share Your Story," accessed April 21, 2014, http://www.arts4choice.com/share-your-story/.

43 Canadians for Choice, "Share Your Story," accessed April 21, 2014, http://www.canadians forchoice.ca/sharestories.html.

44 Silent No More Awareness Campaign, accessed May 21, 2013, http://www.silentnomore awareness.org.

45 Lindy West, "I Set Up #ShoutYourAbortion Because I Am Not Sorry, and I Will Not Whisper," *The Guardian,* September 22, 2015, http://www.theguardian.com/commentisfree/2015/sep/22/i-set-up-shoutyourabortion-because-i-am-not-sorry-and-i-will-not-whisper.

46 Amelia Bonow, quoted in West, "I Set Up #ShoutYourAbortion Because I Am Not Sorry."

47 Detractors of the movement also used online venues to decry abortion, draw comparisons between abortion and genocide, and threaten women. While the Internet can be a tool of activism, it is certainly not a safe space for many. See Patricia Kozicka, "'Shout Your Abortion' Movement Sparks Death Threats From Anti-abortion Activists," *Global News,* September 23, 2015, http://globalnews.ca/news/2235119/shout-your-abortion-movement-sparks-death-threats-from-anti-abortion-activists/.

48 #TogetherForAbortion, accessed January 16, 2016, http://togetherforabortion.com/.

49 In May, NDP leader Tom Mulcair reiterated his party's commitment to reproductive rights, saying: "In the NDP, no MP is ever going to vote against the woman's right to choose. No one will be allowed to run for the NDP if they don't believe that it is a right in our society for women to make their own choices on their reproductive health. Period." Liberal leader Justin Trudeau explicitly stated his party's position going forward in May and June, maintaining, "the policy going forward is that every single Liberal MP will be expected to stand up for women's rights to choose." When asked, then prime minister Stephen Harper once again reiterated that, under his leadership, the Conservative Party would not reopen the debate on abortion in the House of Commons. Andrea Janus, "No Anti-abortion Candidates Allowed to Run for NDP: Mulcair," *CTVnews.ca,* May 8, 2014, http://www.ctvnews.ca/politics/no-anti-abortion-candidates-allowed-to-run-for-ndp-mulcair-1.1812400#ixzz3ND6JdSiG; Laura Payton, "Justin Trudeau Clarifies Abortion Stance for Liberal MPs," *CBC News,* June 18, 2014, http://www.cbc.ca/news/politics/justin-trudeau-clarifies-abortion-stance-for-liberal-mps-1.2679783.

50 Kelly Grant, "As Morgentaler Clinic Closes, New Brunswick Abortion-Rights Group Turns to Crowdfunding," *Globe and Mail,* July 18, 2014, http://www.theglobeandmail.com/news/national/as-morgentaler-clinic-closes-new brunswick-abortion-rights-group-turns-to-crowdfunding/article19679632/.

51 "New Brunswick Abortion Restriction Lifted by Premier Brian Gallant," *CBC News,* November 26, 2014, http://www.cbc.ca/news/canada/new-brunswick/new-brunswick-abortion-restriction-lifted-by-premier-brian-gallant-1.2850474.

52 Wayne Thibodeau, "Premier Robert Ghiz: 'I Am Pro-choice,'" *Charlottetown Guardian,* December 22, 2014, http://www.theguardian.pe.ca/News/Local/2014-12-22/article-3985311/Premier-Robert-Ghiz%3A-I-am-pro-choice/1.

53 "Abortion Access in Canada Needs to Be Equalized, Says Health Minister," *CBC News,* November 17, 2015, http://www.cbc.ca/news/canada/prince-edward-island/abortion-access-jane-philpott-1.3322296.

6

The Dark, Well-Kept Secret

Abortion Experiences in the Maritime Provinces

Katrina Ackerman

Many excellent Canadian studies highlight the barriers to abortion services that remained after the federal government liberalized the law governing abortion in 1969, and yet the experiences of women living in the Atlantic region have received minimal attention in historical research.[1] In this chapter, I draw on women's narratives gleaned through in-person and telephone interviews I conducted with women who lived in the Maritime provinces in the 1970s and 1980s, as well as Canadian Abortion Rights Action League researcher Nancy Bowes's study *Telling Our Secrets*, which includes twenty-five oral interviews with women who sought abortions in Nova Scotia between 1985 and 1989.[2] I also use government records and medical research to offer insights into the challenges women faced when trying to obtain abortions in tight-knit rural communities. The abortion experiences discussed in this essay occurred during a period in which pro-life activists relentlessly lobbied hospital corporations and charitable organizations, tirelessly disseminated anti-abortion petitions, and set up educational booths at community events to increase membership in anti-abortion organizations.[3] Exploring Maritime women's abortion experiences illuminates extralegal barriers residents commonly encountered in their efforts to terminate a pregnancy and the psychological, physical, and economic costs that arose from the lack of access to abortion services.

Maritime women's voices are largely absent in Canadian abortion studies because of the taboo nature of the subject in the region. By drawing on women's experiences in hospital and free-standing abortion clinics, it is possible to explore not only the barriers to the procedure in the region, but also the impact of the shame and stigma of seeking an abortion on women's lives. The majority of abortions performed in the Maritime provinces occurred in Nova Scotia because of the comparatively liberal abortion stance of Halifax's Victoria General Hospital. An examination of Maritime women's abortion narratives demonstrates the extent to which regionalism and pro-life activism shaped access to abortion services, as well as women's reluctance to disclose their experiences.

Therapeutic Abortion Committees and the Ambiguity of the Abortion Law

The liberalization of the Canadian abortion law in 1969 merely created the illusion of access. In 1969, after years of public debate and political deliberation, Prime Minister Pierre Trudeau's Liberal government amended the *Criminal Code of Canada* to create greater access to abortion services. Accredited hospitals were permitted to establish Therapeutic Abortion Committees (TACs) and approve requests to terminate pregnancies that could endanger the life or health of the woman. However, the liberalization of the abortion law in 1969 did not receive widespread support within the hospital system, and access to the procedure remained limited throughout the Maritime region. A woman who worked in the operating room at the former Miramichi Hospital in Newcastle, New Brunswick, in the 1970s remembered that the staff only performed a couple abortions annually; moreover, many of the women she worked with did not like being involved in the procedures and vocalized their opinions.[4] Hospital staff's opposition to abortion did not go unnoticed. According to Nova Scotia psychiatrist Charles J. David, hospital staff, including nurses, residents, and interns, communicated their disapproval of abortion procedures in "verbal and non-verbal ways" and contributed to patients' "post abortion psychiatric sequelae."[5] For patients who already encountered psychological difficulties prior to the abortion procedure due to ambivalence or guilt, judgment from physicians and hospital staff perpetuated the abortion stigma and inhibited patients from seeking support after the operation. Throughout the 1970s, it was clear to both hospital staff and women seeking abortions in the Maritimes that the operation was not a standard procedure within the medical community.

Since hospitals were not required to form TACs, the voluntary nature of the system ensured unequal access to the procedure throughout the region. Women who attempted to obtain abortions within the TAC system sometimes faced harrowing abortion experiences, as described in an interview with Judith Wouk, a former employee for Halifax's Family Planning Association in the 1970s. Wouk quickly learned that a patient needed the support of five doctors to receive an abortion: a family doctor or referral doctor, a surgeon to perform the procedure, and at least three members of a TAC.[6] However, the number of referrals and doctors required to approve an abortion request remained unclear throughout the 1970s and 1980s.[7] Hoping to ease the challenge of finding willing physicians, the Family Planning Association sent a survey to clinics to find out who was willing to perform the procedure. When few responded to the survey, Wouk called doctors directly to find out their position on abortion. She discovered that one doctor referred his patients for abortions but did not want to be on a list, whereas other doctors stated that they would never refer anyone or perform abortions themselves.

When asked if TACs rejected many applications, Wouk recalled that getting access to the committee was the primary challenge because family doctors often stalled women.[8] Many times, family doctors either were misinformed or did not want to be responsible for recommending abortions that were not medically necessary, so they stalled the process by transferring women to psychiatrists for abortion referrals. The need for a psychiatrist's referral created barriers for women who wanted abortions for socioeconomic reasons and were unwilling to perform a mental illness to get a referral.[9] Eighteen-year-old Katherine McDonald did not obtain an abortion in Nova Scotia in 1972 because the psychiatrist she saw for a referral deemed her healthy and capable of carrying a child to term. The psychiatrist told McDonald that to make her eligible for a therapeutic abortion he would need to declare her mentally ill, and he warned her that this label would follow her throughout the rest of her life. McDonald had witnessed mental illness in her own family, and the notion that she would also carry this stigma stopped her from going back to her family doctor and asking for a second opinion. After she decided to keep the baby, against her parents' wishes, McDonald was sent to live at a family cottage in New Brunswick and later to live with a cousin. Eventually, she went to Birthright, an organization established to provide women with alternatives to abortion, and lived with a pro-choice family that housed eighteen unwed women.[10] She originally planned to give her baby up for adoption, but was fortunate to give birth to her son during the period in which the province established social assistance for unmarried mothers and thus was able to keep him.[11] While McDonald was ultimately happy that she did not have an abortion, her experience highlights the psychological pressure women faced while attempting to obtain the time-sensitive procedure.

The ambiguous nature of determining the validity of a woman's abortion request without the definition of health provided to practitioners meant that many psychiatrists were concerned about their new legal responsibility. As the *Criminal Code* amendment did not define *health,* medical professionals became responsible for deciding how broadly or narrowly to apply the term on a case-by-case basis. In an article published in the *Nova Scotia Medical Bulletin* in 1973, psychiatrist Charles J. David offered an overview of the challenges facing psychiatrists when attempting to assess abortion requests under the amended abortion law. David highlighted the complexity of "satisfying the criteria as laid down by the new law," which resulted from the ambiguity of the legal wording, such as that regarding the assessment of health and what constituted normality, which was not easy to determine within the medical profession.[12] David also argued that personal beliefs, the taboo of abortion in the medical profession, and social values influenced medical professionals' willingness to approve abortion requests. Psychiatrists were accustomed to applying traditional criteria to abortion requests, including patients having a history of "precipitated post-partum psychotic reactions," schizophrenia, lobotomy, and suicidal or homicidal inclinations. However, the ambiguity of the new abortion law left room for a "second set of criteria": women with mild suicidal ideation, mild neurosis, "pronounced emotional or intellectual immaturity," and socio-economic issues that would foster "serious psychological hardship" might also be eligible for an abortion.[13] David outlined a multitude of reasons as to why women of all ages requested abortions, and argued that psychiatrists needed to provide help and support due to the "personal, familial, and social conflicts" patients encountered while making the decision.[14]

In addition to the challenge of applying the term *health* to a broad range of abortion requests, doctors faced the unenviable task of determining if parental consent was required for abortion requests from minors. Parental consent policies for people under the age of majority varied only by province and territory, which created challenges and concerns for doctors tasked with approving abortion requests from minors.[15] Due to the ambiguity regarding the age of consent for abortion procedures, the Canadian Medical Association recommended in 1972 that all provinces and territories lower the age of consent to sixteen for medical, surgical, and dental care and expressed concern over legal uncertainty pertaining to family planning procedures.[16] However, not all provincial governments agreed with lowering the age of consent to accommodate abortion requests, and the necessity for parental consent often created stress for the parties required to participate in the decision-making process due to the time-sensitive nature of the procedure.[17]

The issue of consenting minors and parental pressure emerged in a New Brunswick woman's abortion experience in the mid-1980s, and created long-lasting regret for the patient involved. When thirteen-year-old Anita Keating found herself confronted with the stigma of teenage pregnancy, she felt she did not have the choice to continue the pregnancy. After going to a reproductive health clinic in Fredericton and discussing the pregnancy with counsellors, Keating and her boyfriend wanted to give the baby up for adoption, but she recalls that her mother's fear of the shame and stigma associated with teenage pregnancy played a central role in her abortion decision. Because of her young age, Keating remembers her mother fearing judgment from their Baptist church congregation, but also from the broader community.[18] Because of the stigma associated with teenage pregnancy and unmarried mothers, this was a likely outcome.[19] Furthermore, there were socio-economic consequences associated with teenage parenthood. If the teenager decided to keep the baby, there was a significant chance that she would drop out of high school.[20] Therefore, it was common for parents to convince their teenage daughters to terminate unplanned pregnancies to avoid such consequences. [21] Keating went through with the abortion, but she has regretted the procedure ever since.

Anti-abortion Activism and the Silent Choice

Although Keating did not attribute her regret to the pervasiveness of pro-life ideology in the region, her recollections signal that local anti-abortion activism at least partially influenced the shame she associated with her abortion. Shortly after the procedure, Keating attended a local Baptist church with her mother and sat through an anti-abortion sermon that became formative in her rejection of institutional religion. During the sermon, the pastor argued that "anybody who had an abortion for any reason was going straight to hell and would never be forgiven."[22] Keating walked out of the Baptist church and never went back. Keating's abortion was performed during the intensification of pro-life activism in New Brunswick. Throughout the 1980s, anti-abortion activists lobbied hospitals to disband TACs, launched campaigns in local newspapers, which included printing graphic images of aborted fetuses in garbage cans to shock and upset citizens, and garnered enough attention to bolster membership in anti-abortion organizations.[23] With the rise in anti-abortion sentiments, public support for pro-choice activism waned. However, Keating's personal experience did not stop her from supporting women who requested abortions. Keating wished she had not had the procedure, but she continued to promote informed choice as well as counselling – a service she did not receive – to ensure that her friends would not regret their decisions.

While many citizens recognized abortion as unavoidable and supported access to services within the hospital system, the strength of anti-abortion sentiments in the region continued to quiet pro-choice support in communities with small populations. When an eighteen-year-old Prince Edward Island woman required an abortion in 1978, her parents were adamant that no one find out about the abortion because they lived in a small, staunchly Catholic, anti-abortion community.[24] The woman grew up in a Protestant household, and while her parents were devastated that she had sex out of wedlock, they supported her abortion decision. However, they advised their daughter to tell her friends that she was in Halifax for the weekend, rather than admitting that she was in the Prince Edward Island Hospital in Charlottetown having an abortion. Eventually, the woman told her friends about the abortion and, despite disapproval from many of her Catholic peers, they remained friends. The secretive nature of abortion access was common because of the polarization of beliefs surrounding the procedure.

Throughout the 1970s and 1980s, anti-abortion sentiments fostered by the pro-life movement influenced medical professionals' behaviour within small communities in the Maritimes and created a stressful experience for medical staff and patients. Due to the rural nature of the communities, doctors and patients feared breaches of confidentiality. While some women were afraid that someone would recognize them at the hospital, others were more concerned about the medical clinic staff reading their charts and telling people about their abortion requests.[25] A breach of confidentiality came to fruition at one clinic when a woman was in her family doctor's waiting room a long time after her therapeutic abortion. In an interview for *Telling Our Secrets,* the woman recalled that the "nurse commented gratuitously: 'It's really no problem having two [children], you know'... She was an older woman ... She was the one that made me feel the worst."[26] While other women did not experience breaches of trust, it was enough of a concern that doctors informed patients that they would not mention the abortion on medical charts. A Cape Breton woman noted that her doctor did not put her abortion on her chart because she lived in a small town and worried that the staff would read the chart. In another case, a woman from Annapolis Valley, indicated that she was lucky to have a female doctor who called her at home to inform her of the appointment so that the office receptionist did not learn about the abortion. This same woman needed another referral and the second doctor offered to write "regular office visit" on her chart to keep the visit confidential.[27] The reported and presumed breaches of confidentiality were unfortunately prominent in women's abortion experiences, as many feared that judgment and negative consequences would arise if their decision became public knowledge.

Once women made it through the administrative barriers and acquired the necessary approval from a TAC for an abortion, some vividly recalled a tense atmosphere in the hospital waiting and operating rooms, as well as varied responses from staff. The waiting room in the Termination of Pregnancy Unit at the Victoria General Hospital in Halifax received the most criticism from women, as it was a tiny, cramped room, which heightened anxiety. The waiting room crammed approximately twenty-five people into a space the size of a bathroom or closet and the hospital staff forced patients to wear hospital gowns in the waiting room, despite their protestations. Four women recalled feeling humiliated when the staff required them to sit in the room in hospital gowns among fully dressed men and women who accompanied the patients seeking abortions. One woman recalled crying when she asked a nurse if she could wait in another room and the employee denied her request. She did not shave her legs and feared judgment, so she chose to stand by the door until it was time for the procedure.[28] The uncomfortably small space created the impression that the hospital did not take their health care needs seriously. A Nova Scotia woman argued that Victoria General Hospital did not treat abortion like "a legitimate medical procedure, so it's sort of been relegated to this ...

storeroom space, with no proper services."[29] Because there was little discussion in the waiting room, patient Regena Russell made a point of talking to a young woman who was very upset in order to break the silence in the room and bring some comfort to the girl before her abortion.[30]

Women who obtained abortion services at the Halifax hospital reported very different experiences with hospital staff, from hostile and harsh to empathetic and considerate nurses and gynecologists. Russell recalled that the doctor who performed her abortion at Victoria General Hospital was judgmental at the first consultation and she left his office in tears because he made her feel like a bad person. Even when she was on the table receiving drugs before the procedure, the doctor paternalistically admonished teenaged Russell for what he called her mistake.[31] Other women who sought the procedure at Victoria General Hospital also reported experiencing the lack of empathy Russell witnessed. Several women recalled experiencing excruciating pain during the abortion and the nurses and doctors ignored their concerns. As a woman from the Metro area recalled, "Nothing really prepares you for this really mean nurse who is busy saying, 'Don't scream, don't scream, you're going to scare the other patients.'"[32]

Unfortunately, several women who obtained abortions at the Victoria General Hospital documented painful experiences and some may have interpreted this as punishment for their decision.[33] Whereas Dr. Henry Morgentaler's abortion clinic in Montreal provided written instructions to patients indicating that they might experience mild to severe cramping during the procedure, it is unclear if local hospitals advised patients on the possibility of pain.[34] In an article on abortion services in Halifax, *The Dalhousie Gazette* described in detail a negative abortion experience at the Termination of Pregnancy Unit, in which a woman they referred to as Linda endured physical pain throughout the procedure despite informing medical staff of her concerns. The doctor performed a pelvic exam and then told Linda that she would feel a "pinch" when he injected a local anesthetic into her cervix. However, Linda's discomfort intensified throughout the procedure:

> The pain is excruciating. Linda tells the nurse she is going to faint, and is told this is a perfectly normal reaction. The numbness in her belly does not last for long. As the instrument dilating her cervix clicks, there are successive spasms of still more pain, despite the anesthetic. The doctor reaches for the curette and she feels pressure as it probes its way into her

> womb. The vacuum suction is flicked on, the cramps become unbearable. Linda clenches her teeth, feels her hands grow cold as she grips the sheet draped over her legs.[35]

Determining whether the inadequacy of local anaesthesia was intentional, a form of punishment for the women's so-called mistakes, is challenging to discern and requires further research due to the "unsharability" of pain and its subjective nature.[36] However, Linda's story and the women's narratives documented in *Telling Our Secrets* indicate that the pain experienced throughout the procedure troubled many patients and prompted questions about the adequacy of health care provided within the Termination of Pregnancy Unit.[37]

The mixed reactions of staff involved in abortion procedures were common in Maritime hospitals and heightened the turmoil many women experienced while having the procedure. Thirteen-year-old Keating, who went for her abortion at Dr. Everett Chalmers Hospital in Fredericton, remembered hostile treatment from the anaesthesiologist. Keating cried as she entered the operating room and remembered the anaesthesiologist having a "kind of shut up you did it to yourself kind of attitude."[38] One nurse came over, hugged her, and wiped the tears off her face as she went to sleep. Keating's negative experience within the hospital system was not unique.[39] Furthermore, the tight quarters and mixed responses from hospital staff throughout the Maritimes, which contributed to the shame and stigma the women experienced, were potentially a reflection of bureaucratic issues within the hospital system.

Abortion Barriers and Complications

Between 1970 and 1988, access to abortion services fluctuated considerably in the region due to numerous hospitals abolishing TACs or increasingly rejecting applications.[40] By the 1980s, the Victoria General Hospital in Halifax performed the majority of abortions in the Maritimes. In 1984, the Halifax hospital performed 1,412 abortions, whereas the largest abortion provider in New Brunswick, Moncton Hospital, performed approximately 175 abortions and the second largest New Brunswick abortion provider, Dr. Everett Chalmers Hospital in Fredericton, performed 74.[41] According to New Brunswick government statistics, residents' requests for publicly funded abortions that occurred out-of-province most often came from those seeking the procedure in the United States and Nova Scotia.[42] Due to the lack of access to abortions in Prince Edward Island, New Brunswick, and rural areas of Nova Scotia, the Victoria General Hospital became responsible for providing Atlantic Canadian women with access to the time-sensitive procedure and this pressure created issues within the hospital system.

The pressure on the Halifax hospital to provide the majority of the abortions in the region created a hotbed for post-abortion complications due to the time-sensitive procedure and the long wait times. Out of the twenty-five women that Bowes interviewed between 1985 and 1989, seven women reported eight post-abortion complications.[43] Two women experienced post-abortion infections. Four women retained products of conception, that is, fetal tissue that was not expelled from the uterus. Fortunately, two of these four women were able to expel the remaining tissue at home. The other two women had to return to the Termination of Pregnancy Unit for dilation and curettage (D and C) procedures. One woman recalled that the staff treated her wonderfully, but both women could not understand why their physicians had not examined the tissue they removed during the initial procedure, which was a central part of performing abortions. Perhaps most surprising, two women's abortions were unsuccessfully performed and they were forced to return for second abortions late in pregnancy. In one case, it took one patient five weeks before the medical staff would believe she was still pregnant and begrudgingly scheduled a second abortion. The woman's fears and stress heightened when she was lying on the operating table and overheard her new gynecologist grumble, "'They botch a job, and I get to do their dirty work."[44] Unfortunately, the ability for doctors to perform abortions without post-abortion complications was difficult because of bureaucratic issues within the hospital system.

Due to the delays created by administrative barriers, a significant number of Canadian patients underwent the procedure in hospitals at an advanced gestational age, which heightened the abortion complications they faced.[45] In *The Report of the Committee on the Operation of the Abortion Law,* the federally commissioned researchers determined that, in 1974, the rate of complications for the most commonly used method for first trimester abortions, suction D and C, was 28.3 percent nationwide.[46] The complication rate nearly doubled for the saline method, which was performed in the second trimester. Second trimester abortions were highest in Newfoundland,

Prince Edward Island, Nova Scotia, and Manitoba, and complications were highest in hospitals that did not perform many abortions.[47]

By the mid-1970s, Nova Scotia researchers recognized an increase in abortion complications provincially due to a high number of abortions performed in the second trimester. Between 1971 and 1974, second trimester abortions increased from 12 to 31 percent, which meant that a number of women were susceptible to greater risk and trauma.[48] Surgeons used the suction D and C method for abortions performed prior to twelve weeks' gestation and the rate of an additional procedure for retained products was 0.7 percent. In contrast, the intra-amniotic saline method, which involved the instillation of saline solution into the amniotic sac to induce uterine contractions, was commonly performed in second trimester abortions because a suction D and C was deemed too difficult after sixteen weeks and the chance of complications increased to 30 percent.[49] In a questionnaire, which patients returned six weeks after having the procedure, many patients identified post-abortion consequences, including bleeding, pain, and "mental disturbance" requiring treatment.[50] Between 1978 and 1982, first trimester abortions increased from 72.3 percent to 78.6 percent, which signalled an improvement in providing access to first trimester abortions.[51] However, considering that the abortion rate increased throughout the 1970s and 1980s, and New Brunswick and Prince Edward Island hospitals either stopped performing abortions or decreased access, it is not surprising that post-abortion complications continued to be an issue at the Victoria General Hospital.

The inaccessibility of abortion services in the Maritime region was not unique. Throughout Canada, access to abortion services depended on individual hospital boards, and hospitals with liberal stances, such as Victoria General Hospital, became overburdened with abortion requests.[52] The ability of anti-abortion pressure groups to decrease access by lobbying hospital boards concerned doctors nationwide, including those who sympathized with the pro-life movement.[53] However, some doctors also criticized the pointlessness of liberal TACs, which "do nothing more than rubber stamp abortion certificate applications."[54] While larger hospitals in major cities, including Toronto and Vancouver, liberally approved abortions, it was not as simple for women residing in rural Canada. Doctors frequently encountered abortion requests from women who were not their patients and some resented the burden.[55]

Abortion Barriers and Travel

In response to the lack of access to abortion services in the Maritime region, grassroots pro-choice groups established abortion referral services to help women obtain the procedure in a regional hospital or reputable abortion clinic after a decade of women using commercial abortion referral agencies. Beginning shortly after the federal government amended the abortion law in 1969, commercial abortion referral agencies, which were located in New York, New Jersey, Michigan, and Pennsylvania, ran advertisements in student newspapers, including *The Dalhousie Gazette*, throughout the early 1970s offering access to abortion clinics: for example, one advertised "Low Cost, Safe, Legal Abortion in New York."[56] According to the *Report of the Committee on the Operation of the Abortion Law*, commercial abortion referral agencies "routinely told [women] that obtaining an abortion was illegal in Canada, misinformation was given about the actual costs involved, and alleged trained counsellors were paid on a commission basis."[57] The report criticized the opportunistic nature of the commercial abortion referral agencies – some charged women money without obtaining confirmation of pregnancy – and argued that the referral agencies existed because "there was a demand for their services which was not otherwise being met."[58]

However, the abortion referral system in Canada was unclear, and the barriers appeared insurmountable for women living in rural communities. In an attempt to avoid the administrative hoops necessary to obtain a provincially funded abortion, women with the financial means went abroad or to illegal clinics in Canada and the United States.[59] When a former Miramichi Hospital employee required an abortion, she went to an illegal abortion clinic in Montreal to keep her identity anonymous and the procedure a secret. The woman's ability to obtain the abortion was, in her words, "pure luck," since her family doctor was new to northern New Brunswick and had out-of-province contacts.[60] She travelled to a house in Montreal run by a women's organization, and the staff helped her line up an abortion for the next day. A doctor performed the abortion in a clinic located in a strip mall and rushed her out the door because of the illegality of the procedure. She remembered feeling as if she was going to faint, but she was grateful that she was able to obtain the procedure quickly.

In what was presumably an attempt to curb the number of women travelling out of the country at high cost for abortion services – many of whom still thought abortion was illegal – the Family Planning Association ran abortion referral service advertisements in *The Dalhousie Gazette* to encourage women to seek abortions in Nova Scotia.[61] In 1980, pro-choice activists established the Abortion Information and Referral Services (AIRS) to ensure women living in the Dartmouth-Halifax area received access to safe and legal abortion services. The organization advertised its voluntary services in a variety of forums, including *The Dalhousie Gazette*, flyers, and pamphlets.[62] The service operated on Mondays, Tuesdays, and Thursdays from five to seven o'clock in the evening and provided women with confidential information, including the names of sympathetic doctors as well as the locations of abortion clinics outside of Nova Scotia. Unfortunately, access to abortion referral organizations did not prevent women from confronting extralegal barriers to abortion services. For instance, a Cape Breton woman travelled to a Halifax family planning clinic to confirm her pregnancy and when she asked about abortion services, the nurse informed her that the clinic did not discuss that subject.[63] Throughout the 1980s, the AIRS telephone line continued to hear stories of family-planning clinics denying women abortion-related assistance.

Due to the AIRS volunteers' inability to ensure that local family planning clinics would provide non-judgmental information on abortion services, women with the financial means travelled out of the country or province for abortion services. A woman from Nova Scotia travelled to an out-of-province clinic in the late 1980s and was grateful for her experience. It was the woman's second abortion, and the positive atmosphere at the private facility pleasantly surprised her: "The whole atmosphere, you know that everybody working there thinks it's an okay thing to do, and they're supporting you, and they're giving you as much information as you want. You know that you can ask them for information."[64] Women's positive experiences in private abortion clinics, as well as the lack of access to abortion services in hospitals outside of Halifax, compelled some residents with the financial means to leave their province for the procedure. Travel remained a central aspect of Maritime women's abortion experiences throughout the 1970s and 1980s because of the restrictive nature of hospital abortion policies. While it is not clear how many abortion requests Nova Scotia and PEI rejected throughout the 1980s, New Brunswick government records indicate that at least 299 women's requests for abortions were denied by TACs between 1982 and 1986.[65] The number of denied applicants who left the province for the procedure is unclear.[66] PEI officials could not determine the exact number of residents who travelled out-of-province for abortions throughout the 1980s, although estimations ranged from 200 to 650 annually.[67] Atlantic Canadian women with the financial means often travelled to legal abortion clinics in Massachusetts, Maine, or New York.[68] For example, an employed and married New Brunswick woman knew that she did not stand a chance of getting an abortion in the province, so she travelled to New York for an abortion in the late 1980s.[69] Some women also chose the illegal route, and went to doctors' offices in Montreal, including Dr. Henry Morgentaler's Montreal clinic, and later to Toronto, after the first clinic opened in 1983.[70] Throughout the 1980s, approximately five hundred Atlantic Canadian women obtained illegal abortions at the Montreal clinic each year.[71]

The Illusion of Access

The significant number of Atlantic Canadian women travelling out of province for abortions in the 1980s magnified the failure of the abortion law. The extralegal barriers to abortion services in the region created emotional, financial, and sometimes physical hardship for women faced with the decision of terminating their pregnancies. The negative reactions of family, friends, and medical professionals exacerbated the stress women experienced while attempting to obtain doctors' referrals and a TAC's approval. The intensity of pro-life campaigns in the region created extralegal barriers to abortions as TACs increasingly disbanded, administrative delays within hospitals increased, and the stress within the termination of pregnancy units intensified. If women were not able to find abortion services in their own province, they faced the additional stress of travelling to another province or country for the procedure. While only one woman interviewed for this study regretted her abortion, the majority of the interview participants lamented the administrative hoops they encountered throughout their abortion experiences.

Hospitals and medical professionals also faced unexpected challenges due to the ambiguity of the abortion law. The federal government's failure to clearly define what constituted *health* in the Criminal Code amendment caused hospitals to implement a number of bureaucratic barriers to ensure that they and their employees were not at risk of performing abortions that could be deemed illegal. The extralegal barriers had many unforeseen consequences, including higher rates of complications due to longer wait times for abortions. In addition to facing hostility from hospital staff for having second trimester abortions, women with abortion complications had to bear the physical costs of delayed procedures.

The stigma surrounding abortion created significant shame in the late twentieth century and, for many women, it remains a taboo subject. Abortion became a "dark" and "well-kept secret" in the Atlantic region, despite the constant news coverage of pro-choice activities in other Canadian regions.[72] When interviewed for the CARAL study in late 1989, one woman indicated that she was ashamed to the extent that "just even the word [abortion], like I use the word when I'm talking about Morgentaler and things in the news, but not when it relates to me."[73] A PEI public servant argued that even in the twenty-first century, three decades after the decriminalization of abortion, "nobody wants to mention the 'A' word" in the PEI government because anti-abortion opposition could lead to the defeat of members of the provincial Legislative Assembly.[74] The PEI government decided to change the status quo on abortion in 2016 by providing access to the service on the Island. In January 2017, abortions were available in PEI for the first time since 1982.[75] Throughout the Maritimes, however, the shame and stigma fostered by the anti-abortion movement remains and illuminates why many women are still afraid to speak about their abortion experiences in the twenty-first century.

Notes

1 Christina Clorey, "Votes and Vetoes: A Discursive History of Abortion Politics in Prince Edward Island from 1980–1996" (master's thesis, McMaster University, 2007); Lianne McTavish, "The Cultural Production of Pregnancy: Bodies and Embodiment at a New Brunswick Abortion Clinic," *Topia: Canadian Journal of Cultural Studies* 20 (2008): 23–42; Rachael Johnstone, "The Politics of Abortion in Canada after Morgentaler: Women's Rights as Citizenship Rights" (PhD diss., Queen's University, 2012); Katrina Ackerman, "'Not in the Atlantic Provinces': The Abortion Debate in New Brunswick, 1980–1987," *Acadiensis* 41, 1 (2012): 75–101; Katrina Ackerman, "In Defence of Reason: Religion, Science, and the Prince Edward Island Anti-abortion Movement, 1969–1988," *Canadian Bulletin of Medical History* 31, 1 (2014): 117–38; and Shannon Stettner, ed., *Without Apology: Writings on Abortion in Canada* (Edmonton: AU Press, 2016).

2 In 2013, I collected one hundred online survey responses with the approval of the University of Waterloo's Office of Research Ethics. I used the online survey to find interview participants for the study, and then obtained additional interviews through a snowball effect. I

interviewed forty-eight people in person or on the telephone, some of whom preferred to remain anonymous. I did not use pseudonyms.

3 Ackerman, "Not in the Atlantic Provinces," 117.

4 Telephone interview, February 4, 2013, northern New Brunswick.

5 Charles J. David, "An Overview of Psychiatric Aspects of Therapeutic Abortion," *Nova Scotia Medical Bulletin* 52, 6 (1973): 249.

6 Judith Wouk, in-person interview, April 4, 2013, Ottawa, Ontario.

7 "The View from the Medical Society," *Dalhousie Gazette*, February 25, 1972; University of Ottawa Archives and Special Collections, Canadian Women's Movement Archives, box 138, file "Women's Information and Referral Service (Halifax, N.S.)," "Understanding the Law: A Guide for Women in Nova Scotia," 1981.

8 Wouk, in-person interview. A statement issued by the Department of Obstetrics and Gynecology at Dalhousie University in 1974 corroborates Wouk's recollection. See "'Information for Physicians in Nova Scotia Regarding Therapeutic Abortions': A Statement by the Department of Obstetrics and Gynecology, Dalhousie University," *Nova Scotia Medical Bulletin* 53, 5 (1974): 168.

9 A Nova Scotia woman discusses her experience performing a mental illness for a psychiatrist in Canadian Abortion Rights Action League (CARAL) Halifax Chapter, *Telling Our Secrets: Abortion Stories from Nova Scotia* (Halifax, NS: CARAL, 1990), 28. Clarissa Hurley also recalls her New Brunswick doctor telling her that she needed a performance, including tears, to convince the TAC that the patient was medically unstable and a good candidate for an abortion in 1988, after the Supreme Court of Canada struck down the abortion law. The doctor also hinted that the patient should mention problems with her sleep and eating behaviours. Clarissa Hurley, in-person interview, February 5, 2013, Fredericton, New Brumswick. Also see Clarissa Hurley, "T.A." in *Without Apology*, 83–89.

10 Louise Summerhill, *The Story of Birthright: The Alternative to Abortion* (Libertyville, IL: Prow Books/Franciscan Marytown Press, 1973), 6.

11 Katherine McDonald, in-person interview, April 3, 2013, Ottawa, Ontario .

12 David, "An Overview of Psychiatric Aspects of Therapeutic Abortion," 247.

13 Ibid, 247–48.

14 Ibid, 249.

15 J.S. Bennett, "Lawyers, Economists, Health Professionals Join to Discuss Health and the Law," *Canadian Medical Association Journal* 113 (1975): 797.

16 "Association Presents Brief on Family Planning to Minister of National Health and Welfare," *Canadian Medical Association Journal* 113 (1975): 341; "Family Planning/Contraception: CMA Policy Summary," *Canadian Medical Association Journal* 133 (1985): 598A.

17 Nova Scotia Archives (NSA), "Hospital Releases 1972," G.G.S., Executive Director of Nova Scotia Hospital Insurance Commission to Administrators of Public and Psychiatric Hospitals, February 11, 1972, unprocessed accession 1992–163/004, 16–0006.2.

18 Anita Keating, in-person interview, February 6, 2013, Fredericton, New Brunswick.

19 Sharon Wall, "They're 'More Children Than Adults': Teens, Unmarried Pregnancy, and the Canadian Medical Profession, 1945–61," *Canadian Bulletin of Medical History* 31, 2 (2014): 49–69.

20 "Abortions Up in Newfoundland, Controversy Continues to Rage," *Sunday Express*, 19 April 1987.

21 David, "An Overview of Psychiatric Aspects of Therapeutic Abortion," 248.

22 Ibid.

23 Ackerman, "Not in the Atlantic Provinces," 83.

24 In-person interview, February 13, 2013, Charlottetown, PEI.

25 Regena Russell, in-person interview, February 14, 2013, Charlottetown, PEI.
26 CARAL, *Telling Our Secrets,* 61.
27 Ibid., 62.
28 Ibid., 41–49.
29 Quoted in ibid., 65.
30 Russell, in-person interview.
31 Ibid.
32 CARAL, *Telling Our Secrets,* 35, v. Seven of the twenty-five women interviewed by Nancy Bowes in Nova Scotia reported post-abortion complications, from infections to incomplete abortions.
33 In his research on anaesthesia and professionalism in the nineteenth century, Martin Pernick argued that while some "saw pain as biologically and emotionally functional, other critics of anesthesia portrayed physical suffering as punishment; in their view anesthesia constituted an attempt to circumvent the chastisements inflicted by some higher power." Martin S. Pernick, *A Calculus of Suffering: Pain, Professionalism, and Anesthesia in Nineteenth-Century America* (New York: Columbia University Press, 1985), 49.
34 The Rooms, MG 1004, 5.01.045, Materials re: Abortion Technique, File, "Instructions for Morgentaler Clinic."
35 "An Ounce of Prevention, a Pound of Cure," *Dalhousie Gazette,* March 10, 1983.
36 Elaine Scarry, *The Body in Pain: The Making and Unmaking of the World* (New York: Oxford University Press, 1985), 4–5.
37 While there is plenty of discussion on fetal pain in the literature, women's pain during abortion procedures, and the reason for the pain, is understudied.
38 Keating, in-person interview.
39 Psychological trauma was common for women pressured by parents or emotionally blackmailed into having abortions. David, "An Overview of Psychiatric Aspects of Therapeutic Abortion," 248. In *Telling Our Secrets,* two stories describe male partners who threatened women with violence if they did not have abortions. See CARAL, *Telling Our Secrets,* 20–21.
40 Ackerman, "Not in the Atlantic Provinces," 95–100; Ackerman, "In Defence of Reason," 126–29.
41 NSA, RG89, vol. 4, file 9, "Choice Is the Issue: A Brief by CARAL/Halifax on Reproductive Choice," March 1987; Public Archives of New Brunswick (PANB), RS765, file 10–3809, "Number of Therapeutic Abortions Performed in N.B. Hospitals (Calendar Year)."
42 PANB, RS765, file 10–3811, "Back-Up Data: Therapeutic Abortions Out-of-Province by Place of Occurrence," March 1986.
43 One of the women experienced two types of post-abortion complications.
44 Quoted in CARAL, *Telling Our Secrets,* 56.
45 A. Wadhera, "Legal Abortions among Teenagers in Canada, 1974 through 1978," *Canadian Medical Association Journal* 122 (1980): 1386–90; Ellen R. Wiebe, "Retention of Products of Conception after Therapeutic Abortion," *Canadian Medical Association Journal* 134 (1986): 505.
46 Complications included retained products of conception, laceration of the cervix, perforation of the uterus, hemorrhage, infection, and, in very rare instances, death. Canada, Committee on the Operation of the Abortion Law, *Report of the Committee on the Operation of the Abortion Law* (Ottawa: Ministry of Supply and Services Canada, 1977), 309–12, 322.
47 Committee on the Operation of the Abortion Law, *Report of the Committee,* 310
48 S.C. Robinson, "The Status of Therapeutic Abortion in Nova Scotia," *Nova Scotia Medical Bulletin* (1977): 11; Glenn Brodie, "Cervical Tears Following Mid-trimester Saline Abortion," *Nova Scotia Medical Bulletin* 56, 1 (1977): 13–14.

49 William E. Brenner and David A. Edelman, "Dilations and Evacuation at 13 to 15 Weeks' Gestations versus Intra-Amniotic Saline after 15 Weeks' Gestation," *Contraception* 10, 2 (1974): 171–80.

50 Claudia Resch and S.C. Robinson, "Therapeutic Abortion and Its Complications in Halifax, N.S.," *Nova Scotia Medical Bulletin* 52, 2 (1973): 67.

51 NSA, file "Abortions January 1985–June 1985," "Nova Scotia Abortions Performed," unprocessed accession 1992–587 (90–33), 16–1002.2.

52 Committee on the Operation of the Abortion Law, *Report of the Committee,* 249.

53 D. Laurence Wilson, "Medical Schools and Affiliated Teaching Hospitals in the '80s," *Canadian Medical Association Journal* 126 (1982): 1335.

54 W.D.S. Thomas, "Address: 1980 Annual Meeting of the Medical Society of Nova Scotia," *Nova Scotia Medical Bulletin* 59, 5 (1980): x.

55 "Abortion: A Life or Death Dilemma," *Dalhousie Gazette,* November 29, 1979.

56 "Abortion: Pregnancies up to 12 Weeks Terminated from $175.00," *Dalhousie Gazette,* January 28, 1972; "The Facts about Abortion Referral Service," *Dalhousie Gazette,* January 28, 1972; "Low Cost, Safe, Legal Abortion in New York," *Dalhousie Gazette,* February 19, 1971. Advertisements were also run in the University of New Brunwick's *The Brunswickan* and University of Prince Edward Island's *Cadre.*

57 Committee on the Operation of the Abortion Law, *Report of the Committee,* 383.

58 Ibid., 385–86.

59 Christabelle Sethna, Beth Palmer, Katrina Ackerman, and Nancy Janovicek, "Choice, Interrupted: Travel and Inequality of Access to Abortion Services since the 1960s," *Labour/Le Travail* 71 (2013): 29–48.

60 Telephone interview, 4 February 2013, New Brunswick.

61 "Abortion Information, Counselling, and Referrals," *Dalhouse Gazette,* March 5, 1971; Committee on the Operation of the Abortion Law, *Report of the Committee,* 128.

62 "Abortion Information," *Dalhousie Gazette,* November 20, 1980; University of Ottawa Archives and Special Collections, Canadian Women's Movement Archives, box 1, file "Abortion Information and Referral Service (Halifax, N.S.), 1979–1981," Donation Letter, 8 March 1981; Pamphlet.

63 CARAL, *Telling Our Secrets,* 26

64 Quoted in ibid., 63

65 Calculating the total number of abortions performed in New Brunswick in the 1980s is challenging due to inconsistencies in statistics. However, one figure indicates that there were 1,360 abortions performed over the four-year period from 1982 to 1986. Ackerman, "Not in the Atlantic Provinces," 95.

66 PANB, RS765, file 10–3809, "Number of Therapeutic Abortions Performed on N. B. Residents outside the Province (Fiscal Year)"; PANB, RS765, file 10–3809, "Hospital Services (from individual hospitals)."

67 Alice Crook, "Abortion: A Pro-choice Perspective," *Common Ground,* May–June 1985, 16; "Abortion Controversy Fires Island Emotions," *The Guardian,* January 12, 1985; "Both Sides Assessing Vote on Committee," *The Guardian,* June 6, 1986; "Abolishing Committee Puts Issue in Spotlight," *The Guardian,* June 6, 1986; Public Archives and Records Office of PEI (PARO), Correspondence from A.C., J.B., and J.M. to Minister Keith Milligan, box 27, 95–003, file "Abortion 1989," April 14, 1989.

68 PARO, PEI Medical Society fonds, Executive Meeting Minutes, June 9, 1976; "Commission to Retain Authority on Abortions," *The Guardian,* February 17, 1977; "Commission under Attack for Position on Abortions," *The Guardian,* February 11, 1977; Marilyn MacDonald and Suzanne Babin, "The Region: Our Abortion Law Doesn't Do What It's Meant to Do," *Atlantic Insight,* July 1980, 10–11; Marian Bruce, "Prince Edward Island: Abortion Squabble

Sours Mixed Hospital Marriage," *Atlantic Insight,* July 1980, 12; NSA, RG25, Planned Parenthood Association of Halifax, "Counselling Procedures for the Undesired Pregnancy," vol. 603, file 3, February 1980.

69 Telephone interview, May 31, 2013, New Brunswick.

70 CARAL, *Telling Our Secrets,* 7.

71 "Doctor Plans to Open Halifax Clinic by June," *The Chronicle Herald,* March 21, 1989.

72 CARAL, *Telling Our Secrets,* 73–74.

73 Ibid., 70.

74 In-person interview, February 13, 2013, Charlottetown, PEI.

75 "Abortion Services Coming to PEI, Province Announces," *CBC News,* 31 March 2016, http://www.cbc.ca/news/canada/prince-edward-island/pei-abortion-reproductive-rights-1.3514334; "Abortion Services," Health PEI, Government of Prince Edward Island, 7 February 2017, https://www.princeedwardisland.ca/en/information/sante-i-p-e/abortion-services.

7

When Research Is Personal and Political

Researchers Reflect on the Study of Abortion

Marion Doull, Christabelle Sethna, Evelyne Morrissette, and Caitlin Scott

Typically, research on human participants engenders justifiable concern related to the participants' care, regardless of the topic involved. The practice of research requires that researchers be well versed in the ethics of care. Institutional research ethics boards are tasked with ensuring that any potential harms that might result for participants from their involvement in research are identified and minimized, especially when the research is on vulnerable populations.[1] However, with some exceptions, little attention is paid to the potential harms of the research process on the researchers themselves.[2] This lack of attention has led to discussions about the risks that researchers face, especially when conducting research on sensitive issues.[3] As E. Milling Kinard states, "Efforts to address these issues would be enhanced by more published accounts of investigators' experiences in dealing with the effects on researchers of conducting studies on sensitive and emotionally laden topics."[4]

Sensitive issues can include phenomena considered private, stressful, stigmatized, frightening, or politically or culturally marginal.[5] Researchers have documented the specific complications of conducting research on sensitive issues such as breast cancer, rape, domestic violence, anger, sexual health, suicide, infertility, and abortion.[6] In these studies, the researchers outline various research strategies; yet only in some cases do they reflect on their own experiences of conducting research on sensitive issues and on the need to adapt research methodologies to encompass those experiences. This chapter focuses on our personal reflections of conducting a qualitative and quantitative study on abortion.

Research on Researching Abortion

In Canada, a divisive political discourse about abortion that positions opponents of abortion as anti-choice or anti-abortion and supporters of abortion as pro-choice or pro-abortion has grown louder over the last two decades in concert with widespread unrest over the issue in the United States.[7] It is estimated that approximately one third of Canadian women will have an abortion during their reproductive years.[8] History has shown that women will procure an abortion regardless of its legality or illegality, indicating that the legal status of abortion does not change demand for the service.[9] Even when abortion is legal, diverse extralegal obstacles, such as mandatory wait periods, counselling sessions, gestational limits, refusal provisions, and parental consent rules for minors, block access to abortion services.[10] Opposition to abortion is often based on moral, ethical, or religious objections to the practice, generally centring on the status of the fetus.[11] By assigning personhood status to the fetus, abortion opponents argue that having an abortion is tantamount to murder regardless of fetal gestational age or viability. They have called technology into service, relying on two- or three-dimensional sonograms to provide evidence of the personhood of the fetus.[12] And if consideration is paid to the mental or physical health of a woman seeking an abortion, it is framed within an anti-abortion context.[13] In contrast, supporters of women's access to abortion focus on the pregnant woman and on her presumed right to make choices about her own body. Inevitably, this position prioritizes the status of the woman over that of the fetus.[14]

Abortion is an essential medical service that is part of a full range of reproductive health care for women.[15] Despite the 2015 election of an overtly pro-choice prime minister, Justin Trudeau, abortion remains a stigmatized medical procedure, abortion services and abortion providers have had to implement safeguards against the threat of violence from opponents of abortion, and volunteer escorts shield women entering clinics from harassment by anti-abortion protesters. Not surprisingly, women often maintain a silence over their decision to have an abortion.[16]

Within this context, research has been conducted to understand disparities in abortion access, women's experiences of accessing abortion services, and the relationship of abortion access to women's health outcomes.[17] However, with few exceptions, there is little published literature on the personal experiences of researchers conducting studies on abortion, adding yet another tier of silence to this sensitive issue.[18]

Those researchers who have tackled the topic of their own experiences of researching abortion describe the emotional, logistical, and ethical demands of this work. Jessica D. Gipson and colleagues report on doing research in international settings where abortion is illegal.[19] Their interviewees appreciated the rare opportunity that the study provided them to discuss their feelings about their abortions. However, interviewers had problems finding supportive individuals with whom they could debrief about their own emotions in relation to the study. Jeannie Ludlow describes her experience working in an abortion clinic.[20] She illustrates how abortion politics in the United States have created a "trauma-tized" territory in which the mundane reasons why women have abortions are suppressed in favour of so-called horror stories to ensure that access to abortion services is not compromised.[21] Like Ludlow, Lianne McTavish also relies on her personal account of working at an abortion clinic in eastern Canada to assess the ways in which bodies and spaces interact at abortion clinics.[22] As a clinic escort assisting women during their appointments, McTavish deals with anti-abortion protestors outside the clinic; importantly, she did not begin her work at the clinic as a researcher but was motivated instead by her pro-choice feminist beliefs.[23] Delese Wear, another researcher, intended to interview American abortion providers about their work and the effects of their work on their personal and professional lives. Yet only seven of the thirty-seven providers she contacted agreed to participate in the study, and none agreed to be tape-recorded, which underscores the confidentiality and safety concerns of those involved in the study of abortion.[24] In examining women's lives after they had abortions in the United States, Rosanna F. Hess describes how she struggled to reconcile her pro-life beliefs with her own research.[25] These studies illustrate that research conducted on abortion is steeped in layers of complexity not only for the participants but also for the researchers themselves.

Our Study

During the period from 2008 to 2011, the authors of this paper were involved in a four-year mixed methods study examining for the first time women's travel to access abortion services at free-standing abortion clinics across Canada. Our study was funded by a Social Sciences and Humanities Research Council grant. It involved (1) archival research on Canada's abortion history; (2) qualitative interviews with clinic staff; (3) qualitative interviews with key stakeholders who worked on issues of abortion access or worked to facilitate access for women in particular; (4) a quantitative and qualitative questionnaire intended for women accessing abortion services at the clinics; (5) qualitative follow-up interviews with women accessing abortion services at the clinics who had filled out the questionnaires and agreed to be interviewed at a later point; and (6) the creation of illustrative maps of women's travel patterns from their home communities to abortion clinics. The study, which was undertaken well before the federal government approved the distribution of the abortion pill (Mifegymiso) within Canada to facilitate the delivery of medical abortion, focused on women's access to abortion services; the geographical distance women travelled to access those services; and women's logistical and emotional experiences of their journeys to free-standing clinics. [26]

The primary investigator, Christabelle Sethna, hired a project coordinator, Marion Doull, as well as a number of graduate and undergraduate research assistants, including Evelyne Morrissette and Caitlin Scott, respectively. Various student volunteers also participated. Everyone working directly with data related to the questionnaires and interviews signed a confidentiality agreement. Each followed ethical guidelines established by the research ethics board of the University of Ottawa. In total, the research team dealt with seventeen abortion clinics, entered data from 1,186 questionnaires, made countless telephone calls, sent and received numerous emails, and transcribed hours of interviews. We engaged in informal personal reflection throughout our study on aspects including clinical settings, interviews, transcription, and data entry. For confidentiality purposes, we do not reveal who among the four of us authored the personal researcher reflections excerpted below.

Researchers, particularly those who wish to do anti-oppressive research, are expected to be self-reflective because, in the words of Karen Potts and Leslie Brown, "anti-oppressive research involves making explicit the political practices of creating knowledge" in the quest for social justice.[27] Autoethnography can be a suitable method of anti-oppressive research as it is intended to recognize researchers as embedded in the research process such that their research designs include personal narratives of the researchers' experiences of conducting the research. This methodological approach permits researchers to be accepted as part of the research process, treats the researchers' interpretations of their own emotional responses as valuable data, and connects the researchers to both those they research and the larger social phenomena under investigation. In this fashion, the articulation of researchers' feelings can be cathartic and/or reassuring to other researchers facing similar situations.[28]

Our Reflections

Although we had anticipated that doing research on abortion could be emotionally taxing for the participants and possibly to ourselves, we were unprepared to deal with the range and intensity of our subjective reactions to research sites, the participants (clinic staff members, stakeholders, and women accessing abortion services at the clinics) we interviewed, the questionnaire data, and the issue of abortion itself.

When visiting clinics to deliver stacks of questionnaires and/or to meet with staff members who had agreed to an interview, we gained a sense of the clinic's physical setting and the strict identification protocols all visitors were required to follow. During a short clinic visit, one of us observed that while the clinic staff created a warm environment on the inside, the protestors demonstrating outside were an indication of the security measures under which clinics functioned:

> Once in the clinic space, it is warm and welcoming, albeit a bit small, but gaining access to the clinic was somewhat intimidating, even though I was only visiting to drop off questionnaires. My name and identification were double checked, and then I was allowed to enter through two sets of locked doors. This brought me into the waiting area, and another locked door brought me through to the office space of the staff. I felt a sense of relief when I got back outside, only to notice the crowd of protesters across the street, and then I just felt angry, angry that women entering the clinic likely also feel intimidated and afraid and angry that the safety of the staff inside needs to be so closely and constantly guarded.

This researcher's experience is a stark reminder of the continued danger facing those who work in abortion clinics. On the one hand, researchers have documented that security measures at clinics can increase feelings of stigma, shame, and secrecy for women seeking pregnancy termination at clinics.[29] By contrast, other researchers have found that these same measures provide an atmosphere of safety.[30]

Interviewing staff involved the complicated coordination of schedules to find available times to speak and to account for time zone differences across the country. Sometimes, the clinic staff was too busy to participate in interviews. Some, but not all of the interviews for this project were conducted inside the clinic space; others were conducted by phone. The clinic staff appeared to be articulate and seasoned professionals who generally situated the provision of abortion services within the broader scope of women's sexual and reproductive health. Sometimes, interviews with the clinic staff, whether conducted on the phone or at the clinic, were challenging to the research team. We focused primarily on the issue of women's travel to abortion clinics. However, the responses of the clinic staff led us to reflect on an uncomfortable disconnection between some of our unquestioned beliefs about abortion and the job of supporting women who seek abortion services.

We each strongly identify as pro-choice feminists, endorse a reproductive justice framework, and believe that women have a right to access safe, affordable, and legal abortion services. However, during the research period in question, not one of us was involved actively in the grassroots pro-choice movement, and neither were we ever involved in the provision of abortion services.[31] Moreover, at the beginning of this study, some of us were quite complacent about a woman's presumed right to choose an abortion within Canada. As has been documented elsewhere, younger generations of women have become somewhat passive about abortion, believing that the battle for abortion rights has been won and that access to services is unproblematic.[32] This complacency has, in part, permitted opponents of abortion to dominate the divisive political discourse about abortion.[33] For some of us, our study brought to light a conflict between our comfortable pro-choice feminist identities and the burdensome realities of staff working on the front lines of abortion services. This conflict was especially acute when it came to providing surgical abortions:

> I remember one of the doctors [at the abortion clinic] talking about the difficulty of finding new doctors to replace the retiring ones. At first I was feeling like that's a shame, and I didn't really see the issue of why a pro-choice doctor would not be willing to do that job. But then she said something that made me reflect more. I realized that if I was myself a doctor, I would probably not be able to actually do those abortions. I felt

> like there is a frontier between being pro-choice and actually doing abortions, removing the fetus. It's not that it made me feel less pro-choice, but I'm so emotional that I think that actually doing the work they do would be too hard, too real.

Late-term abortions raised another layer of complexity that led us to interrogate our pro-choice beliefs more closely. In Canada, the overwhelming majority (90 percent) of abortions are performed prior to twelve weeks' gestation; late-term abortions (after 20 weeks' gestation) make up just 0.4 percent of all abortions performed. Late-term abortions may occur because of grave physical impairments to the fetus or because life-threatening health issues arise for the pregnant woman. These are not routine procedures and they are undertaken after much medical consultation.[34] One of us, who was privy to information about a late-term abortion during an interview with a clinic staff member, had the following reaction:

> I just transcribed an interview, and the lady was talking about the women that go to New York to get [a late term] abortion. She said that it was not for everyone to help these women because they arrive with the big belly, and they come out of the hospital with much less belly and no babies. I started to question if I was really pro-choice or if I was only pro-choice just for some instances. I reflected a lot about this, and it made me feel even stronger in my beliefs about abortions. I also felt like I should get more involved in defending abortion access.

As indicated in the passage above, some Canadian women must travel to other jurisdictions in the United States to have a late-term abortion. However, inadequate access to late-term abortion services in parts of Canada has not sparked widespread calls to make the procedure more available. Rather, opponents of abortion have used the issue of late-term abortion to press for renewed federal legal restrictions on abortion access in general. Some Conservative politicians have even asked the Royal Canadian Mounted Police to investigate late-term abortion as a case of criminal homicide.[35] These reflections about the shifting meanings of pro-choice in theory and in practice point to the need to encourage dialogue about the reality of abortion provision from the perspectives of clinic staff, women seeking abortions, and researchers who study abortion.

In a few instances, the interviews we conducted with stakeholders raised many mixed feelings in us. When one of us met with a counsellor staffing a help line for women seeking information about abortion, a telephone call from a client interrupted our face-to-face interview. The counsellor indicated that she wanted the researcher to listen to the caller. However, the caller was not informed of the researcher's presence, creating a dilemma for the researcher:

> I heard a distraught woman on the phone explain that she would have to travel from Canada to the United States for an abortion because she was past the gestational limit at a hospital close to her. She was worried about how to care for her young daughter, where she would stay when across the border, and how she would make the trip there and back. She said she had no one to help her. Listening to her shaky voice and to the counsellor trying to calm her down filled me with anger, anger that it was so awful for this woman wanting an abortion and for the counsellor who was trying to help her. I also felt anxious about listening to the caller; I wasn't sure if that was ethical. When I signalled that I would leave her office, the counsellor shook her head to indicate that I should stay. I think she wanted me to hear what she had to deal with every day.

Interviews with women who had accessed abortion services at the clinics and agreed to follow-up interviews after filling out the questionnaires were, in some cases, the most emotionally trying for the researchers. All of the follow-up interviews were conducted by telephone and most of the calls were placed within two months of the women's abortions. Hearing the stories behind their abortions made some of us react with a combination of anger, frustration, and sadness. Recalling an interview with one woman, one of us stated that it was impossible to remain dispassionate when listening to the participant:

> The intense sadness in her voice on the other end of the line was difficult to deal with; I could not offer any words of advice or comfort – my researcher brain was reminding me not to become involved, to stay neutral, unbiased. Listening to her sense of longing for a third child, in spite of the profound [ill] effects on her health, was heartbreaking. Knowing that she arrived at her decision to abort because it was her only option,

to preserve her health and life in order to raise her two toddlers, made me so angry, so angry at all those people who judge, stereotype, and condemn women seeking abortions. Each [woman's] path is unique and never without intense personal consideration.

I got off the phone, and I was exhausted, so tired. I just wanted to cry. I wanted to cry for all the women who need to make such difficult decisions and all the women who are judged, belittled, and punished. I was also angry, so angry at the guy [responsible for the pregnancy] – I wondered if he ever thought about it, ever had nightmares, and doubted it. Where is society's scorn for him? For his indiscretion? I was so angry and sad.

At times, the women we interviewed elicited feelings of pride in us. When one of us interviewed a woman who made what she considered to be a serious decision to have an abortion, she cast her as brave:

> She certainly did not take her decision [to have an abortion] lightly, and I was overwhelmed with feelings of admiration and sadness for her – she was so young and should not have to deal with such an intense decision. Who knows how she ended up being pregnant; there was no mention of the young man involved – only of her mother. She felt very badly for having burdened her mother with helping her – but mentioned that she could not imagine having to arrange it [the abortion] without her mother.

However, when some of us interviewed women who appeared to have made an untroubled decision to have an abortion, or who appeared to have accessed abortion services quickly and easily, we felt unsettled. We are unsure why. The 1969 restrictions on legal abortion services enforced by Therapeutic Abortion Committees in hospitals compelled some women to overstate their distress to convince the committees to grant their abortion requests (see Ackerman, this volume). In addition, the protracted efforts to maintain access to abortion services even after the 1988 Supreme Court of Canada decision that struck down the 1969 law has led some pro-choice advocates to stress repeatedly the obstacles women continue to face in accessing abortion services.[36] Perhaps because of this history, we expected to hear typically sensational stories of women's abortion experiences and were disappointed when we did not. We may have even felt annoyed when the women we interviewed seemed to display little awareness of the very real obstacles to abortion access that so many women do face, especially if living in remote Northern or Eastern Canada.[37] And we admit that the women's stories about wrestling with the decision to have an abortion or about overcoming obstacles to access abortion services were most affecting emotionally, leaving us to question the actions of women who seemed to have experienced little hardship at all. Indeed, in some instances there was a fine line between our conscious acknowledgement that women should not have to suffer for abortion access and our own unconscious judgmental attitudes towards some of the participants. In this vein, one researcher was confused by her own positive and negative reactions to one woman she interviewed:

> When she answered the phone, she sounded busy, like she was doing dishes, very matter of fact, no big deal. I don't know why I think I found her a bit too matter of fact. I don't know why I expected her to say at some point it [the abortion] was hard, there was some deliberation, offer some reasoning. Strange, because I don't really need or want any of these things. I guess after interviewing Cleo [a young woman who encountered several challenges] who really seemed to grasp the limitations of the systems and the limits on her choice, Susan was so different. She was older and married. She thought that travel was no big deal – as long as it [the abortion service] was available somewhere. I kind of wanted to say, well, it is a big deal for a lot of women, but then again I couldn't really say this. She had the means to get to the clinic, to enact her choice. I was happy for her, happy for her that she was so sure, so unaffected, so clear.

Entering the questionnaire data provoked similar responses from the researchers. This data focused primarily on the logistics of women's travel to the clinics, including information about transportation. The questionnaire also provided space for the women to include their own comments about their travel experiences to the clinics. Women living in Canada's major urban centres generally have access to several abortion clinics and to extensive transportation networks. As a result, their travel was relatively stress-free. These women reported taking public transit, walking, or taking taxis to clinics at very little financial and personal cost. The stories they told about these journeys could be described as unremarkable, which once again surprised some of us:

> I didn't expect there to be so many stories that were somewhat mundane/non-sensational. I remember thinking that so many of them did seem to be quite ordinary and uneventful, and that this sort of came as a surprise to me. Obviously, this has a lot to do with the fact that people don't talk about abortion, and at the time I really didn't have a concept of it in my day-to-day life, other than media portrayals; I'm thinking the *Degrassi High* [a popular Canadian television drama about high school students] type narrative, which is often not reflective of many people's real experiences.

The majority of women who agreed to the follow-up interviews described uncomplicated journeys to the abortion clinic. For this reason, we should be cognizant of telling all women's abortion stories, rather than emphasizing only those that follow a sensationalized script.

Nevertheless, not every travel account involved a routine journey. Many women lived outside urban centres, making access to abortion services problematic. Despite the relatively limited qualitative detail reported in the questionnaires, researchers made pointed observations about the obstacles to abortion access that some of the women reported. Here, Canada's geography played a key role, as one of us recognized in her comments:

> One case stands out to me. It was a young girl that lived in a remote town in Alberta and had travelled a long distance to the clinic with her social worker driving her. It's such a stark contrast from the experience of a young person living in a city and shows the vulnerability of certain groups to barriers such as judgmental gatekeepers and unknowledgeable staff.

The length of this journey reinforces not only the logistical challenges posed by a country of Canada's size but also the clear split between urban and rural regions in terms of access to abortion services.

As researchers we are aware of the limits of objectivity even when employing seemingly objective research methods, such as questionnaires. We recognize that our subjectivity as researchers influences the questions we ask and the ways in which we interpret the data. Some of our reflections indicate that we tried to maintain a distance from the qualitative and quantitative questionnaire data we collected. The maintenance of this distance may also have been a way of protecting ourselves from the emotionality of the stories evident even in the raw qualitative data that emerged in sections of the questionnaire. When recalling her experience of reading the questionnaires that women had filled out, one of the researchers remarked:

> I do remember reading some of the questionnaires and getting quite upset/emotionally involved. It was obvious in some of the [replies to the] questionnaires that it was a hard and emotional experience for the person filling out the questionnaire, and even though I was only really interacting with the raw data, it's hard not to imagine what that person went through and feel for them. I found I really felt for those [women represented in the] questionnaires where the person had travelled alone. I guess because if I was going through an abortion, I wouldn't want to be alone and, in some cases, it seemed that they didn't really want to be there alone either.

Although this researcher had no direct contact with the participants in our study, the raw data affected her deeply, thus confirming the affective impact that research on sensitive issues can have.

In hindsight, this first-time study of abortion travel yielded not only data that illustrates women's uneven access to abortion services in clinics across Canada, but also four critical lessons for researchers working on the sensitive issue of abortion.[38] We suggest that these lessons should be considered when planning research on abortion generally, and when determining how abortion research can support political advocacy efforts to maintain and improve access to abortion services even in contexts where abortion is legal.

First, the stigmatization of abortion as a medical practice makes research on abortion challenging to arrange. Gipson and colleagues report on the process of conducting research on abortion in international settings where the illegality of the practice means that finding local collaborators can be frustrating.[39] In the American context, Wear reports on the difficulty of recruiting abortion providers to participate in her study, even when abortion is legal.[40] Our experience with the abortion clinics that agreed to participate in our study was complicated. The clinic staff was generally very supportive of our study and accepted the need for research to give voice to their work. However, the daily workload pressures the clinic staff faced, often functioning under conditions of scarcity – namely, a shortage of time, funds, personnel, and support – meant that, understandably, our study could not be a priority. The threat of violence and harassment to which the clinics are attuned required the development of trust and credibility between us and the clinic staff, thereby adding to the study's timeline. And, because not every clinic has been able to establish a buffer zone that protects the immediate vicinity of the clinic from anti-abortion protestors, we had to be aware of security measures that clinics had put into place. More experienced researchers on a research team should handle the initial arrangements with the clinics, and all research team members need to be briefed ahead of time on security measures so that they can respect identification protocols for gaining physical entry to clinics.

Second, as researchers, we need to reflect critically upon our own beliefs about abortion. Self-reflection is vital to dealing with the emotional weight of the data and to interpreting that data such that we do not reproduce inadvertently the divisive political discourse about abortion. We came to understand that a dearth of information about the wide range of women's abortion experiences has contributed to that divisiveness. Follow-up interviews with women who had had abortions at the clinics led us to move beyond tracking the mere ease or difficulty of women's travel to the clinics and toward a diversity of stories about accessing abortion services. Paying close attention on this diversity is essential, especially when opponents of abortion discount or seek to recriminalize the reproductive choices women make.

As Ludlow discovered in her research on abortion in the United States, there is no one-size-fits-all abortion story.[41] Women told us about repeat abortions, fetal abnormalities, and uncooperative doctors while recounting their difficult journeys to abortion clinics in the developed, democratic, prosperous nation of Canada. Sensational stories of accessing abortion services are emotionally taxing to hear, transcribe, and analyze. While we honour the participants who lived through them, they were a minority in our study. Like Ludlow, we encountered many more stories of travel to access abortion services in clinics that were unremarkable. Of the 1186 women who filled out our questionnaire, a majority indicated that their journey was easy.[42] In these stories, women experienced an unwanted pregnancy, called a clinic, made an appointment, went to the clinic, and had an abortion. As Ludlow so cogently argues, the lack of unremarkable accounts about access to abortion services magnifies abortion horror stories. The latter are used to reinforce the need to safeguard access to safe, affordable, and legal abortion services and to create "a hierarchy of abortion narratives from a pro-choice political perspective."[43]

Focusing solely on sensational stories might play into the divisive political discourse about abortion in Canada, possibly acting against the creation of an environment in which the provision of abortions is destigmatized. Normalizing the unremarkable stories of access to abortion services on the domestic scene as commonplace medical procedures might counter the gruesome messaging about butchered fetuses put forward by some anti-abortion advocates.[44] Conversely, there is a need to highlight the fact that an estimated 68,000 women die globally every year as a result of unsafe abortion.[45] It is vital to document the consequences of unsafe abortions, which are often the result of legal and extralegal obstacles to access to abortion services, in order to promote national and international policy changes that help women access abortion services worldwide.

Third, original study designs for research on sensitive issues like abortion need to prepare researchers in advance to cope with the discomfiting emotions that they will undoubtedly encounter. Although the four authors of this chapter vary in terms of age, personal life histories, disciplinary backgrounds, and professional status, we each felt varying degrees of anger, frustration, confusion, and sadness while working on this study. Sethna and Doull concentrated on meeting the requirements of the stringent university research ethics board review. The board's permission is necessary to conduct research on human participants. It assesses the care of participants taking part in research according to the *Tri-Council Policy Statement* (TCP). The TCP insists upon three ethical principles: respect for persons, concern for human welfare, and justice. These principles take into consideration the "intrinsic value of human beings," the "physical, mental and spiritual health" of individuals, and the "obligation to treat people fairly and equitably."[46]

To complete the ethics review we were asked to provide a list of counselling resources (such as a national toll-free support hotline) to which participants could turn if they so desired after completing their interviews. Albeit well-intentioned, this requirement institutionalizes the notion that abortion can be a traumatic experience for women. However, the research ethics board never calls attention to the need for the self-care of the researchers, even though those who conduct research on abortion have been known to encounter situations that are uncomfortable at best and life-threatening at worst.[47] Sethna and Doull informed students who wished to work on the study that doing research on abortion could be emotionally taxing; yet some students expressed confidentially a desire to work on the project precisely because of their own past abortion experiences. Unfortunately, no formal provisions were put in place to deal with the self-care needs of the research team members during the study beyond requesting written notes of our reflections. The researchers dealt with a variety of emotions that arose over the course of the study admittedly on an ad hoc basis with debriefing sessions occurring periodically, mostly in response to issues arising spontaneously or after particularly upsetting interviews with research participants.

In hindsight, we now know that other researchers have documented the affective impact of working in abortion clinics on health professionals and report emotions similar to those we experienced.[48] Some have recommended frequent standardized debriefing sessions for research teams.[49] This recommendation is particularly important, as Gipson and colleagues point out that in settings where abortion is illegal or stigmatized, researchers have few opportunities to debrief about their work.[50] Furthermore, university-based researchers tend to hire graduate and undergraduate students as research coordinators or assistants. Given the age of most of these students, it is possible that they may have already had an abortion, or supported a friend or relative through an abortion decision, or could be pregnant at some point during the course of the study. Therefore, formal provisions should be incorporated into the research design at the early stages to help deal with the emotional toll that research on sensitive issues can take on individual researchers, especially when they are younger and inexperienced.[51] These often overlooked provisions might include setting aside funds in research budgets for therapeutic support of researchers, monthly debriefings with research team members, and peer counselling.

Finally, researchers need to strike a balance between acknowledging the emotional work of research on abortion and presumptions of researcher objectivity.[52] Kristin Blakely notes that the emotional responses of researchers doing feminist research offers up a rich source of data that questions the existence of objectivity.[53] Others researchers have also struggled with maintaining any presumptions of objectivity when conducting research on abortion. Hess, who researched women's post-abortion experiences, described a "role-conflict" between her roles as researcher and nurse.[54] As a nurse, she wanted to counsel her research participants, whereas as a researcher, she wished to stay neutral and objective. When conducting interviews for our study, we were aware of the need to maintain boundaries between our beliefs about abortion and the women's experiences of accessing abortion services. Although the research was emotionally taxing at times, we prioritized our roles as researchers. Following the research ethics board requirements, we provided the participants we interviewed with consent forms and interview guides to maintain consistency for both participants and researchers. We also provided the participants with contact information for counselling resources, as required, at the end of each interview. In this manner we showed support for the participants in our study without stepping out of our own roles inappropriately.

Researchers' reflections on conducting research, especially on sensitive issues, are rarely documented. Giving space to these reflections, as this chapter does, is a first step in documenting the unique considerations that research on sensitive issues requires. This chapter adds a vital dimension to this knowledge base and also yields lessons for those engaged in research on sensitive issues. In particular, the interface of the personal and political in abortion research points to matters of self-care to which researchers should attend, notably in regard to junior and student research assistants. In addition, pro-choice feminist researchers need to be transparent about their beliefs regarding abortion but in ways that do not play into the divisive political discourse about abortion.

Notes

1 Alice S. Demi and Nancy A. Warren, "Issues in Conducting Research with Vulnerable Families," *Western Journal of Nursing Research* 17, 2 (1995): 188–202; T. James and H. Platzer, "Ethical Considerations in Qualitative Research with Vulnerable Groups: Exploring Lesbians' and Gay Men's Experiences of Health Care – A Personal Perspective," *Nursing Ethics* 6, 1 (1999): 73–81; Colin Murray Parkes, "Guidelines for Conducting Ethical Bereavement Research," *Death Studies* 19 (1995): 171–81; Linda Weaver Moore and Margaret Miller, "Initiating Research with Doubly Vulnerable Populations," *Journal of Advanced Nursing* 30, 5 (1999): 1034–40.

2 Virginia Dickson-Swift, Erica L. James, Sandra Kippen, and Pranee Liamputtong, "Doing Sensitive Research: What Challenges Do Qualitative Researchers Face?" *Qualitative Research* 7, 3 (2007): 327–53; James and Platzer, "Ethical Considerations in Qualitative Research"; Claudia Malacrida, "Reflective Journaling on Emotional Research Topics: Ethical Issues for Team Researchers," *Qualitative Health Research* 17, 10 (2007): 1329–39; Louise Rowling, "Being In, Being Out, Being With: Affect and the Role of Qualitative Researcher in Loss and Grief Research," *Mortality* 4, 2 (1999): 167–81; Jacqueline H. Watts, "Emotion, Empathy and Exit: Reflections on Doing Ethnographic Qualitative Research on Sensitive Topics," *Medical Sociology Online* 3, 2 (2008): 3–14.

3 Dickson-Swift et al., "Doing Sensitive Research;" Kathleen B. Rager, "Self-Care and the Qualitative Researchers: When Collecting Data Can Break Your Heart," *Educational Researcher* 34, 4 (2005): 23–27; Kristin Blakely, "Reflections on the Role of Emotion in Feminist Research," *International Journal of Qualitative Methods* 6, 2 (2007): 59–68.

4 E. Milling Kinard, "Conducting Research on Child Maltreatment: Effects on Researchers," *Violence and Victims* 11, 1 (1996): 69.

5 Heather McCosker, Alan Barnard, and Rod Gerber, "Undertaking Sensitive Research: Issues and Strategies for Meeting the Safety Needs of All Participants," *Forum Qualitative Sozialforschung / Forum: Qualitative Social Research,* 2, 1: http://www.qualitative-research.net/index.php/fqs/article/viewArticle/983.

6 Rager, "Self-Care and the Qualitative Researchers"; Sue Cannon, "Social Research in Stressful Settings: Difficulties for the Sociologist Studying the Treatment of Breast Cancer," *Sociology of Health and Illness* 11, 1 (1989): 62–77; Janet G. Alexander, Mary de Chesnay, Elaine Marshall, Arthur R. Campbell, Sharon Johnson, and Rebecca Wright, "Parallel Reactions in Rape Victims and Rape Researchers," *Violence and Victims* 4 (1989): 57–62; Sevaste Chatzifotiou, "Conducting Qualitative Research on Wife Abuse: Dealing with the Issue of Anxiety," *Sociological Research Online* 5, 2 (2000): http://www.socresonline.org.uk/5/2/chatzifotiou.html; Kathleen deMarrais and Kit Tisdale, "What Happens When Researchers Inquire into Difficult Emotions? Reflections on Studying Women's Anger through Qualitative Interviews," *Educational Psychologist* 37, 2 (2002): 115–23; Gillian Elam and Kevin A. Fenton, "Researching Sensitive Issues and Ethnicity: Lessons from Sexual Health," *Ethnicity and Health* 8, 1 (2003): 15–27; Ben Fincham, Johnathan Scourfield, and Susanne Langer, "The Impact of Working with Disturbing Secondary Data: Reading Suicide Files in a Coroner's Office," *Qualitative Health Research* 18, 6 (2008): 853–62; Jessica D. Gipson, Davida Becker, Joanna Z. Mishtal, and Alison H. Norris, "Conducting Collaborative Abortion Research in International Settings," *Women's Health Issues* 21, 3 (2011): S58–S62; and Katherine Carroll, "Infertile? The Emotional Labour of Sensitive Feminist Research Methodologies," *Qualitative Research* 13, 5 (2012): 546–61.

7 Kathleen McDonnell, *Not an Easy Choice: Re-examining Abortion* (Toronto: Second Story Press, 2003); Ingrid Peritz, "Despite Being Legal, Abortions Still Not Accessible for All Canadians," *Globe and Mail,* June 18, 2010, http://www.theglobeandmail.com/news/national/abortion-access-unequal-across-country/article1215524/; Gloria Galloway, "Tory MP's Call to Revisit Rights-of-Unborn Law Fuels Abortion Debate," *Globe and Mail,* December 21, 2011, http://www.theglobeandmail.com/news/politics/ottawa-notebook/tory-mps-call-to-revisit-rights-of-unborn-law-fuels-abortion-debate/article2279143/; CBC, "How the Abortion Debate Has Reared Its Head in Parliament," *CBC News,* April 26, 2012, http://www.cbc.ca/news/canada/story/2012/04/26/f-abortion-woodworth-motion-parties.html; and Nora Caplan-Bricker, "What the Anti-Abortion Movement Has Won," *New Yorker*, 28 January 2017, http://www.newyorker.com/news/news-desk/what-the-anti-abortion-movement-has-won.

8 Wendy V. Norman, "Induced Abortion in Canada 1974–2005: Trends over the First Generation with Legal Access," *Contraception* 85, 2 (2011): 185–91.

9 Angus McLaren and Arlene Tigar McLaren, *The Bedroom and the State: The Changing Practices and Politics of Contraception and Abortion in Canada, 1880–1997* (Toronto: Oxford University Press, 1997); David Grimes, "Unsafe Abortion: The Silent Scourge," *British Medical Bulletin* 67 (2003): 99–113; David A. Grimes, Janie Benson, Susheela Singh, Mariana Romero, Bela Ganatra, Friday E. Okonofua, and Iqbal H. Shah, "Unsafe Abortion: The Preventable Pandemic," *The Lancet* 368, 9550 (2006): 1908–19.

10 Guttmacher Institute, *State Policies in Brief: An Overview of Abortion Laws, as of June 1, 2012* (New York: Guttmacher Institute: 2012).

11 Tracy A. Weitz, "Rethinking the Mantra That Abortion Should Be Safe, Legal and Rare," *Journal of Women's History* 22, 3 (2010): 161–72; Mary Ann Castle, "Abortion in the United States' Bible Belt: Organizing for Power and Empowerment," *Reproductive Health* 8, 1 (2011): doi:10.1186/1742-4755-8-1.

12 Mercedes Allen, "Parliament to Debate Abortion in April," *Rabble,* March 15, 2012, http://rabble.ca/blogs/bloggers/mercedes-allen/2012/03/parliament-debate-abortion-april and Joanne Boucher, "The Politics of Abortion and the Commodification of the Fetus," *Studies in Political Economy* 73 (2004): 69–88. See also Lisa M. Mitchell, *Baby's First Picture: Ultrasound and the Politics of Fetal Subjects* (Toronto: University of Toronto Press, 2001).

13 See Paul Saurette and Kelly Gordon, *The Changing Voice of the Anti-Abortion Movement: The Rise of "Pro-Woman" Rhetoric in Canada and the United States* (Toronto: University of Toronto Press, 2015).

14 Kate Parsons, "Feminist Reflections on Miscarriage, in Light of Abortion," *International Journal of Feminist Approaches to Bioethics* 3, 1 (Spring 2010): 1–22.

15 Anna Glasier, A Metin Gulmezoglu, George P. Schmid, Claudia Garcia Moreno, and Paul F.A. Van Look, "Sexual and Reproductive Health: A Matter of Life and Death," *The Lancet* 368, 9547 (2006): 1595–607.

16 Hanna Söderberg, Christina Anderson, Lars Janzon, and Nils-Otto Sjöberg, "Selection Bias in a Study on How Women Experienced Induced Abortion," *European Journal of Obstetrics and Gynecology and Reproductive Biology* 77 (1998): 67–70, and Lianne McTavish, "The Cultural Production of Pregnancy: Bodies and Embodiment at a New Brunswick Abortion Clinic," *Topia* 20 (2008): 23–42. See also Heather Mallick, "Ottawa Police Won't Protect Abortion Clinic Despite Pleas," *Toronto Star,* 19 April 2017, https://www.thestar.com/opinion/commentary/2017/04/19/ottawa-police-wont-protect-abortion-clinic-despite-pleas-mallick.html, and Laura Stradiotto, "Not the Right Time," *Chatelaine,* September 2016, 75–76.

17 For disparities in abortion access, see Christabelle Sethna and Marion Doull, "Far from Home? A Pilot Study Tracking Women's Journeys to a Canadian Abortion Clinic," *Journal of Obstetrics and Gynaecology Canada* 29, 8 (2007): 640–47; Jessica W. Kiley, Lynn M. Yee, Cassandra M. Niemi, Joseph M. Feinglass, and Melissa A. Simon, "Delays in Request for Pregnancy Termination: Comparison of Patients in the First and Second Trimesters," *Contraception* 81 (2010): 446–51; Christabelle Sethna and Marion Doull, "Spatial Disparities and Travel to Freestanding Abortion Clinics in Canada," *Women's Studies International Forum* 38 (2013): 52–62. For women's experiences on accessing abortion, see Katrina Kimport, Kate Cockrill, and Tracy A. Weitz, "Analyzing the Impacts of Abortion Clinic Structures and Processes: A Qualitative Analysis of Women's Negative Experiences of Abortion Clinics," *Contraception* 85 (2012): 204–10. For the relationship between abortion access and health outcomes, see Glasier et al., "Sexual and Reproductive Health."

18 Jeannie Ludlow, "The Things We Cannot Say: Witnessing the Trauma-tization of Abortion in the United States," *Women's Studies Quarterly* 36, 1–2 (2008): 28–41.

19 Gipson et al., "Conducting Collaborative Abortion Research."

20 Ludlow, "The Things We Cannot Say."

21 Ibid., 28.

22 McTavish, "The Cultural Production of Pregnancy."

23 Ibid.

24 Delese Wear, "From Pragmatism to Politics: A Qualitative Study of Abortion Providers," *Women and Health* 36, 4 (2002): 103–13.

25 Rosanna F. Hess, "Postabortion Research: Methodological and Ethical Issues," *Qualitative Health Research* 16, 4 (2006): 580–87.

26 Kelly Grant, "Long-Awaited Abortion Pill Mifegymiso Makes Canadian Debut," *Globe and Mail,* January 20, 2017, http://www.theglobeandmail.com/news/national/long-awaited-

abortion-pill-mifegymiso-rolls-out-in-canada/article33695167/. See also Kristina I. Vogel, Kathryn J. LaRoche, Julie El-Haddad, Andréanne Chaumont, and Angel M. Foster, "Exploring Canadian Women's Knowledge of and Interest in Mifepristone: Results from a National Qualitative Study with Abortion Patients," *Contraception* 94 (2016): 137–42.

27 Karen Potts and Leslie Brown, "Becoming an Anti-oppressive Researcher," in *Research as Resistance: Critical, Indigenous, and Anti-oppressive Approaches,* ed. Leslie Brown and Susan Strega (Toronto: Canadian Scholars' Press, 2005), 255.

28 For example, see Deborah K. van den Hoonaard, *Qualitative Research in Action: A Canadian Primer,* 2nd ed. (Don Mills, ON: Oxford University Press, 2015), 144–45. See also Carolyn Ellis, "Sociological Introspection and Emotional Experience," *Symbolic Interaction* 14, 1 (1991): 23–50; and Rebekah Widdowfield, "The Place of Emotions in Academic Research," *Area* 32, 2 (2000): 199–208.

29 Kimport, Cockrill, and Weitz, "Analyzing the Impacts of Abortion Clinic Structures and Processes."

30 Jeanelle N. Sabourin and Margaret Burnett, "A Review of Therapeutic Abortions and Related Areas of Concern in Canada," *Journal of Obstetrics and Gynaecology Canada* 34, 6 (2012): 532–42; Gene Grabiner, "A Question of Choice," *Reproductive Health* 8, 20 (2011): 1–7.

31 To avoid any conflict of interest, Christabelle Sethna resigned from the board of the Ottawa-based organization, Canadians for Choice, before embarking upon this research.

32 J. Baumgardner, "The Pro-choice PR Problem," *The Nation*, March 5, 2001, http://www.thenation.com/article/pro-choice-pr-problem?page=0,1; Gloria Feldt, *The War on Choice: The Right-Wing Attack on Women's Rights and How to Fight Back* (New York: Bantam Dell, 2004).

33 Rachael Johnstone, *After Morgentaler: The Politics of Abortion in Canada* (Vancouver: UBC Press, forthcoming 2017).

34 Abortion Rights Coalition of Canada, "Position Paper #22: Late Term Abortions (After 20 Weeks)," July 2005, http://www.arcc-cdac.ca/postionpapers/22-Late-term-Abortions.PDF.

35 Tonda MacCharles, "Conservative MPs Ask RCMP to Investigate Late-Term Abortions as Homicides," *Toronto Star,* January 31, 2013, http://www.thestar.com/news/canada/2013/01/31/three_tory_mps_ask_rcmp_to_investigate_some_abortions_as_homicides.html.

36 Canadian Abortion Rights Action League (CARAL) Halifax Chapter, *Telling Our Secrets: Abortion Stories from Nova Scotia* (Halifax, NS: CARAL, 1990); CARAL, *Protecting Abortion Rights in Canada: A Special Report to Celebrate the 15th Anniversary of the Decriminalization of Abortion* (Ottawa: CARAL, 2003); Jessica Shaw, *Reality Check: A Close Look at Accessing Abortion Services in Canadian Hospitals* (Ottawa: Canadians for Choice, 2006); and Shannon Stettner, ed., *Without Apology: Writings on Abortion in Canada* (Edmonton: Athabasca University Press, 2016).

37 See Sethna and Doull, "Spatial Disparities."

38 Ibid.

39 Gipson et al., "Conducting Collaborative Abortion Research."

40 Wear, "From Pragmatism to Politics."

41 Ludlow, "The Things We Cannot Say."

42 Sethna and Doull, "Spatial Disparities."

43 Ludlow, "The Things We Cannot Say," 29.

44 "Harper's Riding Targeted with Graphic Anti-abortion Cards," *CBC News,* May 14, 2013, http://www.cbc.ca/news/canada/calgary/harper-s-riding-targeted-with-graphic-anti-abortion-cards-1.1315361.

45 Grimes et al., "Unsafe Abortion."

46 Will C. van den Hoonaard, "Ethics on the Ground: A Moral Compass," in *Qualitative Research in Action,* ed. by Deborah K. van den Hoonaard (Don Mills, ON: Oxford University Press, 2015), 55–56.
47 Virginia Dickson-Swift, Erica L. James, Sandra Kippen, Prannee Liamputtong, "Risk to Researchers in Qualitative Research on Sensitive Subjects: Issues and Strategies," *Qualitative Health Research* 18, 1 (2008): 133–44.
48 Warren M. Hern and Billie Corrigan, "What About Us? Staff Reactions to D & E," *Advances in Planned Parenthood* 15, 1 (1980): 3–8; Lisa Hope Harris, Michelle Debbink, Lisa Martin, and Jane Hassinger, "Dynamics of Stigma in Abortion Work: Findings from a Pilot Study of the Providers Share Workshop," *Social Science and Medicine* 73 (2011): 1062–70.
49 Gipson et al., "Conducting Collaborative Abortion Research."
50 Ibid.
51 Rager, "Self-Care and the Qualitative Researchers."
52 Blakely, "Reflections on the Role of Emotion in Feminist Research."
53 Ibid.
54 Hess, "Postabortion Research."

Part 3
Politics

8

Functionally Inaccessible

Historical Conflicts in Legal and Medical Access to Abortion

Frances E. Chapman and Tracy Penny Light

Landmark challenges to abortion laws in Canada and the United States grew out of the social and cultural shifts of the 1960s, which reconsidered the role of women and their reproductive rights and consequently argued for increased access to surgical abortion.[1] Prior to the 1960s, women in both countries who wished to terminate their pregnancies quietly sought out practitioners to perform the procedure illegally. These were often allopathic practitioners who were willing to help women out of their "trouble," and only occasionally did their practices attract the attention of the law. However, when the services did attract the attention of the law, it was often the women themselves who suffered.[2]

During the period of its illegality, the morality of abortion was a serious consideration, and women who sought to terminate unwanted pregnancies were forced to inquire covertly among those they knew to find someone willing to perform the stigmatized procedure.[3] For physicians who adhered to a traditional notion of the fetus as a living being possessed of a soul or as a rights-bearing person, the practice remained problematic despite contrary views present in the early twentieth century.[4] Even when the mother's life was at risk, most physicians turned their prospective patients away throughout the period of the procedure's illegality. Whether the patient would receive assistance was dependent, however, on many factors, including the patient's geographic location and proximity to a provider, her socio-economic and marital status, and her race or ethnicity. We know, for instance, that women who were members of wealthier families and therefore had the economic means to pay for a procedure had a much better chance of finding a competent practitioner than did racialized or working-class women.[5]

The issue of viability also continued to be an important aspect of access because there were variations in practice in terms of when, and up to what point in gestation, a procedure could be performed in different jurisdictions. In this way, the history of abortion access links moral determinations of when life begins to the ability of doctors to perform the procedure within a judicial regulatory framework, which included the age-old discussion of viability. By the 1960s, however, wider liberation movements in North America that highlighted inequalities – in the case of abortion, those that related to the fact that women did not possess the right to control their own bodies – together with support from medical professionals who advocated for their ability to protect their patients' health, fostered an examination of abortion laws. As a result, these laws eventually were changed.

In Canada, abortion law was first liberalized in 1969. When it became clear that women were still seeking out operations in unsafe conditions and, at times, in other countries, legal challenges eventually led to the repeal of the 1969 law.[6] Specifically, the case of *R v Morgentaler* in 1988 challenged the constitutionality of having a panel of doctors decide what happened with a woman's body under section 251 of the *Criminal Code*. The *Morgentaler* decision was framed around section 7 of the *Canadian Charter of Rights and Freedoms* that protects life, liberty, and the security of the person. The Supreme Court of Canada decided that the legal requirement implemented by the 1969 law for a woman to obtain a positive judgment from a Therapeutic Abortion Committee in order to be able to have an abortion violated her security of the person. In the United States, the case of *Roe v Wade* (1973) focused on a woman's right to privacy in seeking to terminate a pregnancy.[7]

Given that these decisions to amend abortion laws were framed in relation to women's right to privacy and the security of their person, it is perhaps unsurprising that many today believe that the decided legality of the procedure ensures abortion access. In reality, however, neither decision has guaranteed that women are able to terminate pregnancies when they desire. As Chris Kaposy points out with respect to the Canadian situation, "numerous practices and policies in place at the various levels of the Canadian health care system and the health policy apparatus ... make abortion inaccessible for many women."[8] Similarly, Marlene Gerber-Fried notes of the situation in the United States that "for tens of thousands of women in the U.S. annually, the lack of access to abortion remains a key obstacle to fully exercising their reproductive rights" and part of the challenge to access is that abortion provision is a dangerous business – physicians who provide the service are under constant threat due to ongoing moral, theological, and religious debates about when life begins.[9]

In order to examine the moral and legal implications in the history of abortion, this essay calls for a new framework to discuss abortion. To do this, it explores the medical and legal aspects of abortion and highlights how, in the past as in the present, the procedure has been fraught with risk and uncertainty for women seeking to terminate their pregnancies. Historical instances in Canada in which doctors were implicated in illegal operations highlight important and enduring themes around viability and access that persist today. We conclude that it is necessary to shift society towards a harm-reduction approach that mediates moral concerns to better protect women's health and allows for more functional access to abortions.

The Legal History of Abortion: Defining the Beginning of Life in Canadian Abortion Law

> If a woman be quick with childe, and by a Potion or otherwise killeth it in her wombe, or if a man beat her, whereby the childe dyeth in her body, and she is delivered of a dead childe, this is a great misprision and no murder; but if the childe be born alive and dyeth of the Potion, Battery, or other cause, this is murder; for in law it is accounted a reasonable creature, *in rerum natura* [in existence], when it is born alive.[10]

This statement, which holds that the right to life begins with a child born alive, was written by Sir Edward Coke in his *Institutes* of 1648. So entrenched is Coke's principle in English common law that Ian Kennedy and Andrew Grubb call the "born alive" rule "unassailable in England."[11] Because of this bright juridical line, jurists in common law traditions avoid any further need to determine when life begins. The born alive rule, moreover, remains an underlying principle in modern Canadian abortion law.

Until 1969, the Canadian *Criminal Code* of 1892, section 271, criminalized killing unborn children as a separate offence. It provided that "every one is guilty of an indictable offence and liable to imprisonment for life who causes the death of any child which has not become a human being, in such a manner that he would have been guilty of murder if such child had been born." The *Criminal Code*, however, made a notable exception to this rule in section 271 (2) for any individual who, "in good faith considers necessary for the preservation of the life of the mother of the child, causes the death of any such child before or during its birth."[12]

Even when those trained in the respective disciplines of medicine, philosophy, and theology were unable to arrive at any consensus about when life began, the judiciary had to grapple with this issue.[13] Although the law is often very nebulous when it comes to moralistic legal matters, it has been very consistent for hundreds of years in the debate about the rights of the fetus. A person is not ascribed the rights and responsibilities of a person until they are born alive. It is only at the time that a child is fully outside the body of its mother that rights and responsibilities are bestowed. There has been a message in the law that any attempt to erode this bright line must be met with derision, and the born alive doctrine is a fundamental principle of the common law system in the criminal law and beyond. Yet, what rights do we ascribe a Canadian woman so that she may have real access to vital medical services?

Despite the apparent clarity as to the start of life offered by the common law tradition, abortion in Canada remains problematic from the perspective of ideas about access to abortion. Although abortion is legal, functional inaccessibility erodes a woman's control over her own body and restricts the security of her person by not allowing her access to a fundamental medical procedure. Even with the seminal case of *R v Morgentaler*, the courts left open a door for the protection of fetal rights. The majority of the Supreme Court of Canada justices who presided on this case recognized that there was a legitimate interest in the state protecting the fetus, but the infringement of the pregnant woman's right to security of the person was infringed upon more than necessary to protect the fetus. Chief Justice Dickson and Justice Lamer stated that although an exhaustive discussion of fetal rights was not necessary, it was necessary to "evaluate the particular balance struck by Parliament in section 251, as it relates to the priorities and aspirations of pregnant women and the government's interests in the protection of the foetus."[14]

The gap between the interests of the woman and the state's potential interest in the protection of the fetus has led to attempts from some modern Canadian politicians to introduce legislation that accords human rights to the unborn fetus.[15] Such legislation is not, however, the only threat to a woman's rights. Physical, emotional, and financial inaccessibility are also effective limits, as is the lack of abortion operations in many parts of Canada. Canadian constitutional law places health care in the jurisdiction of the provinces, and not the federal government. This naturally results in inequalities from province to province. All of these factors distort, limit, and pervert the law by ascribing rights to women in name only.[16] Given that this is an equality issue that goes to the core rights of women in Canada, careful regulation in terms of functional access to abortion in each province is needed, especially now that the growing majority of abortions take place outside of public hospitals.[17] Just as equality was fought for women to control their own bodies under law, this right must be upheld for all women. Women should not have difficulty seeking basic medical care, or have to travel great distances to obtain it, as they did before 1969 and, arguably, still have to do in the post-*Morgentaler* period.[18] A discussion of the history of access illuminates historical issues that women continue to face when seeking to access abortion today.

Historical Access to Abortion: The Morality of Women and Doctors in the Eyes of the Law

The history of women seeking abortions to terminate unwanted pregnancies is long, and several themes emerge in the legal cases that document Canadian women's experiences. The first is that of women searching and travelling to find an abortion provider. A second is that socio-economic factors were an important consideration for women seeking a reputable and safe provider. Even when women had money to pay for abortions, however, there was no guarantee they would escape the procedure unharmed. A third is that morality was at play – married women were often viewed by physicians and the courts more sympathetically than unmarried women seeking to terminate pregnancies, and women who were immigrants and/or not white were viewed even less positively. These themes point to the intersectional ways that gender, class, religion, and race or ethnicity work together to limit women's access to abortion both historically and today. The following cases highlight these factors.

One of the first legal decisions in Canada on the matter of abortion travel was that given in *R v Browne* (1881).[19] Archibald W. Browne was arrested for murdering Cynthia VanAllan McCrae and her unborn child, and faced extradition to the State of New York from the Canadian province of Ontario. Mr. Browne and Ms. McCrae both lived in Chatham, Ontario, but left the province for a hotel in Buffalo, New York, in search of an abortion provider. The final legal decision in the case clearly states that Mr. Browne was a married man, and Ms. McCrae an unmarried woman who was six or seven months pregnant at the time of the trip. The couple held themselves out to be man and wife under the names of Mr. and Mrs. Clarke. The various reports of this case are not fully clear about the "ailment" for which they allegedly sought treatment, stating only that they went to visit a doctor in Buffalo named Pynchon. When the couple went to Dr. Pynchon's office, Ms. McCrae was treated with "electricity," and they were given a bottle of "fluid extract of *nux vomica,*" for which they paid one dollar.[20]

The couple returned to Dr. Pynchon for additional treatments, which were described as "the application of one electrode of the battery over the stomach where she complained of pain, and one to the back of the neck."[21] Mr. Browne then returned to Chatham while Ms. McCrae stayed in Buffalo. Several days later Dr. Pynchon was called to Ms. McCrae's temporary boarding house where she was described as having "congestive chill," which he treated with "brandy, quinine, and chloroform."[22] Dr. Pynchon claimed that the night of this visit was the first time that Ms. McCrae revealed she was pregnant.[23] Ms. McCrae dictated a telegram to Mr. Browne sending a cryptic message urging him to return to Buffalo. She subsequently miscarried a few days later. Dr. Pynchon eventually called in another doctor to consult on the matter, but concealed the fact that a miscarriage had taken place. Ms. McCrae died three days later, and the Ontario Court of Common Pleas later found that her death was the result of "inflammation consequent upon the miscarriage," which was found to be a result of the "application of electricity."[24] Pynchon had collected in excess of $42 for the fatal services he performed.

The Ontario Court of Common Pleas found Mr. Browne to be an accessory to the murder of Cynthia McCrae and her unnamed infant and, ultimately, the Ontario Court of Appeal affirmed the judgment, although on other grounds. The arguments made by the Ontario Court of Common Pleas and Ontario Court of Appeal differed in that the first found Mr. Browne guilty of being an accessory after the fact, which was not an extraditable offence, and the latter found him guilty of being an accessory before the fact, which was an extraditable offence. Having exhausted the appellate process, the Canadian system remanded Mr. Browne for extradition to the United

States as an accessory before the fact in the murder of Ms. McCrae, and he was extradited under section 14 of the *Imperial Extradition Act* of 1870.[25] Dr. Pynchon, conversely, appears to have escaped all legal responsibility as no record exists to indicate he was ever charged, prosecuted, or sentenced. The Ontario Court of Appeal judge, Justice Patterson, noted that Dr. Pynchon had "innocently treated a woman for neuralgia" and, unbeknownst to him, she had been pregnant. Therefore, there had been "no intent to procure her miscarriage" and, indeed, the patient had applied the electric instrument herself. Thus, Ms. McCrae intended to commit a felony, and Mr. Browne was an accessory to that crime.[26] In this case, not only did the physician, Dr. Pynchon, escape all liability, but also the appellate court blamed the victim for her role in facilitating her own miscarriage.[27]

Incriminating women for facilitating their own miscarriages was not uncommon. Women were often blamed for any harm that came to them as a result of procuring an abortion. Another case describing a woman travelling to procure an abortion was brought against Dr. Benjamin E. Hawke. Dr. Hawke was charged with performing an abortion on seventeen-year-old Florence Watson in Toronto in 1910.[28] Ms. Watson testified at the trial that she paid Dr. Hawke $25 to perform an operation. She stated that she had come to Toronto from Orillia, Ontario, specifically for the purpose of an abortion. She explained that "she did not know of any particular doctor to whom she could go, and just happened to go to Dr. Hawke in her search of a physician after she had been turned away by several others. She said that Dr. Hawke had examined her and then operated on her with an instrument."[29] Ms. Watson survived the operation and was a witness against Dr. Hawke. However, Dr. Hawke was acquitted and a newspaper article reported that "the whole tone of the Judge's charge was favourable to the accused. The character of the girl, he said, was none too good, while Dr. Hawke had a good standing and reputation."[30] The woman who was pregnant with an illegitimate child was no match for an established medical doctor in this case. Less than two years later, Dr. Hawke was prosecuted for the death of another abortion patient before he fled the country.[31] What these and many other cases indicate is that women would go to great lengths to find access to an abortion provider when determined, for whatever reason, to terminate an unwanted pregnancy.[32]

The decriminalization of abortion, as others have shown, has not caused this searching to cease. Indeed, it may have exacerbated the problem because the lack of legal prohibitions on the practice of abortion leads many to assume that access is not only possible but readily available. It is often not until a woman is in need of a procedure that she may realize that finding a safe, qualified, and local provider, even today, can be challenging. For women who are not only economically and geographically vulnerable but also may have other factors, such as age, race, or ethnicity, limiting their access to abortion, the difficulty they face often results in harm. The case against Dr. Hawke illustrates that the challenges women face today are based on longstanding discriminations. For instance, in the judge's comments related to the acquittal of Dr. Hawke in 1910, it is clear that women on the margins were viewed with disdain – not only did they not have the right to control their own bodies, but they were also viewed as immoral for wanting to do so. As the judge noted, the character of the single girl pregnant with an illegitimate child was "none too good, while ... [the doctor] had a good standing and reputation."[33] Yet when the same physician was charged less than two years later for the death of a married woman who had implicated him in her ante-mortem statement, a different view of the doctor was taken.[34] In this case, the woman's husband was charged with her murder, but later acquitted, and the judge in the case noted:

> The jury has taken a merciful view of your case, and I don't disagree with their verdict. I am sorry for the position in which you have been placed during the trial of this case as the result of the death of your wife. I am also sorry for the revelations which have been made of thc ease with which women are able to procure illegal operations of this kind from medical men ... One thing that I am sorry for is the fact that the medical man who performed this wrongful act in this case, and caused the death of your wife, has fled the country. It would have been more satisfactory if he had been here, and if it had been he instead of you in that dock, because I am satisfied that on this evidence if he had been there in your place I would have had the grave duty of sentencing him to death.[35]

While the College of Physicians and Surgeons of Ontario unanimously voted to remove Dr. Hawke from its register because of his "infamous and disgraceful conduct," what this case and others point to is how rare it was for doctors to be prosecuted for illegal abortions and the tendency of the court to focus on the actions of the women seeking out the procedure throughout the long period when abortion was illegal.[36]

In most of the abortion cases where legal actions were pursued, the court's time was mostly taken up with procedural matters rather than with prosecuting those doctors who negligently performed abortions on vulnerable women. For example, the case of *R v Sparham* (1875) was concerned with the admissibility of the victim's dying declaration and the evidence permitted in reply.[37] Dr. Sparham was convicted of the murder of Sophia Elizabeth Burnham through using an instrument to produce an abortion and thereby causing her death. Because Dr. Sparham was convicted of a felony, his name was erased from the register of the Ontario College of Physicians and Surgeons. Although Dr. Sparham was sentenced to death, the sentence was commuted and he was released after a few years in prison. Ten years after being convicted of murder and sentenced to death, Dr. Sparham was charged with practising without being registered. However, there was some confusion about the penalty imposed for practising while unlicensed, and the conviction was quashed.[38] It is not clear whether Dr. Sparham continued to practise medicine after this; however, it is entirely possible.

The decision in *Sparham* seems to have departed radically from the case of *Stinson v College of Physicians and Surgeons.*[39] In that case, the College of Physicians and Surgeons found that although Dr. Albert W. Stinson had been acquitted of performing an abortion on Emma Dale in 1909, the facts of the misconduct had been proved: "[W]hether such misconduct be a crime or not so long as it is infamous or disgraceful in a professional respect, it is quite the same as if the medical man has been convicted of a crime ... if only he has been astute or lucky enough to escape prosecution or if prosecuted to escape conviction."[40] The College of Physicians and Surgeons filed a motion to investigate whether any professional disgraceful conduct had occurred, but the motion was dismissed, and it is unclear whether Dr. Stinson was formally removed from the register from the reported decisions.

Historian Constance Backhouse discovered another example of a doctor being investigated by the College of Physicians and Surgeons in *Re Robert Telford* (1905), where Dr. Telford's name was erased from the register of medical practitioners, despite his acquittal on charges of abortion.[41] Backhouse notes that within the cases she studied involving procuring an abortion there were as many not guilty as guilty verdicts, but she does not separate doctors and other individuals. There are some cases of doctors receiving prison time, however. One particularly interesting case is that of Dr. O.C.J. Withrow, who was charged for manslaughter jointly with B.J. Brooks, fiancé of the victim, Ruth Dembner. Brooks appealed his case to the Supreme Court, and his fate was decided on procedural issues. Dr. Withrow did not appeal his conviction and was sentenced to seven years for an illegal operation on Ms. Dembner and her resultant death. It was reported in the *Ottawa Citizen* on May 18, 1927 that Dr. Withrow had collapsed just before being sentenced in court and that he was suffering from a "serious mental condition." Dr. Withrow said that the operation had been performed according to usual practice but that he might have "made a slip" that perforated her uterus. He maintained, however, that he had been unaware that the girl was pregnant. The manslaughter charge was dropped, and Withrow was convicted on the charge of performing an illegal operation.[42]

Similarly, in *R v Tass* (1946), Dr. Tass was convicted of taking a woman to an abortion practitioner because he did not want to perform the abortion himself.[43] Dr. Tass was convicted of an attempt to procure a miscarriage by injection of a noxious fluid and use of instruments to procure a miscarriage, which resulted in the death of Agnes Laderoute. He was sentenced to three years' imprisonment.[44] Despite the fact that these cases are decades apart, it is clear from a survey of existing legal materials that the successful prosecution and imprisonment of abortion doctors was extremely rare, even when a death of the patient ensued. What they also point to is the importance for physicians to distinguish themselves from those practitioners who were willing to perform abortions. This was an aspect of morality that was a central feature of the rhetoric contained in the medical discourse on abortion in the period before 1930.

Women, Doctors, and Morality Rhetoric in the Late Nineteenth and Early Twentieth Centuries

At the beginning of the nineteenth century, Canadian society did not view a woman's involvement in procuring an abortion, whether by her own hand or with the help of an abortionist, as an important issue. It was not considered immoral for a woman to regulate her reproduction.[45] There were many methods of mechanical and herbal contraception available to couples in this period and it appears that, prior to the criminalization of abortion, it was widely accepted that women regulated their fertility and controlled their reproduction.[46] Women continued to seek out ways to terminate pregnancies, even when it became illegal to do so. However, the evolution of criminal sanctions against abortion over the course of the nineteenth century gradually placed more attention on the ways that women regulated their reproduction as abortion was reframed as not only illegal but also immoral.[47] The role that doctors played in this reframing was important because their expertise on the body helped to reinforce the legal perspective by providing the courts with scientific evidence about why the practice was wrong (see Johnstone, this volume).

As doctors established themselves as experts who derived their knowledge from science, they were increasingly able to proclaim that their perspective on the body was the only legitimate one. Their arguments that abortion was immoral were, they asserted, based on scientific "facts." For instance, Dr. R.V. Pierce noted in his 1888 medical text, *The People's Common Sense Medical Adviser in Plain English or Medicine Simplified,* that "it should be remembered that *life begins with conception*, and, at whatever period of pregnancy abortion is committed, *life is destroyed*."[48] Other doctors noted that abortion was the "murder of the innocents" and that abortion practitioners were "traffickers in human life [who] live and flourish on the blood they spill."[49] Such doctors' application of scientific approaches offered a new way of viewing the practice of abortion, which in turn provided them with a forceful means to differentiate themselves from abortion providers. They did so by claiming that only non-allopathic practitioners, classified as uneducated or irregular, performed abortions, despite the fact that there was evidence that many regular doctors, or those educated in science-based medical school, did indeed provide abortions. Those abortions that were performed, doctors argued, were necessary to protect the health of the mother, and only properly trained physicians could make a determination about what was medically necessary.[50] The ability to differentiate themselves in this way was crucial to these doctors' maintenance of both their economic and social status, even if the differentiation was more rhetoric than reality.[51] As Kristin Luker notes, "what the physicians did, in effect, was to simultaneously claim both an *absolute* right to life for the embryo (by claiming that abortion is always murder) and a *conditional* one (by claiming that doctors have a right to declare some abortions 'necessary')."[52] In other words, their position on abortion helped regular doctors, whether they opposed abortion or not, to separate themselves from the irregulars and facilitated their claim to superiority. At the same time, such claims by the regulars strove to call into question any knowledge held either by irregular practitioners or by women regarding how to control reproduction – a common practice given that abortion had only been a crime since the beginning of the nineteenth century (see Burnett, this volume). By labelling the practice of abortion immoral and by rooting their stance on the practice in science, regular doctors were able to strengthen their position, both practically and socially.

Doctors' desire to regulate the morality of both their profession and their patients reflected their class status. They believed that, because of their status in society, they had the ability to dictate moral values to their patients. As with the rhetoric of science, such claims were more representative of the theory than the practice since we know that many regulars, despite their claims, were really unsure of their status as professionals. The medical profession was overcrowded, which created financial pressures for doctors and threatened their middle-class position in society.[53] Nonetheless, their ability to instruct their patients about how to conduct themselves in society was part of the discourse they used to promote their own profession. For instance, Dr. Alfred A. Andrews of Windsor, Ontario, made the analogy between physicians and ministers in terms of the role that doctors played in helping their patients uphold their morality. He noted the difference between Protestant and Catholic patients:

> I had for many years noted and wondered at the fact, that of the married women who sought my co-operation, nearly all were Protestants. Being myself a Protestant of the broadest Orange stripe, and not ready to acknowledge any marked moral inferiority in my co-religionists, I was for a long season puzzled, but I think the solution is this. The Pulpit is debarred, but the Roman Catholic Priesthood, have in their confessional an opportunity of instructing and warning their flock. Protestant women do not go there, but we, and we only, have the private and confidential ear of the whole sex, and it is, I conceive our duty, to lose no opportunity of diffusing the information we possess in this regard. Let us purify the moral atmosphere.[54]

Dr. Andrews's statement of the moral superiority of doctors over their patients and the need for doctors to guide patients in their daily lives is clear. In the case of abortion, doctors believed that it was their duty to ensure that their patients did not stray from the moral prescriptions for women at the time (that they were made to be mothers), and in so doing, could separate themselves from irregular practitioners who were willing, or were perceived to be willing, to perform the procedure. Dr. Andrews's statement also points to another distinction between different groups of doctors, however. In noting the supposed difference between his Catholic and Protestant patients, he implied that it was Protestant women, rather than Catholic ones, who sought termination of their pregnancies, necessitating counselling by Protestant doctors. Catholic doctors presumably did not need to counsel their patients against the evils of abortion because the patients received such advice from their priests. While there is evidence to suggest that some Catholic women sought to terminate unwanted pregnancies in this period, this statement suggests that there was a difference between doctors of religious backgrounds.[55] Regardless of whether or not regular doctors were Protestant or Catholic, however, they shared the desire to promote the status of their profession.

In the late nineteenth and early twentieth centuries, rhetorical strategies that focused on the immorality of abortion were also common among other members of the professional classes such as those in the legal profession. For instance, at the sentencing of Bridget Blasdell, an abortionist from Hamilton, Ontario, Judge Armour noted that the crime committed by Blasdell

> is an offense which, in my mind, is the worst offense that can be committed – the procuring of an abortion upon the person of another. It is an offense against society; it is an offense against God. If there were no persons such as you who procure abortions, such offenses would die out; but the effect of your carrying out this nefarious trade is that persons are more willing to get into that condition that necessitates or impels them to seek your services than they otherwise would be ... Abortion is a crime that is on the increase in the country, and it is a crime which ought to be put a stop to in the interests of society.[56]

In this view, the practice of abortion was affecting not only individual women and the regular profession of medicine, but also society as a whole. This was an important observation and one upon which doctors capitalized as they sought to regulate their profession in the late nineteenth and early twentieth centuries. The historical cases above point to the ways that women who wished to have an abortion were forced to take their lives into their own hands by seeking out a practitioner amidst moral, medical, and legal debates about the practice. At the same time, there were few safeguards from the state charged with protecting their well-being and prosecuting their deaths.

Morality and Inaccessibility: Current Legal Issues in Canada

While the perspective of some doctors about the immorality of abortion began to shift by the 1930s as connections emerged between abortion and women's health and welfare, the notion that abortion is immoral persists in the present and helps to ensure that abortion is often functionally inaccessible to women in need, fundamentally putting them at risk. The same issues of viability and the timing of abortion that have been discussed for centuries still plague the discussion. Today, the Canadian Medical Association (CMA) defines induced abortion as "the active termination of a pregnancy before fetal viability."[57] The CMA policy on induced abortion goes on to note that the decision to have the procedure is made "confidentially between the patient and her physician within the confines of existing Canadian law" after examination of all of the other options, and that the procedure should be performed "only in a facility that meets approved medical standards, not necessarily a hospital."[58] After the hard-fought battles to legalize abortion, the procedure has been assimilated into the medical system as a medical procedure.

Abortion is meant to be treated like all other medical procedures in Canada and "legally integrated into the health system and governed by the laws, regulations, and medical standards that apply to all health services." As Joanna Erdman notes, however, "abortion can be a health service like any other, but it is not."[59] Immediately after the decriminalization of abortion, inequalities regarding access to abortion continued to surface because of variations in provincial laws and regulations that limit women's access to abortion. While Ontario and Quebec provide funding for abortion under their provincial health insurance policies, all other provinces have a history of restricting or withdrawing funding for this procedure since 1988 making it unclear where abortion is truly available in Canada today.

It is difficult to believe that there continues to be limited access to clinics or hospitals, particularly in Prince Edward Island, Yukon, Northwest Territories, and Nunavut. The Morgentaler Clinic in New Brunswick recently closed but was reopened in January 2015 after the success of lobbying and fundraising efforts, which highlights that access to abortion is still a fraught issue in Canada.[60] Even where services are technically available, there are often other barriers, including quotas, referrals by family physicians (which are not possible for all women, especially those without a family practitioner), and strict gestational time limits. All of these impede access.[61] Many have noted that these barriers create real issues for women and make access to services a reality only for the wealthy. The delay and absence of real access increases physical complications, not to mention the emotional and mental toll it takes on women. It has been aptly noted that although "denied funding does not necessarily prevent poor and low-income women from accessing care, it does prevent their safe and timely access."[62] Because women are the only ones physically requiring these services, the inequities of these limitations on access are absolutely bound to gender, poverty, and true choice.[63]

The courts have recognized this inequality. In the case of *Manitoba v Jane Doe I* in 2004, Justice Oliphant at the Court of Queen's Bench stated that legislation in Manitoba

> that forces women to have to stand in line in an overburdened, publicly-funded health care system and to have to wait for a therapeutic abortion, a procedure that probably must be performed in a timely manner, is a gross violation of the right of women to both liberty and security of the person as guaranteed by s. 7 of the *Charter*.[64]

However, the decision in this case was overturned on appeal. Erdman has noted that a message is being sent that women do not deserve public funding for women's services and that women are not "full and equal members of Canadian society."[65]

It is important to remember that simply the fact that there is no *Criminal Code* provision prohibiting abortion does not mean that abortion is accessible to women because other non-legal impediments also limit women's ability to exercise reproductive choice. As Chris Kaposy and Jocelyn Downie note, when barriers to access exist, a woman who wishes to abort may still be forced to have a child against her will.[66] Thus, more than simply the economic factors must be fully understood to decide if there is true choice among women. Fears of an abusive spouse, or issues with substance abuse and poverty, are as important as wording in the *Criminal*

Code. Some describe what has been called the "liberty argument," which has been defined by Kaposy and Downie. They argue that

> on the one hand, the liberty argument offers the prospect of a justification of the continued decriminalization of abortion in the face of future attempts at re-criminalization – a justification that is broader and stronger than the argument that relies on the right to security of the person. However, if judges believe that women automatically have the ability to make reproductive choices as long as the criminal law is not prohibitive, then they will be less able to see the hardship created by other barriers to reproductive choice, or they may be more inclined to see autonomous choices being made in cases where the capacity for exercising autonomy has actually been restricted ... the capacity to exercise autonomy can be limited in various ways: through external forces, such as a combination of poverty and clinic fees, or through internal forces, such as diminished sense of self-worth that results in an inhibited ability to make major life-decisions for oneself.[67]

Thus, legality cannot necessarily be equated with availability and the Canadian system is not really fulfilling the promise of the autonomy of women and their reproductive choices. Simply having the optics of a Canadian landscape where abortion is "available" does not make it so, especially for the disenfranchised.

Today, the majority of abortions in Canada are procured in clinics rather than hospitals. The 2014 statistics from the Canadian Institute for Health Information (CIHI) reported that of the approximately 91,000 reported abortions in Canada, 39,000 were reported by hospitals, and 52,000 were done at clinics.[68] In other words, almost 60 percent of abortions in Canada occur in private clinics, which means that women are at times limited in their ability to access the procedure in their own communities and must travel to find a practitioner willing and able to provide an abortion.[69] Even with available legal abortions, the risk of having a system where access is still almost impossible for many women is not real equality. Given the restrictions to abortion in Canada, Christabelle Sethna and Marion Doull suggest that women will continue to participate in what they call abortion tourism and seek out abortions elsewhere, which allows politicians to avoid having to deal with the controversy associated with abortion issues, hospitals limiting space for abortion services, medical schools leaving out abortion training in their curricula, and doctors avoiding having to address the issue of referrals or performing the procedure themselves, thereby avoiding possible harassment by anti-choice protesters.[70] Is this really any different than Ms. McCrae seeking her American abortion 136 years ago? The barriers that exist for women who for a variety of reasons desire to terminate their pregnancies today have not shifted significantly from those that were in place during the period of the procedure's illegality, and these continuities around access, safety, viability, morality, and timing signal the need for a new discussion of the practice in Canada.

Better Access through Harm Reduction

In the wider debates about abortion including those in the medico-legal landscape, what is clear is that the dichotomy that exists between pro-life and pro-choice, of which the bright line of being born alive is a part, is a major factor in whether abortion access is available. In the eastern Canadian provinces, the ability of pro-life groups to effectively block the provision of services that are part of the suite of services that all Canadians are supposed to receive through medicare suggests that a polarization continues to exist that factors into the access issue.[71] Recent work by philosopher Shannon Dea posits that we might be able to change the landscape of abortion in Canada if we shift the debate away from rights – which the history demonstrates has been intertwined with morality – towards a focus on reducing or minimizing harm to both the woman and the fetus, something that pro-life and pro-choice advocates agree upon.[72] Indeed, as the cases presented here demonstrate, there are a variety of abortion-related harms (to fetuses at different stages of termination as well as to women) that could be avoided, according to Dea, by a systemic approach to reducing abortion "that combines liberal abortion laws, access to safe abortions, and a broad suite of sexual health and social services" that all women are able to access.[73] Prohibition of, or a limitation of access to, abortions, she argues, has the opposite effect and in fact exacerbates the harms related to both women and fetuses. This is certainly borne out by the historical evidence we have that indicates that, despite issues of illegality and access, women intent on "getting rid of their trouble" will find ways to do so. Perhaps most importantly, the reframing of the debate removes the issue of morality from the issue of access.

If women are to be equal members of Canadian society, the *Charter of Rights and Freedoms* must be interpreted and applied in fulfillment of a broader commitment to transform social and political institutions – including the health care system – in an egalitarian direction wherein women are not only perceived as full members of Canadian society, but believe themselves to be.[74] Instead of paying lip service to equality and pretending that there is a functional system of abortion in Canada, the recognition that there is, at best, functional inaccessibility demonstrates that there is much more work to be done.

Notes

1 *R v Morgentaler* [1988] 1 SCR 30; *Roe v Wade,* 410 US 113 (1973).

2 Tracy Penny, "'Getting Rid of My Trouble': A Social History of Abortion in Ontario, 1880–1939" (master's thesis, Laurentian University, 1995).

3 Angus McLaren and Arlene Tigar McLaren, *The Bedroom and the State: The Changing Practices and Politics of Contraception and Abortion in Canada, 1880–1980* (Oxford: Oxford University Press, 1997); Leslie Reagan, *When Abortion Was a Crime: Women, Medicine and Law in the United States, 1867–1973* (Oakland: University of California Press, 1997); Tracy Penny Light, "Shifting Interests: The Medical Discourse on Abortion in English Canada, 1850–1969" (PhD diss., University of Waterloo, 2003).

4 See Penny Light, "Shifting Interests," and Katrina Ackerman, "In Defence of Reason: Religion, Science, and the Prince Edward Island Anti-abortion Movement, 1969–1988," *Canadian Bulletin of Medical History* 31, 2 (2014): 117–38.

5 See Angus McLaren, "Illegal Operations: Women, Doctors and Abortion, 1886–1939," *Journal of Social History* 26, 4 (1993): 797–816; Constance Backhouse, "Involuntary Motherhood: Abortion, Birth Control and the Law in Nineteenth-Century Canada," *Windsor Yearbook of Access to Justice* 3 (1983): 61; and Penny, "Getting Rid of My Trouble."

6 See Canada, Committee on the Operation of the Abortion Law, *Report of the Committee on the Operation of the Abortion Law* (Ottawa: Minister of Supply and Services, 1977); Angus McLaren and Arlene Tigar McLaren, *The Bedroom and the State*; Janine Brodie, Jane Jenson, and Shelley A.M. Gavigan, *The Politics of Abortion* (Toronto: Oxford University Press, 1992); Penny Light, "Shifting Interests."

7 Chris Kaposy, "Improving Abortion Access in Canada," *Health Care Analysis* 18 (2010): 17–34; McLaren and McLaren, *The Bedroom and the State.*

8 Kaposy, "Improving Abortion Access," 18.

9 Marlene Gerber-Fried, "Abortion in the United States: Barriers to Access," *Health and Human Rights* 4, 2 (2000): 176–77.

10 Sir Edward Coke, 3 Co. Inst. (1648) 50. *In rerum natura* was a phrase used historically in alleging a party was a "fictitious person, and therefore not capable of bringing the action." See Henry Campbell Black, ed., *Black's Law Dictionary,* 7th ed. (St. Paul, MN: West Pub. Co., 1999). For a thorough review of the history of the "born alive" rule, see Gerard Casey, *Born Alive: The Legal Status of the Unborn Child in England and the U.S.A.* (Chichester, UK: Barry Rose Law Publishers, 2005).

11 Ian Kennedy and Andrew Grubb, *Medical Law,* 3rd ed. (London: Oxford University Press, 2000), 1487.

12 *The Criminal Code of Canada*, SC 1892, c 29, s 271. Also see s 272, s 273, and s 274. Section 272 declared: "Every one is guilty of an indictable offence and liable to imprisonment for life who, with intent to procure the miscarriage of any woman, whether she is or is not with child, unlawfully administers to her or causes to be taken by her any drug or other noxious thing, or unlawfully uses any instrument or other means whatsoever with the intent." According to s 273, "Every woman is guilty of an indictable offence and liable to seven years' imprisonment who, whether with child or not, unlawfully administers to herself or permits to be administered to her any drug or other noxious thing, or unlawfully uses on herself or permits to be used on her any instrument or other means whatsoever with intent to procure miscarriage." And s 274 stated: "Every one is guilty of an indictable offence and liable to two years' imprisonment who unlawfully supplies or procures any drug or other noxious thing, or any instrument or thing whatsoever, knowing that the same is intended to be unlawfully used or employed with intent to procure the miscarriage of any woman, whether she is or is not with child."

13 *Roe v Wade*.

14 *Morgentaler*, para 59.

15 Jennifer Ditchburn, "Motion 312: Stephen Woodworth's Controversial Motion on Life Defeated," *Huffington Post*, November 25, 2012, http://www.huffingtonpost.ca/2012/09/26/motion-312_n_1915171.html.

16 This inequality is important, as historians, physicians, and health care experts have noted. For instance, see Ackerman, "In Defense of Reason"; Wendy V. Norman, Judith A. Soon, Nanamma Maughn, and Jennifer Dressler, "Barriers to Rural Induced Abortion Services in Canada: Findings of the British Columbia Abortion Providers Survey (BCAPS)," *PLoS ONE* 8, 6 (2013): 1–7.

17 As Norman and her colleagues note, while most urban abortions adhere to evidence-based guidelines and are performed outside of hospital settings, rural abortions are performed in hospitals where physicians have played a role in how women experience abortion, particularly in terms of moral issues (harassment, stigma, conflict) associated with the procedure. See Wendy V. Norman, Judith A. Soon, Nanamma Maughn, and Jennifer Dressler, "Barriers to Rural Induced Abortion Services in Canada: Findings of the British Columbia Abortion Providers Survey (BCAPS)," *PLOS ONE* 8, 6 (June 2013): 5.

18 For instance, see Penny, "Getting Rid of My Trouble"; Penny Light, "Shifting Interests"; Childbirth by Choice Trust, *No Choice: Canadian Women Tell Their Stories of Illegal Abortion* (Toronto: Childbirth by Choice Trust, 1988); Beth Palmer, "'Lonely, Tragic, but Legally Necessary Pilgrimages': Transnational Abortion Travel in the 1970s," *Canadian Historical Review* 92, 4 (2011): 637–64; Christabelle Sethna, "All Aboard? Canadian Women's Abortion Tourism," in *Women's Health History in North America*, ed. Cheryl Krasnick Warsh (Waterloo, ON: Wilfrid Laurier University Press, 2011), 89–108; and Christabelle Sethna and Marion Doull, "Accidental Tourists: Canadian Women, Abortion Tourism, and Travel," *Women's Studies: An Interdisciplinary Journal* 41, 4 (2012): 457–75.

19 *R v Browne*, [1881] OJ No 244 (Ont Ct Com Pl) affirmed by [1881] OJ No 30, (ONCA).

20 Ibid., para 4. *Nux vomica* is a strychnine derivative and homeopathic remedy used to treat a variety of disorders.

21 Ibid., para 6.

22 Ibid., para 9.

23 Although Ms. McCrae was as much as seven months pregnant, the court never commented that Dr. Pynchon had knowledge of her pregnancy, or should have had knowledge of her pregnancy.

24 *R v Browne*, para 10–12.

25 *Brown*, CA.

26 *R v Browne,* para 24.
27 See Penny, "Getting Rid of My Trouble."
28 See Benjamin E. Hawke, Archives of Ontario (AO), RG 22–392, box 268, York County, 1910.
29 "Dr. Hawke Not Guilty: Jury Acquits Local Physician of Serious Charge," *The Globe,* November 9, 1910, 6.
30 Ibid.
31 "Flight Saved Doctor from Death Penalty," *The Globe,* May 11, 1912, 1.
32 See Penny, "Getting Rid of My Trouble."
33 "Dr. Hawke Not Guilty," *The Globe,* November 9, 1910, 6.
34 An ante-mortem statement, also called a "dying declaration," is admissible in court as an exception to the hearsay rule. The individual's death must be imminent when the declaration is written, and the statement must be about the cause or circumstance of the death.
35 "Flight Saved Doctor," *The Globe,* May 11, 1912, 1.
36 College of Physicians and Surgeons of Ontario, *Announcement of the College of Physicians and Surgeons of Ontario, 1913–1914, Report of Proceedings of Ontario Medical Council* (Toronto: Registry Office, College of Physicians and Surgeons of Ontario, 1913).
37 *R v Sparham,* [1875] OJ No 109 (Ont Ct Com Pl).
38 *R v Sparham,* [1885] OJ No 292 (Ont H Ct J).
39 *Stinson v College of Physicians and Surgeons (Ontario)* (1910), 22 OLR 627 (Ont SC Judicature – H Ct J).
40 Ibid., para 14–16.
41 *Re Robert Telford* (1905), 11 BCR 355 (BCSC). Constance Backhouse, "Physicians, Abortions, and the Law in Early Twentieth-Century Ontario," *Canadian Bulletin of Medical History* 10, 2 (1993): 229n34.
42 "Toronto Doctor Sentenced to Seven Year Term," *Ottawa Citizen,* May 18, 1927.
43 *R v Tass,* [1946] 2 WWR 97 (Man CA), appealed on evidentiary grounds at *R v Tass,* [1946] SCJ No 39 (SCC).
44 Ibid., para 2.
45 Shelley Gavigan, "The Criminal Sanction as It Relates to Human Reproduction: The Genesis of Statutory Prohibition of Abortion," *Journal of Legal History* 5 (1984): 20–43.
46 Angus McLaren, "Birth Control and Abortion in Canada, 1870–1920," *Canadian Historical Review* 59 (1978): 323–28. See also Constance Backhouse, "Involuntary Motherhood." In the United States, see Linda Gordon, *Woman's Body, Woman's Right: Birth Control in America* (New York: Penguin, 1990); Janet Farrell Brodie, *Contraception and Abortion in 19th-Century America* (New York: Cornell University Press, 1994); and Reagan, *When Abortion Was a Crime.*
47 Abortion was defined as a crime punishable by law for anyone who attempted to procure, assisted in procuring, or supplied the means of abortion, including the woman obtaining the abortion, whether she was actually pregnant or not. See Penny Light, "Shifting Interests," Chapter 1.
48 R.V. Pierce, *The People's Common Sense Medical Adviser in Plain English or Medicine Simplified* (Buffalo, NY: World's Dispensary Printing Office and Bindery, 1888), 750.
49 Editorial, "Abortionists," *Canada Lancet,* 21 (1889): 217; Editorial, "Criminal Abortion," *Canada Lancet,* 4 (1871): 185.
50 Criminal Case files from Ontario between 1880 and 1929 indicate that there were two categories of abortionists – those considered to be professionals (who had a history of performing the procedure) and those who were non-professionals (who had not performed abortions before). The number of non-professionals greatly outweighed the number of professionals, representing 72 percent of the total number of charges. Many of these were either

women or men who were the partner or spouse of the woman on whom the abortion was attempted or performed. Others were family members, friends, or acquaintances who, for one reason or another, decided to help the woman out of her trouble. At least fifteen individuals who were charged with abortion were considered to be professionals. While some of these were irregulars, at least seven were regular doctors and accounted for 28 percent or 30 of the total 108 charges. See Penny, "Getting Rid of My Trouble," especially Chapters 2 and 3.

51 Peter J. Mitham, "For 'The Honour and Dignity of the Profession': Organized Medicine in Colonial New Brunswick, 1793–1860," *Canadian Bulletin of Medical History* 13 (1996): 83–108; Wendy Mitchinson, *The Nature of Their Bodies: Women and Their Doctors in Victorian Canada* (Toronto: University of Toronto Press, 1991), 139. See also Michael McCulloch, "'Dr. Tumblety, the Indian Herb Doctor': Politics, Professionalism, and Abortion in Mid-Nineteenth-Century Montreal," *Canadian Bulletin of Medical History* 10 (1993): 49–66.

52 Kristin Luker, *Abortion and the Politics of Motherhood* (Los Angeles: University of California Press, 1984), 32.

53 The American Medical Association estimated that a doctor needed two thousand patients to earn an adequate living yet in Canada in 1891, the ratio of doctors to the population was 1:1079. Penny, "Getting Rid of My Trouble," 54. See also Mitchinson, *The Nature of Their Bodies,* 29.

54 Alfred A. Andrews, "On Abortion," *Canada Lancet* 7, 9 (1875): 291. A similar statement was made by Dr. J.C. in Andrew Nebinger, "Criminal Abortion: Its Extent and Prevention," in *Abortion in Nineteenth-Century America,* ed. Charles Rosenberg and Carroll Smith-Rosenberg (New York: Arno Press, 1974), 9.

55 Joseph G. Ryan has noted, for instance, the difference between Catholic and Protestant physicians when it came to the practices of craniotomy and embryotomy in obstetrics. Craniotomy is the perforation and destruction of the fetal skull with cutting instruments, which is generally followed by embryotomy or the removal of the fetus in pieces. Both were employed to remove a fetus in cases of caesarian section for obstructed birth. Catholics condemned craniotomy if it was performed prior to the death of the fetus because they believed it to be immoral and improper to sacrifice the life of an innocent being. The challenge of waiting, however, was that the death of the mother might occur. See "The Chapel and the Operating Room: The Struggle of Roman Catholic Clergy, Physicians, and Believers with the Dilemmas of Obstetric Surgery, 1800–1900," *Bulletin of the History of Medicine* 76 (2002): 461–94. See also Wendy Mitchinson, *Giving Birth in Canada, 1900–1950* (Toronto: University of Toronto Press, 2002), 236. Similarly, birth control practices were also illegal and were employed by both Protestants and Catholics. See Diane Dodd, "The Canadian Birth Control Movement on Trial, 1936–1937," *Histoire sociale/Social History* 16, 32 (1983): 411–28.

56 *The Hamilton Spectator,* March 18, 1881, 4.

57 Canadian Medical Association, *CMA Policy: Induced Abortion* (Ottawa: Canadian Medical Association, 1988).

58 *CMA Policy.*

59 Joanna N. Erdman, "In the Back Alleys of Health Care: Abortion, Equality and Community in Canada," *Emory Law Journal* 56 (2007): 1093.

60 Tracy Glynn, "Service Restored: New Abortion Clinic Opens in Fredericton," *Rabble.ca,* http://rabble.ca/news/2015/01/service-restored-new-abortion-clinic-opens-fredericton.

61 Erdman, "In the Back Alleys of Health Care," 1095.

62 Ibid., 1096.

63 Ibid.

64 *Manitoba v Jane Doe I,* (2004) 248 DLR (4th) at 564. This case involved a class action against the province of Manitoba because women were having disparate dealings with the system, and those on public assistance were receiving reimbursement while others seeking an abortion at a private clinic because of wait times were not.

65 Erdman, "In the Back Alleys of Health Care," 1100.

66 Kaposy and Downie, "Judicial Reasoning about Pregnancy and Choice," *Health Law Journal* 16 (2008): 281, 296. The authors go on to note, at 297–98, that inability to pay financially may be coupled with other factors to prevent access to an abortion. They note that, in reference to a statement made by a judge in a recent case, "Prince Edward Island has no abortion providers, and a woman may have to travel over 400 km to reach the nearest centre providing abortion. In situations in which a woman must incur the costs of travel to access an abortion, take time off work or school and overcome the difficulty of coming up with excuses for her absence, the fact that she must additionally pay for the abortion out of pocket could work in concert with these other barriers to deny the choice to terminate ... We are making a plea for the courts to be aware of the various impediments that continue to inhibit reproductive choice even though abortion is decriminalized in Canada."

67 Kaposy and Downie, "Judicial Reasoning," 302–3.

68 Canadian Institute for Health Information (CIHI), February 2014, https://www.cihi.ca/en/ta_10_alldatatables20120417_en.pdf.

69 A recently updated list of abortion clinics in Canada compiled by the Abortion Rights Coalition of Canada (ARCC) shows that most communities do not have an abortion clinic so women must travel to access these services if they need them. See http://www.arcc-cdac.ca/list-abortion-clinics-canada.pdf.

70 Sethna and Doull, "Accidental Tourists," 471. See also Gerber-Fried, "Abortion in the United States: Barriers to Access."

71 Ackerman, "In Defence of Reason."

72 Shanon Dea, "A Harm Reduction Approach to Abortion" in *Without Apology: Writings on Abortion in Canada,* ed. Shannon Stettner (Edmonton: Athabasca University Press, 2016), 321.

73 Ibid., 327.

74 Erdman, "In the Back Alleys of Abortion," 1155.

9

Morgentaler and the Technological Production of Embodiment

Jen Rinaldi

THE CASE OF *REGINA v Morgentaler* set the tone for Canadian reproductive rights for over twenty-five years in two respects relevant to this essay.[1] First, reproductive rights were grounded in the *Canadian Charter of Rights and Freedoms* section 7 right to security of the person, which is a personal right to corporeal control. Second, and intimately connected, these rights were situated in a medical context and exercised within a reified relationship between physician and patient; as a result, reproductive issues became health issues. While an important step, the *Morgentaler* precedent reflects a problematic understanding of the scope and nature of reproductive rights, and this understanding has resulted in damaging implications for women.[2]

I show how legal terminology and medical tools have circumscribed the body boundaries of rights-bearers. Using feminist scholarship as my lens of analysis and the *Morgentaler* ruling as my springboard into this analysis, I argue that the tethering of reproductive rights to narrow, liberal notions of autonomy has not captured particular nuances to reproductive decision-making. Further, the individuation of the fetus and the medicalization of the pregnant body have proven ineffectual frames for understanding embodiment, and have led to the mistaking of medical compliance for reproductive freedom. I hope to shed light on how reproductive technologies have been used to crystallize these concerns and how their purposes and processes might be transformed.

Morgentaler and the Autonomy Precedent

In 1983, Dr. Henry Morgentaler, Dr. Leslie Frank Smoling, and Dr. Robert Scott were charged with illegally inducing miscarriages at a Toronto clinic. They were accused of being in violation of section 251 of the *Criminal Code*, according to which abortion was considered an indictable offence unless it was performed in a hospital by a doctor and was approved by a committee of physicians who determined that the medical treatment would serve the purpose of saving a pregnant woman's life or health.[3] The Supreme Court of Canada considered whether section 251 of the *Criminal Code* infringed on the Charter's section 2 (a) right to freedom of conscience; section 7 rights to life, liberty, and security of the person; or section 12 right not to be subjected to cruel and unusual punishment. In 1988, a Supreme Court majority of five to two agreed that section 251 infringed on women's section 7 right to security of the person, and that the deprivation of this right was not in accordance with the principles of fundamental justice.[4]

The justices in the majority wrote three concurrent rulings.[5] Chief Justice Brian Dickson and Justice Antonio Lamer wrote that section 251 "forces women to carry a foetus to term contrary to their own priorities and aspirations and which imposes serious delay causing increased physical and psychological trauma."[6] For Justice Bertha Wilson, the only female Supreme Court justice at the time, section 251 violated section 7 rights to security of the person and liberty: "liberty in a free and democratic society does not require the state to approve the personal decisions made by its citizens; it does, however, require the state to respect them."[7] Justice Wilson went on to write that the decision to terminate a pregnancy was "essentially a moral decision, a matter of conscience" and thus section 251 also violated the Charter's section 2 (a) right to freedom of conscience.[8]

Justice Wilson cited autonomy when ruling that section 251 violated the right to liberty: "the right to 'liberty' contained in section 7 guarantees to every individual a degree of personal autonomy over important decisions intimately affecting their private lives."[9] She held that at the core of every Charter right and freedom was the notion that "the state will respect choices made by individuals and, to the greatest extent possible, will avoid subordinating these choices to any one conception of the good life."[10] Therefore, every right and freedom entails respect for autonomous decisions to the extent that autonomy is interpreted as the condition by which people make choices freely.

Granted, the other justices in the majority did not argue that section 251 of the *Criminal Code* violated the Charter's section 7 right to liberty, nor did they argue that the section 7 right to security of the person should be interpreted so widely as to include the promotion of autonomy despite the argument made by the defence. The appellants' counsel, Morris Manning, had used American constitutional theory to argue their case: "[section 7] is a wide-ranging right to control one's own life and to promote one's individual autonomy. The right would therefore include a right to privacy and a right to unfettered decisions about one's life."[11] Manning was referring to the landmark American case on abortion rights, *Roe v Wade* (1973), according to which the Fourteenth Amendment's Due Process Clause grants women entitlement to privacy in reproductive contexts, at least until the fetus becomes viable at twenty-eight weeks of pregnancy.[12] In response to counsel, Chief Justice Dickson (penning the ruling with which Justice Lamer was in agreement) cautioned against interpreting section 7 through the lens of American theories: "we would, in my view, do our own Constitution a disservice to simply allow the American debate to define us, all the while ignoring the truly fundamental structural differences between the two constitutions."[13] He held, in other words, that it would be problematic to draw a one-to-one comparison between the Canadian principle of security of the person and the legal principle of privacy in the United States, where the latter principle is more expansive and directly tied to autonomy interests.

It might help to unpack the differences between the two principles. Within the 1973 *Roe v Wade* ruling, privacy was linked to "personal 'liberty' embodied in the Fourteenth Amendment."[14] Although the term is not explicitly found in the United States Constitution, "the Court ... recognized that a right of personal privacy, or a guarantee of certain areas or zones of privacy, does exist under the Constitution."[15] This was possible because the right to privacy was understood to have broad applications: "the Constitution nowhere mentions a specific right of personal choice in matters of marriage and family life, but the 'liberty' protected by the Due Process Clause of the Fourteenth Amendment covers more than those freedoms explicitly named in the Bill of Rights".[16] The concept of privacy broadly, at least in the United States, has been applied in an effort to protect individuals from interference when making decisions. In contrast, in Canadian law, the security of the person interest that grounds reproductive rights has a more specific application: "'security of the person' is a more circumscribed interest [which] ... at most relates to the concept of physical control, simply protecting the individual's interest in his or her bodily integrity."[17] In other words, security of the person protects persons strictly from physical and psychological harm.

Despite Chief Justice Dickson's caution, we might still interpret section 7 in a way that incorporates the concept of reproductive autonomy. Canadian theorist Carolyn McLeod considers the effect of interference with reproductive autonomy and demonstrates that there is a connection between autonomy and reproductive control: "If little respect is given to women's autonomy ... they will lack control over how they reproduce or attempt to reproduce."[18] Reproductive decisions thus necessarily involve or affect women's bodies, and the extent to which those decisions are freely made impacts women physically and psychologically. We might also look to bioethicist Laura M. Purdy, who argues that women's autonomy interests are upheld when they possess corporeal control: "autonomy is particularly important for women ... because reproduction still takes place in women's bodies."[19] Women may experience hardships related to unwanted pregnancies, such as bodily transformations, health risks, distress, stigma, and poverty, because – as Chief Justice Dickson held – the criminalization of abortion ran contrary to women's priorities and aspirations. The chief justice acknowledged that, in reproductive matters, reproductive control involves a degree of self-direction, of acting in accordance with one's own values. Therefore, though his ruling does not so explicitly reference autonomy as Justice Wilson's did, even his narrow definition of the right to security of the person may be framed with concepts associated with autonomy.

Autonomy, Liberalism, and Gender

The *Morgentaler* case marks a historic victory, but how the decision was argued matters. An analysis of the arguments – as legal scholar Sanda Rodgers puts it, of the "rights-based, neo-liberal, privatized argumentation that characterizes the Supreme Court jurisprudence on reproductive autonomy" – points the way to the work yet to be done.[20] So far, we know that the rhetoric employed in this case alludes to autonomy, which has a long conceptual history. The term – derived from the Greek *autos* (self) and *nomos* (government or law) – is especially prominent in liberal theories and is understood to refer to self-rule or self-government.[21] Autonomy is a property of persons that pertains to their motivations to act; they may be motivated by particular interests, purposes, reasons, values, and so forth, but the point is that they are self-motivated, rather than moved by external factors or constrained from action by other people.

Though not entirely synonymous, the concepts of autonomy and liberty are intimately related; while autonomy refers to the states and motivations involved in choice, liberty is more generally the ability to make meaningful, independent choices. Negatively and most simply construed, the ability to act requires freedom from the restraint of human interference, formally the space needed for making a decision.[22] Theorizing autonomy, Thomas Hobbes claimed that only coercion constitutes an impediment to free action, and that influence, manipulation, pressure, or anything other than coercion as physical force does not render man unfree.[23]

The theoretical work done on autonomy, then, has posited a certain sort of self: one who is self-sufficient and independent, one who is radically isolated when making decisions, and one who is entirely responsible for the decisions made. The self is thought to be purest when it is decontextualized and neutralized, and yet it bears striking resemblance to the traditional masculine identity. Feminist political philosopher Marilyn Friedman lists characteristics associated with autonomous selves – rationality, independence, outspokenness – and notes that these characteristics tend to be framed as masculine, while "traits popularly regarded as feminine, by contrast, have no distinctive connection to autonomy – social interactiveness, for example."[24] Women have been bracketed out of the category of autonomous agent because they have been more explicitly framed within social networks rather than as isolated individuals. They have functioned within family and household relationships, and have been socially, politically, and economically rendered dependent. Further, the category of woman is associated with pregnancy, an experience that is corporeally incompatible with the conceptual qualifications of autonomy. The autonomous self, for all his rugged individualism, is defined by body boundaries, by the skin that serves as insulation and isolation from all that is other. Pregnancy, in contrast, "defies a sharp opposition between self and other, between the inside and the outside of the body."[25] The pregnant woman is simultaneously one and two.[26]

The problem with grounding reproductive rights in autonomy language is that jurisprudence based on notions of autonomy reflects liberal traditions that cannot properly account for women's decisions and embodiments: "The language of the *Morgentaler* judgments of the majority was a ringing restatement of an *individual* right ... and is thus consistent with the emphasis on abortion as a private and individual matter."[27] Since *Morgentaler*, Canadian women have been guaranteed the right to decisions related to corporeal control, the right to autonomous decision-making in matters pertaining to their bodies. There is another implication to explore, and in so doing we reintroduce the medical context within which decisions are being made.

The Medicalization of Pregnancy and Labour

Legal scholar Shelley A.M. Gavigan is critical of the autonomy rhetoric used in the *Morgentaler* ruling, and also the framing of reproductive matters as strictly medical: "the victory was ... contradictory in that the Court reinforced the notion that abortion is a medical matter."[28] The case questioned the guilt of physicians performing abortions, not the women seeking out abortions. The decision rendered was meant to protect not only women from constraints on their freedom, but primarily physicians from unjust indictment. Indeed, the way in which the case was argued and decided reflects how intimately involved physicians are in reproductive decision-making processes. They need not be, for they have not always been. As midwifery and bioethics scholar Barbara Katz Rothman explains, "the transition from almost all births taking place at home to almost all births taking place in the hospital took just over two generations. In those two generations, birth changed from being an event in the life of a family to being a medical procedure."[29] This transition was due to physician lobbying, which displaced the role of midwives in the birthing process. The argument made at the time was that pregnancy and labour might be conducted more safely and with lowered mortality rates if supervised by physicians.[30] Physicians argued, in other words, that they were needed.

This invention of a need for doctors and the consequential medicalization of pregnancy and labour have had the effect of decontextualizing women-turned-patients, of removing them from their original decision-making contexts and situating them instead in dyadic exchanges with medical practitioners. Within medical spaces, reproductive autonomy is enacted only insofar as women consent to or refuse treatments, choose to heed or neglect physician advice, or avail themselves of or decline health care services. Decisions have come to be made relative to the medical services physicians provide or recommend.

Current health care models, within which pregnancy is now squarely located, frame health care resources as the means and entitlements by which people might cure, repair, or manage biological conditions that function as impediments to meaningful social opportunities. The condition of pregnancy under such models, though not quite identical to pathology, is a functional limitation that women manage via gynaecological appointments, dietary recommendations, and prenatal vitamins, all of which are meant to stave off complications and reduce risk.[31] Though pregnant bodies cannot be cured outright, they are considered unruly enough to be in need of maintenance. While health care provisions are offered on the basis of need, the language of risk in association with pregnancy constructs women's need, and builds a relationship of dependency on medical professionals.[32]

Pregnant women's exercise of autonomy in health care spaces is limited, then, for it occurs within closed contexts based on the information that physicians deem reasonable, and it involves very little agency. That is, limiting the exercise of autonomy to the making of decisions about consent "reinforces the intrinsically passive nature of patient 'participation.'"[33] When discussing the physician–patient encounter, feminist and disability scholar Susan Wendell describes how medical practitioners have the power "to describe us to ourselves and others."[34] In her example, a patient may consult a physician regarding symptoms, but if the physician cannot discern a physical cause the patient is told nothing is wrong with her. In effect, the physician invalidates the pain, the fatigue, and the dizziness that the patient has been experiencing. Wendell elaborates:

> The cognitive and social authority of medicine to describe our bodies affects how we experience our bodies and our selves, how our society describes our experiences and validates/invalidates them, how our society supports or fails to support our bodily sufferings and struggles, and what our culture knows about the human body ... The authority of medicine tends to delegitimize our experiences of our bodies as sources of knowledge about them, because the authoritative, that is, the medical and scientific, descriptions of our bodies are third-person descriptions of physical conditions.[35]

In other words, patients lack the citational force physicians have to call medical conditions by name, and without that force their embodied experience goes unrecognized.

Physicians therefore describe and explain their patients' bodies, and in so doing, they claim, control, and reshape those bodies – a practice which is possible thanks to legal interventions that have been used to make sense of phenomena like pregnancy. Legal rules structure interactions between patients and medical practitioners and regulate patients' bodies within these interactions.[36] A legal scholar interested in reproductive bodies, Isabel Karpin, claims that "in the process of regulating the female body, the law legislates its shape, its lineaments, and its boundaries ... [The law] collaborates with other defining discourses such as science."[37] That is, legal and rights-based rhetoric has the effect of circumscribing and defining body boundaries and this is accomplished in collaboration with medical practitioners and the paradigms within which they operate.

Technological Intervention and the Separation of Woman and Fetus

In order to unpack what medical discourses contribute to the ideological delineation of embodiment, it is important to note that health care contexts are rife with gadgetry: "The primary characteristic of the modern medical model of health and illness in general is that it is based on the ideology of technology ... with its values of efficiency and rationality, practical organization, systematizing, and controlling."[38] Especially in the case of reproductive health, the relocation of women to hospital settings has increasingly witnessed technological intervention and innovation.

A key example, ultrasound technology, was introduced to reproductive health in the late 1950s (thus coinciding with the trend towards hospital-based births) and has since become "one of the most common rituals of pregnancy in the late twentieth-century urban North America."[39] Developed by obstetrician and gynaecologist Ian Donald, the technology applies sound waves to a woman's body and produces a screen image in a form that has become iconic. Medical historian Malcolm Nicolson and engineer John E.E. Fleming, who developed the first mass-produced ultrasound scanner, suggest that "the ultrasound scanner does not reveal the fetus directly or unproblematically."[40] What the technology can yield is an image that is coded according to socially produced meanings.[41]

Fetal imagery produced via ultrasound technology has captured the imagination of our visually-dominated culture.[42] More than that, interpretations of this imagery have fuelled the cultural imagination regarding fetal–maternal identities and relationships. The tool may be used to render public that which is private: "the technological removal of the fetus from the 'secrecy of the womb' through ultrasound and other prenatal procedures gives the fetus social recognition as an individual separate from the mother."[43] The technology facilitates or forces the confrontation of a pregnant woman with the contents of her body, and personifies those contents. Ultrasound has thus been described as a technological quickening, compared to the phenomenon wherein a woman feels fetal movements.[44] Whereas quickening once signalled pregnancy and has been described as rendering pregnancy real, the ultrasound appointment has now replaced this experience as the means by which pregnancy reportedly feels real. Women come to know they are pregnant now not through bodily experience but by medical validation: "meeting" the fetus, or seeing a visual representation of the fetus, mediated by medical practitioners who produce and interpret the image.[45] Physicians have taken on the role of describing pregnancy to their patients.

Although the use of the technology to monitor and regulate pregnancy is meant to reduce parental anxiety and forge an emotional relationship with the fetus, the ritualizing of ultrasound procedures has had the effect of influencing compliance with physician recommendations regarding prenatal care, including food, cigarette, and substance use.[46] Feminist philosopher Rebecca Kukla explains how reproductive rituals like ultrasound have helped shape both fetal identity and the mother's role, which in turn has affected the politics of abortion: "as a shared pregnancy narrative becomes canonized, and the inside of the pregnant body is transformed into a public arena, the individuals outside of pregnant bodies are rendered permeable and transparent."[47] The ultrasound appointment as ritual legitimizes cultural understandings of the fetus as fragile and vulnerable, and the womb as a hostile environment for fetal development, as long as prospective mothers fail to comply with medical counsel. The bifurcation of woman and fetus has thus led not only to the personification of the fetus, but also to the corollary: the vilification of the woman when her interests collide with fetal health, when she is unable or unwilling to maintain and discipline her body for the sake of the fetus.[48]

Katz Rothman considers the ideological underpinnings that shape motherhood and pregnancy, including technology. Ideologies have the power to frame identities and relationships to the extent that they are internalized, becoming "part of common sense"; the internalization of oppressive ideology has a deleterious effect on reproductive decision-making.[49]

Katz Rothman explains how individuation has been accomplished through the use of technology in a culture that inferiorizes women: "in patriarchy, the sense of separation of the fetus and mother was already there as a concept; the new technology allows the separation to be reified."[50] Maternal responsibility, understood as dedication to pregnancy monitoring and maintenance, might appear to be autonomously carried out, at least through a liberal lens that understands all action absent of coercion to be free, but instead happens as a result of the internalization of ideological systems that are designed to control reproduction.

The liberal autonomy of Canadian jurisprudence cannot do the work needed to counter discourses that would seek to limit women's reproductive control, for liberal autonomy requires that we isolate and medicalize pregnant bodies, that we understand pregnant women to be locked in a rights conflict with that which they are carrying. This conflict, predicated on the conceptual separation of woman and fetus, does not properly convey the intercorporeal, interrelational experience of pregnancy, but instead reflects the effects of ideologies that have become ingrained in public consciousness such that they have set the terms of the moral disagreement over abortion. This has been a problem to the extent that early and ardent proponents of reproductive autonomy have let the terms of the debate be set for them. Liberal feminist positions have sought to address or invalidate a rights conflict between woman and fetus. For instance, some have claimed that the fetus may have the right to life, but not the right to make use of the body of an unwilling woman.[51] Others have argued that the fetus has no moral status, and thus has no stake in the rights conflict as long as a number of conditions for personhood are not met.[52] The underlying assumption that the abortion debate can be framed according to who has rights and which rights take priority has had the effect of rooting reproductive rights in personal, competitive notions of autonomy. The arguments made in the *Morgentaler* ruling are not surprising, then, for they are part of a long conceptual history – one in which assumptions have been reified by the ways technological interpretations have defined women's body boundaries.

Relational Reproductive Autonomy

Feminist scholar Elizabeth Wolgast rejects rights discourses because they require that persons be atomistic, self-interested, and in competition with others.[53] Similarly, Carol Gilligan and Nel Noddings stress the value of interpersonal relationships over moral entitlements, seeking to build codes of ethics along lines of relations rather than according to distribution among individuals.[54] In order for the concept of reproductive autonomy to be compatible with these feminisms, it cannot be a concept derived from liberal ideologies.

How does a relational interpretation of autonomy apply to reproductive experiences? We might consider how feminist bioethicists and litigators have been drawing attention to the necessarily relational nature of pregnancy. The "imperative to describe the woman and fetus as either one being or two, but not both one and two," Karpin argues, "indicates the limitations of logocentric and phallocentric discourse."[55] Contrasting with this interpretation of bodies, women – especially in relation to pregnancy – experience their bodies as resistant to "an optics of the skin."[56] Along similar lines, Katz Rothman holds that the experience of pregnancy challenges arguments rooted in personal autonomy:

> We have motherhood, the physical embodiment of connectedness. We have in every pregnant woman the living proof that individuals do not enter the world as autonomous, atomistic, isolated beings, but begin socially, being connected. And we have in every pregnant woman a walking contradiction to the segmentation of our lives: pregnancy does not permit it. In pregnancy the private self, the sexual self, familial self, announces itself wherever we go. Motherhood is the embodied challenge to liberal philosophy, and that, I fear, is why a society founded on and committed to liberal philosophical principles cannot deal well with motherhood.[57]

While many feminist perspectives on reproductive autonomy acknowledge that fetal existence and welfare cannot be understood as separate from the pregnant woman, they fail to account for the implication that liberal interpretations of reproductive autonomy require that the woman and fetus be understood as separate and in conflict.[58] The erection of borderlines around the woman, and the continued characterization of the maternal–fetal relationship as oppositional, runs counter to the phenomenology of pregnancy. The fetus could have moral value, then, not due to abstract notions of individualism, but instead as a result of being "related to the human community in and through the bodies of the women who gestate them."[59]

In her later work, feminist philosopher Mary Anne Warren argues that birth is a morally significant event that should have bearing on the question of reproductive rights. In her own words:

> Birth is morally significant because it marks the end of one relationship and the beginning of others. It marks the end of pregnancy, a relationship so intimate that it is impossible to extend the equal protection of the law to fetuses without severely infringing women's most basic rights. Birth also marks the beginning of the infant's existence as a socially responsive member of the human community. Although the infant is not instantly transformed into a person at the moment of birth, it does become a biologically separate human being.[60]

Consider in the above passage that Warren is not saying that birth marks the individuation of persons; she is not recommending a new cut-off point for assigning moral significance, alongside viability, self-awareness, and the like. She is instead arguing that birth marks a transition in relationships, a shift from the profoundly intimate bond between woman and fetus, two bodies as one, to a situation of engagement with others within a greater network of, if not intercorporeality, at least interconnectivity.

When we introduce notions of relationships and responsibility to discussions about pregnancy, we may well be painting a more accurate picture of women's experiences, thereby erasing the body boundaries that are foundational to rights conflict rhetoric. But do these notions so complicate reproductive autonomy as to render the principle useless? Philosopher and women's studies scholar Anne Donchin argues that, to the contrary, reproductive autonomy can be strengthened with a more central focus on connectivity and community: "a relational perspective can weave its way through shifting relationships and novel reproductive arrangements without jeopardizing the reproductive autonomy of the individuals involved."[61] The intercorporeal experience of pregnant bodies should disrupt conceptions of self, such that we no longer limit autonomy analysis to the sphere of individuals. This is because instances of intercorporeality should deconstruct normalized embodiments, rather than simply be understood as exceptions to them. With this frame of reference in mind, we can more readily account for how reproductive decision-making happens within a vast context of interrelations. As Sara Goering writes:

> Interpersonal connections and influences from intimates can enable rather than present obstacles to an individual's autonomy. If our selves are connected in this way, the requirements for autonomy cannot simply exclude the needs and interests of our loved ones from influencing our decisions. Though relational autonomy theorists can recognize that the influence of some intimates can present obstacles to autonomy ... they also argue that supportive personal relations provide the conditions under which autonomy is even possible.[62]

When identity is no longer understood to be singular when boundary lines between persons blur, decision-making comes to be seen as more nuanced and collaborative, where autonomy is borne out of the support and advice and respect of others, with an emphasis on relationality over responsibility. A refashioned concept of autonomy would consider concerns like: grandmother raised me Catholic, and an abortion would break her heart; my mother is ecstatic about my pregnancy, even offered to move in and help; my boyfriend and I are just not ready to settle down yet; or my wife and I have been trying to have a baby for years. As a result, it would recognize other people as much more relevant to decision-making. Such a perspective opens up the dyadic relationship women have with medical practitioners, and perhaps in so doing complicates our medical paradigms.

It is important, too, to re-embody our discourses, to remember that reproductive decisions, which have been protected thanks to a Charter right to corporeal control, revolve around a sort of corporeality that has not been imagined well in theory and law. Disability and bioethics scholar Margrit Shildrick believes it is possible to restructure legal protections by dropping all our discourses on principles and rights entirely and taking the body as our starting point, for the body more accurately conceived displaces what it means in liberal theory to be an autonomous self: "any critique of consent which takes health care as its substantive field must inevitably come up against the materiality of the body."[63]

Technology Reoriented

I posit that while reproductive technologies have been used to reinterpret and restrain the body, they also have the power to reveal the complexities of embodiment. Sociologist Nikolas Rose says of the potential of reproductive technologies: "these new technologies, then, do not just seek to cure organize damage or disease, nor to enhance health ... Their key feature is their forward vision."[64] What is this new way forward? If we are to continue to take ultrasound as our example, and if we strip away the social work that fetal imagery has thus far accomplished, we see that the intentions and design motivating ultrasound's invention almost immediately got away from its inventor. Ian Donald meant ultrasound to affirm fetal life and to contribute to the abortion debate as a response to any possible defence of abortion. He even employed the machinery to manipulate patients seeking abortions, to convince them to change their minds, thinking they would be incapable of terminating pregnancy if only they saw the fetus. But the tool became essential to diagnosing pregnancy early, and diagnosing fetal impairment; it has served as a starting point, in other words, on roads that lead to termination, much to Donald's chagrin.[65] This would seem to suggest that the interpretive work ultrasound imagery accomplishes is not fixed but fluid – it is complex, contradictory, and contingent.

Indeed, the imagery yielded by ultrasound is not just fetal; it is simultaneously one body and two, even one becoming two. With the development of new technologies and their interpretation via a feminist lens, we could see "the emergence of a new form of person": the shifting relationship between genetics and identity deeply undermines any concept of the moral agent as an autonomous sovereign subject.[66]

This emergent, transgressive embodiment, though constantly being contained through medical and legal discourses, has the power to challenge those discourses by confronting the abstract self, that impossible regulatory standard. Through this confrontation, we see that "the subject is always irreducibly embodied."[67] That is, technology that can show us our insides and contents may ground us in a body that philosophical tradition has worked to distance us from. The fact that our interiors are no longer so esoteric, and are now possible to access and visualize, might help support an understanding that our corporeal experiences are not necessarily contained within our subjective frame, but situated within and extending into our worlds.

Reproductive technologies paired with a feminist lens might reshape body boundaries, especially those of pregnant bodies, eliciting a complex redefinition of self. Says Karpin: "[our technology-derived] discourses, indifferent to the surface of the body as a marker of identity, demand a more complex understanding of the self in law. What happens, for instance, when [they] reveal that we are all 'leaky,' boundaryless, and transgressive?"[68] The fetus need not be rendered in sharp relief – with lines of delineation so crisply drawn – if the uterus, the placenta, and the umbilical cord were reincorporated into our visual rhetoric as something other than environment. The depiction of the fetus in situ has the power to illustrate human vulnerability and the necessity of our situatedness. In other words, imagery of bodily interiors, especially those of pregnant bodies – where multiple, developing, and necessarily connected subjectivities can be contained in the same skin – could reorient our discourses "in order to open a space for subjects who are connected, vulnerable, and dependent [or in other words] who cannot shed their dependencies in order to become the liberal subject."[69]

We have seen how ultrasound technology has been wielded in problematic ways, but the technology itself, its meaning and purposes, are contingent on how it is used, and I believe it can be used in the service of reconceptualizing the legal and medical self. Such a self could transgress the boundary lines that carve out rights-bearers, their discrete entitlements, and their responsibilities. Such a self could suggest that decision-making cannot happen in a vacuum any more than the early stages of human life can develop in empty open space. If such a self took hold in the cultural imaginary, the questions posed around abortion access and the arguments grounding it might shift such that we could concern ourselves less with removing all obstacles in the way of atomistic decision-making and instead consider more closely the conditions that make reproductive decisions possible, conditions that surround us like amniotic fluid.

o o o

I suggest that technology both undergirds current paradigms and may function as a catalyst for paradigmatic shifts. Perhaps technology has the power to alter legal discourse as law and policy are catching up to innovation. Regulation of reproductive technologies in Canada consists of recommendations and guidelines offered by medical colleges, as well as legislation already at risk of being outdated.[70] The scope of this paper is limited to ultrasound, an early development in the story of reproductive technologies. Left unmentioned are the genetic screening and testing technologies that see little regulation outside international treaties, as well as pre-implantation genetic diagnosis and in vitro fertilization, which change the very processes of conception. While our courts have been loath to intervene and legislate the medical profession, their hands may well be forced as we find ourselves coming to terms with what reproductive technologies tell us about bodies and selves.

Can work on reproductive technologies, even just a more careful examination of jurisprudence regarding reproductive technologies, embody the principle of autonomy and render it feminist? While some scholars mentioned here recommend the dismissal of rights-based rhetoric entirely, such a thing may not be immediately possible in the mammoth, incrementally moving legal system we have built up. Perhaps autonomy can still serve as an effective tool, if only recalibrated and recontextualized. Such a tool can complicate reproductive technologies and the rituals that have formed around their use. An autonomy reconceived may shed its liberal baggage, which often confuses privilege for the ideal self – a self that is atomistic and isolated, unencumbered by historical and systemic disadvantage, and compliant with medical discourses. Without such baggage, autonomous reproductive decisions and practices can be taken up by impoverished women who require access to reproductive services, by disabled women no longer so concerned by their children's inheritance, and by queer persons interested in developing their families. The imagery technology produces may never be politically neutral, may never be vacant of social meaning, but it can be imbued with new meaning. Rather than pitting mother against child, it can instead tell a story of a deeply embedded, interconnected subject that reaches into the womb and out past the skin.

Notes

1 *R v Morgentaler* [1988] 1 SCR 30, https://scc-csc.lexum.com/scc-csc/scc-csc/en/item/288/index.do [*Morgentaler*].

2 Although I use the term "woman" throughout this essay, I'd like to recognize that pregnancy is not limited to women. Trans, genderqueer, and gender nonconforming bodies can experience pregnancy and have a place in conversations about reproductive justice.

3 From Pierre Elliott Trudeau's legislative reforms in 1969 until the *Morgentaler* case in 1988, the *Criminal Code's* s 251 (1) read as follows: "Every one who, with intent to procure the miscarriage of a female person, whether or not she is pregnant, uses any means for the purpose of carrying out his intention is guilty of an indictable offence and is liable to imprisonment for life." The only exceptions to this rule could be found in s 251 (4), which outlined the process for acquiring written documentation from a medical practitioner certifying that the pregnancy endangered the woman's life or health, and subsequently seeking approval for an abortion from a Therapeutic Abortion Committee. The plaintiffs in *Morgentaler* challenged the narrow limitations found in this section.

4 The ruling in *Morgentaler* further determined that the violation of women's right to security of the person did not satisfy s 1 of the Charter. Cases alleging Charter violations involve a two-step process. First, the court determines whether a Charter right has been violated. If there has been a Charter violation, the court then determines whether the violation can be saved by s 1, which reads: "The *Canadian Charter of Rights and Freedoms* guarantees the rights and freedoms set out in it subject only to such reasonable limits prescribed by law as can be demonstrably justified in a free and democratic society."

5 There were three concurrent rulings in total, but in this chapter I focus on rulings written by Chief Justice Dickson and Justice Lamer and Justice Wilson. In the ruling I have not addressed here, Justices Jean Beetz and Willard Estey wrote that by amending s. 251 in 1969, Parliament had acknowledged that "the objective of protecting the foetus is not of sufficient importance to defeat the interest in protecting pregnant women"; s 251 was "manifestly unfair" because it failed to meet Parliament's objective. See *Morgentaler.*

6 *Morgentaler*, 63.

7 Ibid., 167.

8 Ibid., 175.

9 Ibid., 37.

10 Ibid.

11 Ibid., 51.

12 *Roe v Wade*, 410 US 113 (1973), https://supreme.justia.com/cases/federal/us/410/113/case.html [*Roe*].

13 *Morgentaler,* 53.

14 *Roe,* 129.

15 Ibid., 152.

16 Ibid., 168.

17 *Morgentaler,* 54.

18 Carolyn McLeod, *Self-Trust and Reproductive Autonomy* (Cambridge, MA: MIT Press, 2002), 2.

19 Laura M. Purdy, "Women's Reproductive Autonomy: Medicalisation and Beyond," *Journal of Medical Ethics* 32 (2006): 287.

20 Sanda Rodgers, "Misconceptions: Equality and Reproductive Autonomy in the Supreme Court of Canada," in *Diminishing Returns: Inequality and the Canadian Charter of Rights and Freedoms*, ed. Sheila McIntyre and Sanda Rodgers (Toronto: LexisNexis Canada, 2006), 275.

It bears noting that Rodgers argues that autonomy – even when conceptualized as relational – does not do enough to ground reproductive rights discourse, and advocates instead for equality as a principle that carries more explanatory force in questions around abortion access and reproductive decision-making. Her argument raises concerns around why theorists even need bother with emphasizing autonomy's relational qualities, and whether we might have more tools available in our arsenal than those that come with long-standing, liberal-coloured histories. While these questions are important in the development of a comprehensive medico-legal framework for protecting and facilitating reproductive decision-making, they fall outside the scope of this chapter. Such a framework would still include some notion of autonomy, even if autonomy is not central, so I believe how autonomy is conceptualized still matters.

21 John Christman, "Liberalism and Individual Freedom," *Ethics* 101, 2 (1991): 344; Gerald Dworkin, *The Theory and Practice of Autonomy* (New York: Cambridge University Press, 1988), 1.

22 Isaiah Berlin, *Four Essays on Liberty* (London: Oxford University Press, 1969), 122.

23 Thomas Hobbes, *Leviathan* (London: Penguin Classics, 1985), 261. The use of male pronouns to indicate neutrality is a common literary device with built-in sexist assumptions

about what has historically been considered neutral, legitimate, and authoritative. Many early modern Western philosophies were arguably not meant to account for women, and this is a significant point to note and to preserve when tracing the history of big concepts like autonomy. For this reason, I do not offer a politically correct, gender neutralized reading of Hobbes, because my critique begins with what lies at the heart of his pronoun use.

24 Marilyn Friedman, "Autonomy, Social Disruption, and Women," in *Relational Autonomy: Feminist Perspectives on Autonomy, Agency, and the Social Self,* ed. Catriona Mackenzie and Natalie Stoljar (New York: Oxford University Press, 2000), 39.

25 Catriona Mackenzie, "Abortion and Embodiment," in *Troubled Bodies: Critical Perspectives on Postmodernism, Medical Ethics, and the Body,* ed. Paul A. Komesaroff (Durham, NC: Duke University Press, 1995), 50.

26 Isabel Karpin, "Legislating the Female Body: Reproductive Technology and the Reconstructed Woman," *Columbia Journal of Gender and Law* 3 (1992–93): 327.

27 Shelley A.M. Gavigan, "Morgentaler and Beyond: The Legal Regulation of Reproduction," in *The Politics of Abortion,* ed. Janine Brodie, Shelley A.M. Gavigan, and Jane Jenson (Toronto: Oxford University Press, 1992), 222.

28 Ibid.

29 Barbara Katz Rothman, *In Labor: Women and Power in the Birthplace* (New York: Norton, 1991), 29.

30 Lisa M. Mitchell, *Baby's First Picture: Ultrasound and the Politics of the Fetal Subjects* (Toronto: University of Toronto Press, 2001), 24.

31 Norman Daniels, *Just Health: Meeting Health Needs Fairly* (New York: Cambridge University Press, 2008), 41.

32 Abby Lippman, "Prenatal Genetic Testing and Screening: Constructing Needs and Reinforcing Inequities," *American Journal of Law and Medicine* 17 (1991): 15.

33 Margit Shildrick, *Leaky Bodies and Boundaries: Feminism, Postmodernism and (Bio)ethics* (London: Routledge, 1997), 85.

34 Susan Wendell, *The Rejected Body: Feminist Philosophical Reflections on Disability* (New York: Routledge, 1996), 24.

35 Ibid., 119.

36 Catherine Frazee, Joan Gilmour, and Roxanne Mykitiuk, "Now You See Her, Now You Don't: How Law Shapes Disabled Women's Experience of Exposure, Surveillance, and Assessment in the Clinical Encounter," in *Critical Disability Theory: Essays in Philosophy, Politics, Policy, and Law,* ed. Dianne Pothier and Richard Devlin (Vancouver: UBC Press, 1996), 233.

37 Karpin, "Legislating the Female Body," 325.

38 Katz Rothman, *In Labor,* 34.

39 Mitchell, *Baby's First Picture,* 3.

40 Malcolm Nicolson and John E.E. Fleming, *Imaging and Imagining the Fetus: The Development of Obstetric Ultrasound* (Baltimore, MD: Johns Hopkins University Press, 2013), 267.

41 Gordon Fyfe and John Law, eds., *Picturing Power: Visual Depiction and Social Relations* (London: Routledge, 1988), 1.

42 Rosalind Pollack Petchesky, "Fetal Images: The Power of Visual Culture in the Politics of Reproduction," *Feminist Studies* 13, 2 (1987): 263.

43 Robert H. Blank, "Maternal-Fetal Relationship: The Courts and Social Policy," in *Bioethics, Justice, and Health Care,* ed. Wanda Teays and Laura Martha Purdy (Belmont, CA: Wadsworth Thomson Learning, 2001), 73.

44 Mitchell, *Baby's First Picture,* 6.

45 Carol Sanger, "Seeing and Believing: Mandatory Ultrasound and the Path to a Protected Choice," *ULCA Law Review* 56, 351 (2008): 368.

46 Mitchell, *Baby's First Picture,* 4.

47 Rebecca Kukla, *Mass Hysteria: Medicine, Culture, and Mothers' Bodies* (Lanham, MD: Rowman and Littlefield Publishers, 2005), 122.

48 The policing of pregnancy is further intensified in cases where the pregnant woman in question is disadvantaged or discriminated against on the basis of age, class, race, disability, gender identity and expression, or sexual orientation. Reproductive technologies differentially impact women who are over thirty-five or disabled insofar as they experience more pressure to diagnose disability in utero on the grounds that they are at higher risk of producing disability. See Lippman, "Prenatal Genetic Testing and Screening," 30. Poor and racialized women are regarded as a danger to the fetuses they are carrying when they cannot afford to maintain ritualized pregnancy practices or are more likely to be exposed to environmental hazards and health conditions. See Lippman, "Prenatal Genetic Testing and Screening," 41; and Katz Rothman, *In Labor,* 132. Women with compounding identity markers such as disability or race have argued that reproductive justice must entail the right to reproduce in the face of social, political, and economic conditions that compromise activities related to conceiving, bearing, and raising children. See Andrea Smith, "Beyond Pro-choice versus Pro-life: Women of Color and Reproductive Justice," *Feminist Formations* 17, 1 (2005): 128. Indeed, racialized, disabled, and queer women share difficulties in accessing reproductive technologies and services in the interest of becoming pregnant and maintaining pregnancy on their own terms. See Candace Johnson, "Reproducing Inequality and Identity: An Intersectional Analysis of Maternal Health Preferences," in *Fertile Ground: Exploring Reproduction in Canada,* ed. Stephanie Paterson, Francesca Scala, and Marlene K. Sokolon (Montreal and Kingston: McGill-Queen's University Press, 2014), 94; and Michelle Walks, "Stratified Reproduction: Making the Case for Butch Lesbians', Transmen's, and Genderqueer Individuals' Experiences in British Columbia," in *Fertile Ground: Exploring Reproduction in Canada,* ed. Stephanie Paterson, Francesca Scala, and Marlene K. Sokolon (Montreal and Kingston: McGill-Queen's University Press, 2014), 74.

49 Barbara Katz Rothman, *Recreating Motherhood: Ideology and Technology in a Patriarchal Society* (New York: Norton, 1990), 27.

50 Ibid., 158.

51 Judith Jarvis Thomson, "A Defense of Abortion," *Philosophy and Published Affairs* 1 (1971): 47.

52 Michael Tooley, "Abortion and Infanticide," *Philosophy and Public Affairs* 2, 1 (1971): 37; Mary Anne Warren, "On the Moral and Legal Status of Abortion," *The Monist* 57, 1 (1973): 43.

53 Elizabeth Wolgast, *The Grammar of Justice* (Ithaca, NY: Cornell University Press, 1987), 41.

54 Carol Gilligan, *In a Different Voice* (Cambridge, MA: Harvard University Press, 1982), 20; Nel Noddings, *Caring: A Feminist Approach to Ethics and Moral Education* (Berkeley, CA: University of California Press, 1984), 3.

55 Karpin, "Legislating the Female Body," 327; Isabel Karpin, "Genetics and the Legal Conception of Self," in *Ethics of the Body: Postconventional Challenges,* ed. Margrit Shildrick and Roxanne Mykitiuk (Cambridge, MA: MIT Press, 2005), 195.

56 Ibid.

57 Katz Rothman, *Recreating Motherhood,* 59.

58 Mackenzie, "Abortion and Embodiment," 49.

59 Rosemarie Tong, *Feminist Approaches to Bioethics: Theoretical Reflections and Practical Applications* (Boulder, CO: Westview Press, 1997), 151.

60 Mary Anne Warren, "The Moral Significance of Birth," *Hypatia* 4, 3 (1989): 62.

61 Anne Donchin, "Toward a Gender-Sensitive Assisted Reproduction Policy," *Bioethics* 23, 1 (2009): 34.

62 Sara Goering, "Postnatal Reproductive Autonomy: Promoting Relational Autonomy and Self-Trust in New Parents," *Bioethics* 23, 1 (2009): 9–19.
63 Shildrick, *Leaky Bodies,* 81.
64 Nikolas Rose, *Politics of Life Itself: Biomedicine, Power and Subjectivity in the Twenty-First Century* (Oxford: Princeton University Press, 2007), 18.
65 Nicolson and Fleming, *Imaging and Imagining the Fetus,* 235.
66 Margrit Shildrick, "Genetics, Normativity, and Ethics: Some Bioethical Concerns," *Feminist Theory* 5, 2 (2004): 152.
67 Ibid., 155.
68 Karpin, "Genetics and the Legal Conception of Self," 195.
69 Ibid., 212.
70 The Society of Obstetricians and Gynaecologists of Canada (SOGC), "Fetal Soft Markers in Obstetric Ultrasound," *SOGC Clinical Practice Guidelines* 162 (2005): 592; *Assisted Human Reproduction Act,* SC 2004, c 2, http://laws-lois.justice.gc.ca/eng/acts/a-13.4/.

10

Between a Woman and Her Doctor?

The Medicalization of Abortion Politics in Canada

Rachael Johnstone

SINCE ITS DECRIMINALIZATION nearly three decades ago, abortion has persisted at the edges of Canadian politics. No longer a criminal matter, access is now dictated by the provinces as a matter of health care. Given this history, it is perhaps unsurprising that one of the most influential frameworks adopted by both the pro-choice and anti-abortion movements, who are collectively responsible for shaping the abortion debate for public consumption, is a medical framework, which seeks to classify abortion in seemingly straightforward and apolitical medical terms. But what is the value, strategic or otherwise, of thinking about abortion in purely medical terms? Moreover, how can a single framework benefit such disparate causes?

The evolution of abortion law in Canada showcases the initial gains provided by a medical lens for the pro-choice movement and highlights early efforts made by the anti-abortion movement to co-opt this framework. This history illuminates the tension inherent within the medical framing of abortion for the pro-choice movement, as both legitimating and potentially threatening access. With these dynamics in mind, this chapter seeks to engage with the medical framing, or medicalization, of abortion. While the Canadian experience suggests that this tactic has proven effective in eliminating certain barriers, I contend that, by artificially separating abortion from other equality rights issues, continuing to rely on this framework also risks undermining these gains, since it predicates access to abortion solely on its value as a medical procedure. I therefore argue for the need to understand abortion as an inherently political issue. Importantly, while such an understanding does not preclude the classification of abortion as a health care issue, it does necessitate government action to guarantee women's equality rights more broadly conceived. After all, it is not enough that abortion is available as a matter of health care. Governments, both federal and provincial, must recognize the importance of women's equality, as well as the significance of abortion to its realization, in order for women's equality rights to be protected and entrenched in Canada. To advance these claims, I rely on document analysis, media coverage, and a selection of one-on-one interviews with social movement activists. These interviews offer insight into the realities of securing access on the ground, thereby highlighting the concerns of activists on the front lines.

Ultimately, the effect of positioning abortion as a medical issue is not only the erasure of its connection with a range of social issues related to society's treatment of women, but also the obfuscation of the role of politics in structuring medical care. In sum, this framework neglects the important and appropriate political oversight of Canada's public health care system as well as the power dynamics at play within the medical profession. While the regulation of abortion as a medical issue has provided the necessary space to realize improved access in many parts of the country, there are still barriers to access that will persist if the political weight of abortion access is not recognized. Despite the pro-choice movement's commitment to securing access to abortion services, a focus on improved access has often positioned abortion as a stand-alone issue, its links to a larger project of women's emancipation secondary to the pressing need to realize access on the ground. Fortunately, a surge in recognition for a reproductive justice approach to abortion access may provide the necessary tools to rethink abortion as a matter of health care in Canada.

Foundations of a Medical Framework in the Development of Canadian Abortion Law

Canada's first abortion law, adopted in 1869, was designed to mimic an existing British law that prohibited abortion without exception.[1] Canada's law first began to take shape as *Lord Ellenborough's Act* in Britain in 1803. The act banned certain types of abortion around the second trimester of pregnancy – after the pregnant woman was first able to detect fetal movement.[2] It was created with the intention of protecting women from unsafe medical practices, often attributed to midwives, and to safeguard the domain of physicians.[3] It was later broadened to include abortion at all stages, a change largely intended to make the law more easily enforceable, although it is important to note that public sympathy for the plight of women facing unwanted pregnancy made the enforcement of this law difficult.[4] These restrictions eventually developed into a complete prohibition of abortion by way of Britain's *Offences Against the Person Act* (1861), which was later adopted into Canada's first *Criminal Code*.

In the decades that followed, jurisprudence coming out of Britain helped to ease the severity of the law. On the heels of an influential 1939 British case, in which a woman's mental state was found to be sufficient grounds to deem an abortion a medical necessity, the barriers for physicians attempting to exercise their professional judgment on the state of women's reproductive health were relaxed.[5] This case provided precedent that would spare physicians from prosecution if they performed an abortion because they deemed the procedure necessary to protect the life or health of a pregnant woman. While this shift signalled some improvement in access, it also foreshadowed a troubling view of abortion that would be repeated in the 1969 amendment to Canada's *Criminal Code,* section 251, which eased restrictions on abortion by creating a means for abortions to be legally sanctioned following approval by a Therapeutic Abortion Committee (TAC).[6] While changes to the law in both Britain and Canada paved the way for improved access to abortion services, they also dismissed the fundamental socio-political reasons women required access to the procedure in the first place – to secure equality.

Following the changes to the abortion law in 1969, the pro-choice movement in Canada was organized and active, working on the front lines to help women access services; keenly aware of the consequences of illegal abortions, those involved in the movement felt the urgency to improve women's reproductive rights.[7] These changes only added to their growing belief that treating abortion as a criminal issue violated women's rights, because the Criminal Code only partially legitimated the treatment of abortion as a medical necessity, drawing attention to the subjectivity of apparent health distinctions.[8] The changes to the abortion law required a woman to plead her case before a TAC in the hopes of being granted a legal abortion to protect her life and health, but what constituted a threat was left to the discretion of the committee. Thus many women continued to be able to access abortions only illegally.

Notably, when the 1969 amendment took effect, the pro-choice movement had few clear tools in politics or law that it could utilize to challenge the new law. Abortion was still a federal matter under the *Criminal Code,* and the constitution contained no individual rights clauses likely to allow for a successful challenge over this jurisdiction. When Dr. Henry Morgentaler, a family physician and growing figure in the pro-choice movement, first appeared in the Supreme Court for a case in which he had been accused of performing an illegal abortion, he claimed medical necessity as grounds to challenge the existing law, but the court ruled against him.[9] Fortunately, the federal government's adoption of the *Charter of Rights and Freedoms* in 1982 soon created new avenues for change. The Charter entrenched individual rights in the constitution, rights that Morgentaler was able to successfully utilize to take on the country's abortion law.[10]

In October 1986, Morgentaler, alongside Drs. Leslie Frank Smoling and Robert Scott, re-entered the Supreme Court to challenge the constitutionality of section 251 of the *Criminal Code.*[11] This time using section 7 of the newly minted *Charter of Rights and Freedoms,* he argued that the existing law violated women's rights to security of the person. This defence turned on the health risks associated with forcing women to either carry unwanted pregnancies to term or seek out illegal abortion services. The consequences of attempting to endure or illegally terminate an unwanted pregnancy were widely understood at the time, despite not being openly discussed. By demonstrating the consequences of uneven and restricted access to abortion services, Morgentaler highlighted the failure of the health care system to effectively protect the health of women under the existing law.

On January 28, 1988, the Supreme Court ruled in favour of Morgentaler, Smoling, and Scott, with a majority decision of five to two. The court found that section 251 of the *Criminal Code,* by requiring "a pregnant woman whose life or health is in danger to choose between, on the one hand, the commission of a crime to obtain effective and timely medical treatment and, on the other hand, inadequate treatment or no treatment at all," was in direct violation of her right to security of the person.[12] Of course, by choosing to strike down section 251 of the *Criminal Code,* rather than modifying it, the court left room for Parliament to create new legislation to regulate abortion access. Jane Jenson contends that this move undermined the treatment of abortion as a medical issue, the framework favoured by the court, inviting new perspectives and thereby freeing the terms of the debate in the political sphere.[13] Attempts by the government of then Prime Minister

Brian Mulroney to create a new abortion law immediately following the decision gave a platform to both the pro-choice and anti-abortion movements to articulate their own frameworks in Parliament.[14]

The Mulroney government moved quickly in its attempts to create a new law in its proposal of Bill C-43, which passed successfully through the House of Commons on May 29, 1990. The bill was originally meant to balance the demands of those advocating both for and against abortion access in Canada, but it soon became apparent that there was no room for compromise. In the end, the bill did not go far enough for either side. Bill C-43 proposed to reintroduce a ban on abortion to the *Criminal Code,* but with exceptions to allow doctors to perform abortions at their discretion should they determine that the woman's health was compromised because of the pregnancy.[15] While the limitations on women's rights validated by this law seemed to support the anti-abortion movement's moralistic attacks on women's autonomy, the exceptions provided for women at risk of negative health consequences added an important escape clause. Mimicking previous restrictions on abortion in Canada, designed to protect physicians, the portrayal of abortion in Bill C-43 was meant to temper the otherwise polarizing debate without overtly challenging the power structures according to which abortion access has been historically restricted. The right to veto a woman's choice to have an abortion still fell under a clear hierarchy preserving "scientific and male privilege."[16]

Despite being passed by the House of Commons, Bill C-43 was met with a rare tie vote in the Senate on July 31, 1991, which signalled its defeat.[17] No federal government has since attempted to create legislation restricting abortion and, in the absence of a new law, the procedure has been reclassified as a health care issue and its jurisdiction shifted to the provinces.[18] The reclassification of abortion as health care following *R v Morgentaler* gave provinces significant discretion in their regulation of the procedure, but it quickly became apparent that the provincial governments were also limited by this classification.

Perhaps the best example of the limitations of the provinces' ability to regulate abortion can be found in Nova Scotia. In 1989, shortly after jurisdiction over the procedure shifted, the government of Nova Scotia implemented a regulation prohibiting the performance of abortions "in any place other than a building, premises, or place approved by the Minister of Health and Fitness as a 'hospital.'"[19] When Morgentaler set up an abortion clinic in the province later that year, he was swiftly charged with fourteen separate counts of breaching the *Medical Services Act*.[20] The case was appealed to the Supreme Court, which ruled in Morgentaler's favour and found the legislation to be an "indivisible attempt by the province to legislate in the area of criminal law."[21] This case makes evident the new parameters within which the provinces must operate to regulate abortion: they must adopt a medical rationale to justify restrictions to abortion access or risk legal action. In federal politics, however, abortion is still open to being reclassified through the creation of a new law, although a medical framework of abortion has also taken hold in the House of Commons.

Limitations of the Medicalization of Abortion

The term "medicalization" is a reference to both the "process and outcome of human problems entering the jurisdiction of the medical profession."[22] Over time, many issues commonly faced by women, ranging from eating disorders to gender identity to reproductive decisions, have been medicalized.[23] This phenomenon is by no means new, but it is significant in a country that prides itself on providing access to universal health care. In many instances, the medicalization of these issues reduces their stigma and increases their legitimacy in the public eye while allowing them to be handled in a more systematic manner. However, the reclassification of these issues can also alter the way we think about and attempt to address them in ways that obscure their socio-political implications. Indeed, implicit in the medicalized framework is the deeply misleading notion that health care is somehow a safe haven from political power and discourse. In reality, health care is deeply intertwined with politics.

In Canada, the relationship of health to politics is further complicated by the federal–provincial division of powers. Health care in Canada falls under provincial jurisdiction, but the provinces do not have the necessary tax base to cover the cost of a universal health care system. To compensate for this shortfall, the federal government transfers money to the provinces annually.[24] Thus, while the provinces have jurisdiction over health care, the necessity of these transfers gives the federal government some influence over their policies. For example, if a province does not abide by the regulations set out in the *Canada Health Act* (1985), it may not receive a full cash contribution from the federal government.[25] While the *Canada Health Act* allows for variance in services and regulations across the country, barriers to abortion access in some provinces clearly fail to satisfy the act's five foundational pillars: public administration, comprehensiveness, universality, portability, and accessibility.[26] The federal government has the power to address these failings by limiting its transfer payments; under the Harper government, however, the federal government opted not to interfere with the decisions of provincial governments in this area.[27]

Many barriers to access are therefore the result of a combination of provincial regulations that restrict access and federal inaction to address problematic regulations. As such, barriers created by provincial governments to restrict access to abortion, which contravene both the *Canada Health Act* and the *Charter of Rights and Freedoms,* often go unchecked. While this may seem to be more a political problem than a health care problem, it is important not to be too quick to treat these domains as separate. The reality in Canada is that medical care is largely a public service and provincial governments are responsible for implementing and overseeing rules and regulations shaping that care. In highlighting this relationship, I do not wish to say that governments should not be responsible for health care; I am merely calling for a deeper understanding of the significance of their role in providing care. Indeed, populations in each province are likely to have different needs and priorities, for which provincial governments are elected to help deliver programs and services. While the appropriateness of government action – and inaction – in the regulation of abortion ought to be scrutinized, suggesting that governments are not, or should not, be tied to health care is troubling. A medical framework may treat the two domains as separate, but the reality in Canada is quite different.

Even if we could imagine the realms of health care and politics as distinct, it is important to note that physicians are not impervious to the charged debates surrounding abortion. Physicians and other medical personnel may hold anti-abortion sentiments and are given significant discretion in how they treat patients. This reality becomes further complicated when we consider that the details of how abortion ought to be regulated in health care are still contentious. Terms like *health* and *medical necessity,* which are presently used to justify the provision of abortion, remain undefined, leaving women's access to abortion largely up to the discretion of individual physicians. Given the continued stigma surrounding abortion in much of Canada, the realities of this discretion continue to allow for uneven access to services for women. When we treat abortion as a purely medical issue, we may reduce the stigma that surrounds it, but we cannot erase it; nor can we guarantee the equal treatment of women by service providers, or provide a deeper understanding of the issues at stake to politicians. Instead, we discount one of the most potent challenges to these restrictions: women's constitutionally guaranteed protection of their equality.

A few notable examples of what access to abortion has looked like in the provinces illustrate the potential range of services – from poor to progressive – that are made available when abortion is relegated to the realm of medicine. Until 2015, New Brunswick had some of the most limited access to abortion services in Canada.[28] For a woman in the province to access an abortion covered under her provincial health insurance plan, she first had to negotiate a complex bureaucratic system – the realities of which were likely unknown to her – without a clear sense of her rights as a patient. Regulation 84–20 of the province's *Medical Services Payment Act,* created in 1989, set out the requirements for an abortion to be funded. According to the act, a woman had to first obtain written permission from two doctors stating that the procedure was medically necessary, a requirement for which there is no medical rationale. Next, she had to secure an appointment with a specialist in the field of obstetrics and gynaecology in an approved hospital. The appointment had to take place before she reached the twelfth week of gestation.[29] Given the average wait times in the province, and the fact that there was no guarantee that doctors would be willing to provide referrals, it was nearly impossible to get access to publicly funded abortion care. Moreover, women encountering anti-abortion physicians would not necessarily have been provided with a clear breakdown of their rights. In effect, the ability of these women to exercise their choices was often contingent on the belief systems of their doctors. In 2015, responding to pressure from reproductive justice activists, the recently elected Liberal Government, under Premier Brian Gallant, amended Regulation 84–20, removing the requirement for two signatures and a specialist to perform the procedure, but retaining the restriction that abortions must be performed in a hospital.

On the other side of the spectrum of the quality of abortion access is the case of Quebec. Abortion in Quebec is covered under provincial health insurance in both hospitals and clinics and does not require a referral. There are also a number of pioneering clinics that are attempting to change the way women experience terminating their unwanted pregnancies from one of fear to one of understanding and respect. Anne Marie Messier is the clinic manager at the Centre de santé des femmes de Montréal, which is one of three clinics in Quebec offering abortion services using a strictly feminist approach grounded in respect for women and their experiences.[30] She explains that women are given some control over the setting during the procedure (e.g., whether they would like to listen to music or have someone to hold their hand and talk with them), and that their knowledge of their own bodies is respected. If a woman is certain of her conception date, for example, she is not required to have an ultrasound.[31]

Quebec is a standout example, however, in large part because of the province's recognition of women's rights. In 2010, the National Assembly of Quebec put forward a motion stating that "the National Assembly reaffirms the rights of women to freedom of choice and to free and accessible abortion services and asks the federal Government and the Prime Minister of Canada to put an end to the ambiguity that persists in relation to this question."[32] Recognition of women's rights in the province, not just as a health issue but also as a broader question of equality, has informed the treatment of abortion in the province. While access to abortion in Quebec is still not uniform, this declaration reflects public sentiment that has allowed medical practitioners room to attempt to improve services and given women a sense of entitlement that helps to guide them through a system meant to help them realize their choices.

The examples of New Brunswick and Quebec represent opposing ends of the abortion access spectrum in Canada, in provinces where access of some sort is available. Note the exception of PEI where, until 2017, no services were available. While every province now provides some level of publicly funded care, understanding access entails looking at a wider range of issues beyond merely hospital or clinic availability. Barriers like distance, time, stigma, and fear continue to influence the reality of the way women experience this access (see Brown, Ehrlich, and MacQuarrie, this volume). Women in PEI, for example, until 2017, when the Prince County Hospital in Summerside began offering services, were only able to have the procedure covered at facilities in other provinces (no services were available in the province), and only if they met strict criteria, but they needed to travel off the Island to have it performed, and travel was not covered.[33] Thus, while levels of access to abortion have dramatically improved across Canada since the procedure was decriminalized, the nature of access that women experience in different provinces is still markedly different. The medicalization of abortion has helped to improve access, but rather than granting more power to women, it has ensured that the agency women are able to access continues to depend on physicians and provincial regulations. Without formal protections, women's rights remain vulnerable.

The above examples make it clear that the medicalization of abortion does not mean the absence of social movement arguments and platforms in its regulation, but it does mean that these justifications for action often go unacknowledged. Governments continue to be active in the regulation of abortion services through both formal restrictions (as in New Brunswick) and value-laden motions (as in Quebec). Locating abortion within medicine does not preclude political engagement with the issue and, I contend, we should not want it to, since health care remains a provincial responsibility and provincial governments are responsible for ensuring that their policies are compliant with the *Charter of Rights and Freedoms*. Rather than attempting to separate politics and medicine to address problems with abortion access, I argue it is better to re-politicize the issue and demand that governments recognize women's equality rights and help to address barriers directly. Certainly, the larger goals of the pro-choice movement would seem to demand such action. Moreover, by adopting this approach, the claims of the anti-abortion movement could be resituated in a broader discussion of women's equality, effectively undermining them.

The Use of Medical Discourse by the Anti-abortion and Pro-choice Movements

While both the pro-choice and anti-abortion movements have incorporated different strategies to achieve their ends, they have converged on a medical rhetoric to address the issue of access to abortion care. In so doing, they have attempted to sidestep or de-emphasize the fundamental issues they believe to be at stake in the abortion debate. The anti-abortion movement has done so in order to gain legitimacy; the pro-choice movement has done so strategically to hold its ground. To be sure, the treatment of abortion as a medical issue may offer some protections for women, for example, by legitimizing the health risks associated with a lack of reproductive choice; however, this framework fundamentally fails to hold governments to account. Rather, the treatment of abortion as a medical issue has been used as a platform to both demand greater access to services and to push for a recriminalization of the procedure, all the while obscuring the political and social implications of these struggles.

In 2012, Conservative member of Parliament Stephen Woodworth introduced a private member's motion calling on the House of Commons to revisit the legal definition of when human life begins. His argument turned on the assertion that human life should be defined in scientific terms. The motion, which was defeated in a vote of 203 to 91, called for the creation of a special committee to assess "what medical evidence exists to demonstrate that a child is or is not a human being before the moment of complete birth."[34] The use of medical language to challenge the existing regulation of abortion in Canada is by no means a new tactic. Indeed, anti-abortion groups have been warning women about the alleged health risks of abortion since the procedure was decriminalized, claiming that abortion causes breast cancer and even assigning the term "post-abortion syndrome" to symptoms not causally linked to abortion.[35] While these claims are without substance, attempts to employ a medical framework to create barriers to abortion access require a closer look at what classifying abortion as a health care issue really entails. Why do anti-abortion activists believe it is advantageous to adopt a medical framework for abortion? As evidenced by the Woodworth example, talking about abortion using medical language is done with the intention of isolating the procedure from its socio-political context. The implication of regulating women's bodies from an allegedly neutral stance, without considering the social, legal, political, and economic consequences of policing the pregnant body, is that women's rights claims can be ignored. In this context, a medical framework is used to present health as a kind of apolitical compromise that does not require a rehashing of the abortion debate and, perhaps most importantly, enables the anti-abortion movement to claim that its opposition to abortion should not be interpreted as an attack on women's rights.

Of course, the aims of the anti-abortion movement are much broader than the recriminalization of abortion. The movement first organized under a pro-family umbrella, which positions "the traditional family as under attack and falling into an ever-deepening crisis because of an overly intrusive state and an ever-expanding secular value system."[36] While abortion remains a central issue, the desire for its regulation is part of a larger wish for a return to traditional gender roles that prioritize women "first and foremost as wives and mothers."[37] The means through which groups believe these changes ought to be achieved, however, vary. In more recent years, Canadian anti-abortion groups have begun to mimic the strategies of their counterparts in the United States, including a new discursive approach that attempts to portray the anti-abortion agenda as inherently pro-woman, by asserting that "abortion harms women."[38] This framework necessitates a focus on shifting values rather than just changing legislation, and may even claim a desire to avoid recriminalizing abortion. However, despite attempts to change the public face of the anti-abortion movement, the underlying platforms of anti-abortion groups remain largely the same – a larger project that includes the maintenance of what are seen as traditional marriage and family structures.[39] While legislation criminalizing abortion is not the sole focus of these groups, it remains a central objective and the logical endpoint of an expansive campaign designed to associate abortion with harm to women. A brief look at anti-abortion activity in federal politics following the decriminalization of the procedure in Canada helps to showcase this strategic evolution.

The anti-abortion movement in Canada began to mobilize as the Canadian abortion law was liberalized.[40] The growing legitimacy of abortion in Canadian society was an important motivator for the movement's attempts to have the procedure recriminalized.[41] While the movement has continued to organize following the decriminalization of the procedure, its initial framing of abortion as the result of the immorality of women was not successful. As a result, many anti-abortion advocates have since shifted their rhetorical approach, instead suggesting the potential danger of abortion to the life and health of women in ostensibly objective terms. This shift is apparent in the numerous backbencher bills put forward in the House of Commons after 1988.

In 1991 and 1996, motions were put forward "to reclassify both embryos and fetuses as human beings, which would make abortion homicide."[42] Both were defeated. In 2002 and 2003, two similarly unsuccessful backbencher motions emerged, but with a perceptible shift in language. These later motions required "that the Standing Committee on Health should fully examine, study, and report to Parliament on a) whether or not abortions are medically necessary for the purpose of maintaining health, preventing disease or diagnosing or treating an injury, illness or disability; and b) the health risks for women undergoing abortions compared to women carrying their babies to full term."[43] Already, the language had changed from a clear attempt to create substantial barriers to abortion access, to a more neutral, inquisitive tone that seems to suggest a desire to get at some universal *truth* about the health care implications of the procedure. This approach was also reflected in other bills. Overt attempts to reclassify abortion as homicide (1991, 1996) and secure fetal rights (1998, 1999, 2001) have been replaced with calls to prevent the coercion of medical professionals and women (2008, 2010), ensure informed consent from women seeking abortions (2003), and create increased penalties for the murder of pregnant women (2004, 2007).[44] While the goals of these motions have remained the same – the eventual recriminalization of abortion services – the language is demonstrative of an understanding that calling on the immorality of women or the rights of *unborn children* does not garner significant public support, particularly given the known consequences of illegal and restricted abortion.

Woodworth's 2012 motion to reconsider the legal definition of what constitutes a human being also showcased a strategy which downplayed the goal of recriminalization while emphasizing an interest in women's health. Woodworth's intention in putting forward the motion was apparent in its third section, which questioned the legal impact of the existing definition of life for "the fundamental human rights of a child before the moment of complete birth" but made no mention of the rights of pregnant women. Nonetheless, Woodworth staunchly defended the motion, arguing that it was not "an attempt to criminalize abortion procedures in Canada."[45] He received strong backing from the anti-abortion community. The executive director of Life Canada, Natalie Sonnen, praised the motion, saying that it was "pushing for something that is very rational, that we have a discussion on this based on the science."[46] Consideration of the consequences for women's rights and status was markedly absent from the motion, which suggests that a purely medical rationale for recriminalizing abortion could be understood as an unbiased move by the House of Commons. Importantly, even when such attempts to legally restrict abortion are unsuccessful, they have the advantage of calling the safety of abortion into question, and regularly reintroducing uncertainty about the safety of the procedure into the public consciousness.

Of course, the medicalization of abortion has not been limited to groups opposing the procedure; the pro-choice movement has also embraced medical rhetoric. Indeed, this framework underpins the watershed moment for the pro-choice movement in Canada, the case of *R v Morgentaler*. Absent a new law on abortion following this case, jurisdiction over the procedure shifted to the provinces where it was categorized as a health care service, a framework that remains the political status quo. Thus, by positioning abortion as a medically necessary service, the pro-choice movement has been able to pressure governments to ensure that women's health care needs are met through the provision of comprehensive health care that includes abortion.

Like the anti-abortion movement, the Canadian pro-choice movement treats abortion as part of a larger project. The movement, which began to mobilize when abortion was still a criminal matter in Canada, continues to work towards the recognition of abortion as a right that is necessary for women's equality. Unlike the anti-abortion movement, however, the pro-choice movement has not had a consistent presence in politics after the 1988 *Morgentaler* decision. In recent decades, the movement's momentum has begun to fade from formal politics, replaced by attempts to counter anti-abortion motions in the House of Commons in an effort to safeguard existing access. This approach is not just representative of the political climate, which became increasingly resistant to women's rights claims under the former prime minister Stephen Harper's Conservatives; it also represents a decreased sense of urgency surrounding issues of abortion access. When it became apparent that a new law was not going to replace section 251 of the *Criminal Code* after the decriminalization of abortion in Canada, many pro-choice groups slowed their mobilization, feeling that they had effectively won the war. As numerous provincial court cases sought to ensure that provinces were providing reasonable access to abortion care, the treatment of abortion as a health issue has been the most effective tool in advancing these cases.[47]

In terms of litigation, the pro-choice movement's focus on health makes a great deal of sense; abortion was decriminalized under a provision for the right to life, liberty, and security of the person, rather than the equality claims endorsed by the movement. The medical model has had significant success in maintaining and improving provincial access. Joyce Arthur, director of the Abortion Rights Coalition of Canada, explains that abortion is "a health treatment, it's medically necessary under the *Canada Health Act,* and I think that's helped a lot in terms of making abortion services more integrated into the healthcare system in general."[48] The fact that Canadians place such value on universal health care also makes this model appealing.

Unfortunately, without the sense of urgency the movement once had, there is a constant struggle to simply maintain existing services. Arthur explains that the fear of losing what services are already in place motivates a certain caution around the issue.[49] Michelle Robidoux, director of the Ontario Coalition for Abortion Clinics, echoed a similar sentiment when asked what kind of changes she would like to see to the regulation of abortion in Ontario: "It's funny because you never get asked 'what do you think would be a really good thing to have'. It's just ... it's rear-guard actions all the time."[50]

In addition, a disturbing trend in silencing the pro-choice movement was particularly prevalent at the federal level during the Harper administration (2006–15). Robidoux explains that the anti-abortion movement has had "access to this government [the Harper Government] in a way that they probably hadn't had for some time in previous governments."[51] Pressure to maintain services rather than push for improved access has led many in the pro-choice movement to strategically focus on the letter of the law, defending abortion as a medical issue, rather than being seen to push for improved recognition and threatening the gains achieved under the existing framework. Although the newly elected Liberal Government under Prime Minister Justin Trudeau has been vocal in its support of the pro-choice position, the exact implications of this stance for abortion access in the provinces are not yet clear.[52]

Pro-choice activity in the political sphere is markedly less common than anti-abortion activity, and tends to arise in opposition to anti-abortion activity rather than originating from pro-choice activists. While pro-choice groups have worked diligently in opposition to the backbencher motions detailed above, they have not attempted to create their own legislation.[53] The difficulties in advancing an equality agenda in federal politics were made apparent in 2010 when Canada hosted the annual G8 summit, in which leaders from the world's eight leading global economies met to discuss important economic and social issues. The agenda for this meeting included discussion on the continuation of a project championed in previous summits designed to promote maternal, newborn, and child health in developing countries, although what the Harper government believed should fall under the header of "maternal health" was not made clear. While Prime Minister Harper argued that his government "would not be 'closing doors against any options, including contraception,'" the pro-choice movement was rightly wary that abortion services would be excluded from the initiative and rallied to press for guarantees of a comprehensive maternal health policy.[54] In response, the movement came up against strong opposition and was cautioned by Senator Nancy Ruth to "shut the fuck up" on abortion, saying, "If you push it, there will be more backlash."[55]

Both the pro-choice and anti-abortion movements have adopted strategies reliant on the medicalization of abortion with the aim of situating the often taboo subject on neutral ground to secure improvements to access, or to challenge the health benefits of the access that is already in place. For pro-choice groups, this strategy has been a particularly successful one, but this framework is a double-edged sword for the movement. While treating abortion as a purely medical issue may seem expedient, producing immediate and positive outcomes, such as more points of access, these outcomes are contingent on the beliefs and actions of individuals within the medical profession. If there were a swell of resistance to performing abortions in the medical profession, or an opening to address women's rights claims in government, it would not be as apparent that physicians are the best gatekeepers of women's rights. After all, medicine is not an institution with the capacity or legitimacy to enforce rights – this is the domain of government. Moreover, the notion that medicine is somewhat insulated from politics is itself misleading.[56] Canada's public health care system falls under the jurisdiction of provincial governments, which are elected to make decisions about the allocation of funding and the enactment of provincial regulations pertaining to health care. While physicians do maintain some independence from government, they are directly impacted by these decisions. As such, when a medical framing is implemented in a political climate that may be resistant to recognizing women's rights claims, it may seem like the only path towards improved access, even as it removes the onus from governments to advocate for women's rights protections. The reality is that abortion is a medical procedure with significant implications for women's equality rights, meaning that who has access to abortion, when, and under what circumstances are important political questions.

Re-politicizing Abortion

The decriminalization of abortion in 1988 was a significant victory for the pro-choice movement, but it did not mark the end of the campaign to realize women's equality. While the policy vacuum surrounding abortion, in which the procedure was relegated to the provinces as a health issue, provided some substantial gains in access, adherence to the language of health remains limited in its ability to improve services and, as evidenced by some anti-abortion campaigns, also provides a potential path towards legitimizing increased barriers to access. Most importantly, in treating abortion as a stand-alone issue, this framework no longer connects the procedure to a range of other social issues. Calls for a national child care program, equal pay for equal work, and an end to intimate partner violence can be positioned as separate issues, rather than necessary to create an environment in which reproductive choice could be realized.

Although the rights rhetoric has not disappeared from the pro-choice movement's discussion of abortion, failing to stake claims on the grounds of equality implies that abortion is better off guided solely by health care than it might be if the debate were to be reopened. The patchwork of services now available in the provinces is treated as a marked improvement over the pre-1988 context; while it is clear that the decriminalization of abortion was a positive step, leaving abortion in the realm of medicine continues to leave the equality of Canadian women vulnerable.

Treating abortion as a stand-alone medical question without pushing for equality protections for women leaves women at the mercy of provincial regulations on abortion access, which may limit the facilities they can access, coverage of the procedure under provincial medicare, and the timeline in which they can access abortion services. Women may also be made reliant on the personal belief systems of doctors, despite the powerful political consequences of these beliefs. In many instances, where details about what access women are entitled to may not be readily available, women may also find themselves at the mercy of other medical gatekeepers. Although many physicians attempt to guide women through their reproductive choices rather than create barriers for them, without formal protections for women who encounter anti-abortion physicians or medical staff, the ability to access abortion services can be compromised.

With these shortcomings in mind, I aim to challenge the medicalization of abortion as a stand-alone framework to advance abortion rights. There are, of course, risks that accompany this challenge to the medical framework, most obviously because the medical framework is seen as the foundation on which so much positive change has been possible. Questioning its value could be seen as risking existing gains. But is the type of access to abortion we have in Canada satisfactory as it is? Women seeking access may have to travel significant distances, navigate barriers created by physicians, and feel silenced by a social climate that stigmatizes abortion.[57] By treating abortion as part of women's emancipation in broader terms, we can create new tools to address the flaws apparent in our treatment of abortion. This is not to say that a medical discourse will or ought to disappear: women's health still matters and abortions will still need to be provided by medical personnel. However, this access will always be fraught with barriers unless it is also protected through rights recognitions.

The reproductive justice movement's emphasis on expanding the definition of choice, to include a range of issues necessary to create real choice, may provide a path to move forward. Legal recognition of a woman's right to choose is not sufficient for equality; women's reproductive freedom must be embraced by society as a whole so that women are able to exercise agency. If abortion remains stigmatized and women are unsure of their rights and safety in attempting to access a legal procedure, reproductive choice has not been realized. Moreover, recognition of women's equality as it relates to pregnancy necessitates a more complete understanding of choice that is not limited to a negative right to abortion.[58] Reproductive justice, with its focus on a larger package of rights – including the right to have children, the right not to have children, and the right to parent existing children with dignity – is grounded in an understanding of existing barriers to reproductive freedom, and may thus provide a productive new lens to explore a range of policies affecting women's health. Its expansive focus may also help to contribute a sense of urgency to issues surrounding reproduction that have not been the focus of previous debates on choice.

This movement is only just beginning to emerge in Canada, but its expansive message is already being endorsed by pro-choice organizations. Reproductive Justice New Brunswick has successfully challenged the New Brunswick government on its restrictive abortion regulation, resulting in significant improvements in the province. Likewise, the PEI Abortion Rights Network, which identifies itself as allied with reproductive justice, recently threatened the PEI government with legal action against its policies, which they alleged violated both the *Charter of Rights and Freedoms* and the *Canada Health Act*, resulting in the province backtracking on its abortion policy and making services available. Indeed, Premier Wade McLauchlan, in defending his government's decision to offer services, admitted that the province's policies would likely not have been defensible because they were "contrary to the Canadian Charter of Rights and Freedoms."[59] By locating abortion issues in a social as well as legal and political context, these movements are once again working to realize women's rights on all fronts. By recognizing that abortion is, indeed, a political issue, as well as a medical, social, legal, and economic one, there is renewed hope that women's abortion rights might be recognized and that governments will finally take their roles in safeguarding the bodies, rights, and freedoms of their citizens seriously.

Notes

1 John Keown, *Abortion Doctors and the Law: Some Aspects of the Legal Regulation of Abortion in England from 1803 to 1982* (Cambridge: Cambridge University Press, 1988), 15.
2 Ibid., 15.
3 Ibid., 18–19; Kate Gleeson, "The Strange Case of the Invisible Woman," in *Gender, Sexualities and Law,* ed. Anna Grear, Rachel Anne Fenton, and Kim Stevenson (New York: Routledge, 2011), 217.
4 Keown, *Abortion Doctors and the Law*, 16, 18–19.
5 Jane Jenson, "Getting to *Morgentaler*," in *The Politics of Abortion,* ed. Janine Brodie, Shelley A.M. Gavigan, and Jane Jenson (Toronto: Oxford University Press, 1992), 24.
6 Therapeutic Abortion Committees were panels of physicians convened voluntarily by hospital boards at accredited hospitals to rule on whether or not women could access legal abortion services. Their uneven operation across Canada, highlighted in a 1977 Royal Commission report commonly known as the Badgely Report, led the Supreme Court to strike down s 251 of the *Criminal Code,* which authorized these committees, in 1988.
7 Judy Rebick, "Freedom of Choice: The Morgentaler Clinics," in *Ten Thousand Roses: The Making of a Feminist Revolution,* ed. Judy Rebick (Toronto: Penguin Canada, 2005), 157.
8 In 1977, the Badgely Report, formally known as the *Report of the Committee on the Operation of the Abortion Law,* found that "procedure provided in the Criminal Code for obtaining therapeutic abortion is illusory for many Canadian women." Quoted in Judy Rebick, "Freedom of Choice: The Morgentaler Clinics," *Ten Thousand Roses: The Making of a Feminist Revolution* (Toronto: Penguin Canada, 2005), 157.
9 *Morgentaler v The Queen,* [1976] 1 SCR 616.
10 Morgentaler previously appeared in provincial courts in Quebec (1973, 1975, 1976) and Ontario (1983) to challenge Canada's abortion law. His 1973 case was appealed as far as the Supreme Court, where he famously challenged the constitutionality of the 1969 law using the defense of necessity. Without any formal individual protections, however, the court focused on the jurisdictional element of the claim and found that the federal government appropriately regulated abortion.
11 Morgentaler's decision to employ the defence of life, liberty, and security of the person was influenced by the success of a similar defence used in the case of *Roe v Wade* in the United States over a decade earlier. *Roe v Wade* (1973) turned on a woman's right to privacy, which the court extended to her decision to have an abortion.
12 *R v Morgentaler,* [1988] 1 SCR 30.
13 Jenson, "Getting to *Morgentaler*," 17.
14 Ibid., 17.
15 Marvin Overby, Raymond Tatalovich, and Donley Studlar, "Party and Free Votes in Canada: Abortion in the House of Commons," *Party Politics* 4, 3 (1998): 383.
16 Melissa Haussman, "Of Rights and Power: Canada's Federal Abortion Policy 1969–1991," in *Abortion Politics, Women's Movements, and the Democratic State: A Comparative Study of State Feminism,* ed. Dorothy McBride Stetson (New York: Oxford University Press), 63–68.
17 Brodie attributes the defeat of Bill C-43 largely to the actions of physicians who, unsure of the implications of the new law, began "voting with their feet"; that is, they stopped performing abortions en masse to pressure the government to reconsider the bill. See Janine Brodie, "Choice and No Choice," in *The Politics of Abortion,* ed. Janine Brodie, Shelley A.M. Gavigan, and Jane Jenson (Toronto: Oxford University Press, 1992), 112.

18 While no government has attempted to create legislation restricting abortion access since the Mulroney government's failed attempt to pass Bill C-43 in 1991, there have been more than forty-five private members' bills since 1988, from both Conservative and Liberal MPs, attempting to restrict abortion access in some capacity. None of these bills were passed. See Abortion Rights Coalition of Canada (ARCC), "Anti-abortion Private Member Bills and Motions Introduced in Canada since 1987," 2016, http://www.arcc-cdac.ca/presentations/anti-bills.html.

19 *R v Morgentaler*, [1990] 99 NSR (2d) 293 (Can), para 55.

20 Ibid., para 2.

21 *R v Morgentaler*, [1993] 3 SCR 463 (Can).

22 Peter Conrad, "Medicalization and Social Control," *Annual Review of Sociology* 18 (1992): 210.

23 Ibid., 222.

24 This annual transfer is known as the Canada Health Transfer (CHT) and consists of both cash and tax credits.

25 *Canada Health Act*, RSC 1985, c C-6.

26 Ibid.

27 Linda A. White, "Federalism and Equality Rights Implementation in Canada," *Publius: The Journal of Federalism* 44, 1 (2014): 157–82.

28 Notably, the changes that were made to New Brunswick's Regulation 84-20 were the product of concerted social activism on the part of Reproductive Justice New Brunswick (RJNB) and are discussed in the final section of this chapter.

29 NB Reg 84-20/1984, s 2 a.1.

30 Anne Marie Messier, interview with author, June 17, 2011, Montreal, Quebec.

31 Messier explained that the women were often more accurate in predicting their conception dates than their sonograms were, a reality which further demonstrates the importance of recognizing the authority of women in making decisions about their own bodies – authority that can be distorted through medicalization.

32 Quebec, National Assembly, Votes and Proceedings, 39th Leg, 1st Sess, No 119 (19 May 2010) at 1335.

33 Health PEI, "Abortion Services." Charlottetown: Health PEI, 2013, http://www.healthpei.ca/abortionservices.

34 House of Commons, Standing Committee on Procedure and House Affairs, Sixteenth Report (March 12, 2012), Chair: Joe Preston.

35 Anti-abortion groups liken post-abortion syndrome to post-traumatic stress disorder (PTSD), in which women who undergo abortions will experience "symptoms of trauma, such as flashbacks and denial, and symptoms such as depression, grief, anger, shame, survivor guilt, and substance abuse." Talk of this alleged syndrome was so prevalent that it was the subject of an American Psychological Association task force report in 2008 that found these links to be based on studies with "often severe" methodological issues. The study concluded that "among adult women who have *unplanned pregnancy* the relative risk of mental health problems is no greater if they have a single elective first-trimester abortion than if they deliver that pregnancy." See American Psychological Association, *Report of the APA Task Force on Mental Health and Abortion* (Washington, DC: American Psychological Association, 2008), 18, 5–6.

36 Chris MacKenzie, *Pro-family Politics and Fringe Parties in Canada* (Vancouver: UBC Press, 2005), 104.

37 Ibid., 104.

38 Paul Saurette and Kelly Gordon, "Arguing Abortion: The New Anti-abortion Discourse in Canada," *Canadian Journal of Political Science* 46, 1 (2013): 157–85.

39 Campaign for Life Coalition, "Campaign for Life Coalition," 2009, http://www.campaignlifecoalition.com/index.php?p=Home.
40 MacKenzie, *Pro-family Politics,* 104.
41 Dallas Blanchard, *The Anti-abortion Movement and the Rise of the Religious Right* (New York: Twayne Publishers, 1994), 36.
42 ARCC, "Anti-abortion Private Member Bills and Motions Introduced in Canada Since 1987."
43 Ibid.
44 Ibid.
45 CTV News, "Backbencher's 'Abortion Motion' Defeated 203 to 91," *CTV News,* September 26, 2012, http://www.ctvnews.ca/canada/backbencher-s-abortion-motion-defeated-203-to-91-1.971640.
46 Jennifer Ditchburn, "Motion 312: Stephen Woodworth's Controversial Motion on Life Defeated," *Huffington Post,* November 25, 2012, http://www.huffingtonpost.ca/2012/09/26/motion-312_n_1915171.html.
47 Some of the more prominent provincial court cases aiming to improve abortion access in the provinces include: *Morgentaler v PEI* (1994), *Morgentaler v NB* (2004), *Nova Scotia (Attorney General) v Morgentaler* (1990), and *R v Lewis* (1996). While equality rights were noted in most of these cases, they did not provide the turning point for the central arguments. One notable exception to this trend was *Doe et al. v The Government of Manitoba* (2004), in which abortion laws were recognized as violating the equality provision in the Charter; this case was later overturned on appeal.
48 Joyce Arthur, interview with author, September 30, 2011, Kingston, Ontario.
49 Arthur, interview with author.
50 Michelle Robidoux, interview with author, March 30, 2011, Toronto, Ontario.
51 Robidoux, interview with author.
52 Laura Payton, "Justin Trudeau's Abortion Policy Keeps People Talking," *CBC News,* September 22, 2014, http://www.cbc.ca/news/politics/justin-trudeau-s-abortion-policy-keeps-people-talking-1.2771828; Michelle Zilio, "Trudeau Defends Abortion Position after Graphic Flyers Target Liberal Leader," *CTV News,* May 13, 2014, http://www.ctvnews.ca/politics/trudeau-defends-abortion-position-after-graphic-flyers-target-liberal-leader-1.2371906.
53 One notable exception to this trend was Quebec's 2010 motion affirming a woman's right to choose.
54 CBC News, "No Abortion in Canada's G8 Maternal Health Plan," *CBC News,* April 26, 2010, http://www.cbc.ca/news/politics/no-abortion-in-canada-s-g8-maternal-health-plan-1.877257.
55 Susan Delacourt, "Aid Groups Advised to 'Shut the F – Up' on Abortion," *The Star,* May 3, 2010, http://www.thestar.com/news/canada/2010/05/03/aid_groups_advised_to_shut_the_f_up_on_abortion.html.
56 A key account of these dynamics is provided by Katrina Ackerman, who details how the Prince Edward Island Right to Life Association (RTLA) lobbied to have Therapeutic Abortion Committees on the island shut down. Ackerman explains that, "by holding key positions within the hospital corporations, pro-life activists ensured that abortion provisions were no longer legally or medically permissible in Island hospitals." Importantly, Ackerman addresses the significant role social activists played in restricting abortion access through medicine. Katrina Ackerman, "In Defence of Reason: Religion, Science, and the Prince Edward Island Anti-abortion Movement, 1969–1988," *Canadian Bulletin of Medical History* 31, 2 (2014): 120.
57 Christabelle Sethna and Marion Doull, "Spatial Disparities and Travel to Freestanding Abortion Clinics in Canada," *Women's Studies International Forum* 38 (2013): 52–62; Chris

Kaposy, "Improving Abortion Access in Canada," *Health Care Analysis* 18 (2010): 17–34; Rebecca J. Cook and Bernard M. Dickens, "Reducing Stigma in Reproductive Health," *International Journal of Gynaecology and Obstetrics* 125, 1 (2014): 89–92.

58 I do not mean to suggest that the pro-choice movement in Canada adopt a strictly negative understanding of choice; indeed, I think the movement in Canada has been very focused on positive rights issues, including access. I simply wish to point out that a more expansive understanding of rights is more explicit in a reproductive justice framework.

59 Sara Fraser and Jesara Sinclair, "Abortion Services Coming to P.E.I., Province Announces," *CBC News*, March 31, 2016, http://www.cbc.ca/news/canada/prince-edward-island/pei-abortion-reproductive-rights-1.3514334.

11

Subverting the Constitution

Anti-abortion Policies and Activism in the United States and Canada

Lori Brown, J. Shoshanna Ehrlich, and Colleen MacQuarrie

As a matter of federal constitutional principle, women in the United States and Canada have the right to terminate unwanted pregnancies. Grounding their decisions respectively in the right of privacy and bodily security, the high courts in both countries, in striking down existing criminal prohibitions, expressly recognized the harms of legally compelled maternity. However, reflecting the dynamic interplay between the contested nature of the right to have an abortion and the complex allocation of jurisdictional authority over abortion between national and subnational political units (namely states and provinces), the lofty conception of rights represented in the decisions to decriminalize abortion has been destabilized by laws, policies, and well-coordinated, well-funded attacks by anti-abortion groups.

Based in a comparative constitutional framework, this essay examines the disjuncture between the decriminalization of abortion and the current experience of abortion access in the United States and Canada. Using Mississippi and Prince Edward Island as case studies that are representative of some of the most egregious infractions against abortion access in each country, it explores how subnational political actors have worked, sometimes in concert with anti-abortion groups, to subvert a federally anchored mandate of respect for a woman's ability to decide for herself whether to carry a pregnancy to term. Although the politics of destabilization have proceeded differently in each country based upon distinguishing structural characteristics, these studies reveal a similarly disturbing disconnect between the express recognition at the federal level that compelled pregnancy deprives women of constitutionally secured rights and the realities of abortion access in each locale.

In 1973 and 1988, respectively, federal Supreme Court decisions in the United States and Canada swept away restrictive criminal laws prohibiting women from obtaining abortions in all but the narrowest of circumstances. However, there is a significant difference between these decisions. As succinctly put by G. Gail Kellough, while women in the United States won "the symbolic right to choice without the corresponding right of access," Canadian women "won a symbolic right to access but without the corresponding right to choose."[1] But given that "the implementation story in Canada and the United States may be characterized as one of massive non-compliance with the law of the land," as illustrated by our cases studies, in the final analysis, this may prove to be a difference without a distinction.[2]

The Context in the United States: Abortion and the Constitutional Right of Privacy

In the seminal 1973 *Roe v Wade* decision, the United States Supreme Court faced a constitutional challenge to a Texas statute criminalizing abortion unless a doctor determined it was necessary to save the life of a pregnant woman.[3] Dating back to 1854, the challenged statute was typical of laws enacted by states during the second half of the nineteenth century in response to a crusade by elite physicians to replace the more relaxed common law approach to abortion with a strict criminal regime.[4] Seeking to enhance their professional status, as Luker argues, elite physicians focused on the evils of abortion in order to be able "to claim *moral stature* (as a high minded, self-regulating group of professionals) and *technical expertise* (derived from their superior training)" to justify their demand for licensing laws that would drive out other healers.[5] This focus also allowed them to assert their authority over women's bodies in order to manage their transgressive behaviour, particularly if the women were of the "better sort." This was deemed an urgent task in order to counter the influence of both the women's rights movement and the growing numbers of immigrants.

The criminal laws resulting from the pressure of elite physicians contained a narrow therapeutic exception permitting abortion where a physician determined it was necessary to save the life of the pregnant woman, which empowered them to determine the boundaries between life and death.[6] However, over time, it became clear that while many doctors hewed to a strict biological definition of life, others were willing to take quality of life considerations into account when deciding whether or not to perform an abortion.[7]

Seeking to manage these diverging practices, during the 1940s and 1950s, hospitals established Therapeutic Abortion Committees (TACs) to police the border between lawful and unlawful abortions.[8] However, as with individual practitioners, a tremendous variability between TACs emerged regarding what constituted a lawful abortion. Accordingly, in addition to the problem of limited and unpredictable abortion access, which was most severe for low-income women and women of colour, women now also faced the indignity of having to offer up intimate details of their lives to an impersonal committee. TACs eventually came under increasing pressure to limit the number of approved abortions and some responded by implementing arbitrary quota systems, which resulted in denials of access even when abortion requests fit within the law's narrow parameters.[9]

Although obtaining TAC approval was not a formal legal requirement, liberal-minded doctors feared prosecution for performing abortions that had not gone through this approval process. This fear, coupled with concerns about the growing restrictiveness of TACs, led some doctors, who were soon joined by other health and legal professionals, to seek reform of the law. Their efforts met with some success and, by 1973, a number of states had liberalized their laws to permit abortion in situations such as those involving rape, incest, or severe fetal anomalies, and four had voted for outright repeal.[10]

Not willing to settle for halfway reform measures that continued to vest decision-making authority in doctors, a rising generation of feminist scholars and lawyers pinned their hopes for sweeping change on the courts, and they began developing legal theories and looking for test cases to challenge the constitutionality of the existing criminal laws.[11] In 1973, their litigation strategy paid off when the United States Supreme Court ruled in the landmark case of *Roe v Wade* that the constitutional "right of privacy ... founded in the Fourteenth Amendment's concept of personal liberty and restrictions upon state action ... is broad enough to encompass a woman's decision whether or not to terminate a pregnancy."[12] Although recognizing the "detriment that the State would impose upon the pregnant woman" by denying her decisional authority over the outcome of her pregnancy, the court nonetheless rejected the argument that the abortion right was absolute, and instead held that a woman's right to terminate a pregnancy must be considered against the interests of *the state* in protecting the health of the pregnant woman and the potentiality of life.[13] Given our comparative approach, it is important to note that the court's focus was properly on the potential regulatory authority of individual states as distinct from Congress, since the federal government is one of limited and enumerated powers, with minimal authority over abortion.[14]

Recognizing, however, that the interests of the state are not of sufficient magnitude throughout pregnancy to justify uniform limits on the abortion right, the court constructed its now famous trimester approach. Accordingly, in the first trimester, neither state interest is deemed substantial enough to justify restrictions on abortion; in the second trimester, when the procedure is potentially riskier, the state's interest in the well-being of the pregnant woman becomes compelling and permits regulations to protect her health; and in the third trimester, the state's interest in the potentiality of life is deemed sufficiently robust to warrant banning abortion, unless necessary to save the life or protect the health of the pregnant woman.

The Canadian Context: Abortion and the Right to Bodily Security

In 1988, in the landmark case of *R v Morgentaler,* the Supreme Court of Canada considered a constitutional challenge to section 251 of the Canadian *Criminal Code,* which prohibited abortion unless a pregnant woman obtained a certificate of approval from the TAC of an accredited or approved hospital establishing that "the continuation of the pregnancy would be likely to endanger [her] life or health."[15] Enacted in 1969, like the liberalized pre-*Roe v Wade* statutes in the United States, this section was intended to address the growing discontent with the strict anti-abortion regime that had been in place since 1892 when Canada's consolidated *Criminal Code* made abortion a federal crime, subject to a narrow and rather discretionary therapeutic life-saving exception.[16]

As in the United States, doctors who performed abortions under a liberal construction of the therapeutic exception but feared prosecution due to its vagaries were the primary agents of change in the first wave of mobilization leading up to the 1969 enactment of section 251 against the strictures of the *Criminal Code*. Seeking to formally encode a therapeutic exception into federal law that would "clarify the ambiguities inherent in the existing judicial language and procedures," the Canadian Medical Association, together with other professional organizations, successfully lobbied for a federal abortion statute that would clearly enable women to obtain abortions when necessary to safeguard their life or health, as determined by a TAC.[17]

Although certainly a move in the right direction, a major feminist objection to this reform law was that it did not transfer decisional authority over abortion to women. Instead, abortion remained a crime, unless obtained in accordance with the strict requirements of the law, which continued to vest ultimate decision-making authority in the TACs.[18] The limits of this approach were made abundantly clear by the 1977 *Report of the Committee on the Operation of the Abortion Law,* as explained in 1988 briefing paper prepared for Parliament:

> The procedure for obtaining a legal abortion under the 1969 law depended entirely upon access to a therapeutic abortion committee at an accredited or approved hospital. In turn, access to a [TAC] depended upon the distribution of eligible hospitals, the location of hospitals with therapeutic abortion committees, the use of residency and patient quota requirements, and the distribution of obstetrician-gynaecologists within and among provinces.[19]

Accordingly, the influential report concluded that "sharp regional disparities in all of these factors meant the *Criminal Code* procedure for obtaining a legal therapeutic abortion was in practice illusory for many Canadian women."[20]

In 1982, as part of a multi-faceted drive to reframe abortion as a women's rights issue, the Ontario Coalition for Abortion Clinics collaborated with Dr. Henry Morgentaler to open a free-standing clinic in Toronto to provide women with abortions in defiance of the TAC requirement. Not unexpectedly, police soon raided the clinic and Morgentaler – along with two colleagues – was arrested and indicted under the *Criminal Code* for performing illegal abortions.

Challenging the indictment, the defendants argued that the criminalization of abortion impermissibly infringed upon a woman's right to life, liberty, and security of the person guaranteed under section 7 of the 1982 *Canadian Charter of Rights and Freedoms.* Declining the opportunity to read section 7 broadly to provide affirmative protection of the abortion right itself, the court focused on the narrower question of whether the *Criminal Code* provisions interfered with the right to security of the person. Explaining that the longstanding respect shown by Canadian law for the inviolability of the human body had been "elevated to the status of a constitutional norm" with the adoption of the Charter in 1982, a majority of the Supreme Court justices concluded that the *Criminal Code* unjustifiably interfered with the protected right to security of the person.[21] As further explained: "forcing a woman, by threat of criminal sanction to carry a foetus to term unless she meets certain criteria unrelated to her own priorities and aspirations, is a profound interference with a woman's body, and thus a violation of the security of the person."[22] As for the TAC process, the court concluded that the "increased physical and psychological trauma" of this scrutiny likewise violated the security of the person.[23]

The majority's approach was soundly critiqued by Justice Bertha Wilson, the Supreme Court's first female justice, who argued that the court should have framed the question before it as implicating a woman's liberty interest in making a decision about a matter so fundamentally integral to her own "dignity and worth as a human being."[24] Insisting that "the flaw in the present legislative scheme goes much deeper" than the imposition of procedural barriers to abortion in contravention of the right to security of the person, she concluded that the "right to liberty guaranteed by section 7 of the *Charter* gives a woman the right to decide for herself whether or not to terminate her pregnancy."[25] In short, she chided the majority for sidestepping the issue of whether women have a protected constitutional right to decide for themselves whether or not to carry a pregnancy to term.

Countervailing Pressures: The Fragility of the Rights Paradigm in a Federalist Context

Although unquestionably altering the terrain of women's lives, the full transformative potential of the *Roe v Wade* and *R v Morgentaler* decisions has been eroded by subnational political actors who have used their jurisdictional authority over abortion to drive a deep wedge between a potentially expansive conception of rights and their actualization. In the context of the United States, the source of this schism is embedded in *Roe v Wade's* recognition of the state's interest in the potentiality of life. Seizing upon this acknowledgment of their potential regulatory authority, as soon as the ink had dried, states eagerly sought to encode limits on abortion rights in the name of the fetus. Until the 1992 *Casey* decision discussed below, the

Supreme Court generally hewed to *Roe v Wade's* trimester framework and invalidated most of these restrictive measures. In a notable exception, however, the Supreme Court upheld laws banning most public funds for abortion based on the view that, although the constitution protects a woman's right to make the abortion *decision* free from governmental compulsion, nothing in it prevents states from making a "value judgment favoring childbirth over abortion" and implementing that judgment "by the allocation of public funds."[26]

Greatly expanding the reach of this pro-natalist jurisprudential shift, in the pivotal 1992 case of *Planned Parenthood of Southeastern Pennsylvania v Casey,* although affirming the fundamental nature of the abortion right, the court concluded that *Roe v Wade* had undervalued the state's interest in potential life. Repudiating the trimester framework, the court held that states were free to enact laws designed to promote the state's interest in the unborn from the outset of pregnancy so long as they do not impose an "undue burden" on the right to abortion. In short, unless a law effectively divests women of the "right to make the ultimate decision," measures, such as waiting periods, that create "a structural mechanism by which the state may express profound respect for the life of the unborn" are permissible even if they increase the "cost and risk of delay of abortions" or the risk of exposure to "the harassment and hostility of antiabortion protestors."[27] States have since responded to the exhortation provided by the *Casey* decision, that they may seek to persuade women to "choose childbirth over abortion," by enacting a variety of laws that would have been invalidated under *Roe v Wade,* including ultrasound image viewing requirements and biased counselling mandates.

In the Canadian context, where Parliament is the appropriate body to regulate abortion based on its constitutional authority over criminal matters, in contrast to the court in *Roe v Wade,* the justices in *R v Morgentaler* did not invite legislative intervention into the abortion decision based on articulated governmental interests. Whether influenced or not by this lack of invitation, and in contrast to the blossoming of restrictive state laws in the United States, Parliament has not enacted restrictive measures, thus signalling, according to Linda A. White, its "compliance with the Supreme Court ruling on the essential legality of abortion."[28]

However, this clearly has not been the end of the matter. With the invalidation of the criminal edifice governing abortion, the regulation of abortion as a medical procedure was effectively entrusted to the provinces based upon their constitutionally designated jurisdictional authority over health care. Underscoring this constitutional allocation of authority, which limits provinces to regulating abortion as a health issue only, the Supreme Court has invalidated provincial laws that purport to be within their jurisdictional authority over matters of health but instead actually seek to regulate abortion "from the viewpoint of public wrongs or crimes" – a viewpoint that lies outside the boundaries of provincial authority.[29]

This constitutional limit on the regulatory authority of the provinces is further complicated by the *Canada Health Act*. Enacted by Parliament in 1985 pursuant to its constitutional spending powers, the *Canada Health Act* guarantees federal funding to the provinces and territories provided that they in turn provide free access to medically necessary health services that meet the basic principles of the act: namely, public administration, comprehensiveness, universality, portability, and accessibility. However, since "the operation of the health delivery system in Canada is primarily reserved for the provinces," the federal government can "only sanction provincial violations of the *Canada Health Act* with financial penalties."[30] Accordingly, "the functioning of health-care service delivery ... is characterized by a competition between national fiscal power and the formal constitutional authority of the provinces to provide for health care," and when it comes to abortion, the entrenched resistance of some provinces has resulted in a system of "uncooperative federalism."[31]

Opting to assume the risk of federal sanction through the loss of transfer payments, some provincial governments have openly rejected the characterization of abortion as a medically necessary service, despite its characterization as such by the provincial and territorial colleges of physicians and surgeons.[32] They have also employed a range of obstructionist tactics in open defiance of the *Canada Health Act*'s governing principals, including the denial of licences for new clinics, the defunding of existing ones, the inclusion of abortion on lists of excluded services with respect to reciprocal billing agreements between provinces, and the refusal to reimburse women for clinic abortions.[33]

The Quest to Make Mississippi an Abortion-Free Zone

Mississippi has a contentious history around access to reproductive health care.[34] Although the *Roe* and *Casey* decisions make clear that women have a federally protected constitutional right to abortion, Mississippi offers a powerful example of how activists at the state level have mobilized to subvert that guarantee. Anti-abortion groups and elected state representatives have made it a goal to eliminate all access to abortion in Mississippi. Republican Governor Phil Bryant has publicly stated: "My goal, of course, is to shut it [the only remaining clinic] down. If I had the power to do so legally, I'd do so tomorrow."[35]

Dating back to the pre–*Roe v Wade* era, the goal of eliminating all access to abortion in Mississippi has been a full-blown, ongoing effort by anti-abortion groups and elected state representatives. A brief synopsis of some of the key restrictive laws that have been enacted since *Roe v Wade* offers a sense of the magnitude and impact of these efforts.

Targeted Regulation of Abortion Providers (TRAP) laws have become one of the primary ways in which anti-abortion groups have been slowly and continually eroding women's access to abortion, and this is especially true in Mississippi. TRAP laws create undue burden on those providing abortion care. According to the Center for Reproductive Rights, these laws "single out the medical practices of doctors who provide abortions, and impose on them requirements that are different and more burdensome than those imposed on other medical practices." Two examples include far more stringent building code requirements for facilities where abortions are performed and the allowance of unannounced state inspections.[36]

Mississippi witnessed many such laws take effect during the 1980s. Two require that abortion providers become licensed abortion facilities, which dictates that they must follow specific licensure stipulations often resulting in building renovation expenses other medical providers are not required to meet. Another statute requires abortions after the first trimester to be performed in ambulatory surgical facilities, hospitals, or abortion facilities that meet the standards for ambulatory care.[37]

Mississippi's abortion restriction onslaught continued throughout the 1990s. A new counselling law mandated the provision of information about medical assistance benefits for prenatal, childbirth, and neonatal care, paternal child support requirements, and alternatives to abortion. Another law requires written consent from both parents for minors, defined as being under eighteen years of age and never married or freed from parental care. Parental consent cannot be waived if the young woman is a victim of rape, incest, or child abuse; however, she is entitled to seek a judicial bypass that states she is mature enough to make her own decision if she cannot turn to her parents. The state also began to allow individuals or entities the right to refuse to provide health care based on conscience.[38]

The 2000s witnessed another dramatic increase in abortion restrictions. For example, public funds can no longer be used to provide abortions for women eligible for state medical assistance or to provide abortion coverage for state employees, except in a narrow range of circumstances; similar limits were placed on the use of public facilities for abortions. In response to the 2010 *Affordable Care Act,* Mississippi enacted a law prohibiting state insurance exchange plans from covering abortion services. A 2012 law requires physicians operating in clinics to obtain local hospital admitting and staff privileges, yet nothing in the law requires hospitals to provide such privileges. At present, a lower court has blocked this measure from going into effect, permitting the clinic to stay open; however, since the Supreme Court 2016 ruling in *Whole Women's Health v. Hellerstedt,* which declared a similar Texas law unconstitutional, the case will be returned to a lower court for action.[39]

When looking more closely at Mississippi's demographic landscape, it becomes clear there are many other factors at work in the attempt to make the state abortion-free. There is only one clinic remaining in the entire state, which means geographical distance has become a major consideration for women, especially poor women of colour. If a woman lives in the far reaches of the state with no near abortion provider across state lines, the distance she must travel becomes significant. The fact that there is a twenty-four-hour mandatory delay between when a woman attends a mandatory counselling session and when she can have an abortion, and that the clinic has a complex scheduling arrangement that, because no doctor is on the clinic premises on a daily basis, requires the flying or driving in of a doctor several times a week, means that the difficulty of access is seriously compounded. As a result of fluctuating variables, some patients have to wait much longer between the state-mandated counselling and their scheduled return to the clinic for their abortion. In addition, women may be subject to the additional burden of lost wages, additional child care costs, and travel expenses, which might well include the cost of overnight accommodations.

Another important abortion research data point for Mississippi is poverty. As has been noted by the Guttmacher Institute, in the United States, poverty and the rate of abortion can be directly connected. According to the American Community Survey five-year census, 15.6 percent of individuals nationally live below the line of poverty. In Mississippi, the average is 22.6 percent. Statistics reveal greater disparity in the percentage of female head-of-households with children under five years of age living below the line of poverty. For example, in the state capital of Jackson, 29.9 percent of people live below the poverty line, but 45.3 percent of female head-of-households live below the poverty line. In Lucedale, 27.2 percent of people live in poverty, but 100.0 percent of female head-of-households live in poverty.[40] Not only are these poverty statistics extremely high, but Mississippi also stipulates that no public funding can be used to provide facilities for abortion unless the abortion is necessary to preserve the woman's life, the pregnancy is the result of rape or incest, or there is a fetal anomaly incompatible with live birth.[41]

Rates of teen pregnancy in Mississippi are also a factor to consider. Although 2010 Center for Disease Control data demonstrate historically low levels of teen pregnancy in the past seven decades this information has been collected, Mississippi has the highest rate of teen pregnancy in the nation.[42] Perhaps not surprisingly, Mississippi also dictates sex education must stress abstinence education.[43] The correlation of the interconnected barriers of state restrictions, barriers to clinic access, and barriers of poverty and teen pregnancy with a lack of accurate sex education makes it extremely difficult for women in Mississippi to exercise their constitutional right to abortion. Of particular concern, women of lower economic status are being disenfranchised in accessing reproductive health care. As the director of Mississippi's only abortion clinic, the Jackson Women's Health Organization (JWHO), mentioned during an interview, the combined result of ongoing and new state restrictions with the health department's capricious interpretations of these restrictions results in the clinic having to constantly adjust the way it provides abortion care in order to follow state laws.[44]

Located in an upscale mixed-use neighbourhood of Jackson, Mississippi, and embedded within a residential community, one of the first things a person encounters upon arriving at the clinic is the number of people protesting outside. On busier patient days, there is typically anywhere between eight and twelve protestors. As the director observed over ten years, there appears to be a protest rotation in effect with different groups participating on different days, as observed over ten years by the director. When the director drives up to the clinic in the morning, she already knows what she is going to hear based on whom she sees standing outside in front of the clinic.

Although all patients are informed about the protesters they may encounter upon arrival, it is shocking and intimidating when experiencing this personally for the first time. Protestors are able to congregate all along the wrought iron fence where they heckle and attempt to pass pamphlets to patients as they make their way from the parking lot to the clinic's front doors. They are also legally able to stand uncomfortably close to patients. The clinic has used industrial fans and music to block the sounds of protesters screaming or singing at the top of their lungs immediately adjacent to it's entrance and lobby area. Often when the noise becomes too loud, police are called to force the protestors to quiet down.

The clinic also has an ongoing problem with insufficient parking. Although it has its own lot on-site, the residential side street once used for overflow patient parking is no longer an option. Several years ago, it became illegal to park along the side street. This is the only street in this area zoned to prohibit parking.[45] Although there is no way of knowing for sure, many suspect that this was done for the purpose of putting further pressure on the clinic and its parking needs.

The serious impact of not having enough parking is directly reflected in patient scheduling and is a continual problem around which the JWHO is forced to work.[46] As dictated by state law, the doctor must first counsel patients collectively with other prospective patients then immediately follow with individual counselling sessions. As a result, the clinic cannot schedule a second group of women for their counselling session until all of the women from the first session have left due to the clinic's limited number of parking spaces. Other states do not require doctors to provide counselling in person or in two different sessions. Rather, counselling is often performed by other staff members and in some states can be done over the phone.

The health department performs clinic inspections on a regular basis in Jackson to ensure the clinic is run according to state mandates. However, it is not uncommon for these inspections to be sudden and unexpected. One particular conflict arose when the health department requested the doctors' schedules. The owner of the clinic would absolutely not provide this information because she firmly believed that doing so would put the doctors at risk. The owner mentioned that she assumed the next time the health department came it would be an intense inspection where the health department workers would be looking for any infraction, minuscule or otherwise, for which the clinic could be written up. One could argue that this is a form of retaliation for not providing the information requested.

Another startling acknowledgment concerns the local police. Both the director and owner of the clinic confirmed that the police often do not do their jobs to the full extent of the law. They do not request pro-choice police officers but merely ones who would hold protesters accountable when they do not abide by the law. Both the director and owner have witnessed preferential treatment and allowances given to protestors making it far more difficult for the clinic to provide care. The protestors are able to get away with far more in obstructing a woman's ability to access the clinic and creating extreme noise than is legal. Once the clinic recognizes an officer doing a good job, this person's assignment is often changed. The director said they have seen this happen time and again.

Mississippi is undermining women's constitutional right to access abortion. The subnational actors of state government combined with anti-abortion activists have placed an undue burden on the women of Mississippi seeking to terminate their pregnancies. Women are systematically deprived of their legal rights and thus placed in a fragile and precarious state.

Prince Edward Island: A "Life Sanctuary"

Prince Edward Island, Canada's smallest province with approximately 145,000 people, illustrates how a province can sidestep federal law to subvert the constitution since provinces have the authority to regulate abortion access through their jurisdiction over matters of health.[47] Using its ability to regulate health matters, the PEI government has been able to continually shirk its responsibility to ensure women's protected right to life, liberty, and security of the person, as powerfully articulated by Justice Bertha Wilson during the *Morgentaler* case.

Reproductive justice requires equality, but the broad picture shows equality for PEI women lags behind equality for women in other provinces. On international measures for socio-economic well-being, PEI consistently ranks last or near last in Canada; the situation is worse for women than for men.[48] Compared to the rest of Canada, there are more households headed by single women and a higher proportion (64.3 percent versus 61.6 percent) of PEI women participating in a low-wage labour force. These women are more likely to live in poverty with their children, and PEI has a provincial child poverty rate at least 2 percent above the national average.[49]

About half of the population in PEI lives in rural areas and only the capital city has public transportation. More than 95 percent of the population is religiously affiliated with the majority religions, split equally between Protestant and Catholic. The Roman Catholic Diocese of Charlottetown encompasses the entire province, is the second oldest English diocese in Canada, and promotes traditional heterosexual roles for women. Violence against women by male partners is a systemic problem reflected in more than seventeen thousand calls for information and support to the Transition House Association in a typical year. The majority of women have experienced violence (51 percent).[50] The status of women in PEI clearly needs attention on economic, social, and legal fronts, which makes the sustained resistance to federal human rights laws a particularly painful experience for PEI women seeking abortion. It adds to the burdens of their inequality.

Although the *Canada Health Act* guides universal medical care on a federal level, the PEI case illuminates how provinces opt to risk federal sanctions, namely the loss of transfer payments, in pursuit of anti-abortion politics. While some provinces, such as Nova Scotia, have been penalized for not funding clinic abortions, PEI was merely threatened with sanctions. This motivates continued operationalization of an anti-choice health regime in flagrant disregard of the principles of Canada's universal health care law.[51]

The provision of medical services in PEI is governed by a public act, and, at the time of the *Morgentaler* ruling, the PEI Hospital and Health Services Commission was vested under public law with broad authority to determine what types of care and procedures qualified as fundable medicare services as stipulated in the *Health Services Payment (HSP) Act Regulations* of PEI. However, individual hospitals, acting through their elected boards, had the authority to determine which specific services they would provide.

It was at the level of these individual hospital boards that the PEI Right to Life Association celebrated its first success in the early 1980s. This success was the removal of the Therapeutic Abortion Committee from the newly amalgamated Queen Elizabeth Hospital (QEH) in the capital city of Charlottetown. The planned construction of the QEH, a single large hospital, resulted in the amalgamation of the Catholic and Protestant hospital boards. The Catholic hospital board had never established a TAC within its hospital while the Protestant hospital board had. Combining the two hospital boards into one to govern the new QEH resulted in a rancorous protracted public battle over the establishment of a TAC and the planned provision of abortion services. Following their success of removing the TAC at the QEH in Charlottetown, anti-abortion advocates targeted the last remaining hospital TAC in the province at the existing Prince County Hospital in Summerside. An intense board membership drive and lobbying by church representatives resulted in the disbanding of the last TAC and the end of access to safe surgical abortion in 1986 – although access had already been compromised as the last termination had been performed in 1982. Since that time, approximately 150 women have been forced to leave the province annually in order to access safe surgical abortion.[52] Substantial resources are necessary to make journeys thousands of kilometers away to Montreal or New York to obtain safe abortions, rendering abortion services mostly unavailable to low-income or younger women without family support. A few women applied to the provincial health department between 1986 and 1995 to have their abortions covered, but few of these requests were granted.[53] Prince Edward Island politicians demonstrated their cavalier ambivalence to women's abortion access in refusing to become engaged in conversations about abortion access, citing the independence of hospital boards as a more important value. The ideological hegemony of the day enabled politicians to sidestep their role as upholders of women's rights in favour of conferring rights to the fetus.[54]

Unfortunately, not much changed in PEI with Morgentaler's Supreme Court victory. Rhetoric and emotions were harnessed in the service of creating PEI as what the PEI Right to Life Association referred to as a life sanctuary, so that by the time the 1988 constitutional ruling came down, Prince Edward Island politicians were spectacularly united in resisting it.[55] On February 3, 1988, PEI's Attorney General stated he had not "received a lot of calls from Islanders pressuring government to take a stand one way or the other."[56] It is compelling that no systematic surveys were conducted to engage public input, yet a few short weeks later a resolution was passed declaring PEI an anti-abortion province. This resolution remained PEI's only legislative response to abortion.

Meanwhile, the number of PEI women journeying to Morgentaler's clinics in other provinces prompted him to act. Morgentaler's lawyer, Ann Derrick, met with abortion activists in Charlottetown to discuss opening a local clinic. Momentum built as Morgentaler won a court case in 1995; he argued the PEI *HSP Act Regulations*, which denied payment for therapeutic abortions unless the Health and Community Services Agency "determined that such abortion was medically necessary and performed in a hospital," overextended the province's jurisdiction and that doctors' fees in his clinics should also be covered. The judge ruled in favour of Morgentaler because the regulations "severely restricted payment for a necessary medical service and effectively prohibited abortions."[57] However, celebrations were cut short in 1996 when this case was overturned on appeal at the

PEI Supreme Court, which ruled that the *HSP Act Regulations* could restrict payment for abortion services if they failed to meet the requirements of the regulations.[58]

In 1995, as the appeal was making its way to the provincial Supreme Court, quietly behind closed doors, the PEI government negotiated an agreement to refer women to the QEII hospital in Halifax, Nova Scotia. Under the new policy, women needed a PEI physician to provide a referral to a physician at the QEII hospital. They also needed to be less than fifteen weeks pregnant, have had an ultrasound, and not have had a previous referral for an abortion. It was a small victory for choice, but it was kept hushed.

Unconscionably, the government refused to educate the public. Throughout the years, pro-choice advocates petitioned government to make information about the potential for referral to the Halifax hospital public, but were ignored.[59] The province relented only when the PEI Reproductive Rights Organization (PRRO), a young feminist group, orchestrated a series of media interviews, garnered national attention, and held the first public rally and outcry in more than twenty years.[60] Finally, in December 2011, the government included access to abortion information on its web page, which was an important step forward for choice in PEI because government had been forced to provide its citizens with information. At long last, more women could know how to obtain an abortion through the public system even if they did not have local access.

Fortuitously, a keystone in the anti-choice arch fell at about the same time. Specifically, a new provincial health act reorganized PEI's health system, which abrogated the ability of individual hospitals to determine which services they would provide, thus cancelling their authority to formally adopt a no-abortion policy. As a result, at least in theory, it seemed possible that an individual physician could terminate a pregnancy in PEI since no individual hospital policy formally prohibited it. However, no physician has offered to perform the service and both the premier and the health minister stated publicly that they wanted to preserve the status quo on abortions, meaning they did not want surgical abortions available within the province. Taking their cue from the government's anti-abortion position, the newly formed Health PEI refused to allow repatriation of abortion care despite legal, economic, and health arguments supporting the provision of this service within the province.[61]

In July 2011, our community-based research project Understanding for a Change was launched to determine the impacts of the abortion access barriers in PEI in both the pre- and post-*Morgentaler* eras. Our work shows that barriers to abortion persisted notwithstanding the *Canada Health Act* and the 1988 *Morgentaler* ruling, thus making PEI an important case study of what happens when women live in an isolated and isolating anti-abortion environment.

We conducted forty-five hour-long research conversations in our community with women who sought abortion services between 1979 and 2013; ubiquitously, they experienced degrees of blocked access to abortion. Most of these women somehow found a way to end their pregnancies. Some left PEI, others – by their own hand or with the help of a boyfriend – tried self-induction, and others used medical abortion to obtain nonsurgical abortions within PEI. However, without the availability of local surgical termination, the medical abortion in at least one case resulted in maltreatment in the local emergency room. Some women were forced to continue their pregnancies, give birth, and parent against their will. We also spoke with friends, family, activists, and medical personnel who assisted women in these situations. Harm was documented in every case. No woman who tried to access abortion in this time period was left unscathed by the obstacles to abortion access. However, younger and lower income women were disproportionately burdened by the lack of local abortion access. All women were adamant that local, safe, and confidential abortion services would have made a difference in their experiences.

To understand the harms these women experienced, we also need to understand the context and culture of barriers created to block access to abortion. Research conversations with participants illustrated an array of barriers pertaining specifically to a lack of knowledge and resources. Many women described a striking dearth of information on how to access abortion both within and outside the health system; some were unaware of the main information telephone number for health services. When physicians refused to give women information, there were few alternatives. Well-resourced anti-choice organizations and crisis pregnancy centres competed with legitimate abortion access information lines and supports, making knowledge barriers more profound as this exemplary quotation from one participant demonstrates:

> It will lead you to things that say *right-to-life* ... There is one in the Bible Society building downtown, a pregnancy centre, and so I didn't know what to do. I just kept on coming up with that end ... because my key search terms were "abortion PEI," and all I was finding was, like, not abortion. Right to life ... (Marcy)

Resource barriers included the obvious lack of local access that necessitated costly travel over water to another province and always required personal supports and financial assets. When a woman did not know about or could not obtain a referral to the public system, she needed to have additional money to pay for the procedure at a private clinic. Significantly, in the years before Morgentaler opened clinics in the Maritimes, significant travel times and costs were incurred to journey sometimes internationally.

In considering the impacts of barriers related to a lack of information and resources, it becomes clear these further introduce more barriers – a continual nesting of barriers. For example, lack of local access means women must travel; however, travel becomes a further barrier. The impact of the barrier of travel varies on women's access to resources. If she has no vehicle, that is an additional barrier, but the impact may be elevated stress, loss of dignity, delay in access, and so on. If she has to negotiate extended time away from work that may be another barrier, but it will also be an impact of previous barriers such as not having local access.

Among the women we spoke with, the barriers to safe abortion and their impacts varied within the context of the women's lives so that they travelled several different paths. None of the women had easy access to abortion; rather, many experienced their attempts to procure an abortion as a needlessly complicated and intensely punishing regime. Some were totally blocked from obtaining an abortion so were parenting children they did not want, and others had tried to bring their periods back through painful procedures and ingesting substances at home. The women who had been able to obtain abortions were later in accessing their abortions than they wanted, sometimes because they delayed having the procedure while they scraped funds together. Health and financial costs were ubiquitous with the delays to access and hurdles to be jumped. All women expressed frustration with their lack of personhood in PEI. As one woman put it:

> 'Cause it's your right in every other province. Therefore, you have access to it. But here it's our right, but it's not really. I mean, only if you jump through the hoops to do it somewhere else. You can do it but go away ... It feels like we're in the stone ages, where it's like you have rights, but you don't, really, and I guess it does kind of feel like a woman's rights issue to the extent that it feels *[laughing]* like we don't actually have, you know, equal rights as, that you would in other places. (Kim)

The status quo of PEI's subversion of the constitution is an enduring reminder that women's equality is fragile. Regardless of a constitution of rights and protections, when a province determines to undermine equality, it is in the hands of citizens to take up the battle. Given the intense anti-abortion climate in PEI, physicians have articulated how unsafe it is for them to be seen as pro-choice, how uncertainty reigns around funding, and that the government's stance is disingenuous in blaming physicians for the lack of abortion services.[62] Renowned and respected constitutional lawyer Clayton Ruby, who worked on the 1988 *Morgentaler* Supreme Court case, states:

> PEI is sufficiently isolated that those women [travelling off-island] are being denied access to safe medical care, and that's what the constitution says governments may not do ... You can decide that you're not going to make abortions a priority, but you've got to have something in place that really does give access to safe medical care. This province does not. Those who can afford to get over somewhere else, they can survive and those without money can't. That's not access.[63]

Ruby charges that the PEI government's persistent emotional reaction to preserving the status quo opens the province to a potential Charter challenge that PEI is likely to lose.

A newly incorporated group, Abortion Access Now PEI (AANPEI), gave official notice on January 5, 2016, of its intention to mount such a challenge. Represented by Nijhawan McMillan Barristers of Halifax, and receiving litigation support from the Women's Legal Education and Action Fund (LEAF), a national equality rights organization, AANPEI's planned legal challenge seeks full and unrestricted access to publicly funded abortion services for PEI women within PEI. On March 31, 2016, the PEI government announced it would not contest the case and that they would provide abortion services within the year.[64] It took longer than expected, however: the first abortion was scheduled for the end of January and performed on January 27, 2017, at the Prince County Hospital in Summerside. One of the authors was in the hospital when a friend passed along the news. That Saturday, she drove past anti-abortion protestors who were restricted to sidewalks leading up to the hospital and not permitted on hospital property. It is clear that the provision of abortion services does not address the cultural milieu impinging on women's freedom of choice. That work continues.

Constitutional Subversion at the Subnational Level

As demonstrated by the case studies of anti-abortion activism in Mississippi and PEI, the transformative power of the *Roe* and *Morgentaler* decisions has been eroded by federalist structures that divide jurisdictional authority over abortion between national and subnational entities, thereby resulting in a pattern of highly uneven access to abortion in both countries. In the United States, as exemplified by Mississippi, more conservative states have seized upon the growing pro-natalist tilt of the Supreme Court to enact ever-increasing statutory restrictions on abortion access. Similarly, in Canada, as illustrated by PEI, access to abortion varies greatly from province to province due to the entrenched resistance of many provincial governments to the requirements of the *Canada Health Act*, even in the face of federal sanctions. Subnational entities have eroded women's rights as they are envisioned by the highest federal court in each nation, pursuant to constitutional understandings of women's right to privacy or bodily security. This erosion has been bolstered by the well-executed and well-resourced campaigns of private actors who are fiercely committed to subverting the federal understandings of women's rights.

This is what constitutional subversion looks like on the ground in federalist systems where national articulations of rights do not necessarily translate into meaningful reproductive control for women. In order to challenge what Tatalovich has characterized as the story of "massive non-compliance with the law of the land," we need to ask ourselves how it has come to pass that a woman's location within a nation should subject her to dramatically different levels of abortion access, given promises made at the federal level? In short, how can we better protect the ideals of a federally enumerated constitutional right in both the United States and Canada in the face of contrarian attacks at a subnational level?

Notes

The authors are listed in alphabetical order and share equal credit for the work.

1 G. Gail Kellough, "Pro-choice Politics and Postmodern Theory," in *Organizing Dissent: Contemporary Social Movements in Theory and Practice,* ed. William Carroll (Toronto: Garamond, 1992), 83.

2 Raymond Tatalovich, "The Abortion Controversy in Canada and the United States," *Canadian-American Public Policy* 25 (1996): 24.

3 *Roe v Wade,* 410 US 113 (1973), 118–19.
4 James C. Mohr, *Abortion in America: The Origins and Evolution of National Policy* (New York: Oxford University Press, 1978), 147–70; Kristen Luker, *Abortion and the Politics of Motherhood* (Berkeley, CA: University of California Press, 1984), 20–27.
5 Luker, *Abortion and the Politics of Motherhood,* 31.
6 Ibid., 30–33.
7 Ibid., 45–46; Leslie Reagan, *When Abortion Was a Crime* (Berkeley, CA: University of California Press, 1998), 61–63.
8 Reagan, *When Abortion Was a Crime,* 174–77.
9 Luker, *Abortion and the Politics of Motherhood,* 57.
10 Lawrence H. Tribe, *Abortion: the Clash of Absolutes* (New York: Norton Press, 1992), 35–49.
11 Linda Greenhouse and Reva B. Siegel, "Before (and After) *Roe v. Wade*: New Questions About Backlash," *Yale Law Journal* 120 (2011): 2028–87.
12 *Roe v Wade,* 154.
13 Ibid., 153–55.
14 See David B. Kopel and Glenn H. Reynolds, "Taking Federalism Seriously: *Lopez* and the Partial-Birth Abortion Ban Act," *Connecticut Law Review* 30 (1997): 59–116.
15 *R v Morgantaler,* [1988] 1 SCR 30, 64.
16 Constance Backhouse, "Involuntary Motherhood: Abortion, Birth Control and the Law in Nineteenth-Century Canada," *Windsor Yearbook of Access to Justice* 3 (1983): 62, 110–17.
17 Jane Jenson, "Getting to *Morgentaler*: From One Representation to Another," in *The Politics of Abortion,* ed. Janine Brodie, Shelley A.M. Gavigan, and Jane Jenson (Toronto: Oxford University Press, 1992). 24–27.
18 Gail Kellough, *Aborting Law: An Exploration of the Politics of Motherhood and Medicine* (Toronto: University of Toronto Press, 1996), 44.
19 Mollie Dunsmuir, *Abortion: Constitutional and Legal Developments* (Ottawa: Parliamentary Information and Research Service, Library of Parliament, 1998).
20 Dunsmuir, *Abortion,* quoting Canada, Committee on the Operation of the Abortion Law, *Report of the Committee on the Operation of the Abortion Law* (Ottawa: Minister of Supply and Services, 1977).
21 *Morgentaler,* 53
22 Ibid., 56.
23 Ibid., 63. It should be noted that the concurring opinion focused more narrowly on the harms to women "who qualify for therapeutic abortions" due to state-imposed delays. Ibid., 105–6.
24 Ibid., 172.
25 Ibid., 173, 172.
26 *Maher v Roe,* 432 US 464 (1977), 475. The court also upheld restrictions on the abortion rights of minors in the pre-*Casey* era. See Shoshanna Ehrlich, *Who Decides? The Abortion Rights of Teens* (Westport, CT: Praeger, 2006).
27 *Parenthood of Southeastern Pennsylvania v Casey,* 505 US 833 (1992), 885.
28 See Linda A. White, "Federalism and Equality Rights Implementation in Canada," *Publius: The Journal of Federalism* 44 (2014): 151–82, 163–64.
29 Quoted Karine Richer, *Abortion in Canada: Twenty Years after R. v. Morgantaler* (Ottawa: Parliamentary Information and Research Service, Library of Parliament, 2008), 8.
30 Howard A. Palley, "Canadian Abortion Policy: National Policy and the Impact of Federalism and Political Implementation on Access to Services," *Publius: The Journal of Federalism* 36, 4 (2006): 565.
31 Ibid., 566, 583. See also White, "Federalism and Equality Rights," 164–68.
32 Richer, *Abortion in Canada,* 7.

33 Palley, "Canadian Abortion Policy," 573; Melissa Haussman, *Abortion Politics in North America* (Boulder, CO: Lynne Rienner Publishers, 2005), 91.

34 The discussion about Mississippi draws upon and extends upon Lori Brown, *Contested Spaces: Abortion Clinics, Women's Shelters and Hospitals* (Surrey, UK: Ashgate Publishing Limited, 2013).

35 David Crary, "40 Years Later, *Roe v Wade* Abortion Ruling's Legacy Is One of Bitter, Unrelenting Division," *Huffington Post,* January 19, 2013, http://www.huffingtonpost.ca/2013/01/19/40-years-later-roe-v-wad_n_2512301.html.

36 Center for Reproductive Rights, "Targeted Regulation of Abortion Providers (TRAP)," March 5, 2009, http://reproductiverights.org/en/project/targeted-regulation-of-abortion-providers-trap.

37 In 1987, public school nurses were prohibited from counselling or referring any student to abortion services. In 1989, the Mississippi Children's Trust Fund, a fund explicitly established to support child abuse and neglect programs and services, forbade spending for abortion counselling or services. As per NARAL, Pro-choice America State Laws Mississippi, https://www.prochoiceamerica.org/state/mississippi/.

38 State Laws Mississippi Abortion Care Policies, NARAL Pro-choice America, 2017, https://www.prochoiceamerica.org/state-law/mississippi/#abortion-policies-providers.

39 State Laws Mississippi Refusals and Guarantees, NARAL Pro-choice America, 2017, https://www.prochoiceamerica.org/state-law/mississippi/#refusals-guarantees.

40 Mississippi, US Census Bureau, 2012.

41 Low-Income Women and Abortion, State Laws Mississippi, NARAL Pro-Choice America, 2017, https://www.prochoiceamerica.org/state-law/mississippi/#abortion-policies-low-income.

42 Brady E. Hamilton and Stephanie J. Ventura, "Birth Rates for U.S. Teenagers Reach Historic Lows for All Age and Ethnic Groups," *NCHS Data Brief* 89 (2012) 1, 4.

43 "Contemporary Health (9-12) Curriculum Unit 4: Human Grown and Development," Mississippi Department of Education, Jackson, MS: Office of Career and Technical Education Mississippi Department of Education, 2012.

44 Interview with author, July 13, 2011, Jackson, Mississippi.

45 Interview with author, July 12, 2011.

46 Ibid.

47 Morris Manning, quoted in Roseanne MacDonald, "Morgentaler Abortion Clinic Possible if Island Throws Obstacles at Women: Province 'Frustrates Federal Law,'" *The Guardian,* February 3, 1988; see also White, "Federalism and Equality Rights," 163–68.

48 Centre for the Study of Living Standards, "The Human Development Index in Canada: Ranking the Provinces and Territories Internationally, 2000–2014," July 2016, http://www.csls.ca/reports/csls2016-14.pdf.

49 Interministerial Women's Secretariat, "Women in PEI: A Statistical Review," 2010, http://www.gov.pe.ca/photos/original/Women_Stat2010.pdf; MacKillop Centre for Social Justice and Poverty, *We Cannot Linger: Background Paper on a Poverty Eradication Strategy for Prince Edward Island* (Charlottetown: MacKillop Centre for Social Justice and Poverty, 2011); PEI Provincial Government, "Preventing and Reducing Poverty in Prince Edward Island: A Strategy for Engagement – Discussion Paper," July 2011, http://www.gov.pe.ca/photos/original/cssl_povertyred.pdf; PEI Advisory Council on the Status of Women, *Response to the Discussion Paper – Preventing and Reducing Poverty in Prince Edward Island: A Strategy for Engagement* (Charlottetown: PEI Advisory Council on the Status of Women, 2012).

50 PEI Advisory Council on the Status of Women, "2006 Purple Ribbon Campaign Against Violence: The Violation of Our Teen Girls," December 6, 2006, http://www.gov.pe.ca/photos/original/acsw_purp2006e.pdf.

51 Kerry Campbell, "Abortion Law Q & A," *CBC News*, January 13, 2012, http://www.cbc.ca/news/canada/prince-edward-island/abortion-law-q-a-1.1242368.
52 McMahon, Tamsin, "P.E.I. Abortion Ban Challenged by New Pro-Choice Movement," *National Post*, November 16, 2011, http://news.nationalpost.com/2011/11/16/p-e-i-abortion-ban-challenged-by-new-pro-choice-movement/.
53 Ibid.
54 Christina Clorey, "Votes and Vetoes: A Discursive History of Abortion Politics in Prince Edward Island from 1980–1996" (master's thesis, McMaster University, 2007).
55 Ackerman, Katrina, "A Region at Odds: Abortion Politics in the Maritime Provinces, 1969–1988" (PhD diss., University of Waterloo, 2015), 85–88.
56 "Morgentaler Abortion Clinic Possible if Island Throws Obstacles at Women: Province 'Frustrates Federal Law,'" *Charlottetown Guardian*, February 3, 1988.
57 *Morgentaler*, 603.
58 Ibid., 611.
59 Advisory Council on the Status of Women, personal communication with author, November 14, 2011.
60 Peter Driftmeir, "No Abortion Services on Prince Edward Island," *Halifax Media Co-op*, March 20, 2012, http://halifax.mediacoop.ca/fr/story/no-abortion-services-prince-edward-island/10285.
61 Josie Baker, "PEI: An Island without Safe Legal Abortion," *Rabble.ca*, November 4, 2014, http://rabble.ca/news/2014/11/pei-island-without-safe-legal-abortion.
62 Des Colohan, "Our Hypocritical Approach to Abortion," *Charlottetown Guardian*, December 2, 2011.
63 Campbell, "Abortion Law Q&A."
64 Sara Fraser and Jesara Sinclair, "Abortion Services Coming to P.E.I., Province Announces," *CBC News*, March 31, 2016, http://www.cbc.ca/news/canada/prince-edward-island/pei-abortion-reproductive-rights-1.3514334.

Part 4

Discourse and Reproductive Justice

12

The Future of Pro-choice Discourse in Canada

Kelly Gordon and Paul Saurette

NEARLY THIRTY YEARS after the *Morgentaler* decision, most Canadians assume that the abortion issue has been settled, that the right to abortion access is firmly grounded in Canadian law, that universal access has been achieved, and that the issue is not seriously debated anymore. To the extent that observers consider the Canadian anti-abortion movement, most assume that the Canadian version is essentially the same as the American movement with one significant difference: they assume that the movement is much weaker, even functionally absent, in Canada in contrast to its powerful and highly visible cousin in the United States. Given this context, many of the abortion rights advocacy efforts of the last several decades in Canada have been focused on increasing concrete access rather than debating abortion policy or challenging laws. This strategy has been crucial to highlighting and addressing the significant challenges that continue to remain around abortion access and is appropriate to a political context in which the laws of the land generally do not represent major legal barriers to access.

Over the past decade, there have been important changes to the strategic orientation of the Canadian anti-abortion movement and the communication strategies it employs, changes that we believe might hold important consequences for the likelihood and nature of future debates around abortion policy. As has been proven in many other issue areas, a transformed communication strategy – if done properly – can dramatically alter the political landscape by attracting large numbers of new supporters, particularly when the issue itself has not been actively debated in several decades, as is the case with abortion in Canada.[1]

What are these changes? And what implications do they hold for abortion rights advocates who want to defend and extend abortion access in Canada? This chapter addresses these questions and suggests that in order to respond to a new political context, a modified reproductive justice framework might offer abortion rights advocates an important resource for responding to future challenges.

The Traditional Portrait of the Anti-abortion Movement

If one asks a group of Canadians to describe the anti-abortion movement, one receives by and large very similar accounts. Most assume that the North American anti-abortion movement is male-dominated, sometimes violent, and religiously motivated; its public discourse explicitly appeals to religious sources to ground its philosophical position; its main arguments are primarily fetal-centric; and the overall rhetoric, framing, and narrative techniques of its discourse embody a distinctly anti-woman tone. As we have outlined elsewhere in detail, this image – one we call the "traditional portrait" of the anti-abortion movement – also dominates most academic and popular accounts.[2]

Michael Cuneo's extensive work on the abortion debate throughout the 1980s, for example, emphasizes not only the organizational role that religious institutions played in the Canadian movement but also the fact that religious grounds were central to the anti-abortion movement's public arguments and its attempts to persuade the broader Canadian public. Most accounts also highlight the fetal-centric nature of anti-abortion discourse. Janine Brodie, Jane Jenson, and Shelley A.M. Gavigan's classic book, *The Politics of Abortion* (1992), underlines the fact that the anti-abortion movement of the 1980s and 1990s countered the pro-choice discourse "with the claim that the right to life of the foetus takes legal and moral precedence over women's rights to self-determination."[3] Shelley Gavigan argues that the effect of the singular focus on the fetus of the "foetal personhood campaign [is] to render women invisible."[4] Janine Brodie is even more explicit, arguing that the anti-abortion movement represents a "discursive campaign against women" in which "control of the womb is of primary importance" and women who choose abortions are represented as "governed by their irrational subjectivity" and "either too selfish to act for the social good or have been tricked and need legislation to protect themselves against themselves."[5]

In many ways, the traditional portrait is an accurate account of the Canadian anti-abortion movement of the 1970s and 1980s. In Canada, almost all of the key anti-abortion actors of that era were men, many of them were publicly and vocally religious, and many of the arguments of high profile anti-abortion activists and politicians reinforced the perception of the movement as anti-woman.[6] In a memo to the Manitoba Legislature, for example, Joe Borowski, a former Canadian politician and one of Canada's most famous militant anti-abortion activists, wrote that "we are being asked to be accomplices in this medieval act of barbarism, forcing our doctors and nurses to commit murder ... so a handful of cheap, third-rate tramps (and also some good women) can escape the consequences of their actions."[7] Even after 1988, many proposed pieces of anti-abortion legislation were framed in ways that often appeared to have an anti-woman tone.

Many contemporary journalistic, activist, and academic perspectives also suggest that this portrait is an accurate representation of the contemporary Canadian context. Consider, for example, a 2003 report written by Joyce Arthur. Arthur, founder and president of the Abortion Rights Coalition of Canada (ARCC), is a highly visible activist and media commenter on the abortion debate in Canada. In 2003, she published a report that sought to offer a portrait of "who comprises the [anti-abortion] movement and ... their underlying motivations and worldview."[8] In it, she describes a profoundly religious and anti-woman movement that opposes abortion because of a fundamentalist belief that abortion kills a human being.

According to Arthur, "the vast bulk of anti-choicers ... [are] *religious fundamentalists*"[9] and their "anti-choice literature is often completely suffused with religious language," even often attempting to "convert women to Christianity."[10] Arthur's report also argues that one of the most elemental characteristics of the anti-abortion movement is its deeply anti-woman position. Arthur contends that "the primary motivation behind the anti-choice agenda is a sexist paternalism that requires control of women and their sexuality"[11] and that the movement's "narrow focus on fetal rights completely excludes and negates women's fundamental right to bodily integrity – and even their right to life."[12] Arthur's portrait is not an outlier, as a variety of academics continue to represent anti-abortion discourse along the same lines. Arthur's account of the anti-abortion movement and its communication strategy is favourably referenced and relied upon by a variety of recent academic articles that tend to reinforce the idea that a central characteristic of contemporary anti-abortion discourse is its anti-woman tone.[13] The traditional portrait, in other words, continues to structure many contemporary understandings of the anti-abortion movement.

The New Face of the Canadian Anti-abortion Movement

Is the traditional portrait a reliable guide to the contemporary anti-abortion movement and its strategies of persuasion? To answer this question, we undertook a comprehensive qualitative and quantitative study of the public discourse employed by the contemporary Canadian anti-abortion movement. Our study combined naturalistic observation of key anti-abortion events, such as marches, speeches, protests, and conferences, with a comprehensive mixed-method critical discourse analysis that systematically analyzed the rhetorical communication strategies of over four hundred documents and many other public statements disseminated by the most influential anti-abortion bloggers, advocacy organizations, and federal politicians in Canada between 2007 and 2014, as well as comparable examples from the United States.[14]

What did our analysis reveal? First, we found that the traditional characterization of the anti-abortion movement as male-led, religiously grounded in its philosophical appeals, fetal-centric in its argument, and anti-woman in its tone likely remains accurate for certain groups and individuals today. The traditional portrait, for example, continues to accurately describe much of the American movement, although there are signs of emerging shifts in the United States as well. In particular, aspects of the traditional portrait correctly identify some of the motivations and a few of the communication strategies of certain contemporary Canadian anti-abortion actors.

That said, our main finding is that contemporary Canadian anti-abortion communication strategies are very different than those suggested by the traditional portrait. Rather than the punitive, religious, and anti-woman discourse that pits the pregnant woman against the fetus, our analysis demonstrates that contemporary anti-abortion activists are increasingly trying to persuade Canadians to adopt an anti-abortion position by presenting the movement as female-led, avoiding religious justifications and language, downplaying and reframing fetal-centric arguments, and, above all, explicitly using a variety of purportedly progressive, feminist, and pro-woman arguments, framing techniques, and narratives to make their case.[15] Rather than rehearse the results of this study, however, allow us to begin by illustrating this shift through an analysis of one of the most recent motions that has been tabled on this issue in Parliament.

On September 26, 2012, Conservative member of Parliament Mark Warawa tabled Motion 408 (M408), which asked Parliament to condemn the practice of sex-selection abortion in Canada. Although the motion was eventually deemed unvoteable in Parliament on March 21, 2013, it received wide media coverage and eventually inspired the 2013 March for Life's "Stop Gendercide" theme.[16] The goal of M408 seemed relatively straightforward. It simply asked Parliament to condemn the practice of sex-selection abortion in Canada. As an exemplar of the communication strategies of the new anti-abortion movement, however, it is fascinating. M408 was not framed against women or even against abortion more generally. Nor was it grounded in any form of religious rhetoric. It did not seek to recriminalize abortion, nor did it seek to directly attempt to criminalize or even vilify women accessing abortion. Instead, it appealed directly to the feminist language of women's and girl's rights. M408 was entirely framed in pro-girl language, its main slogan being "Protect Girls, Stop Gendercide." The website created to promote M408 also invoked seemingly feminist arguments about discrimination, stating that sex-selection abortion is a "form of discrimination against women and girls is abhored [sic] by Canadians, who value equality and stand up for human rights."[17] Moreover, as illustrated in the image below, the imagery characterizing the official website and marketing materials used to promote the motion dramatically reinforce this thematic.

What is particularly fascinating about these arguments and visuals is that they draw on both traditional and feminist female symbolism, with the slogan typed in pink lettering and designed around the symbol of Venus generally used to represent women. It is also notable that the visual marketing of the motion showcases a photograph of three female toddlers of different racialized backgrounds. Neither the motion itself nor its marketing made any reference to the fetus at all. Instead, each appealed directly to the language and visuals of already born girls.[18]

M408 – and its pro-woman anti-abortion argumentation – highlights the insufficiency of the traditional understanding of anti-abortion discourse. First, at least in its language, it does not read as anti-woman. It does not explicitly attack or vilify women. In fact, its core message is entirely framed through the language of women's rights, with its expressed goal being to protect girls. Second, nowhere in this motion is the fetus even mentioned. Instead, the motion skips over the fetus and focuses solely on already-born girls with both its choice of visuals and language. And finally, there are no references to religion anywhere in this motion. Rather than appealing to religion, this motion uses the progressive language of anti-discrimination, asserting that M408 is "the anti-discrimination motion against sex-selection."[19]

The framing and argumentation of M408 alone suggests that the traditional portrait of anti-abortion activism is no longer sufficient to capture important elements of new anti-abortion communication strategies. However, M408 is only the tip of the iceberg. The type of pro-woman language evident in M408 has also increasingly characterized other pieces of recent private member bills, including Bill C-484 and Bill C-510. Consider, for instance, the pro-woman language employed by Conservative member of Parliament Ken Epp in his tabling of private member's Bill C-484 in 2007. Dubbed the "Unborn Victims of Crime Act," Bill C-484 sought to protect fetuses from third-party attacks. While critics of Bill C-484 argued the bill was a way for anti-abortion lawmakers to entrench some form of fetal personhood into Canada's *Criminal Code*, anti-abortion activists countered that the bill was in fact designed to buttress women's rights and safety. Ken Epp himself argued that the proposed act "goes very narrowly at one issue – where the woman has made the choice to have the child, and that choice is taken away unilaterally, without her consent and usually with violence."[20]

The increasing usage of seemingly pro-woman anti-abortion arguments is not limited solely to the legislative realm either. In fact, we have found that anti-abortion advocates at both the grassroots and organization levels are having explicit and open discussion about new anti-abortion strategies that seek to introduce a woman-focused perspective into the anti-abortion discussion.[21] The Canadian blog ProWomanProLife (PWPL) – founded by anti-abortion activist and program director at the social conservative think tank Cardus, Andrea Mrozek – is often home to such debate. Echoing a common PWPL line of argumentation, one blogger suggests that while she has her "own beliefs about the sanctity and rights of an unborn baby," she doesn't think the anti-abortion movement will "change many minds by arguing about that." Instead, she stresses that "we need more discussion, then, of abortion as a women's issue. Abortion damages women."[22] Even controversial *National Post* columnist Barbara Kay has advised anti-abortion activists to "mov[e] away from the rights of the fetus, which arouses defensiveness and hostility," and instead to "focu[s] the debate on women's health, [which] would occupy the moral high ground feminists claim as their particular precinct."[23]

Ultimately, we have found that these new approaches characterize the communication strategies of the anti-abortion movement well beyond the formal sphere of federal politics. Across the board, activists on the ground and anti-abortion organizations are using communication strategies that are challenging our traditional understanding of the anti-abortion movement. The public face of the new anti-abortion movement is increasingly diverse. It is no longer led primarily by older men. Many of the most creative and influential voices of the movement are highly articulate, telegenic, and thoroughly modern-seeming young women. Once again, take the PWPL blog as an example. Not only does the very name of the blog point to the existence of a new anti-abortion orientation, but so do its bloggers and content.

At the time of writing, PWPL was composed of fourteen female bloggers, and its explicit mission was to "develop a nationwide network of mentors, 'big sisters,' who can speak confidently to their views on why abortion is not a woman's right, and help other women to understand the same."[24] If you peruse the "who we are" page of the PWPL website, you see young, attractive women of different ethnicities, backgrounds, and political persuasions, although they are all, obviously, anti-abortion. According to founder Andrea Mrozek, the motivation behind starting the blog was to "be able to discuss abortion with complete and total freedom, and to highlight how uncompassionate abortion actually is, from a woman's perspective."[25] The blog's entries stress the position that the PWPL bloggers are "pro-life *because* they are pro-woman."[26] They do not want to recriminalize abortion as much as make Canada free of abortion "not by coercion but by choice."[27]

Influential anti-abortion organizations have also increasingly employed these strategies. One of the most popular, and historically effective, feminist charges against the anti-abortion position is that its strict focus on the fetus renders the woman invisible. As Joyce Arthur puts it, "the invisibility of women to the anti-choice movement reflects yet another major blind spot, one that the entire movement has suffered from since the beginning."[28] The Canadian anti-abortion movement seems to have taken note of this, however, and shifted its strategy accordingly. For instance, Campaign Life Coalition (CLC) – the organizer of the annual March for Life – has made a concerted effort to include a female perspective on its website. CLC has two web pages explicitly devoted to the topic of women and abortion. The first of these outlines the harm that abortion inflicts on women, arguing that a woman "certainly has a right to know" about the potential harms of abortion.[29] The next is a page dedicated to the testimonial of women who regret their abortions. CLC writes that, "in the hopes of warning other women, [these women's testimonials] describe the devastating emotional, spiritual and physical suffering which the choice to abort caused in their lives."[30]

This approach is also paralleled in the arguments and principles that other actors in the anti-abortion movement are using. Yes, fetal-centric arguments are still important. For instance, Conservative Member of Parliament Stephen Woodworth's Motion 312 called for a study of the definition of what constitutes a *human being* with the relatively explicit goal of defining fetuses as legal persons meriting legal protection. But increasingly, an argument we call the "abortion-harms-women" argument – which argues that we should be against abortion because it hurts women in various ways – is becoming predominant.[31] In our study of over four hundred documents, we found that the abortion-harms-women argument was present in 43 percent of the cases, whereas fetal-centric arguments were employed in only 38 percent of cases.[32] Perhaps even more surprising is that the predominance of the abortion-harms-women argument became even more evident when we measured the total number of words each argument represented, the idea being that the more words devoted to an argument, the more impactful it would be on the reader. Here we found that while 8 percent of the total words of the four hundred documents were devoted to fetal-centric arguments, more than 21 percent of the total words were devoted to abortion-harms-women arguments. In other words, abortion-harms-women arguments were given almost three times as much attention as were fetal-centric arguments.[33]

Our analysis also revealed that in very few cases (less than 2 percent) were religious themes appealed to – either explicitly or implicitly.[34] This does not mean that religion is not a primary motivator for many activists; it may be for some or many. Nor does it mean that religious language is not used sometimes, especially in less public arenas; in fact, it is. But it does mean that much of the new public anti-abortion discourse carefully and consciously avoids appealing to religion.

We have found that anti-abortion activists are also adopting and redefining other key values traditionally seen as being progressive. The principle of choice itself, once the exclusive purview of abortion rights activists, is increasingly employed by the anti-abortion position. The traditional stories told by the anti-abortion movement, which tended to demonize pregnant women seeking abortions as selfish and promiscuous, are being replaced by new archetypal stories in which pregnant women are portrayed as victims, coerced into abortions by partners, a pro-abortion culture, and the abortion industry. These stories depict women as being in need of support and protection that only the anti-abortion movement can provide.

What our analysis has uncovered, in sum, is that the contemporary Canadian anti-abortion movement is an increasingly sophisticated movement interested in self-consciously managing its own political communication to the broader public by using rhetorical strategies that are very different than those described by the traditional portrait. It is now a movement that seeks to present itself as more pro-woman than feminism, banking on the fact that there are many people in Canada who would be open to considering some restrictions on abortion if the anti-abortion position was not viewed as anti-woman and old-fashioned. Regardless of the truth of the issue, new strategies such as these can have very powerful rhetorical effects and thus potentially shift the public opinion and political context that surrounds the abortion debate.

A New Strategy in Support of Abortion Access

Since the 1991 defeat of Bill C-43, there has been much less visible need for activists who support access to abortion to invest enormous amounts of energy to mobilize in the formal political and legal realm in Canada. The formal legal barriers to abortion in Canada today are much lower than they were in Canada prior to 1988, and much lower than in many parts of the United States. Many issues and inequalities around abortion access still exist in Canada, however.[35] Accordingly, most activity in favour of abortion rights throughout the past twenty years has revolved around ensuring medical education of abortion providers, establishing abortion care in PEI (which was finally secured in 2016), extending the medical coverage of abortion in New Brunswick and transprovincially, and reducing barriers to access related to socio-economic, cultural, and geographic factors.

However, given the increasing public contestation of the status quo by anti-abortion groups, a new conservative leader (Andrew Scheer) who has made his anti-abortion views known, the apparent growing sophistication and coordination of their efforts, and the fact that anti-abortion activists now routinely speak about their own eighteen year plan (the amount of time between the first abortion caravan in 1970 and the *Morgentaler* decision in 1988), it is perhaps an opportune time to consider whether, and in what ways, activists who support strong access to abortion should respond to the new strategies employed by the anti-abortion movement. This is especially the case if one believes, as we do, that the struggle to frame political issues is an important, ongoing, and contested process between cooperating and competing organizations whose effects can be quite different depending on the historically specific context. If this is true, then the act of strategically and thoughtfully "choosing the appropriate language to talk about issues" is a continuous task that is never over, even if one believes the status quo is more or less acceptable.[36] Which is to say, just because someone won a debate previously, with certain language, does not mean they will not have to re-argue it again in the future. Or that the results will be the same.

So how might abortion rights advocates respond to these new discursive developments? There are, of course, many possibilities. The way in which a reproductive justice framework is being used by other North American activists to argue in favour of abortion access suggests that these strategies might also be useful in a Canadian context characterized by the new rhetorical strategies of the contemporary Canadian anti-abortion movement, but that this framework must be critically adapted to the Canadian context.

The Reproductive Justice Framework as a Starting Point

In considering Canadian pro-choice activism, the emerging literature surrounding reproductive justice has had an undeniable impact on both feminist scholarship and abortion-related activism, particularly in the United States. A reproductive justice analysis and activism first emerged from women of colour in the United States. One of their main assertions is that a variety of structural conditions contextualize the nature and limit the reality of formal choice, and therefore it is not sufficient to simply protect formal choice alone.[37] The language of reproductive justice – with its willingness to frame the question of abortion around protecting the right to reproduce as well as the right to not reproduce, along with its ability to highlight a vision of justice that defends these rights and their structural conditions – has created a robust perspective that defends access to abortion in a way that might be capable of countering the new pro-woman discourse of the anti-abortion movement.

The core of a reproductive justice framework has as its focus the ways that social, political, and economic inequalities affect various communities of women differently. In addition, it takes into account a wider range of reproductive issues, arguing that activism around reproductive rights should not only focus on abortion access. In this respect, reproductive justice concerns "complete physical, mental, spiritual, political, economic, and social well-being of women and girls, and will be achieved when women and girls have the economic, social, and political power and resources to make healthy decisions about our bodies, sexuality, and reproduction for ourselves, our families, and our communities in all areas of our lives."[38]

A reproductive justice approach to abortion politics links reproductive rights to a larger social justice perspective, placing abortion rights "within the context of achieving a spectrum of human rights rather than only privacy to make a decision to legally access abortion."[39] Given that the bulk of the reproductive justice literature has emerged out of the American context, this argument often articulates itself through a critique of the 1973 *Roe v Wade* decision that legalized abortion in the United States. Responding to this judgment, reproductive justice advocates argue "the liberal approach's narrow focus on the formal right to reproductive choice doesn't *just* miss the fact that governmental nonintervention in reproductive decision-making can actually harm some women and perpetuate inequalities. It also obscures the role of biased legal and governmental policies in *creating the contexts* in which women's choices are made in the first place."[40] In this sense, a reproductive justice perspective disrupts the idea that the abortion debate can be easily divided into two separate and diametrically opposed camps.

On the one hand, the reproductive justice critique of the anti-abortion perspective typically argues that the anti-abortion movement in the United States relies exclusively on the argument that the fetus is a life, and thus abortion should be criminalized to protect the right to life of the fetus. Andrea Smith, for instance, argues that the pro-life position means maintaining a "commitment to criminal justice intervention in reproductive justice issues," which overlooks the systemic ways in which criminalization more generally "individualizes solutions to problems that are the result of larger economic, social, and political conditions."[41] In other words, Smith argues that criminalization is not something that solves anything, but instead has the effect of merely growing the prison industrial complex, which further marginalizes those who are victims of "larger economic, social, and political conditions."[42] Reproductive justice advocates thus reject any attempt to prohibit, criminalize, or limit access to abortion, and groups founded on the principles of reproductive justice, such as SisterSong, officially endorse access to healthy and affordable abortion care for all women.

On the other hand, reproductive justice advocates also argue that the historical language and attitudes of the pro-choice movement are insufficient, as their focus on the rhetoric of choice runs the risk of overlooking certain key issues. First, reproductive justice advocates highlight that in many respects, abortion access has always been more easily available for women who are socially and economically privileged. However, particularly with the passing of the *Hyde Amendment* in 1976 – which prohibits the use of any federal money to fund abortion – economically marginalized women's choice to terminate a pregnancy does not translate into the actual ability to exercise that choice. Because the *Hyde Amendment* is tied to Medicaid – the program that provides low-income individuals and families in the United States with access to health care – the effects of the bill are almost exclusively felt by low-income women and families. According to the Guttmacher Institute, 20 to 35 percent of Medicaid-eligible women who carry their pregnancies to term would choose abortion if the public funds were available.[43] Moreover, the lack of federal spending on abortion can force low-income women to delay their abortion procedures while they try to gather funds, postponing their abortions to times when the costs and health risks can be higher.[44] Thus, reproductive justice advocates often suggest that the pro-choice movement has done too little to address the inequalities of systematic barriers to real choice, and argue that the pro-choice movement has been willing to accept incomplete solutions that do not address the realities of the lack of reproductive choice related to race, class, and other systemic factors.

Second, reproductive justice activists argue that parts of the pro-choice movement have been historically willing to accept a variety of classist and racist views (for instance, those of the eugenics and population control movements) that "essentially blame third-world women for poverty, war, environmental damage, and social unrest, without looking at the root causes of all these problems."[45] Reproductive justice advocates suggest that these views have meant that the pro-choice movement has been too silent on important issues – such as the ways that hormonal contraception with "dubious safety records" (e.g., Norplant and Depo-Provera) were "frequently promoted in communities of color and often without informed consent,"[46] or the fact that Planned Parenthood and the National Association for the Repeal of Abortion Laws opposed restrictions against sterilization abuse despite the thorough documentation of the forced sterilization of thousands of American women of colour – citing that they considered speaking out on such issues as "interfering with a woman's 'right to choose.'"[47]

Third, if reproductive justice advocates reject the anti-abortion position because it "pits fetal rights against women's rights," they find the pro-choice position insufficient because it merely "argues women should have freedom to make choices rather than possess inherent rights to their bodies regardless of their class standing."[48] As such, theorists such as Smith are interested in looking beyond the "us versus them" framework, in cases where it might be possible to "work with people with whom we may have sharp disagreements, but who may, with different political framings and organizing strategies, shift their positions."[49]

The Limitations of the Reproductive Justice Framework in Canada

But what, in practice, does a movement founded on the premises of reproductive justice look like? How might the premises of a reproductive framework work in a uniquely Canadian context? While a reproductive justice framework is often touted as the future of the pro-choice movement, there are three important and noteworthy issues that might limit its indiscriminate applicability in Canada. By understanding these limits – and the larger differences between the abortion debate in the United States and Canada – we believe that we can begin to more concretely implement certain elements of the reproductive justice literature into a uniquely Canadian context.

First, because it understands the anti-abortion position as one that "pits fetal rights against women's rights" and does not engage with other anti-abortion arguments and perspectives that do not rest entirely on this foundation, reproductive justice literature does not offer much explicit guidance in terms of how to respond to the new anti-abortion argumentation that increasingly characterizes the Canadian landscape.[50] While traditional fetal-centric arguments have not disappeared in Canada, as we argued above, Canadian anti-abortion discourse is diverse and characterized to a much greater degree by the use of abortion-harms-women frames, as opposed to fetal-centric ones. This abortion-harms-women discourse operates in different ways than do fetal-centric arguments. In our view, developing arguments and framing strategies that will effectively challenge the new anti-abortion discourse requires us to take into account the nature of these new anti-abortion tactics and develop different strategies. We cannot assume that the same arguments and strategies that work best to counter fetal-centric arguments will be the best ones to counter the new discourse that frames itself as much more pro-woman and modern. Up to this point, however, the heavily United States–focused reproductive justice perspective has not explicitly considered nor responded to this new discourse.

The applicability of the American reproductive justice literature to Canada is also limited due to the substantial difference in the degree to which, and ways in which, accessibility to abortion has been limited in Canada and the United States. While many Canadian scholars have rightly argued that abortion is not equally accessible to all Canadian women, major gains in the accessibility to abortion have been made, and preserved, since the 1970s.[51] The 1988 *Morgentaler* decision, for instance, declared the existing abortion law (section 251 of the *Criminal Code*) unconstitutional precisely because of the uneven accessibility of abortion and, up to this point, there has been no subsequent large-scale legal or political backtracking of abortion access. In fact, later legal decisions, such as *Tremblay v Daigle* – which affirmed that the fetus has no legal standing in Canada as a person – further cemented the gains of the abortion rights movement.

In contrast, since the 1973 *Roe v Wade* decision in the United States, the American anti-abortion movement has proven increasingly successful in chipping away at abortion access. From 1973 through to 1988, 571 abortion-related bills were introduced into Congress, with 94 percent advancing the anti-abortion agenda.[52] The three major Supreme Court decisions following *Roe v Wade* – the *Hyde Amendment, Webster v Reproductive Health Services,* and *Planned Parenthood of Southeastern Pennsylvania v Casey* – have all successfully challenged fundamental tenets of abortion accessibility outlined in *Roe v Wade*.[53] Moreover, at the state level, many American states have also been successful in limiting abortion access through the implementation of informed consent laws and forced wait times.[54] In 2011 alone, 1,100 anti-abortion bills were introduced at the state level. Of those 1,100 bills, 135 were successfully enacted, 68 percent of which were aimed directly at restricting abortion.[55]

It is also true that the experiences of American and Canadian women differ greatly in accessing abortion. While barriers to abortion access continue to exist for many Canadian women, these barriers are generally limited to several provinces or territories (New Brunswick, PEI, and the northern territories) or largely mirror other barriers to general health care access experienced by rural women. Perhaps even more notably, Canada has no piece of legislation that even closely resembles the *Hyde Amendment*. Instead, Canadian health care covers the majority of abortion procedures throughout Canada.

Given the American context, it is not surprising that to the extent that the existing reproductive justice literature considers political strategies, it largely focuses on reversing the *Hyde Amendment* and its ban on the federal funding of abortion, as this is a significant driver of unequal access to abortion.[56] In contrast, since in Canada the formal legal and political right to abortion has been largely uncontested for the last thirty years, there is no clear galvanizing legal or political lightning rod for the movement to challenge. Of course, ensuring equal access to abortion has always remained a site of abortion rights activism. However, in Canada, the barriers to access are more informal and structural (i.e., related to geography, stigma, and culture), and thus require very different types of efforts to overcome than would legal barriers.

Finally, the significant differences between the legal and political structure of opportunity in Canada and the United States also limit the applicability of the American reproductive justice framework. These variations in access combined with substantial differences between Canadian and American public opinion on the issue of abortion itself have shaped anti-abortion activism in very different ways. The most obvious of these contextual differences is the different role that the legislative process continues to play in the regulation of abortion in the two countries. While in 2011 alone, 1,100 anti-abortion bills that sought to limit women's access to abortion were introduced at the state level in the United States, no Canadian government has tabled *any* abortion-related bill further limiting abortion access since the defeat of Bill C-43 in 1991; all subsequent bills and motions were tabled by private members, and none successfully passed through Parliament. No prime minister – including former Prime Minister Stephen Harper, who enjoyed a Conservative majority from 2011 to 2015 – has expressed any interest in reopening the abortion debate in Parliament since Brian Mulroney in 1991. Even recent complaints from backbenchers and the social conservative base in reference to the ruling that Motion 408 could not be voted upon did not shift Harper's position.[57] In Canada, there are clear legal decisions that declare the fetus to have no Charter rights (e.g., *R v Morgentaler* and *Tremblay v Daigle*) – which is why at least one recent motion (M312) has aimed at changing the legislative definitions of a what constitutes a human being to include fetuses, something which could potentially change the way the Supreme Court would, in the future, interpret Charter rights.

The difference in legislative strategies between the two countries is also mirrored in the considerable differences between American and Canadian public opinions when it comes to the acceptability of abortion. In the United States, abortion remains as politicized and polarized as ever, with 45 percent of Americans self-identifying as pro-life.[58] Conversely, the vast majority of Canadians seem to accept the notion that abortion is a private medical decision between a woman and her doctor, as only 6 percent of Canadians believe that abortion should not be permitted under any circumstance.[59]

The differences in both the legal and political opportunity structure and public opinions between the two polities has meant that Canadian anti-abortion efforts vary greatly from their American counterparts. As we have argued elsewhere, the Canadian anti-abortion movement is not only focused on driving legislative change on abortion.[60] There are, of course, elements of the movement that continue to seek to introduce various types of legislation restricting abortion (see, for instance, the "We Need a Law" campaign). But given the current political and legal opportunity structure, the short-term prospects of this type of recriminalization seem much less likely. In light of this, Canadian anti-abortion activists seem more focused on changing the deep values and beliefs of Canadians. As noted by one PWPL blogger, "top-heavy legislation that might criminalize abortion, for example, gets us nowhere with a culture of women who believe abortion to be anything from a necessary evil, to a compassionate act, to completely neutral."[61] It is thus not surprising that when we examined all of the cases we collected that discussed the overall strategy of the movement (a total of forty-three documents), we found that that only 25 percent of anti-abortion discourse that directly discusses strategy focused on the realm of legislative change alone. In contrast, 58 percent championed non-legislative change, with the remaining 15 percent discussing both legislative and non-legislative change together.[62]

The lesson here is that for the Canadian anti-abortion movement, politics on Parliament Hill are just the tip of the iceberg – and in Canada, it is possible that the more important anti-abortion efforts are focusing on cultivating a set of deep values that would both change Canadians' individual views, actions, and choices in regard to abortion, and possibly build the groundwork for legislative change in the future, perhaps with a government that is more receptive than that of Stephen Harper and with a public opinion more favourable towards a carefully framed bill. Thus, the limitation of the American reproductive justice framework and its almost exclusive focus on the legislative sphere is that it does not offer much assistance in strategizing about how to react to an anti-abortion movement that is working primarily outside the formal political sphere.

Moving towards a Uniquely Canadian Reproductive Justice Movement

While we must delineate the important differences between anti-abortion activism in Canada and the United States and the impact that this has on the implementation of a reproductive justice framework in Canada, there are nevertheless important insights that the American reproductive justice literature can offer Canadians in thinking about abortion rights activism. To be clear, we are in no way claiming that abortion rights/reproductive justice activism is not currently happening in Canada, nor are we suggesting that the discursive strategies we advocate below are brand new. The abortion rights movement in Canada is not monolithic and has always employed multiple and varying strategies. However, we do believe that some strategies that might be effective in certain circumstances might prove inadequate in others. Moreover, given a growing strategic reorientation on the part of the Canadian anti-abortion movement, we believe abortion rights advocates need to be increasingly strategic about the public arguments they invoke.

First, the reproductive justice literature reminds us to evaluate our own history more critically, and to be clear about the injustices of the past.

While the ties between the eugenics and pro-choice movements in Canada are not as strong as in the United States, we nevertheless need to ask the hard question about our own complicity in the forced sterilization of marginalized communities.[63] For instance, from 1928 until 1972, the Alberta government sterilized over 2,800 individuals deemed as "mentally deficient" without their consent.[64] Indigenous communities, while representing only 2 percent of the province's population, made up 6 percent of those individuals sterilized, and thus disproportionately felt the impact of coerced sterilization in Alberta.[65] Understanding the impact of this type of reproductive coercion, particularly within Indigenous and minority communities, must be at the centre of our theorization around reproductive rights.

However, in thinking about this issue, we also believe it is crucial to understand that there are different types of political spheres. While understanding the ways in which some historical abortion rights activists in Canada may have been willing to support other problematic policies is important, from a contemporary standpoint, the more important question is how to ensure that today's movement is free from any such linkages and practices. This means seriously evaluating contemporary practices with the critical insights of reproductive justice in mind, and ensuring providers and abortion rights advocates are in close internal conversation with advocates of reproductive justice as well as voices and experiences of all communities of women so that contemporary practices address historical inequalities and do not perpetuate new ones.

Not surprisingly, the reproductive justice framework has already greatly impacted pockets of the abortion rights movement in Canada. Jessica Danforth, for instance, highlights that reproductive justice is something that Indigenous peoples have believed, lived, and practised for generations in Canada. She also rightfully suggests that while "many people and communities don't know about it," reproductive justice "is no longer something that only a select few people are talking about ... [it] has been taken up by students, midwives, men, Two-Spirited people, sex workers, mothers and daughters, pro-life and pro-choice activists."[66]

Following Danforth, we also believe that the voices and experiences of women – especially Indigenous and minority women – must be included in a more public conversation about reproductive justice. Publicizing women's abortion experiences is not a new strategy either. Not only was it a popular and influential strategy in the initial struggle for the liberalization of abortion (for instance, the 1972 "We Had Abortions" campaign led and signed by Gloria Steinem), but it also continues to be an influential strategy throughout North America (see for instance, www.arts4choice.com, and www.naf.org). However, given that the anti-abortion movement has started to very publicly promote the selective voices of women who regret their abortions, the abortion rights movement must seek to publicly promote the diverse voices of the vast majority of women whose experiences attest to the fundamental importance of abortion access to their lives. We also agree with scholars such as Jessica Shaw, who believe that publicizing the stories and realities of abortion providers in Canada is a crucial avenue to defending abortion access in Canada.[67] Moreover, to ensure that the new anti-abortion movement cannot successfully claim to speak for all women, abortion rights advocates must actively promote a vision of how the contemporary pro-choice movement promotes rights that most women view as crucial to their lives.

Second, a reproductive justice framework is especially helpful in understanding the limits of a discourse centred on the idea of choice. The reproductive justice literature does an excellent job of highlighting that choice, devoid of a structural analysis of the reality of implementing that choice, can be an insufficient response to the issues highlighted by reproductive justice. Moreover, by stressing the ways that formal choice does not necessarily translate into the ability for all communities of women to effectively exercise reproductive choice, the reproductive justice framework is very helpful in underlining the ways in which some Canadian women continue to face informal barriers to abortion access, as well as limits on other reproductive choices.

In this respect, although we believe that a discourse centred on choice will continue to be an indispensable element for abortion rights activists, it is also likely to be insufficient. The feminist theorization of the concept of choice has deep roots in women's mobilizations. The concept of choice has a long history of being rhetorically tied to feminist activism, literature, and ideology. The framing of choice has become a focal point of feminist discourse. Recognized feminist thinkers, from Simone de Beauvoir to Judith Butler, have advanced numerous feminist articulations, constructions, and criticisms of the concept of choice. Constant reference to choice has ultimately transformed the term into a rhetorical foundation of feminist discourse. It also resonates widely and deeply with contemporary Canadian political culture.

We therefore believe the continued usage of the framework of choice, in this feminist vein, is indispensable. Not only does it appeal to the strong history of feminist thought, but it also continues to be a central frame around which activism has mobilized. However, as we are beginning to see with the tabling of legislative efforts like Bill C-484 and C-510, a choice rhetoric that is void of a structural analysis that places choice within the wider reality of the actual ability to implement these choices inevitably runs the risk of being co-opted by anti-abortion activists and discourse.

Given this co-optation, employing the reproductive justice strategy of linking choice around abortion with other progressive choices might pay significant dividends in terms of allowing for increased political mobilization and more persuasive public discourse. The creation of a national child care program in Canada, for instance, provides one of the most politically salient examples of this type of potential linkage.

In 2005, then Prime Minister Stephen Harper scrapped any immediate hope of the creation of an affordable national daycare program in Canada. Citing a respect for parents' choices, Harper maintained that Canadian women did not want or need national child care. Instead, he insisted that women should be able to make their own choices when it comes to raising their children.[68] Harper's use of the (feminist) concept of choice is highly questionable in this context. Not only is there a dismal number of child care spots for Canadian children – meaning that women cannot even find child care if they can afford it – there is also no current federal regulation around daycare. For this reason, the price of child care often forces women to stay home to care for their children, or conversely, have fewer children or none at all.

To many, it seemed clear that such a policy did not respect many women's choices. And while the feminist response to Harper's rejection of a national child care program was strong, it rarely made the explicit argument that linked this issue with abortion and reproductive choice. Moreover, as reproductive justice scholars argue, mainly low-income women and families who cannot afford private child care feel the effects of these types of policies. Ultimately, women need child care options in order to be able to make reproductive choices.

Examining the explicit links between these types of political issues provides an important opening for a Canadian reproductive justice movement. Governmental policies that impact women's abilities to freely make decisions regarding their family size and reproductive health provide an important opening for pro-choice/reproductive justice mobilization. Linking a whole series of reproductive choices, including abortion, under the theme of women's broader reproductive health is thus timely and necessary.

The third insight we can draw on from the reproductive justice literature is in thinking about abortion *access,* both in its formal and informal capacity. While Canada does not have legislation comparable to the *Hyde Amendment* in the United States, as we have seen throughout this essay and others within this volume, informal barriers to abortion access still exist. Since the *Morgentaler* decision, addressing these inequalities has been perhaps the main focus of both scholarship and grassroots activism in Canada.

Feminist scholars have done an excellent job of highlighting the barriers that continue to exist for women in accessing abortion. Rachael Johnstone has traced the ongoing legislative battle for funded abortion in New Brunswick.[69] Christabelle Sethna and Marion Doull have documented the geographical barriers to abortion access throughout Canada.[70] And Chris Kaposy has addressed the lack of abortion providers in PEI, along with other access issues, in his deliberations over how to improve abortion access in Canada.[71]

Activism in this domain, often by medical providers, has also been strong. For instance, the Kensington Clinic, Calgary's free-standing abortion clinic, in collaboration with the National Abortion Federation Canada (NAF Canada), has built a travel fund for low-income women from rural areas who have to travel long distances to access abortion. Abortion clinics have also been able to provide women with low- or no-cost birth control.[72]

Building on this literature and activism, and ensuring that abortion rights activism continues to link abortion *rights* to the actual ability to concretely *access* abortion care, is thus an obvious and important site for continued reproductive justice activism. From a reproductive justice perspective, this also means focusing on the ways that different communities of women (based on race, class, geography, age, ability, etc.) experience abortion in different ways. Understanding that accessing abortion, contraception, and prenatal health care – or even health care more generally – is more difficult and arduous for women in some communities than it is for others must centre our approach as advocates and academics.

Finally, the reproductive justice framework highlights the value of linking the pro-choice position to wider social justice movements in Canada. Building political linkages between the pro-choice and other progressive movements is not a new idea, of course. In the 1960s and 1970s, the emergence of the New Left – and its ties to the Canadian labour movement – were extremely influential in the emergence of the Canadian pro-choice movement, primarily in its opposition to section 251 of the *Criminal Code*. By the late 1970s, when mass mobilization became the aim of the pro-choice movement, unions began passing pro-choice motions within their congresses, demonstrating support of various pro-choice initiatives.[73] Unions also knew how to mobilize masses of people – something that was increasingly important as the battle for abortion access intensified. As Beth Palmer argues, the alliances between labour and pro-choice movements played a key role in winning the battle of the "silent majority."[74]

In the contemporary context, unions have continued to play a role in opposing anti-abortion efforts. In 2012, the anti-abortion movement mobilized what it referred to as an anti-abortion caravan, an effort that mirrored the pro-choice abortion caravan of 1970. It was met by strong counter-protests across the country, partially due to the organizing efforts of the Canadian Auto Workers union.[75] The continued ability of unions to mobilize people, as well as the historically strong female leadership of the labour movement, means that unions remain crucial sites for pro-choice collaboration.

A reproductive justice framework might also help abortion rights advocates proactively investigate and develop solutions for some of the potential issues highlighted by the new anti-abortion discourse. Take the supposed issue of sex-selection abortion in Canada, for example. The anti-abortion movement asserts that it is a significant problem and that it demands a solution. The temptation for a traditional pro-choice perspective is to reject the issue entirely and claim that a woman's choice is inviolable regardless of the situation. This may not be the only, or even the best, strategy to use to confront the issue in the public sphere, however. A reproductive justice framework could (a) acknowledge that systematically gender-biased sex-selection is, in principle, problematic; (b) properly investigate whether the alleged problem actually exists and if so, its root causes; (c) develop an understanding of the various policy options for addressing it, if it is found to be a significant issue; (d) identify a solution that addresses the root causes while still unequivocally protecting a woman's right to choice; and (e) justify and champion its approach publicly so that the anti-abortion movement cannot present its preferred response (i.e, condemning and banning abortion) as the only option.

Reproductive coercion is another important area that would fall into this category. One of the major frames of contemporary anti-abortion discourse in Canada is that of abortion coercion. In 2010, for example, Conservative Member of Parliament Rod Bruinooge tabled Bill C-510, a private member's bill that sought to fight abortion coercion in Canada. Named after Roxanne Fernando, a woman who was killed for allegedly not procuring an abortion, this bill appropriated women's stories and voices to advance a decidedly anti-abortion position. Moreover, it was marketed using language that carefully replicated feminist critiques of violence against women, with Bruinooge arguing that his bill sought to give "protection to pregnant women, empowering them to press charges should someone coerce them into ending their pregnancy."[76]

Feminists and abortion rights advocates were of course horrified by these events and strongly condemn abortion coercion when it occurs. But without the proper language, this issue puts abortion rights advocates in the difficult position of condemning both violence against women and the use of coercion to convince women to have an abortion while simultaneously strongly defending abortion access. Once again, the language of reproductive justice might help. Such a framework would allow defenders of access to (a) strongly assert their condemnation of all types of gendered violence; (b) link this to a condemnation of all types of reproductive coercion (e.g., birth control sabotage, forced pregnancy, forced abortion, child support default, lack of regulated and affordable child care spaces, etc.); (c) outline a variety of policy solutions to all of these issues in ways that protect a woman's right to choice; and (d) publicly champion these so that activists and politicians have clear and better alternatives to suggest in reaction to the anti-abortion movement's attempts to broaden its appeal by claiming ownership of progressive-sounding policy issues.

There are certainly signs that this type of work is being done. One report – released as a collaboration between Planned Parenthood Ottawa, Ottawa Coalition to End Violence Against Women, Canadians for Choice, and the Canadian Federation for Sexual Health – seeks to fuse feminist advocacy against violence against women and advocacy around women's sexual health, including access to contraception and abortion.[77] The report also introduces the concept of reproductive coercion as a potentially important frame around which supporters of abortion access might mobilize. While this report primarily speaks to abortion providers, we believe that some of the basic ideas it promotes might be effective with a broader audience as well.

The common portrait of the anti-abortion movement as anti-woman, fetal-centric, and profoundly religious continues to inform contemporary thinking around Canadian anti-abortion activism. This traditional portrait, however, is no longer an accurate representation of contemporary Canadian anti-abortion communication strategies. Increasingly, anti-abortion activists are appropriating a variety of progressive and feminist tropes to argue that its movement is one that represents women's interests and rights.

Given this shift in anti-abortion discourse, we believe that it is necessary for abortion rights advocates to rethink how to respond at a strategic level. In particular, we believe that advocates need to understand the ways in which the anti-abortion position is currently being argued, framed, narrated, and circulated in Canada, and develop a strategic response that is effectively calibrated against this new reality. While the American literature of reproductive justice provides solid groundwork in this type of thinking, in itself it does not account for the nuances of the Canadian context. However, following the work of Danforth and others, we believe that building on a home-grown Canadian reproductive justice perspective that takes into account the specific nuances of the Canadian context might offer important and effective additional resources to abortion rights advocates.

Notes

1 The work of Alexa Degagne, for instance, has shown how neoliberal shifts in the discourse advocating for marriage equality in the United States has suddenly transformed the debate, and public opinion, over same-sex marriage in the United States. See Alexa Degagne, "Queer Bedfellows of Proposition 8: Adopting Social Conservative and Neoliberal Rationalities in California's Same-Sex Marriage Fight," *Studies in Social Justice* 7, 1 (2012): 107–24.

2 For our discussion of the traditional portrait of the anti-abortion movement, see Paul Saurette and Kelly Gordon, "Arguing Abortion: The New Anti-abortion Discourse in Canada," *Canadian Journal of Political Science* 46, 1 (2013): 157–85, and Paul Saurette and Kelly Gordon, *The Changing Voice of the Anti-abortion Movement: The Rise of "Pro-woman" Rhetoric in Canada and the United States* (Toronto: University of Toronto Press, 2015). For examples of this portrait in academic and popular accounts, see Mark Steiner, *The Rhetoric of Operation Rescue* (New York: T & T Clark, 2006); Mark Herring, *The Pro-life/Choice Debate* (Westport, CT: Greenwood Press, 2003), especially Chapter 5; Keith Cassidy, "The Right to Life Movement," in *The Politics of Abortion and Birth Control*, ed. Donald Critchlow (University Park, PA: Penn State University Press, 1995), 128–51; Dallas Blanchard, *The Anti-abortion Movement and the Rise of the Religious Right* (New York: Twayne Publishers, 1994); Ted Jelen and Marthe Chandler, eds., *Abortion Politics in the US and Canada* (Westport, CT: Praeger, 1994), especially Chapters 3, 6, and 7; Maureen Muldoon, *The Abortion Debate in the United States and Canada* (New York: Garland Publishing, 1991); Michael

Cuneo, *Catholics against the Church: Anti-abortion Protest in Toronto* (Toronto: University of Toronto Press, 1985); Janine Brodie, Shelley A.M. Gavigan, and Jane Jenson, *The Politics of Abortion* (Toronto: Oxford University Press, 1992); Marci McDonald, *The Armageddon Factor* (Toronto: Random House Canada, 2010); and F.L. Morton, *Morgentaler vs. Borowski* (Toronto: McClelland and Stewart, 1992).

3 Janine Brodie, "The Politics of Abortion," in *The Politics of Abortion*, 5.

4 Shelley A.M. Gavigan, "Beyond *Morgentaler*: The Legal Regulation of Reproduction," in *The Politics of Abortion*, 146.

5 Janine Brodie, "Choice and No Choice in the House" in *The Politics of Abortion*, 81, 83–84.

6 Morton, *Morgentaler vs. Borowski*; Cuneo, *Catholics against the Church*.

7 Morton, *Morgentaler vs. Borowski,* 66.

8 Joyce Arthur, "Where Is the Anti-choice Movement Headed?" *Pro-choice Press*, 2003, http://www.prochoiceactionnetwork-canada.org/prochoicepress/03summer.shtml.

9 Ibid., 8.

10 Ibid., 7.

11 Ibid., 5.

12 Ibid., 24.

13 See, for example, Christabelle Sethna and Marion Doull, "Accidental Tourists: Canadian Women, Abortion Tourism, and Travel," *Women's Studies: An Interdisciplinary Journal* 41, 4 (2012): 457–75; and Jessica Shaw, "Full-Spectrum Reproductive Justice: The Affinity of Abortion Rights and Birth Activism," *Studies in Social Justice* 7, 1 (2013): 143–59.

14 For a detailed discussion of our methodology, see Saurette and Gordon, "Arguing Abortion"; and Saurette and Gordon, *The Changing Voice of the Anti-abortion Movement.*

15 Saurette and Gordon, "Arguing Abortion"; Saurette and Gordon, *The Changing Voice of the Anti-abortion Movement*; Gordon, Saurette, and Trevenen, "From Jezebel to Snow White."

16 Paul Saurette, "Conservative MP Mark Warawa's Motion 408 Is about Abortion, Not Free Speech," *Toronto Star,* April 3, 2013, https://www.thestar.com/opinion/commentary/2013/04/03/conservative_mp_mark_warawas_motion_408_is_about_abortion_not_free_speech.html.

17 Defendgirls.ca, "Motion 408," http://defendgirls.ca/motion-408/.

18 Huffington Post, "Mark Warawa's Motion 408 Aimed at Condemning Sex-Selection Abortion," *Huffington Post,* September 27, 2012, http://www.huffingtonpost.ca/2012/09/27/mark-warawa-motion-408-abortion_n_1920769.html.

19 Ibid.

20 Quoted in ProWomanProLife, "The Question That Nobody Is Asking," *ProWomanProLife*, January 5, 2008, http://www/prowomanprolife/org/2008/01/05/the-question-nobodys/asking/.

21 Saurette and Gordon, "Arguing Abortion."

22 ProWomanProLife. "Why I'm Prowomanprolife," *ProWomanProLife,* February 4, 2008, http://www.prowomanprolife.org/2008/02/04/why-im-prowomanprolife/.

23 Barbara Kay, "Women Deserve Better Than Abortion," *National Post,* February 4, 2009, http://www.barbarakay.ca/articles/view/23.

24 ProWomanProLife, "The Plan," *ProWomanProLife*, 2008, http://prowomaprolife.org/the-plan/.

25 Ibid.

26 Ibid.

27 Ibid.

28 Arthur, "Where Is the Anti-choice Movement Headed?" 24.

29 Campaign For Life Coalition, "Harm to Women," http://www.campaignlifecoalition.com/index.php?p=Harm_to_Women.

30 Campaign For Life Coalition, "Women Speak Out," http://www.campaignlifecoalition.com/index.php?p=Women_Speak_Out.
31 It should be noted that the argument that abortion harms women often relies on dubious, non-peer reviewed research. For a full discussion of this topic, see Saurette and Gordon, *The Changing Voice of the Anti-abortion Movement,* especially Chapter 12.
32 Saurette and Gordon, "Arguing Abortion."
33 Ibid.
34 Ibid.
35 Christabelle Sethna and Marion Doull, "Spatial Disparities and Travel to Freestanding Abortion Clinics in Canada," *Women's Studies International Forum* 38 (2013): 52–62.
36 Zakiya T. Luna, "Marching toward Reproductive Justice: Coalitional (Re) Framing of the March for Women's Lives," *Sociological Inquiry* 80, 4 (2010): 555.
37 See Andrea Smith, "Beyond Pro-choice versus Pro-life: Women of Color and Reproductive Justice," *Feminist Formations* 17, 1 (2005): 119–40; Zakiya T. Luna, "From Rights to Justice: Women of Color Changing the Face of US Reproductive Rights Organizing," *Societies without Borders* 4 (2009): 343–65; Luna, "Marching toward Reproductive Justice"; Zakiya T. Luna, "'The Phrase of the Day': Examining Contexts and Co-optation of Reproductive Justice Activism in the Women's Movement," *Research in Social Movements, Conflict and Change* 32 (2011): 219–46.
38 Asian Communities for Reproductive Justice, *A New Vision for Advancing Our Movement for Reproductive Health, Reproductive Rights, and Reproductive Justice* (Oakland, CA: Asian Communities for Reproductive Justice, 2005).
39 Luna, "Marching toward Reproductive Justice," 556.
40 Nancy Ehrenreich, ed., *The Law, Medicine, and the Reproductive Construction of Motherhood Rights* (New York: New York University Press, 2008), 4.
41 Smith, "Beyond Pro-choice versus Pro-life," 123.
42 Ibid.
43 Guttmacher Institute, "State Funding of Abortion under Medicaid," *Guttmacher Institute,* 2013, http://www.guttmacher.org/statecenter/spibs/spib_SFAM.pdf.
44 National Abortion Federation, "Public Funding for Abortion: Medicaid and the Hyde Amendment,"http://www.prochoice.org/about_abortion/facts/public_funding.html.
45 Smith, "Beyond Pro-choice versus Pro-life," 132.
46 Ibid., 130.
47 Ibid.
48 Ibid., 134.
49 Ibid., 133.
50 Ibid.
51 See, for instance, Rachael Johnstone, "Framing Reproductive Rights: The Politics of Abortion Access and Citizenship in a Post-*Morgentaler* Era" (paper presented at the Annual Canadian Political Science Association Conference, Montreal, Quebec, June 1, 2010); Sethna and Doull, "Spatial Disparities"; and Chris Kaposy, "Improving Abortion Access in Canada," *Heath Care Analysis* 18 (2010): 17–43.
52 Raymond Tatalovitch, *The Politics of Abortion in the US and Canada* (New York: M.W. Sharpe, 1997), 95–96.
53 Melody Rose, *Abortion: A Documentary and Reference Guide* (Westport, CT: Greenwood, 2008).
54 Ibid.
55 Guttmacher Institute, "Laws Affecting Reproductive Health and Rights: 2012 State Policy Review," *Guttmacher Institute,* October 1, 2013, http://www.guttmacher.org/statecenter/updates/2012/statetrends21012.html.

56 Smith, "Beyond Pro-choice versus Pro-life."
57 Saurette, "Conservative MP Mark Warawa's Motion 408."
58 Gallup Politics, "Americans Still Split along 'Pro-choice,' 'Pro-life' Lines," May 23, 2011, http://www.gallup.com/poll/147734/americans-split-along-pro-choice-pro-life-lines.aspx.
59 National Post, "New Poll Shows Most Canadians Support Abortion – With Some Restrictions," *National Post,* April 7, 2012, http://news.nationalpost.com/2012/07/04new-poll-shows-most-canadians-support-abortion-with-some-restrictions.
60 Saurette and Gordon, "Arguing Abortion."
61 ProWomanProLife, "The Story," 2007, http://prowomanprolife.org/the-story/.
62 Saurette and Gordon, "Arguing Abortion."
63 Angus McLaren, *Our Own Master Race: Eugenics in Canada, 1885–1945* (Toronto: McClelland and Stewart, 1990).
64 Douglas Wahlsten, "Leilani Muir versus the Philosopher King: Eugenics on Trial in Alberta," *Genetica* 99 (1997): 185–98.
65 Jana Grekul, Arvey Krahn, and Dave Odynak, "Sterilizing the 'Feeble-Minded': Eugenics in Alberta, Canada, 1929–1972," *Journal of Historical Sociology* 17, 4 (2004): 358–84.
66 Jessica Danforth, "Reproductive Justice – For Real, For Me, For You, For Now," November 6, 2010, http://jolocas.blogspot.ca/.
67 Shaw, "Full-Spectrum Reproductive Justice."
68 *CBC News*, "Tories Promise New Childcare Allowance," December 5, 2005, http://www.cbc.ca/story/canadavotes2006/national/2005/12/05/elxn-conservatives-child-care.html.
69 Johnstone, "Framing Reproductive Rights."
70 Sethna and Doull, "Spatial Disparities."
71 Kaposy, "Improving Abortion Access in Canada."
72 Jamie Komarnicki, "Low Cost Birth Control Available Again at Clinics," *Calgary Herald,* May 7, 2013, http://www.calgaryherald.com/health/cost+birth+control+available+again+clinics/8345684/story.html.
73 Beth Palmer, "Choices and Compromises: The Abortion Movement in Canada 1969–1988" (PhD diss., York University, 2012).
74 Ibid.
75 *LifeSiteNews*, "Canadian Auto Workers Union Battles 'New Abortion Caravan' Pro-life Campaign," June 11, 2012, http://www.lifesitenews.com/news/canadian-auto-workers-union-battles-new-abortion-caravan-pro-life-campaign/.
76 Canada, House of Commons, November 1, 2010.
77 Sunny Marriner, "Bridging Services for Women: Coordinating a Community Response to Violence against Women and Sexual and Reproductive Health," *Planned Parenthood Ottawa, Ottawa Coalition to End Violence against Women, Canadians for Choice, Canadian Federation for Sexual Health*, 2013, http://www.ppottawa.ca/cms/upload/dir/ppo/Documents/Bridging%20Services%20For%20Women.Final.PubReady.pdf.

13

Reproductive Justice in Canada

Exploring Immigrant Women's Experiences

Laura Salamanca

Freedom is what happens when possibilities are allowed to unfold, not what happens when a plan is properly conceived and efficiently executed.

– Maren Klawiter, "Using Arendt and Heidegger to Consider Feminist Thinking on Women and Reproductive/Infertility Technologies"

Despite significant progress made by women's movements, reproductive justice issues continue to be areas of tension wherein the interests of women are not always well protected. Sexual health services such as testing and treatment of sexually transmitted and blood-borne infections, birth control, and abortion, despite illusions to the contrary, are not uniformly accessible in many countries that purport to value gender equality, including Canada. In relation to the general population, women, racialized minorities, and those of lower socio-economic backgrounds disproportionately encounter inadequate sexual health services and care. This essay is an ethnographic exploration designed to shed light on the state of reproductive freedom in Canada, through an examination of women who are underserved by the current social service and health care system.[1] Looking at the experiences of immigrant women exposes the inadequacy and limits of the current theoretical frameworks that inform sexual and reproductive health issues in Canada, and the ways in which many women's reproductive decision-making is not well supported.

The framework of reproductive justice illustrates some limitations of the liberal human rights discourse that has shaped advances in reproductive health policy at the international level. This human rights discourse constructs and reinforces hegemonic ideas about what it means to be a modern woman, the onus that is placed on individual women to be responsible for managing their fertility, and the role that hormonal contraception plays in how the dominant society perceives pregnancy risk. Human rights discourse central to pro-choice philosophy erroneously reduces women's oppressions to gender discrimination, ignores intersecting factors, and mistakenly presumes that choice is uniformly available to all. For immigrant women, various intersectional oppressions affect their ability to participate in making reproductive health decisions, including the diverse socio-cultural and legal contexts of pregnancy and abortion in their countries of origin, changes in their personal relationships brought about by processes of migration, and changes in the availability of economic and social supports in their new country. The experiences of immigrant women illustrate the need to tackle sexual health issues not as philosophical matters of individual choice, but as central to equity and reproductive justice.

Exploring the Experiences of Immigrant Women

For this study I interviewed twenty-one immigrant women of various ethnic backgrounds from thirteen different countries living in the Greater Toronto Area in the summer and fall of 2012.[2] Eleven women came from continental Africa (Angola, Egypt, and Tanzania), four from Asia (Tajikistan, China, Bangladesh, and India), two from the Middle East (United Arab Emirates and Qatar), two from the Caribbean (Grenada and Trinidad and Tobago), and two from Europe (Germany and Romania). All participants had lived in Canada for more than five years, with most having lived here for ten to fifteen years. Half of the participants came to Canada through family sponsorship, and the other half through refugee settlement programs or by applying as professionals. All participants voluntarily chose Canada as their long-term destination, or were invited to migrate because of their, or their partner's, professional qualifications. Most women who participated in this study were between the ages of forty-one and fifty-two, and all were or had been sexually active with men. Thus, most had had experiences with pregnancy (85.7 percent) and childbirth (80.9 percent), and some had had experience with abortion (23.8 percent) or miscarriage

(14.0 percent).[3] All participants came to Canada after the age of thirteen, and most migrated after their eighteenth birthday (85.7 percent). For this study, I selected women who had migrated after reaching sexual maturation to capture the process of adjusting to life in Canada as an adolescent or young adult, particularly regarding fertility, pregnancy, and abortion.

The questions that prompted this study arose from my own experiences of migration and maturation, and from bearing witness to young immigrant women with similar trajectories to my own making reproductive health decisions that I considered in my early twenties to be contrary to feminist values. Immigrant women becoming pregnant as teenagers in an age where highly effective contraceptives are supposedly easily available, becoming young mothers while still in school, or getting married due to parental pressure were all events I thought should not happen, or ones I would not choose for myself. For me, keeping an unplanned pregnancy or getting married young meant the end of a woman's career prospects and hope for a better and different life – the very reasons immigrant parents often cite for bringing their children to Canada.

Margaret Sanger once wrote that "no woman can call herself free, until she can choose consciously whether she will or will not be a mother."[4] Like Sanger and other first-wave feminists, I believed that conscious decision-making in motherhood is the true measure of women's freedom, and I interpreted many of my peers' decisions as passive acceptance of motherhood and marriage. To me, this begged the question: Why would women, upon arriving in a seemingly emancipated country, choose to maintain cultural normativity by allowing their reproductive obligations to limit them? My interpretation of these events was dramatically transformed throughout the course of this study. Many conversations with immigrant women and my involvement in clinical work as a sexual health peer educator and abortion counsellor completely reformulated my perception of how ordinary people make reproductive health decisions, and of the priorities that inform them. These experiences have enabled me to arrive at a more nuanced understanding of the rationale that fuels popular stereotypes regarding immigrant women as anti-feminist, culturally bound, or victims of micro-patriarchies within an otherwise egalitarian Canada.

My judgment of young immigrant women's reproductive experiences did not consider their own aspirations and reproductive goals regarding marriage and family. Instead, I prioritized participation in the workforce and worried that they could not be mothers while also pursuing successful careers. I judged them to be irresponsible for potentially misusing contraception and for choosing to continue unplanned pregnancies with limited resources. My initial reaction to their choices was derived from hegemonic attitudes that hold women individually responsible for regulating their fertility, force them to choose between motherhood and career advancement, and shame them for reproductive decisions without considering the significant complexities of birth control use, or the social meanings of pregnancy in relation to women's own reproductive goals. The misogynistic attitudes permeating my initial judgment are ubiquitous in North America and are part of seemingly liberal beliefs about women and our responsibilities in regulating our fertility that immigrants are compelled to embrace as they integrate into Canadian society. Thus, my intention in undertaking this study was not to measure immigrant women's straightforward pre- and post-migration sexual health literacy, but to encourage open and self-reflexive accounts of their experiences of health and engagement with sexual health services in Canada. My approach to women's narratives was directed by the following questions: To what extent does migration impact women's conceptualizations of themselves, their bodies, and their roles in society? What is *their* vision of healthy sexuality?

Reproductive Justice in Canada

Over the last several decades, feminist scholars have turned their attention to the role medical discourses have played in shaping the female body and how social conditions and inequities often determine health outcomes. While an analysis of gender and its significance has broadly shaped the ways in which we understand health policy and research health issues, persistent inequities demand a paradigm shift towards a more nuanced understanding of intersectionality in women's lives. Canada's history as a colonizing power and settler society, its unique approach to multiculturalism, and its popularity as an immigration destination for people from around the globe mean that the circumstances that shape women's health in Canada are not only extremely diverse, but also have relevance beyond national borders.[5] Most of the white, middle-class women who dominate feminist movements in industrialized nations have chosen to remain silent about reproductive injustices at home because they intersect with socio-economic, racial, and political inequities that challenge their own socio-economic and racial privilege. For Canadian feminist movements to take into account the health of marginalized women in Canada, a postcolonial understanding of current health disparities is required, as well as what Susan Sherwin calls a relational conceptualization of human autonomy: that is, an understanding of autonomy as socially situated, and thus contextualized by multiple personal and public relationships with political dimensions that structure an individual's selfhood.[6] This formulation of autonomy is fundamentally antithetical to liberal human rights discourse and pro-choice philosophy, which locate rights and choice primarily within the individual citizen body.

Feminists in the global South and racialized women in industrialized nations have critiqued pro-choice movements for portraying women as overly autonomous and self-interested actors, and for failing to pay sufficient attention to women's historical and contemporary embeddedness in their social contexts.[7] Intellectual currents informed by critical race theory (particularly by women of colour in the United States) have, over the past twenty years, expanded discussions of reproductive rights to conceptualize *reproductive justice* as the complete physical, mental, spiritual, political, social, and economic well-being of women and girls.[8] For example, the American organization SisterSong: Women of Colour Reproductive Health Collective discusses reproductive justice as linked to the ability of any woman to determine her reproductive destiny in relation to the conditions in her community, and not just as a matter of individual choice and access.[9] For Indigenous women and women of colour, it is equally important to fight for the right to have children, the right not to have children, and the right to safely parent the children we have.[10] In a society where women earn less than men, where quality and affordable daycare and housing are scarce, and where racism is systemic, the opportunities for women to realize their goals are complex and systemically regulated.[11] Thus, drawing on reproductive justice as a theoretical framework is important because it shifts the focus to reproductive oppression – "the control and exploitation of women, girls and individuals though our bodies, sexuality, labour and reproduction."[12] We have only just begun to grapple intellectually with how processes of migration and adjustment complicate women's reproductive lives.

For immigrant women in Canada, issues of reproductive justice are nestled within broader processes of settlement. For instance, since the 1980s, research has shown that recently arrived immigrants, especially those of non-European origin, statistically have had *lower* rates of negative health outcomes than other Canadians, such as low life expectancy, disability prevalence, incidence of chronic health conditions, depression, smoking, and obesity.[13] However, immigrants who have lived in Canada for longer than a decade report a decline in health status and begin to resemble the Canadian-born population. Women, particularly from non-European source countries, are most likely to report the steepest decline in self-rated health status compared to Canadian-born women and men.[14] Dubbed *the healthy immigrant effect,* this phenomenon clearly illustrates the impact of social determinants of health and well-being in Canada.

Other studies suggest that higher education and income, the ability to communicate in an official language, a spousal relationship, and the presence of a support network operate as prophylactic factors against a decline in health status.[15] Unfortunately, immigrants are disproportionately poorer than the general population; 65 percent of immigrants become low-income within their first decade in Canada, *regardless of educational attainment.*[16] The likelihood of being poor is fifty times higher for immigrants than members of the dominant society, and more likely for those coming from non-European countries.[17] A loss of social networks and support, de-skilling and de-professionalization, as well as disruption and changes in power dynamics within families and couples, are common across all immigrant ethnicities in Canada.[18] It is through processes and experiences of immigration that women often witness a decline in health, socio-economic status, and access to social support networks. From a reproductive justice perspective, considering the political consequences of migration and changes in socio-economic status and access to support is central to understanding how immigrant women make reproductive health decisions. Moreover, considering these issues is imperative when determining the substantive kinds of supports immigrant women need in order to be served equitably by our health care system.

While some feminists are offended by the assertion that conceptualizing reproductive rights as a matter of choice is not inclusive, I challenge them to consider the socio-economic privilege involved in seeking to dominate those narratives women of colour use to express our experiences and shape reproductive activism.[19] Focusing exclusively on choice is insufficient, and leads to making individuals personally responsible for creating and coping with larger systemic problems related to reproduction, motherhood, and sexuality.[20] The language of reproductive justice offers tools to build theoretical bridges and integrate intersectionality into reproductive rights movements so that people can engage with matters of reproductive oppression, even if they feel alienated by the overly moralistic and sensational debates surrounding abortion. Especially in academic settings, diluting conversations about reproductive oppression down to abortion and individual freedoms draws attention away from the systemic cultural and socio-economic inequity that results in imbalanced opportunities to participate in cultural discourse and public policy decisions about women's health. In contrast to the practical emphasis on abortion rights of the pro-choice movement, a framework of reproductive justice not only engenders conversations about the necessity of creating those conditions of possibility that enable the realization of fairness in reproductive rights, but also allows for room to conceptualize the individual as embedded within diverse communities and contexts.

Reproductive Rights in International Context

Perhaps the clearest illustration of privilege in the voices dominating discussion about reproductive rights is in the international context of commitments made toward the improvement of women's health and reproductive health issues since the beginning of the millennium. A number of influential international women's conferences were held in the 1990s, most notably the 1994 International Conference on Population and Development (ICPD) in Cairo and the 1995 United Nations Fourth World Conference on Women in Beijing, in which discourse on reproductive health came to be understood within the framework of human rights, gender equality, and the empowerment of women.[21] Advocates established the application of human rights standards to sexual and reproductive health issues, gaining the formal recognition of some sexuality and reproduction rights as outlined by documents such as the *Yogyakarta Principles on Sexual Orientation and Gender Identity,* and the International Planned Parenthood Federation's *Declaration on Sexual Rights.*[22]

The sense of imminent change felt by the international community at the time was reinforced when concern with reproductive health issues was dominant in conceptualizing the United Nations Millennium Development Goals (MDGs), where reduction of child mortality, maternal mortality, and HIV/AIDS was part of the agenda. Specific targets called for significant improvements between 1990 and 2015: to reduce by three-quarters the maternal mortality ratio, to reduce by two-thirds the under-five mortality rate, and to have halted and begun to reverse the spread of HIV/AIDS.[23] UN member states recognize that most maternal deaths arise from complications of childbirth, in the immediate postpartum period, or after unsafe abortion.[24] These deaths are linked with the absence of skilled health personnel during childbirth, lack of services able to provide emergency care and deal with "complications of unsafe abortion," and ineffective referral systems.[25] At the international level, advocacy for the provision of safe abortion, and not merely the elimination of unsafe abortion, is carefully spoken about as limited "to the extent allowed by law."[26]

International human rights law has a tendency towards fragmentation; for the sake of realizability, we limit the protections that can be afforded by any one right in isolation. Given the lack of official arbiters across political and expert bodies, considerable tensions between United Nations member states have stalled the realization of standardized applications of established human rights law to address reproductive health problems.[27] Measures of maternal mortality, widely regarded as the most important indicator of the status of women and their access to adequate health care, show that we are nowhere near achieving the goals of the ICPD Programme of Action, or of the Millennium Summit of 2000.[28] In fact, none of the Millennium Development Goals (MDGs) in relation to reproductive health were met by 2015. At the global level, maternal mortality decreased by less than 1 percent per year between 1990 and 2005.[29] By 2015, the maternal mortality ratio had declined by 45 percent worldwide,[30] falling well short of the target reduction of two-thirds, or 66 percent. Reproductive health has not fared as well as originally hoped by member states, and the international community remains far from achieving agreed upon targets.[31]

In practice, maternal health is a poor indicator of women's reproductive health. As countries concentrated on maternity, they focused on health care for women giving birth to ensure mothers remained alive for their children. Maternal health became linked to newborn mortality.[32] Berit Austveg, Senior Adviser of the Norwegian Board of Health Supervisors, asserts that maternal health, rather than encompassing only the health of women giving birth and their newborns, was meant to be about pregnancy and all its possible outcomes: miscarriage, delivery of stillbirth, living child, or abortion.[33] However, these latter dimensions were lost through the interpretation and use of this measure as an overall indicator.

While the International Conference on Population and Development (ICPD)'s application of human rights to reproductive rights was pivotal in advancing international discourse, so was its discussion of abortion. Removed from its reality, the ICPD's discussion of the procedure was couched in moralistic language regarding its undesirability. The ICPD

Programme of Action reads: "Prevention of unwanted pregnancies must always be given the highest priority and every attempt should be made to eliminate the need for abortion ... In circumstances where abortion is not against the law, such abortion should be safe."[34] In effect, instead of treating abortion as a legitimate health service and means of fertility regulation, the Programme of Action recommends that we prioritize preventing unwanted pregnancies, and not the provision of abortion on demand.[35] Once again, a narrow focus on pregnancy decision-making and national imperatives to constrict the actions of individual women dominated the discussion, ignoring the approximately 8 million women who suffer life-threatening complications related to pregnancy each year worldwide[36] and the estimated 68,000 women globally who die each year from unsafe abortion complications.[37]

Further, preventing unwanted pregnancies is not, statistically, a feasible task. As Marge Berer asserts, "contraceptive methods are not perfect and people are not perfect users of them ... in some cases men stop women from using contraception, while in other cases rape, sexual abuse and coercive sexual relations" are the reason for pregnancy.[38] Moral judgment of abortion consistently undermines the public health directive to save women's lives – the language of initiatives such as the 1994 Programme of Action is simply not based on evidence of what is required to reduce women's mortality. Indeed, this stigmatizing language was felt by those at the table to be the only way in which a conversation about abortion could be included in the ICPD at all. International discourse asserting that contraceptive technology negates the need for safe abortion is saturated both with an inflated expectation about the effectiveness of the newest modes of birth control, most notably the contraceptive pill, and a blind belief in scientific and technocratic solutions to social problems. The pervasive ideology of the power of technology both to depoliticize and fix problems of power inequity is maintained by wilful ignorance of statistical and ethnographic data on the suitability and efficacy of contraception, violence against women, and the complex and socially determined ways in which human sexuality is negotiated.

Controlling Fertility: A Matter of Choice?

Since the so-called sexual revolution of the 1960s, widespread acceptance of hormonal birth control has created a pernicious climate in which women's decisions *not* to "just take the pill" are perceived as irresponsible, silly, or uneducated. Most popular in industrialized countries such as New Zealand, Australia, Britain, and the United States, within five years of its launch in the 1960s, the pill was being taken by nearly eleven million women across the world every year.[39] The new technology was lauded as a dream come true. In the words of an American journalist: "Modern woman is at last free, as a man is free, to dispose of her own body, to earn her living, to pursue the improvement of her mind, to try a successful career."[40]

Although the theoretical need to control conception in the name of women's freedom was part of the rhetoric of birth control advocates such as Margaret Sanger and Simone de Beauvoir since the 1920s, historian Lara Marks asserts that the pill significantly altered people's expectations about contraception and what it should be able to achieve, both in terms of efficacy and in terms of user responsibility.[41] Contraceptive appliances already popularized at the time of the pill's inception, such as the external condom and the diaphragm, are very effective with perfect use, but their typical effectiveness hovers around 84 to 85 percent. Couples in the earlier part of the twentieth century accepted an element of risk in contraceptive techniques and, believing they could not entirely control fertility, did not expect to be able to plan family size with absolute certainty.[42] The introduction of the pill dramatically altered this view for individuals, and for the international population control movement that enthusiastically popularized the idea that fertility is amenable to careful planning and control. From its launch, pharmaceutical companies have promoted the pill as at least 99 percent effective – often without explanations that this maximum efficacy is only made possible by individual women's abilities to take the medication every day at the same time, use backup contraception when mistakes are made, withstand the pill's potential side effects, and accept elevated risks of cardiovascular complications.

Notwithstanding its drawbacks, efficacy of the pill made the *perceived level of risk* regarding pregnancy an important question when it came to contraceptive choice.[43] By raising expectations about the effectiveness of contraceptive techniques in general by providing seemingly near-perfect coverage, the pill also influenced reproductive behaviour; planning the size of families enabled couples to pursue other priorities – such as education, women's careers, and financial stability – and delay having children until it was convenient.[44] The importance of these other goals, and the fact that they can most often be achieved by women in capitalist economies only through careful control of their fertility, raises questions about the degree to which taking the pill is a matter of choice. Sociologist Kara Granzow explains, "if control of her reproductive capacity is what grants her 'freedom' then the question of 'choice' is brought immediately to bear: with freedom at stake, the 'choice' is one between being free and not being free – a dubious 'choice.'"[45] Given the necessity of women's participation in the workforce, and the perceived dearth of options for birth control, the social imperative to take what is lauded as the world's most effective (temporary) contraceptive feels for many like an obligation.[46]

Since the 1990s, feminist theorists have started to problematize this conceptualization of women's freedom as stemming directly from their disassociation from the body and its banal capacities of reproduction. Causal links between the advent of the pill and women's so-called liberation are persuasive only if we accept the premise that various forms and histories of gender oppression are universally due to women's essential biological inferiority.[47] Eco-feminist critiques have highlighted the ubiquity of what Lealle Ruhl calls the "paradigm of the willed pregnancy" and illustrated some of the punitive consequences for women who decline (or worse, fail) to prove their possession of personal responsibility by planning and controlling their fertility.[48] Neoliberal paradigms have made acting responsibly when it comes to reproduction synonymous with being in control of biological functions (as if this were entirely possible). Planned reproduction is idealized as the manifestation of women's ultimate freedom (from the body), and unplanned pregnancy conceptualized as individual moral failure to control the body – lack of choice in pregnancy is consequently a lack of freedom.[49]

The inescapabilty of this discourse of personal responsibility stems from the historical reality that women's reproductive capacities have been the bases of their exclusion from public life. Western feminism has historically accepted that the theoretical foundations of the rational actor are severed from natural and physical domains; women's escape from the binds of birthing and child rearing would lead to their status as autonomous and rational actors in the elusive public sphere.[50] For the liberal subject, the need to control the body is not a choice, but a condition of being accepted as human: autonomous, of rational intellect, and possessing free will.

Present-day ideology around reproduction positions pregnancy as a matter of choice within a general "fetishization of the will," as well as the mind/body split characteristic of modern liberalism.[51] The willed pregnancy rehabilitates pregnancy – and therefore women – for liberalist autonomy; (self-)control is imposed on a biological process widely held to be beyond human control and the scope of liberal theory.[52] In efforts to control their fertility, women's practical engagement with contraceptive technologies (including the pill) can be challenging and dissatisfying because of the latter's inability to reconcile rational planning with the lived experience of sexuality and the body. While women's trajectories arriving at a suitable method of birth control and difficulties in doing so merit academic study on their own, I broach this subject here briefly to destabilize the common assumption I have encountered clinically in sexual health counselling that the sexual revolution and availability of the pill have made women's sexual lives straightforward, an assumption that Marks documents historically.[53]

Sexual Health and Social Realities: Experiencing Fertility

One of the guiding assumptions initially directing this research was my contention that abortion should always be considered in cases of unintended pregnancy. This misguided attitude obscures the ordinary nature of unplanned pregnancy, the fact that not all such pregnancies are also unwanted, and the reality that reactions to unintended pregnancy are as varied as the people who have them. Whatever the conditions of abortion accessibility, various factors dictate whether a pregnancy will produce a decision-making process in which abortion is considered at all. A significant factor related to this study is that, for many immigrant women, pregnancy and fertility may be nestled in conceptual contexts where these events are not necessarily methodically planned and controlled, as is expected in the norms of Western fertility regulation. Rather, pregnancy may be accepted and expected as a natural progression after marriage, and for many it is a spiritual occurrence not meant to be individually controlled.[54] When discussing their pregnancies, many immigrant women who shared their experiences with me recalled not making concrete plans to control when and how many pregnancies they expected. I asked if their pregnancies were planned and if they wanted all of them:

> Um, they were wanted, but were they planned? *[chuckles]* I would say in a way they were planned, because they were wanted. I wanted to have kids, right? After I got married, then ... I guess I wanted – of course that's

> a natural thing. You start having kids. So was it planned that I would have the kid ... but, um, in this year? Not really.
>
> – Angela, fifty-one, migrated from Grenada, human resources manager and mother of three[55]

> We didn't plan to ... my husband came [to Tajikistan] for the second time after we got married to ... fix the documents and everything, and I got pregnant very quickly. I went for the tests to the doctor, for when I applied to come here, and the doctor was like, um, we have to check if you're pregnant or not, and I said, "No, I'm not pregnant." And I got the pills to start that day, but then the doctor said, "No, you're pregnant!" ... I always wanted ... but not at that time, because I had to come here to settle [when I was seven months along].
>
> – Stella, twenty-four, migrated from Tajikistan, homemaker and mother of two

> I never planned for anything, you know *[chuckles]* all of them! Here, when I had my daughter, my son after her, maybe a year and seven months, but I don't plan for that. Like, I start to use my tablets [birth control pills] the same, I don't know what happened to me. I ... found the tablets not good. I have to go for my doctor to tell her that. Before I go, I find myself pregnant.
>
> – Anna, forty-four, migrated from Egypt, homemaker and mother of four

In addition to accepting the anticipation of pregnancy after marriage, women in many parts of the world may not necessarily have concrete contraceptive knowledge before their first pregnancy. This is partly because contraceptives are conceptualized as technologies used less to prevent pregnancies, and more to achieve a couple's desired space between them. Many immigrant women share the sentiment that couples should wait to consider using a birth control method in order not to interfere with the natural conception process of the first pregnancy and to ensure they will have no fertility challenges.

> Because [in Egypt] they think if you're having any method, then it's gonna prevent you in the future from having any children, so they try at least for the first child to have nothing. Just have the first child, then do

> whatever you want ... Even though now it's different, some people will wait, and not all people will have problems afterwards.
>
> – Nala, twenty-eight, migrated from Egypt, chemical engineering student and mother of two

Many participants pointed out the irony that most women's lives in North America are permeated by inflated fears of an untimely pregnancy in their teens and early twenties and difficulties in achieving pregnancy in their late twenties and into their thirties. For example, Grace expressed worry that her daughter, who was born and raised in Canada, was delaying her first pregnancy too long in hopes of establishing her career. She explained:

> They say, "Listen, you don't know whether you can conceive or not. You don't have to wait that many years, because maybe you not conceive ... You have to try from now." It's not that, oh, I want next year, and for sure you'll conceive. It depends, right? For some ... it's not that easy to get pregnant.
>
> – Grace, forty-nine, migrated from Tanzania, support services staff and mother of three

Whatever their knowledge of contraceptives, women's experience of their fertility is shaped by conceptualizations of its social (and personal) value. The existence of extensive social support makes the birth of potential children less of an individual or couple's burden, and more of an extended family and community endeavour. For example, Anna married after completing her first year of university in Egypt and became pregnant shortly after. While she was scared at the prospect of her first pregnancy, and even though she was in the middle of an undergraduate program, keeping the pregnancy was not a choice made after a conscious decision-making process. Anna had a network of relatives who seamlessly collaborated on child care after the birth of her child. She continued her studies without much difficulty and eventually graduated with a bachelor's degree in business administration.

The importance of changes in social support in the lives of immigrant women cannot be overstated, as the loss of personal networks and changes in socio-economic status during migration to Canada mean that pregnancies may be experienced with more hardship here than in the countries from which they immigrated. Under liberal discourses of personal responsibility, this may be reason enough to start carefully managing one's fertility; however, for many immigrant women, hardships experienced in Canada are not caused by the birth of their children, but by the economic failings of Canadian society. For example, in addition to the loss of the support of extended family, women also experience the forced separation of families because of a spouse's employment elsewhere (for example, in Dubai or Alberta), which has implications for women's health that researchers have not begun to investigate in relation to pregnancy. One woman explained:

> I had an abortion. I got pregnant when he came for a visit and ... I didn't want the baby because ... first of all, I was almost forty. That was one reason ... But on the other hand, my husband was still not ready to move and stay with us, and I thought, no, I don't want to go through the whole thing again, taking care of two girls ... then with a new baby without any support. I discussed [it] with my husband. I told him, "If you move here, then we keep the baby," 'cause he was very, very excited ... But he wasn't ready to move then, and I wasn't ready to do everything on my own. I didn't have my parents, my mother, everybody was still back home.
>
> – Rita, fifty-one, migrated from Tanzania, dental clerk and mother of two

Another woman recalled:

> It was very hard the first year when I came. I was pregnant. I had my baby, and we are alone. Nobody ... I feel very bad ... My husband, he doesn't find job, and everything is very bad, you know? When we came from there, they told us we can find job here, and we can find everything ... But nothing ... Through the [UN] program that we came, they help us for one year. But after that, you have to look for job ... I have my daughter (maybe she's four months), and we find that life here, we need money, and nobody help us *[pause]*, but I can't find at that time a permanent job. Like, sometimes, three days they call you, the agency, sometimes two days.
>
> –Anna, forty-four, migrated from Egypt, homemaker and mother of four

After having good experiences with pregnancy in Egypt, Anna had considerable difficulties in Canada – not because of the pregnancies themselves, but because of her and her husband's struggle, given their experience and education, in finding suitable employment. Even when nuclear families are in Canada together, for many people who do not have enough resources to comfortably raise children, the problem is not the number of children they have, but the inability to attain employment that is commensurate with their qualifications. With a bachelor's degree in science, Zola was formerly a quality assurance specialist for the dairy industry in Egypt. Now a community peer outreach worker, her comments are representative of people's experiences of deprofessionalization and de-skilling in Canada:

> I never found a job that was with my qualifications, so, although what I'm doing now is a bit of office work, anything you can think of, I work. Security guard. I worked as deliver [sic]. I work as packer, picker. I work as cleaner. I work as cashier in coffee shops, McDonalds, like, everywhere! And I never find a job in my field. That's what irritated me. This is the major purpose I came to Canada. My thinking is, I'm an educated person. As soon as I come to Canada, I will find a job in my field, have a better life ... no. This is not the reality. It's not an easy experience ... I was expecting it to be very easy because, you know, the First World country – it's Canada. Everything is very easy. So I find everything *is* easy *except* finding a job in your field, and I believe this is the top priority.
>
> – Zola, forty-one, migrated from Egypt,
> peer outreach worker and mother of two

Aside from economic resources and the level of emotional and practical support, another factor that engenders significant anxiety when coping with pregnancy is the perception of available choices. For immigrant women, difficulties in accessing abortion may be confounded by their previous engagement with information on options or legal restrictions in their country of origin. For example, Jane experienced considerable difficulties in her adjustment to life in Canada. When she became pregnant, her perceived options were informed not only by her limited engagement with Canada's medical system, but also by popular discourses of abortion in China:

> *Jane:* Abortion available [in China] and, actually, because there's a child policy, lots of women have to go through abortion, even they want kids, but they need a quota to have a kid, so ... Even they want the kid, they're pregnant, they have to go through the abortion ... Also, I heard some stories that abortion was ... the women were treated badly and as if they did something really bad for having sex, and now they got themselves

into trouble ... It was like they're kind of, um, product. It was like one on the bed, and done! Another one on the bed, gone! It was just like doesn't have dignity, so that's why I was so scared after hearing and reading so many things about abortion. I didn't know how that works in Canada, and ... just, like, the idea to have abortion is terrifying me, and so I didn't want an abortion.

I always wanted children but *[pause]* while I never doubt that I'm going to have children, it seems like it came faster than I would like, and it was overwhelming. The pregnancy wasn't planned.

LS: How did you feel when you found out you were pregnant?

J: [Pause]. Shocked, scared, and then it's a hard decision whether to keep the baby or not. Uh, yeah, it was a hard decision. I know I had the option, but, um, I don't want to have abortion. That sounds scary, too.

LS: If you had wanted to do that, would you have known where to go to get an abortion?

J: No, I didn't. Yeah, that's also another thing – I found it so confusing, to get the information or to talk with somebody to make an informed decision ... I guess that I didn't know how the system works, and I didn't know where to find the information. At that time, it was before I find my family doctor ... after I decided that I'm going to keep the baby. I realized I need a doctor, then I started to look ... So the doctor only got into the picture after I decided I'm going to keep the baby.

– Jane, forty-two, migrated from China,
self-employed and mother of one

It is a common reality that prenatal care is the first time many immigrant women receive primary health care in Canada. Although counselling for pregnancy options is available through some sexual health clinics, Jane's difficulty in accessing this service was related not only to the limited availability of information about our health care system, but also to the highly politicized attitude of shame surrounding the issue of abortion in Canada at the time when Jane arrived in the early 1990s. Even if she had been able to find a family doctor, information and support regarding pregnancy options are not routinely offered as part of medical care. We cannot be sure that her physician would have taken the time to discuss her situation and her thinking around her options or to provide appropriate referrals for her to access abortion or adoption services. I do not mean to suggest that Jane would or should have had an abortion if she felt the service was a caring one in Canada, but to point out that, even if she had still chosen to continue her pregnancy, her decision-making could have been better supported.

Justice and Reproductive Freedom

In this essay, I have described some issues that are pertinent when considering current tensions permeating international, national, and community ethical and modernist discourses regarding women's roles in society, the control of our fertility, and our responsibility in participating in economic and political life. My purpose was to shed light onto issues of reproductive justice in Canada to problematize pro-choice and liberal discourse, technologies that supposedly make women's lives straightforward, and systems that are thought to be egalitarian. The conceptual seeds of this study were planted by my own experience of migration and exposure to diverse ways of thinking about fertility management, pregnancy, and women's roles in the family and society. I undertook this inquiry with the misguided intention of uncovering a feminist awakening of sorts in immigrants who came from countries where women seem to be worse off. Instead, the immigrant women who shared their spaces and stories with me over the course of this study taught me that differing worldviews about how fertility should be managed, pregnancy experienced, and families raised, do not (and need not) magically change with migration. While the international rhetoric that has brought reproductive rights to the attention of governments employs individual human rights discourse and narrow abortion rights discussions, it is clear that making reproductive decisions is, in the lived experience of women, not an endeavour they undertake as rational and completely autonomous actors.

Thinking of the women I serve at sexual health clinics, and those who were interviewed for this study, I am humbled by the thoughtful way in which they make decisions about their reproductive health, by the difficulties they face in coping with emotional complexities, and by their resilience in striving to reconcile their own goals, hopes, and fears, constrained by the choices available to them. Like many other women, immigrant women do not see pregnancy and career aspirations as either/or scenarios. Rather, they aspire to be able to pursue meaningful work as they raise their families and contribute to local communities. Past experiences of varied socio-cultural and legal contexts of pregnancy and abortion in their countries of origin may lead some immigrant women to feel like they have no choice. Changes brought about by migration, such as spousal separation, loss of social support networks, and decline in socio-economic and health status, often mean that pregnancies are experienced with greater hardship in Canada. These changes are the result of systemic barriers experienced by immigrant populations in general, yet they are seldom discussed as issues of reproductive justice. In my view, the decline in health that women and men experience in their adjustment to living in Canada is linked to their experiences of reproductive events under oppressive conditions. The stories of racialized women speak to the importance of working within a framework of reproductive justice – not only for increased access to abortion but also for the right to mother, to be free from violence, to find suitable employment, and to receive adequate wages so we can keep our families together. Like other women in Canada, when immigrant women create and provide for our families, use current tools available to them to regulate fertility, and contribute to the fabric of Canadian society, we are not following carefully constructed plans. From my perspective as an immigrant woman, reproductive justice in Canada entails economic opportunity, equitable access to health care and, as Maren Klawiter suggests, the freedom to allow possibilities to unfold.

Notes

1 This chapter is based on "Social Realities of Sexual Health: Conversations with Immigrant Women in Toronto," submitted in 2013 in fulfillment of requirements for the Master of Arts in Anthropology at the University of Toronto.

2 The countries from which participants migrated refer to those where they resided immediately before coming to Canada. Many participants in my study were not born in the countries from which they migrated.

3 I discuss here only the experience of cisgendered women who have been or are currently sexually involved with cisgendered men. I did not specifically discuss sexual orientation or gender identity with research participants; thus a properly queer reading of findings is beyond the scope of my data.

4 Margaret Sanger, *Woman and the New Race* (New York: Brentano's, 1920), 4.

5 Colleen Varcoe, Olena Hankivsky, and Marina Morrow, "Introduction: Beyond Gender Matters," in *Women's Health in Canada: Critical Perspectives on Theory and Policy*, ed. Marina Morrow, Olena Hankivsky, and Colleen Varcoe (Toronto: University of Toronto Press, 2008), 4.

6 Susan Sherwin, "A Relational Approach to Autonomy in Health Care," in *The Politics of Women's Health: Exploring Agency and Autonomy* (Philadelphia: Temple University Press, 1998), 25–39.

7 See, for example, Sonia Corrêa in collaboration with Rebecca Reichmann, *Population and Reproductive Rights: Feminist Perspectives from the South* (London: Zed Books, 1994).

8 Loretta Ross, "Understanding Reproductive Justice: Transforming the Pro-choice Movement," *Off Our Backs* 36, 4 (2006): 14.
9 Ibid.
10 Ibid.
11 Carolyn Egan and Linda Gardner, "Racism, Women's Health and Reproductive Freedom," in *Gender Relations in Global Perspective,* ed. Nancy Cook (Toronto: Canadian Scholars' Press, 2007), 302.
12 Ross, "Understanding Reproductive Justice," 14.
13 Samuel Noh and Violet Kaspar, "Diversity and Immigrant Health," in *The World in a City,* ed. Paul Anisef and Michael Lanphier (Toronto: University of Toronto Press, 2003), 323; Ilene Hyman, "The Mental Health and Well-Being of Immigrant and Refugee Women in Canada," in *Engendering Migrant Health: Canadian Perspectives,* ed. Denise Spitzer (Toronto: University of Toronto Press, 2011), 101.
14 Denise L. Spitzer, "Introduction," in *Engendering Migrant Health: Canadian Perspectives,* ed. Denise Spitzer (Toronto: University of Toronto Press, 2011), 3, 4; Hyman, "The Mental Health and Well-Being of Immigrant and Refugee Women," 100; Bilkis Vissandjée, Wilfreda Thurston, Alisha Apale, and Kamrun Nahar, "Women's Health at the Intersection of Gender and the Experience of International Migration," in *Women's Health in Canada: Critical Perspectives on Theory and Policy,* ed. Marina Morrow, Olena Hankivsky, and Colleen Varcoe (Toronto: University of Toronto Press, 2008), 226; James Dunn and Isabel Dyck, "Social Determinants of Health in Canada's Immigrant Population: Results from the National Population Health Survey," *Social Science and Medicine* 51 (2000): 1574.
15 Spitzer, "Introduction," 4.
16 Hyman, "The Mental Health and Well-Being of Immigrant and Refugee Women," 114; Spitzer, "Introduction," 246
17 Spitzer, "Introduction," 15.
18 See, for example, Khosro Refaie Shirpak, Eleanor Maticka-Tyndale, and Maryam Chinichian, "Post Migration Changes in Iranian Immigrants' Couple Relationships in Canada," *Journal of Comparative Family Studies* 42, 6 (2011): 751–70; Carolyn F. Sargent, "Reproductive Strategies and Islamic Discourse: Malian Migrants Negotiate Everyday Life in Paris, France," *Medical Anthropology Quarterly* 20, 1 (2006): 31–49; Mehrdad Darvishpour, "Immigrant Women Challenge the Role of Men: How the Changing Power Relationship within Iranian Families in Sweden Intensifies Family Conflicts after Immigration," *Journal of Comparative Family Studies* 33, 2 (2002): 271–96; Sepali Guruge, Khosro Refaie Shirpak, Ilene Hyman, Margareth Zanchetta, Denise Gastaldo, and Souraya Sidani, "A Meta-synthesis of Post-migration Changes in Marital Relationships in Canada," *Canadian Journal of Public Health* 101, 4 (2010): 327–31.
19 Ross, "Understanding Reproductive Justice," 15.
20 Abby Lippman, "Foreword," in *Fertile Ground: Exploring Reproduction in Canada,* ed. Stephanie Paterson, Francesca Scala, and Marlene K. Sokolon (Montreal and Kingston: McGill-Queen's University Press), xiv.
21 Berit Austveg, "Perpetuating Power: Some Reasons Why Reproductive Health Has Stalled," *Reproductive Health Matters* 19, 38 (2011): 26.
22 Alice Miller and Mindy Roseman, "Sexual and Reproductive Rights at the United Nations: Frustration or Fulfillment," *Reproductive Health Matters* 19, 38 (2011): 102.
23 World Health Organization, "Reproductive Health Strategy to Accelerate Progress towards the Attainment of International Development Goals and Targets" (Department of Reproductive Health and Research, 2014), 7.

24 Ibid., 11.
25 Ibid.
26 Ibid., 22.
27 Miller and Roseman, "Sexual and Reproductive Rights at the United Nations," 106; Austveg, "Perpetuating Power," 26.
28 Austveg, "Perpetuating Power," 28; Jyoti Shankar Singh, *Creating a New Consensus on Population: The Politics of Reproductive Health, Reproductive Rights and Women's Empowerment*, 2nd ed. (London: Earthscan, 2009), 199.
29 Singh, *Creating a New Consensus*, 199.
30 United Nations, "The Millennium Development Goals Report 2015," https://mdgs.un.org/unsd/mdg/Resources/Static/Products/Progress2015/English2015.pdf.
31 Austveg, "Perpetuating Power," 27.
32 Ibid., 29.
33 Ibid., 28.
34 International Conference on Population and Development, *Report of the International Conference on Population and Development Cairo, 5–13 September, 1994* (New York: United Nations, 1995), 41.
35 Marge Berer, "The Cairo 'Compromise' on Abortion and Its Consequences for Making Abortion Safe and Legal," in *Reproductive Health and Human Rights: The Way Forward*, ed. Laura Reichenbach and Mindy Roseman (Philadelphia: University of Pennsylvania Press, 2009), 153.
36 World Health Organization, "Reproductive Health Strategy," 10.
37 Ibid., 14.
38 Berer, "The Cairo 'Compromise,'" 154.
39 Lara V. Marks, *Sexual Chemistry: A History of the Contraceptive Pill* (New Haven, CT: Yale University Press, 2001), 183.
40 As quoted in Marks, *Sexual Chemistry*, 183.
41 Lealle Ruhl, "Dilemmas of the Will: Uncertainty, Reproduction, and the Rhetoric of Control," *Signs* 27, 3 (2002): 641–63; Marks, *Sexual Chemistry.*
42 Marks, *Sexual Chemistry*, 192.
43 Ibid.
44 Ibid.
45 Kara Granzow, "The Imperative to Choose: A Qualitative Study of Women's Decision-Making and Use of the Birth Control Pill," *Social Theory and Health* 6 (2008): 5.
46 I say "perceived" because there are actually many birth control options available in the Canadian market. However, doctors tend to push the pill as the most convenient choice, and not to provide comprehensive birth control counselling.
47 Granzow, "The Imperative to Choose," 6.
48 Ruhl, "Dilemmas of the Will," 643.
49 Kara Granzow, "De-constructing 'Choice': The Social Imperative and Women's Use of the Birth Control Pill," *Culture, Health and Sexuality* 9, 1 (2007): 50.
50 Ibid., 46.
51 Ruhl, "Dilemmas of the Will."
52 Ibid., 660.
53 Marks, *Sexual Chemistry*, 183–215.
54 The notion that fertility either *is* not or is not *meant to be* under individual control is popular in the global South. As one of my participants put it, you have "as many children as God will give you."
55 All research participant names are pseudonyms.

14

Toxic Matters

Vital and Material Struggles for Environmental Reproductive Justice

Sarah Marie Wiebe

On November 11, 2013, the *Globe and Mail* published the findings released by a team of scientists led by Dr. Nil Basu. The results of Basu's study noted that elevated levels of hormone-blocking chemicals, known as endocrine disruptors, were found in the bodies of mothers and children of the Aamjiwnaang First Nation, located in one of Canada's most industrialized regions.[1] This research is reportedly the first to scientifically prove the community's fears of heightened exposure to pollutants in its atmosphere, homes, and bodies. The effects of these pollutants penetrating women's and children's bodies prompt the following question: How can we make sense of the corporeal impacts of these chemicals on human lives – in theory, policy, and practice? The local site-specific concern in Aamjiwnaang has much to tell us about the study of reproductive justice in Canada and beyond. When Indigenous communities are faced with a struggle to reproduce, the very vitality of their culture is at stake. This reality signals the need for innovative insights in reproductive justice theorizing in order to take us in new directions beyond a sole focus on abortion and reproductive choice. Reproductive justice is an intersectional analytical lens that fuses concepts of reproductive health, rights, and justice. It entails an emphasis on gender equality and extends beyond a libertarian framework to move away from an overemphasis on the right to reproductive health. In doing so, its orientation shifts from an overemphasis on the language of individual choice towards one rooted in place-based justice.[2] As defined by the Black Women's Caucus in 1994, reproductive justice combines reproductive rights and social justice, which requires service delivery, addressing legal issues, and movement building.[3] Reproductive justice is based on equality, the right to have or not have a child, and the right to birth and to parent children. It emphasizes an awareness of structural (i.e., geopolitical, legal, socio-economic) and discursive constraints on individual agency, respect for social location, and recognition of the importance of creating the conditions necessary to realize reproductive rights. This requires respectful state–citizen relations that make reproductive experiences safe, affordable, and accessible.[4] Building on the 2005 Asian Communities for Reproductive Justice (ACRJ) declaration, Loretta Ross, the national coordinator for SisterSong, stated that "reproductive justice is the complete physical, mental, spiritual, political, social and economic well-being of women and girls, based on the full achievement and protection of women's human rights."[5]

In this essay, drawing upon the experiences of Indigenous women living at the front lines of pollution exposure, in an area known as Canada's Chemical Valley, I contend that a place-based and relational environmental reproductive justice framework takes us even further beyond the instrumental language of rights and choice. A relational, place-based approach to reproductive justice is structural and discursive. It provides procedural access to pathways for self-determination and conceptually brings the inextricable connection between physical and cultural vitality to the fore. Creating such pathways is not limited to documenting and raising awareness about the visceral impacts of environmental violence, but also includes the development of intersectional public policies that enhance environments so that they can be physically and culturally safe.[6] To be clear, such a reproductive justice approach requires an imperative shift away from the abortion movement's historical focus on the language of *choice*.[7] An attunement to social location and place draws into focus how reproductive justice is not simply a matter of choice or lack of choice, but also a matter of interrogating how environmental factors impact an individual or community's ability to physically and culturally reproduce.[8] Environmental reproductive justice is a place-based, relational approach to reproductive justice that enhances environmental justice by shifting the lens away from the individual body and the advancement of individual rights towards an emphasis on building healthy and sustainable communities.

To advocate for a relational, place-based reproductive justice framework that entails environmental reproductive justice, my core argument is twofold: first, we must take seriously the lived realities where citizens confront ongoing environmental assaults and injustices, which prompt new directions for the theory, practice, and method of reproductive justice; second, we must move away from an overemphasis on choice towards an intersectional and contextually specific analysis of the inextricable connection between physical and cultural survival – and not just of individuals but also of entire communities. Such a framework aligns with and enhances an intersectionality-based policy analysis lens, which emphasizes the importance of lived experiences for more equitable policy making.[9] Accounting for the importance of lived experiences is a profoundly political undertaking, as it addresses fundamental questions about the relationships between human and non-human environments.

Assessing the potentially harmful, turbulent, and disorderly effects of non-human pollutants is also a deeply political process. As Jane Bennett asks, "so how would political responses to public problems change were we to take seriously the vitality of (nonhuman) bodies?"[10] Given that citizens in Aamjiwnaang live in a constant state of uncertainty and insecurity about their daily exposure to a polluted atmosphere, it is not a vulnerable non-human world that is in need of protection, but the placed, affected body that calls for a political intervention. As recent debates about intersectionality and affect theory highlight, the material, physiological processes experienced by bodies cannot be explained by language alone.[11] Shifting our attention towards local experience, and carefully examining some of the ways in which bodies are rendered vulnerable to toxins reorients the central axiom of reproductive justice scholarship away from a pluralist emphasis on individuals or institutions towards a focus on situated communities whose bodies are at the front lines of pollution exposure. In this manner, I seek to address both discursive and material consequences of changing environmental conditions that impact local communities in very specific corporeal, lived, affective ways by interrogating the implications of this reproductive injustice at the human/non-human interface.

To do so, I turn to the grounded, place-based lived experiences of citizens from the Aamjiwnaang First Nation, which is a community encircled by a region known as Canada's Chemical Valley. As it is on both sides of the border, this region is home to over sixty-two petrochemical and polymer facilities on both sides of the Canada–United States border.[12] Aamjiwnaang is a tiny reserve encircled by a toxic bubble at the southernmost point of Lake Huron, near Sarnia, Ontario, adjacent to the Canada–United States border.[13] Companies with facilities surrounding the community include Imperial, Shell, and Suncor, among numerous others. In 2000, Health Canada designated seventeen communities around the Great Lakes as "Areas of Concern," due to high levels of toxins in the surrounding environment with potential adverse health effects.[14] Aamjiwnaang is located within the St. Clair River Area of Concern and is continuously exposed to both incidental and accidental emissions.[15]

In this context, the ground, as a material force, is not passive or distinct from robust community life; rather, it is co-constituted through citizen engagement and encounters with toxic matter.[16] Citizens sense and experience their environment as an affective atmosphere; they encounter atmospheres by interacting with soil, air, and water, through their seeing, hearing, smelling, tasting, and feeling bodies.[17] The affective atmosphere is never finished – it is always looming, becoming, penetrating, transforming. The atmosphere is felt through lived experience. A focus on toxins at the body's boundary troubles distinctions between human and non-human vitality and prompts an examination of some of the ways in which things pass through bodies. As an intersectional lens, environmental reproductive justice reveals how silent, chronic, and sometimes even invisible toxic exposures interrupt any rigid human/non-human binary and affect bodies.

The connection between physical and cultural survival constitutes the crux of a relational, place-based approach to reproductive justice within an Indigenous context. Elizabeth Hoover and her colleagues, as well as SisterSong, discuss environmental reproductive justice as the right and ability to reproduce in culturally appropriate ways: "for many Indigenous communities to reproduce culturally informed citizens requires a clean environment."[18] Defining environmental reproductive justice underscores the ways in which physical, material vitality is tethered to cultural survival.

Reproductive In/Justice in Canada's Chemical Valley

In Aamjiwnaang, birth complications are also commonplace. Of 132 women surveyed in the community in 2005, 39 percent had at least one stillbirth or miscarriage.[19] Furthermore, there's a constant odour issue; many people just do not want to be outside.[20] In the Chemical Valley, structural and material constraints affect the Aamjiwnaang First Nation's ability to live a life free from pollution. Institutional configurations and existing policies intersect with discursive, embodied, lived, felt, and *affective* constraints such as the penetration of human reproductive bodies by toxic non-human agents. As much intersectionality scholarship points out, taking a cue from feminist and critical race theory, systems of inequality – that is, colonialism, racism, sexism – are bound up within intersecting forms of gendered, racialized, and class-based forms of oppression.[21] In Aamjiwnaang, these intersecting forms of oppression are embroiled within material toxicity.

A turn towards Aamjiwnaang's everyday concerns illuminates current struggles and draws into focus issues around physical and cultural survival in Canada's colonial present. As articulated by the Native Youth Sexual Health Network (NYSHN) during its intervention before the National Energy Board on the Line 9 Pipeline proposal, we cannot talk about reproductive justice in general without an awareness of environmental violence.[22] NYSHN's submission to the National Energy Board affirmed the importance of lived experience, relationships rooted in place, social context, and intergenerational effects of large-scale development projects. "Indigenous women and children often bear the brunt of negative consequences of resource extraction and are suffering the detrimental, devastating, multi-generational, and deadly impacts of environmental toxins and contaminants. This particular impact of environmental racism on Indigenous women and children is increasingly referred to as 'environmental violence.'"[23] The submission further depicted how social stressors linked to resource extractive industries also strain existing social and economic systems. Consequently, "these social stressors cause severe psychological, relational, emotional, and economic damage to mothers, families and communities."[24] Moreover, though reproduction is not distinctly a women's issue, women often bear the responsibility for physical and cultural reproduction in their communities. This is particularly relevant within Indigenous communities like Aamjiwnaang, a community with long-standing concerns about its vitality while situated in a highly polluted hot spot surrounded by heavy industrial manufacturing.

NYSHN's intervention in response to the Line 9 Pipeline proposal resonates with ongoing concerns facing citizens of the Aamjiwnaang First Nation. As Dayna Scott argues, "The Aamjiwnaang experience is marked by the individual trauma of repeated miscarriage and the collective loss of a viable future."[25] Though women's physical, material bodies are at the forefront, the whole community is affected.

As Dr. Basu's bio-monitoring study revealed, the toxic bubble of the Chemical Valley surrounding the Aamjiwnaang First Nation has viscerally affected, and continues to viscerally affect, the reproductive bodies of citizens living in the midst of Canada's worst air pollution hot spot. This bio-monitoring study emerged in response to a previous community-based health study released in 2005, which documented a skewed male to female birth ratio and highlighted concerns regarding a sharp decline in male births.[26] Toxins spewing over the community from the adjacent smokestacks have largely been identified as the cause of this decline, which has been referred to as a "slow violence."[27] Health concerns related to the community's atmosphere can be considered as incidental to living within what has been called a toxic sacrifice zone in a climate of state withdrawal with limited policy intervention.[28] In this colonial context, the Aamjiwnaang First Nation fights to exist as a distinct group of people while also fighting for physical survival. As the site of the Chemical Valley's location surrounding the Aamjiwnaang First Nation reveals, pollution is a geopolitical problem rendering citizens of Aamjiwnaang more vulnerable to long-term exposure than are the surrounding citizens in the adjacent City of Sarnia.[29]

Following the whirlwind of media attention that poured over Aamjiwnaang in the wake of the sex ratio study's release in 2005, Lambton County's Community Health Services Department, Health Promotion, and Program Support Unit produced their own reproductive health report in 2007 that showed no correlation of a skewed birth ratio when scaled from the local population of Aamjiwanang to the county as a whole.[30] While the report's findings did not address the acute features of Aamjiwnaang's reproductive health concerns, representatives from Aamjiwnaang began to enter into conversations with stakeholders, community leaders, and policy makers within the City of Sarnia about persistent health concerns on reserve and elsewhere within the county. Between 2005 and 2007, informal meetings evolved into the formation of a Board of Directors comprised of spokespeople representing First Nations, unions, community associations, and labour, industry, occupational health, and public health organizations. From this, the Lambton Community Health Study (LCHS) was born with a mandate to study the health effects associated with exposure to environmental emissions as a public health priority.

In January 2012, the LCHS entered into a partnership with the provincial Ontario Health Study, thus widening out the scale even further away from the situated reproductive health concerns in Aamjiwnaang.[31] Community members refer to this troubling phenomenon as the "politics of dilution."[32] As a result, several alternative options emerged as possible avenues through which Aamjiwnaang could potentially seek acknowledgment of its ongoing health concerns. These include focused bio-monitoring studies in partnership with organizations such as the Assembly of First Nations or liaising with university researchers like Dr. Basu, whose scientific study of the impacts of chemicals and metals, including polychlorinated biphenyls, on forty-three mother–child pairs honed in on the impacts of toxins on local population health.[33] The study's findings revealed elevated rates of PCBs and metals, including mercury and cadmium, and indicated that some perfluorinated chemicals and the pesticides hexachlorocyclohexane and DDT were also located within the bodies of mothers and children.[34] Blood, hair, and urine samples served as biomarkers of the community's reproductive vulnerability to contaminated, toxic matter affecting its atmosphere, homes, and bodies.

A locally situated analysis of citizens' experiential knowledge is crucial to enrich our understanding of contemporary injustices. Surely, pollution is a global problem, with uneven consequences. Yet, bodies in Aamjiwnaang are uniquely affected by the intergenerational penetration of toxic matter. The land is central to Indigenous communities' wellness and cultural survival. When the land is affected, so too is the health of the community. As environmental justice scholars point out, it is commonly known that some communities bear a disproportionate burden of modernity's adverse effects.[35] In order to resolve the contemporary effects of toxic contamination, these scholars draw attention to the uneven distribution of hazards along the lines of race, class, and gender. Such intersectional thinking highlights some of the ways in which certain bodies confront toxic matter and thrust into view a new way of imagining environmental reproductive justice.

Reframing Reproductive Justice: Culture, Reproduction and the Environment

To further develop the theory of reproductive justice, we have much to learn from existing environmental justice scholarship. Environmental justice theory often pivots around three axes: procedural, distributive, and discursive dimensions. *Procedural* dimensions of environmental justice involve structural and participatory processes that bring citizens into conversation with institutions. Such deliberative processes generally begin by recognizing the scope and parameters of existing injustices; identifying citizen concerns, needs, and wants; and, furthermore, gesturing towards mitigating and responding to citizens' rights. A concrete example of this comes to light given the official responses to Aamjiwnaang's controversial birth ratio study.

A turn towards the *distributive* dimensions of environmental justice theorizing draws into focus the uneven distribution of environmental harms. As David Schlosberg and environmental justice scholars in a Canadian setting discuss in greater detail, the distributive dimension of environmental justice highlights how "some communities receive more environmental risks than others."[36] In broad terms, distributive justice generally refers to the "distribution of benefits and burdens."[37] Theories of distributive justice generally make reference to what resources are distributed and how, describe the principles of allocation, identify sites for struggle, and examine the conditions under which citizens make their claims. This approach tends to focus on state–institutional parameters for redistribution among a citizenry. Following Alex Sager, "Institutions that play a casual role in systematically disadvantaging and harming people demand close moral scrutiny."[38] These concerns of structural injustice resonate environmental justice theory and practice, as the experience of Aamjiwnaang's involvement in the LCHS highlights.

With respect to distributive justice and environmental theory, much of this scholarship originates within the American context to examine the disproportionate burden of harms borne by communities of colour. As such, distributive equity, fairness, and restorative justice offer key reference points for communities of colour seeking environmental justice and redress. In this respect, questioning the ways in which social location puts certain communities at risk in the face of environmental contamination and pollution underscores the intersections of race and injustice. Both the experiences of impoverished African American citizens in the wake of Hurricane Katrina and the experiences in Aamjiwnaang illuminate this systemic, asymmetrical risk exposure.

Racializing environmental justice highlights how certain harms and risks impose themselves upon marginalized communities. The notion of environmental racism emerged out of the United Church of Christ's Commission on Racial Justice under the leadership of Benjamin Chavis, and the publication of his seminal study *Toxins, Waste and Race.*[39] From then onward, as Schlosberg notes, the practice and experience of racism has been at the heart of the environmental justice movement in the American context. Much of the scholarship reflecting upon this racialization of marginalized communities exposed to heavy industrial pollution acknowledges the detrimental effects of industries and governments seeking the path of least resistance to development.[40] Given the location of the Aamjiwnaang First Nation reserve, the uneven distributional effects of environmental emissions are difficult to dispute.[41] Without question, this community's social location reveals how citizens confront contamination in particular ways in comparison to their predominantly non-Indigenous neighbours in Sarnia and Lambton County. The affective atmosphere of Chemical Valley – sensed through the smell of pollution, the drone of a warning siren, or the vibrations of flares, to name but a few dimensions – characterizes the unique, situated features of daily life in Aamjiwnaang, unlike lived realities elsewhere.[42] Conceptualizing Aamjiwnaang's social and geopolitical location as an affective atmosphere accentuates the importance of assessing the lived and felt dimensions of environmental reproductive justice to account for experiential knowledge.

Finally, the third, *discursive* dimension of environmental justice moves us towards thinking about human/non-human relationships in terms of embeddedness rather than binary opposition. Building upon the conceptual groundwork laid by Schlosberg, reproductive justice must "expand the sphere of a discourse" horizontally, outwards from institutions to communities, not to erase structural constraints but to include the material force of both our laws and economy, which shape and constrain individual agency.[43] Structural and discursive dimensions cannot be separated from one another. Attention to the local context cannot be removed from the vertical scale out from communities to the global realm. Highlighting the uneven distribution of capitalism in an advanced industrial society, Ulrich Beck famously claimed, "poverty is hierarchic, while smog is democratic."[44] To move away from hierarchical framings between communities, institutions, and toxins, locating, documenting, and understanding how environmental harms uniquely affect situated communities is critical. Shifting environmental justice theorizing horizontally towards communities and vertically towards the global sphere are equally important features of environmental justice; however, a turn to community practices on the ground, situated at the global/local interface, locates the placed and affected body at the forefront of this intersection.

Turning to the discursive dimension, deliberative processes reveal the manner in which struggles over knowledge regarding human/non-human relations emerge. These processes illuminate how certain knowledges become marginalized. Concretely, the LCHS can be understood as a deliberative health study, as it involved a sustained period of citizen engagement, including an online and phone survey, as well as five town hall–style open houses and ongoing monthly board meetings. Significantly, deliberative health studies are not neutral. They actively (re)produce discursive regimes, which shape and constrain citizen action. There is a wide and vast literature discussing the deliberative turn and promise of the public arena for reasonable communication, interaction, and governance.[45] However, as Chantal Mouffe cautions us, the promise of the deliberative sphere as a rationally ordered realm oriented to consensus-based deliberation often falls short of its democratic promise.[46] As the LCHS reveals, institutional processes are mechanisms that reproduce discourses and knowledges, which in turn structure and constrain the parameters and possibilities for recognition and justice.

Creating conditions for intersectional place-based policy making is one avenue through which we can begin to cultivate space for thinking about lived experience and to bring in the vitality of women's bodies, experiential knowledge, and reproduction to engage in a much more productive conversation than evidenced by present occlusions. Environmental reproductive justice recentres the narratives of women's affective dimensions of injustice and brings their knowledges and voices into the fore. As such, a vibrant reproductive justice approach hones in on the agency of the lives of those directly affected by the injustices of inequitable toxic exposure. Such a rewriting both embodies and territorializes the discursive dimensions of environmental reproductive justice.

Centring an analysis of environmental justice upon the embedded relationship between bodies (human) and pollutants (non-human) expands the conventional framing of environmental justice to account for reproductive justice in unsettling ways. As Schlosberg discusses, the traditional, liberal rights-based frame for justice is frequently individualistic. In contrast to this liberal framework, reproductive justice reveals how the co-constitution of individuals and communities is at stake.[47] Taking this a step further, the environmental reproductive justice framework offered here responds to Schlosberg's call to expand the sphere of a discourse and critically interrogates the classic dividing lines that separate humans from nature, and individuals from community. With respect to the predominant pollution story in Aamjiwnaang, there is a great need to reconceptualize rigid binaries between reproductive bodies, toxins, and the non-human environment. As such, environmental justice theorizing must expand the discursive dimensions towards the reproductive body, and, moreover, the dynamic intersections between bodies and toxic matter. An environmental reproductive justice framework makes clear how it is not solely a harmed non-human environment that is to be the primary focus for redress, but also an interconnected, relational, intersectional, placed, affected body.

Coping with catastrophe is a normalized everyday reality in Canada's Chemical Valley, which affects the bodies of those who reside nearby. Adding to this sense of living in a sacrificial zone, it is commonplace to hear the shrill of a siren either during weekly Monday morning tests or in the incident of an accidental release of chemicals. These are frequent. Aamjiwnaang's location within Canada's Chemical Valley can thus be read as an affective atmosphere in the following ways. Atmospheres are necessary conditions for life. They are forces to be reckoned with, affecting spatial inhabitations. Such a phenomenological account attends to the affective qualities of lived, breathed, felt, and sensed atmospheres. This reading emphasizes non-representational properties of social life beyond human dimensions to include the intersections between technologies, matter, and bodies.[48] An affective atmosphere remains unregistered in the human consciousness but configures the backdrop of everyday life. Affect must be distinguished from emotion. While emotion can be named – i.e., hope, love, and fear – affect is unregistered, unconscious; it does not necessarily constitute a "sensible phenomen[on]."[49] It may not be immediately felt.

An affective atmosphere is marked by ambiguity. It is a spatialized geopolitical assemblage, a mixture of policies and their visceral impacts; it is an interstitial zone between presence and absence, subject and object, definition and lack thereof.[50] These impacts are not easily fathomable. They are often silent, chronic, and slow-moving. As such, toxins act as communicative registers that play out beyond the clearly articulated "grammars and vocabularies of discourse."[51] Affective atmospheres touch citizens deeply in their everyday lives as they struggle to make sense of these ongoing impacts. These atmospheres register through the sensing body while remaining diffuse, ethereal, and in the air. As such, an affective atmosphere is associated with that which is uncertain, tenuous, precarious, disordered, shifting, and contingent. It is that "which never achieves the stability of form."[52] Such an ominous depiction of affective atmospheres prompts many questions about how toxins shape our everyday lives, while unevenly affecting some communities more than others.

Reproductive Justice and Physical Survival

Affective atmospheres intersect with the *wounding* and *becoming* of corporeality. As Dayna Scott discusses: "When synthetic chemicals, uninvited, take over for hormones, binding with available receptors and orchestrating physiological processes, it has real, tangible, material consequences for bodies. When this happens in the context of reproduction, it has gendering consequences."[53] As the reproductive injustices in Aamjiwnaang demonstrate, this affective atmosphere impacts the physical becoming of the gendered body.[54] Moreover, the effects of hormone-disrupting chemicals are not only gendered but also *gendering.*

An environmental reproductive justice framework takes into consideration not only Aamjiwnaang's disproportionate burden of toxic exposure, but also the way in which contamination affects this community's ability to reproduce future generations. This intersectional orientation to the body underscores the significance of geopolitical location and points to "the hidden and insidious workings of power through the structures of everyday life."[55] Such a critical positioning examines the ways in which local knowledges become marginalized by mainstream political processes. As the lived experiences in Aamjiwnaang suggest, women's bodies are uniquely enmeshed within these affective un/conscious processes. As Dr. Basu's study highlights, the incessant exposure to toxins in Aamjiwnaang impacts the maternal body in particular ways and incites a further investigation of the distinct ways in which women's bodies encounter more-than-human entanglements. Beginning with women's bodies in Aamjiwnaang provokes a reconceptualization of justice, with women at the centre of knowledge production.

Exposure to heavy metals takes an invasive turn for citizens of Aamjiwnaang. The lived reality demonstrates that humans cannot escape their embeddedness in social and synthetic contexts, both material and discursive, that shape and affect daily life. According to Elizabeth Grosz, a feminist, ethical, and aesthetic orientation looks to the body with the intention of devising a politics adequate for non-dualistic accounts of subjectivity.[56] An affective consideration of the body as such opens up possibilities for new ways of thinking about corporeal agency. In this vein, connecting affect scholarship to vital materialism troubles the view that individuals are discretely able to control or master their bodies and the non-human world.[57] This fusion of affect theory and new materialism emphasizes a haunting affinity between human and non-human matter. In so doing, it heightens an appreciation for the agential powers of toxic matter and its harrowing impacts on human agency.[58] What is more, this approach highlights the assemblage of coalescing bodies, environments, and pollutants. Rather than gauging the value of the non-human world for human ends, this relational, place-based approach to environmental reproductive justice unsettles the human/non-human divide with an attunement for material-semiotic interactions.[59] This unsettling act prompts a critical inquiry into some of the promiscuous pathways in which toxins transcend these binaries.

Ontologically, this orientation moves away from conceiving of the non-human world as passive. On the contrary, it participates in a "dance of agency" including human, non-human, nature, and artifice.[60] Acknowledging the agential powers of non-human artefacts troubles the egoism of anthropocentric theorizing about human/non-human life. Opening up conceptions of agency to the material, non-human world complicates romantic Western ways of thinking about nature as pristine, untouched, and in need of protection.

An affective, relational, place-based approach to environmental justice reconceptualized as environmental reproductive justice turns our focus towards an assemblage of myriad spaces and bodies as they become entangled within synthetic environments. As Teena Gabrielson and Katelyn Parady make clear, "not all human bodies are similarly positioned or equally opened to the multiple and material flows that form the networks of life (and death)."[61] Marginalized bodies may encounter affective atmospheres, unaware. Though quite real and powerful, invisible pollutants in the air, soil, and water can be physically difficult to represent, yet no less tangible, with material consequences.

Thus, how can we account for the un-representability of invisible toxic matter that affects reproductive bodies? What must we do when toxins embed bodies from within? Are there avenues to ethically disentangle bodies from toxic matter? Confronted with the invisible effects of pollution, it is presumptuous to assume that one can be above or "outside a nonhuman 'environment.'"[62] While Jane Bennett contends that there is a need to move away from a hierarchical relationship between human and non-human life, it is evident that some communities disproportionately encounter and confront hazardous, synthetic non-human life. The uneven context within which certain bodies encounter hazardous material affects community vitality. In an Indigenous setting, these entanglements have considerable implications for cultural survival.

Reproductive Justice and Cultural Survival

Environmental reproductive justice is clearly articulated in this statement by an Aamjiwnaang First Nation community member during a Lambton Community Health Study Townhall Forum meeting in 2010: "We are losing our people, losing our history. Our environment is affecting all life, not just humans."[63] The effects of pollution on this community's way of life pertains to humans, animals, land, and water. As this community member states: "We used to be able to go into areas to hunt and fish that are now blocked off with fence lines that say 'No Trespassing.' Centuries of industrial development have impacted traditions and land use."[64] Aamjiwnaang citizens increasingly worry about the pollution of their reserve. In addition to the notion that the environment has a physical impact on the body, pollution also has cultural, spiritual, and emotional effects. As an Ecojustice report highlights, community members express a growing sense of fear – of the sirens, outdoors, air, water, and so on. "These chemicals and related incidents have significant impacts on their cultural life, including hunting, fishing, medicine, gathering and ceremonial activities. Health impacts include asthma, reproductive effects, learning disabilities and cancer. The most common reported impact was fear. People on the reserve feared the outdoors, the warning sirens and unreported incidences."[65] When toxins are found in food and wildlife, avoidance becomes impossible, and exposure is an everyday reality.

Environmental reproductive justice underscores the importance of lived experience, representation, identity, and relationships to place, which entails the critical connection between physical and cultural reproduction. This lens draws together material and ideational dimensions of justice. Aamjiwnaang is an Indigenous community that is uniquely affected by a compromised environment. Environmental reproductive justice is a framework that seeks to ensure that a community's reproductive capabilities are not inhibited by environmental contamination, which compromise a community's ability to reproduce cultural knowledge. Individuals must have the ability to reproduce in culturally appropriate ways. As such, environmental reproductive justice fuses health and environment at the nexus of human and non-human relations, which cannot be separated from the need to protect culture and knowledge.

The situation in Aamjiwnaang reveals how these toxins have a life force of their own, which affects the reproductive body in material and post-material ways. The chronic penetration of toxins pressing upon the reproductive body can be interpreted as a kind of vibrant – yet haunting – matter.[66] Assessing the agency and vibrancy of matter, Bennett assesses the capacity of certain properties, certain things, which act and produce certain effects. Drawing from Bruno Latour's conception of an actant – a source of action, either human or non-human – Bennett accompanies this vocabulary to characterize the "efficacious powers of particular material configurations."[67] This turn underscores the intimate and intricate relationships between humans and non-human matter, which shape and constrain subjectivity and collective agency.

Theorizing the relationship between human and non-human matter is complicated by the situation wherein bodies in Aamjiwnaang cannot escape exposure to the vibrant matter of toxins. By discussing the dangerous effects of toxins affecting the reproductive body, this material discussion highlights how bodies are porous, resistant, plural, and connected. As such, it troubles and deconstructs a rigid nature/culture divide.[68] Noting the ways in which contaminants act on bodies, my aim is to broaden the scope of what constitutes the grounds for reproductive justice theory while also being geopolitically situated, local, relational, and place-specific.[69] Policy makers within Lambton County would benefit significantly from this place-based approach to the problem of ongoing environmental reproductive injustice.

Asking What Matters

The ongoing reproductive health concerns in Aamjiwnaang highlight how bodies are more than surfaces or performative sites. Their experiences are physical and cultural and merit an inquiry into the parameters of how we come to understand environmental reproductive justice in particular, and environmental justice broadly speaking. Citizens in Aamjiwnaang do not simply have the *choice* to reproduce in culturally safe and appropriate ways when they reside in a compromised environment. The environmental reproductive justice lens presented here to examine ongoing injustices seeks to make everyday experiences visible, while acknowledging that the body is not a blank slate for discursive inscription. As a carrier of local knowledge, and a producer of corporeal meaning, bodies are profound political forces. They are material and immaterial, combining matter and sense.

Reframing reproductive justice weaves together everyday experiences with broader national and global processes of environmental injustice.

Finally, it is important to reiterate that advancing environmental reproductive justice entails discursive and structural dimensions. As a matter of procedural justice, this involves shifting away the burden of responsibility from citizens to ask how our institutions can appropriately respond. In the Canadian context, this raises questions about jurisdiction and responsibilities. As deliberations within the LCHS revealed, the procedural and distributive issues of funding, federal–provincial jurisdictional responsibility, resource allocation, and fiduciary responsibility for on-reserve health led to a structural power imbalance in the community's struggles for recognition and redress, signifying the limits of a deliberative approach to justice. According to Aamjiwnaang's environmental officer Sharilyn Johnston, the community is looking to the regulators; "they're the ones who are allowing these standards that reduce pollution among our people."[70] A continuous challenge is determining who has legal and administrative responsibilities for the policy assemblage of on-reserve environmental health, leaving Indigenous citizens in jurisdictional limbo. To move these struggles forward in pursuit of justice, a reproductive health policy approach that is attuned to place is a crucial starting point for democratizing and decolonizing policy. Structurally and discursively, this requires making space for local voices and situated bodies of knowledge in decision-making processes.

Going forward, grounding situated discourses in ongoing policy deliberations is critical for environmental reproductive justice. This underscores an emphasis on local capacity and the involvement of communities themselves as agents for meaningful engagement and dialogue.[71] To ensure such dialogue, emphasizing a policy framework that accounts for local, experiential situated knowledge is a critical preliminary conceptual intervention on inequitable systemic political processes. Specifically, in practice, environmental reproductive justice must encourage citizen input from diverse backgrounds, highlight local expertise, and engage grassroots communities through action-based research in pursuit of collaboratively designed solutions. In this context, it is imperative to develop policy directions where it is Indigenous peoples who identify and implement the solutions.[72] Accessing diverse knowledges through a participatory process to create a kind of participatory policy approach to knowledge production will lead to the democratization and decolonization of expertise while inviting in a wider range of voices and experiences. This requires policy makers across global and local scales to emphasize locality and the specificity of knowledge in order to respectfully and reciprocally pursue pathways towards justice.

Notes

1 Benjamin Shingler, "Ontario First Nation Exposed to High Level of Pollutants, Study Finds," *Globe and Mail*, November 24, 2013, http://www.theglobeandmail.com/news/national/ontario-first-nation-exposed-to-high-levels-of-pollutants-study-finds/article15577533/.

2 See Laura Briggs, Faye Ginsburg, Elena R. Gutiérrez, Rosalind Petchesky, Rayna Rapp, Andrea Smith, and Chikako Takeshita, "Roundtable: Reproductive Technologies and Reproductive Justice," *Frontiers* 24, 3 (2013): 102. See also Greta Gaard, "An Ecofeminist, Environmental Justice Perspective on the Rhetoric of Choice," *Ethics and the Environment* 15, 2 (2010): 103–29.

3 Loretta Ross, "What Is Reproductive Justice?" The Pro-choice Public Education Project, http://www.protectchoice.org/section.php?id=28; SisterSong, "What Is RJ?" Women of Colour Reproductive Justice Collective, 2015, http://www.sistersong.net/.

4 SisterSong, "What Is RJ?"

5 Ross, "What Is Reproductive Justice?"

6 Native Youth Sexual Health Network (NYSHN), "Environmental Violence and Reproductive Justice," Native Youth Sexual Health Network, accessed April 16, 2015, http://www.nativeyouthsexualhealth.com/environmentalviolenceandreproductivejustice.html.

7 For an overview of the scope and breadth of abortion debates in Canada, see the Aboriginal Rights Coalition of Canada (ARCC), http://www.arcc-cdac.ca/home.html, and the Pro-Choice Action Network, http://www.prochoiceactionnetwork-canada.org/aboutus/aboutus.shtml. To carry out their mandates, these networks seek to build a broad-based political movement that promotes public education on the right to choice on abortion, supports the establishment of mutually beneficial relationships between clinics, hospitals, physicians, health care workers, women's groups, pro-choice groups, and other groups who further the right to choose. In their political work, these groups advocate for government funding of health services related to reproductive health in community-based clinics and hospitals, including surgical and medical abortion services and the defeat of any law that criminalizes women's access to abortion services. In British Columbia, the Pro-Choice Action Network seeks to see the implementation of the *Access to Abortion Services Act* to promote women's access to services within an atmosphere of dignity and respect. These networks adhere to the principles outlined in the 1998 *Canada Health Act* and promote federally guaranteed access to abortion in all regions of Canada. For an in-depth examination of contemporary abortion debates in Canada, see Paul Saurette and Kelly Gordon, "Arguing Abortion: The New Anti-abortion Discourse in Canada," *Canadian Journal of Political Science* 46, 1 (2013): 157–85; see also Rachael Johnstone, this volume. Further discussion of abortion debates in a global context appears in "Contraception and Abortion: Not a Matter of Choice," special issue, *Global Public Health* 6 (2011).

8 Elizabeth Hoover, Ron Plain, Katsi Cook, Kathy Sanchez, Vi Waghiyi, Pamela Miller, Renee Dufault, Caitlin Sislin, and David Carpenter, "Indigenous Peoples of North America: Environmental Exposures and Reproductive Justice," *Environmental Health Perspectives* 120, 12 (2012): 1645–49.

9 Olena Hankivsky, ed., *Health Inequities in Canada: Intersectional Frameworks and Practices* (Vancouver: UBC Press, 2011); Olena Hankivsky, ed., *An Intersectionality-Based Policy*

Analysis Framework (Vancouver: Institute for Intersectionality Research and Policy, Simon Fraser University, 2012).

10 Jane Bennett, *Vibrant Matter: A Political Ecology of Things* (Durham, NC: Duke University Press, 2010), viii.

11 Ann Pellegrini and Jasbir Puar, "Affect," *Social Text 100* 27, 3 (2009): 35–38.

12 Ecojustice, *Exposing Canada's Chemical Valley* (Toronto: Ecojustice, 2007). In addition to textual analysis, the methodology employed in research for this essay included participant observation during the LCHS town hall meetings in the fall of 2010, preceding a year-long period of field immersion in the Chemical Valley, from January to December 2011. The latter included attending monthly Board meetings as an observer. Upon invitation and with consent, immersion also included attending open houses, events, and gatherings in Aamjiwnaang. After viewing a CBC documentary, *The Disappearing Male*, I began a research assistant position that led me to work with Indigenous youth in Aamjiwnaang on a 'PhotoVoice' project. Sarah Flicker, Beth Savan, Brian Kolenda and Matto Mildenberger, "A Snapshot of Community-Based Research in Canada: Who? What? Why? How?" *Health Education Research* 23, 1 (2008): 106–14; Dayna Scott and Adrian Smith, "The Green Teens of Aamjiwnaang Make the Connection," *Canadian Dimension* 6, 1 (2012): 20–21. During my field research, I lived in Sarnia and continued volunteering with the Aamjiwnaang Green Teens as an informal adviser while building trust and rapport with community members. Together, we co-produced a documentary film, *Indian Givers,* publicly available online. See Indian Givers, *Kiijig Collective*, 2012, http://www.youtube.com/watch?v=pot411GJzdM. My continued involvement with the community includes collaborating with local and international artists on various visual media projects to document concerns and draw these into focus.

13 Isaac Luginaah, Kevin Smith, and Ada Lockridge, "Surrounded by Chemical Valley and 'Living in a Bubble': The Case of the Aamjiwnaang First Nation, Ontario," *Journal of Environmental Planning and Management* 53, 3 (2010): 353–70; Sarah Marie Wiebe and Erin Marie Konsmo, "Indigenous Body as Contaminated Site? Examining Reproductive Justice in Aamjiwnaang," in *Fertile Ground: Exploring Reproduction in Canada,* ed. Francesca Scala, Stephanie Paterson, and Marlene Sokolon (Montreal and Kingston: McGill-Queen's University Press, 2014), 325–58.

14 Luginaah, Smith, and Lockridge, "Surrounded by Chemical Valley," 353.

15 Further details about ongoing, cumulative impacts to the Aamjiwnaang First Nation's territory, ecosystems health, and culture are documented in the community's Traditional Land Use Study findings. For details, see Aamjiwnaang Environment Department, "Traditional Land Use Study: An Aamjiwnaang First Nation Perspective," http://www.thamesrevival.ca/wp-content/uploads/2014/12/TraditionalLandUse-SJohnston.pdf.

16 The ground itself is not monolithic. Following David Schlosberg, different discourses of justice correspond with multiple experiences and articulations of injustice, which inform how the concept of *on the ground* is used, understood, articulated, and demanded in practice. See David Schlosberg, "Theorizing Environmental Politics: Expanding the Sphere of a Discourse," *Environmental Politics* 22, 1 (2013): 37–55. Engaging with articulations of on the ground thus adds considerably to the study of the discursive dimensions of justice. In the analysis presented here, the ground, materially and post-materially, is in question. This article is thus intended to produce an innovative way of thinking about the ground in theory and practice, at the nexus of affect, corporeality, and environmental politics.

17 Ben Anderson and John Wylie, "On Geography and Materiality," *Environment and Planning A* 41 (2009): 318–35.

18 Hoover et al., "Indigenous Peoples of North America," 15; SisterSong, "What Is RJ?"

19 Brian Bienkowski, "Contaminated Tribe: Hormone-Blocking Chemicals Found in First Nation Families," *Environmental Health News,* November 11, 2013, http://www.environmentalhealthnews.org/ehs/news/2013/contaminated-tribe; Ecojustice, *Exposing Canada's Chemical Valley.*

20 Sharilyn Johnston, Environmental Officer, Aamjiwnaang First Nation, quoted in Bienkowski, "Contaminated Tribe."

21 Rita Dhamoon, "Considerations on Mainstreaming Intersectionality," *Political Research Quarterly* 64, 1 (2011): 230–43; Hankivsky, *Health Inequities in Canada,* 212; Mary Hawkesworth, *Feminist Inquiry: From Political Conviction to Methodological Innovation* (London: Rutgers University Press, 2006); Jessica Yee, *Feminism for Real: Deconstructing the Academic Industrial Complex for Feminism* (Ottawa: Canadian Centre for Policy Alternatives, 2011).

22 Native Youth Sexual Health Network, "NYSHN Statement to National Energy Board Regarding Line 9 Proposal," statements and press releases, October 18, 2013, http://www.nativeyouthsexualhealth.com/october182013.pdf, 2.

23 Ibid.

24 Ibid., 3.

25 Dayna Scott, "'Gender-Benders': Sex and Law in the Constitution of Polluted Bodies," *Feminist Legal Studies* 17, 3 (2009): 247.

26 CBC Radio, *The Disappearing Male,* October 23, 2008, http://www.cbc.ca/player/Shows/Doc+Zone/ID/1233750780/; Constanze Mackenzie, Ada Lockridge, and Margaret Keith, "Declining Sex Ratio in a First Nation Community," *Environmental Health Perspectives* 113, 10 (2010): 1295–98.

27 Rob Nixon, *Slow Violence and Environmentalism of the Poor* (Cambridge, MA: Harvard University Press, 2013).

28 Steve Lerner, *Sacrifice Zones* (Cambridge, MA: MIT Press, 2010).

29 Sarah Marie Wiebe, *Everyday Exposure: Indigenous Mobilization and Environmental Justice in Canada's Chemical Valley* (Vancouver: UBC Press, 2016).

30 CBC Radio, *The Disappearing Male;* Barri Cohen, dir., *Toxic Trespass,* documentary, 2007, http://www.cinemapolitica.org/film/toxic-trespass; LCHS, Lambton Community Health Study, http://www.lambtonhealthstudy.ca; Martin Mittelstaedt, "Pollution Debate Born of Chemical Valley's Girl-Baby Boom," *Globe and Mail,* November 15, 2005; Martin Mittlestaedt, "Where the Boys Aren't," *Globe and Mail,* July 31, 2004.

31 An article from the *London Free Press* noted that, with limited funding available to move into the third phase, community members are considering turning to industry or the province for funds. See Cathy Dobson, "Politicians Question If Industry Should Invest," *London Free Press,* April 17, 2013. The Lambton Community Health Study has debated at length the issue of who should fund the study, with suggestions, including local businesses, provincial authorities, and Federal authorities. As Dobson writes, the *Ontario Health Study,* "one of the world's most ambitious health studies," is a voluntary province-wide study seeking to assess population health; however, Sarnia and Lambton County are not listed as priority communities within the study. Carly Weeks, "Are You Ready? Massive Ontario Health Study Begins Second phase," *Globe and Mail,* November 29, 2012.

32 Anonymous community member comment, personal correspondence, May 10, 2015.

33 As noted by Nil Basu and his colleagues, "The industrial facilities surrounding Aamjiwnaang are primarily involved in the petrochemical, polymer, and chemical manufacturing sectors. In 2009 these facilities collectively released more than 110 million kilograms of pollution into the air. About 60% of these releases occurred within 5 km of Aamjiwnaang. The released chemicals are complex mixtures of metals (e.g., mercury, lead, cadmium, manganese,

aluminum), volatile and persistent organics (e.g., benzene, polycyclic aromatic hydrocarbons), and dust and particulate matter. Emerging chemicals of concern (e.g., brominated flame retardants, perfluorinated chemicals) also exist in the region. *All these chemicals are potent neurotoxicants, carcinogens, and/or endocrine disruptors* [my italics]." Moreover, Basu and his colleagues explain the biomarker approach used in their study: "Despite a strong belief that chronic exposures to toxic chemicals impacts health and causes persistent uneasiness in Aamjiwnaang, and surrounding areas, little is known about direct human exposures. As such, the current community-based study was conducted to assess exposures to various chemical pollutants. Using a scientific biomarker approach chemical pollutants were analytically measured in blood, urine, and hair samples from participating individuals." Nil Basu, Diana Cryderman, Fiona Miller, Sharilyn Johnston, Christine Rogers, and Wilson Plain, *Multiple Chemical Exposure Assessment at Aamjiwnaang, McGill Environmental Health Sciences Lab Occasional Report 2013–1*, 3.

34 Ibid.

35 Ulrich Beck, *Risk Society: Towards a New Modernity* (London: Sage, 1992); Robert Bullard, *Confronting Environmental Racism: Voices from the Grassroots* (Boston, MA: South End Press, 1993); Luke Cole and Sheila Foster, *From the Ground Up: Environmental Racism and the Rise of the Environmental Justice Movement* (New York: New York University Press, 2001); Schlosberg, "Theorizing Environmental Politics."

36 Schlosberg, "Theorizing Environmental Politics," 38; Julian Agyeman, Peter Cole, Randolph Haluza-Delay, and Pat O'Riley, eds., *Speaking for Ourselves: Environmental Justice in Canada* (Vancouver: UBC Press, 2009).

37 Alex Sager, "The Implications of Migration Theory for Distributive Justice," *Global Justice: Theory, Practice, Rhetoric* 5 (2012): 58.

38 Ibid., 59.

39 United Church of Christ, *Toxins, Waste and Race,* 1987, https://www.nrc.gov/docs/ML1310/ML13109A339.pdf.

40 Scholsberg, "Theorizing Environmental Politics," 39.

41 Ecojustice, *Exposing Canada's Chemical Valley.*

42 Wiebe, "Everyday Exposure," 2016.

43 Schlosberg, "Theorizing Environmental Politics," 40.

44 Beck, *Risk Society,* 36.

45 John Dryzek, *Deliberative Democracy and Beyond: Liberals, Critics, Contestations* (Oxford: Oxford University Press, 2000); Frank Fischer, "Deliberative Policy Analysis as Practical Reason: Integrating Empirical and Normative Arguments," in *Handbook of Public Policy Analysis,* ed. Frank Fischer, Gerald J. Miller, and Mara Sidney (Boca Raton, FL: CRC Press, 2007), 223–36; Frank Fischer, *Reframing Public Policy* (Oxford: Oxford University Press, 2003); Frank Fischer and John Forrester, *The Argumentative Turn in Policy Analysis and Planning* (Durham, NC: Duke University Press, 1993).

46 Chantal Mouffe, *The Democratic Paradox* (London: Verso, 2005).

47 Schlosberg, "Theorizing Environmental Poltics,"43.

48 David Bissell, "Passenger Mobilities: Affective Atmospheres and the Sociality of Public Transport," *Environment and Planning D: Society and Space* 28, 2 (2010): 272.

49 Anderson and Wylie, "On Geography and Materiality," 78.

50 Ibid., 77.

51 Bissell, "Passenger Mobilities," 284.

52 Anderson and Wylie, "On Geography and Materiality," 78.

53 Scott, "'Gender-Benders," 246–47.

54 Elizabeth Grosz, *Volatile Bodies: Toward a Corporeal Feminism* (Bloomington: Indiana University Press, 1994); Gilles Deleuze and Felix Guattari, *A Thousand Plateaus: Schizophrenia*

and Capitalism (Minneapolis: University of Minnesota Press, 1987), 256; Scott, "Gender-Benders."

55 Lorraine Dowler and Joanne Sharp, "A Feminist Geopolitics?" *Space and Polity* 5, 3 (2001): 167.

56 Grosz, *Volatile Bodies.*

57 Teena Gabrielson and Katelyn Parady, "Corporeal Citizenship: Rethinking Green Citizenship through the Body," *Environmental Politics* 19, 3 (2010): 380.

58 Ibid., 382.

59 Donna Haraway, "Situated Knowledges: The Science Question and the Privilege of Partial Perspective," *Feminist Studies* 14, 3 (1988): 575–99.

60 Andrew Pickering, cited in Gabrielson and Parady, "Corporeal Citizenship," 383.

61 Gabrielson and Parady, "Corporeal Citizenship," 384.

62 Bennett, *Vibrant Matter,* 120.

63 Quoted in Basu et al., *Multiple Chemical Exposure.*

64 Sharilyn Johnston, Environmental Officer, Aamjiwnaang First Nation, quoted in Bienkowski, "Contaminated Tribe."

65 Ecojustice, *Exposing Canada's Chemical Valley.*

66 Bennett, *Vibrant Matter.*

67 Ibid., ix.

68 Gabrielson and Parady, "Corporeal Citizenship."

69 Scott, "Gender-Benders," 261.

70 Bienkowski, "Contaminated Tribe."

71 Daniel Wilson and David Macdonald, *The Income Gap between Aboriginal Peoples and the Rest of Canada* (Ottawa: Canadian Centre for Policy Alternatives, 2010).

72 Ibid.

Conclusion

Kristin Burnett and Shannon Stettner

In 1985, a Canadian journalist described abortion as "the issue that won't go away."[1] Thirty years later, this statement remains true. Although a generation of women have grown up since the 1988 Supreme Court decision removed federal restrictions on abortion, unequal access to safe abortion on request across Canada ensures that abortion continues to be a central pillar in the slate of issues linked to women's equality and status. For many women, abortion remains taboo – full of stigma and personal shame – and even today very few people talk about or admit to having made "the choice." Much of this silence is tied to fallacious beliefs about the success of medical science in guaranteeing the ability of individual women to control their fertility and moral judgments about personal bodily and social responsibility. This pervasive silence affords abortion opponents continued strength. The chapters in this collection, while offering fresh insight into the histories and politics of abortion in Canada, also suggest new ways of moving forward and lenses through which to examine the issue. Legal access to abortion is the least of what we should be fighting for, and essays like those in the final section of this book show us how much farther we need to go.

Studying Abortion

The essays in the section "History" make important contributions to our understandings of abortion history. Kristin Burnett reminds us that, although we often examine abortion in isolation, or as an act and choice that is highly individualized, in truth it is interwoven into many aspects of the lives of women and their communities. Drawing on colonial and critical race theory, Burnett shows how "non-Indigenous scholars have rarely seen Indigenous reproductive knowledges *as knowledge,* and in this way often fail to see these practices as sites of learning and areas fit for scholarly inquiry." She also reminds us that there is much still to learn. Rebecca Beausaert's work likewise touches on a rarely examined topic in the history of abortion – its place in African Canadian communities during the nineteenth century. Her piece is an important reminder of how invisible race has been until very recently in abortion histories in Canada. Beausaert's study of the social construction of race, gender, justice, rumour, and respectability moves abortion history into new areas, complicating the dominant narratives. Erika Dyck's chapter examines the response of Catholics, both clergy and lay members, in western Canada to a modernizing society and the desire of Canadian Catholic women to employ effective contraception. Dyck's work has begun to flesh out religious ideas, specifically those understandings held by women, in relation to abortion, which has been understudied thus far in Canadian abortion history. Together, these essays offer new ways of exploring the historical meanings of abortion and birth control in the geographic area that came to be known as Canada.

Legal scholar Shelley A.M. Gavigan once reminded us that "the history of restrictive abortion legislation is also the history of women's resistance to it."[2] The chapters in the second section, "Experience," illuminate the complexities of women's experiences in relation to and beyond the legislation of abortion. By centring women's experiences and women's voices, these chapters help to correct a historiography that has, for too long, been concerned with the legal status of abortion and not with the impact that inaccessibility has had on women's everyday lives. Shannon Stettner's chapter centres women's voices during the 1960s, which was a critical decade for discussions about abortion law reform. Her work shows the transformative power that sharing abortion stories can have for women and how the retelling of their reproductive struggles shaped the final report of the Royal Commission on the Status of Women (RCSW), which called for abortion on request during the first twelve weeks of pregnancy.[3] This eagerness to be heard and to shape abortion law continued after the 1969 law changes, as Beth Palmer's contribution demonstrates. Like women who shared their stories with the RCSW, Palmer illustrates the power of publicly sharing abortion experiences. In the two decades leading up to the 1988 Supreme Court decision, feminist activists worked to make abortion part of the public dialogue, while, simultaneously, the anti-abortion movement increasingly worked to stigmatize abortion, representing it as an unspeakable act. Consequently, women are much less likely to share their abortion experiences in a public forum today. Palmer's work encourages activists to recentre the sharing of abortion experiences in political activism.

Katrina Ackerman's chapter examines how the stigmatization experienced by women seeking abortion is further complicated when they reside in small, tight-knit, rural communities that are dominated by anti-abortion sentiments. Ackerman's work helps to flesh out how abortion politics played out in the Maritime provinces where abortion is harder to access and the anti-abortion movement is extremely vocal. Feminist scholars are also exploring the contemporary politics and the experiences of women who access abortions in Canada. The decision of academics to pursue abortion research has not always been an easy one. The chapter by Marion Doull, Christabelle Sethna, Evelyne Morrissette, and Caitlin Scott outlines some of the costs of studying abortion, especially when women's efforts to access abortion are complicated by distance, a lack of resources, and negative attitudes. Their findings are important to future studies and suggest that abortion remains a taboo topic in many arenas of Canadian society, even those believed to be more progressive. Women struggle to assert control over both the embodied experiences of having abortions but also the meaning and knowledge produced about those experiences.

The four chapters in the section "Politics" look at how the 1988 Supreme Court decision has affected the ability of women to access abortion services across the country. Frances Chapman and Tracy Penny Light weave together an analysis of the legal provisions governing abortion with historical examples of its inaccessibility despite the lack of a federal abortion law. Their essay ends by borrowing from the work of philosopher Shannon Dea and calling for the recentring of the abortion framework from a focus on the right to an abortion to a harm reduction model in order to bridge the gap between opposing sides. In the next two chapters, Jen Rinaldi and Rachael Johnstone examine the implications of the *Morgentaler* decision's grounding in section 7 of the *Canadian Charter of Rights and Freedoms'* right to security of the person. In particular, both illuminate the complications that arise from viewing abortion as a private health care decision between a woman and her physician. Rinaldi especially draws our attention to the ways in which the medicalization of pregnancy and technological advances have eroded perceptions of women's bodily autonomy, while Johnstone fleshes out the grounds for a stronger claim to abortion rights. Finally, the section ends with a comparative study of abortion access in Prince Edward Island and Mississippi to show how federal regulations in Canada and the United States have both been subverted at the provincial and state levels as well as by actors outside of the government. Such transnational comparisons as this one by J. Shoshanna Ehrlich, Lori Brown, and Colleen MacQuarrie are important, especially when, internationally, Canada is considered to be a liberal state when it comes to abortion laws. As their analysis shows, reproductive oppression of women in both locations "is what constitutional subversion looks like on the ground in a federalist system where national articulations of rights do not necessarily translate into meaningful reproductive control for women."

In the final section, "Discourse and Reproductive Justice," the authors employ a reproductive justice framework and illuminate new ways forward for abortion studies and activism. Picking up on the implications of new rhetorical strategies like "abortion harms women," used by the anti-abortion movement, Kelly Gordon and Paul Saurette argue that the pro-choice movement in Canada needs to adapt its discursive strategies to combat new anti-abortion tactics. To that end, they examine the applicability of a reproductive justice framework in Canada, and suggest ways to reframe the abortion debate. Picking up the challenge to look at and consider abortion in a new light, Laura Salamanca suggests that we need to do a better job of looking at how women experience reproductive choices differently depending on their identity and social location. Using an ethnographic approach for her study of immigrant women's abortion experiences, Salamanca illuminates the need to look at women as not simply autonomous and self-interested but rather as subjects with "historical embeddedness in social contexts." Salamanca's work highlights how focusing solely on abortion ignores the complex and multi-faceted terrain of women's lives and identities.

Finally, Sarah Marie Wiebe's chapter is an exciting contribution not only to this collection, but to future studies about women's reproductive lives. Incorporating an evaluation of environmental impacts and harms within the concept of reproductive justice, Wiebe shows us one way to move "beyond the instrumental language of rights and choice to provide access to pathways for self-determination and cultural vitality." She challenges us to reconsider what we envision as part of the spectrum of women's reproductive health issues and reminds us that definitions of reproductive freedom have diverse meanings depending on one's location and identity. Wiebe illustrates how complicated constellations of access, choice, and justice can be; for the Aamjiwnaang First Nation, reproductive autonomy has very little to do with access to abortion on request and instead centres on the right of the community to exist and be well. Thus, the demands and strategies employed in this context look very different from the efforts of many of those who organize to guarantee that an abortion clinic remains open and access to it is equitable. Wiebe's work forces us to consider that women do not live compartmentalized lives and that it is only by embedding women's need for and recourse to abortion within broader social, political, cultural, and environmental contexts that we can fully overcome reproductive oppressions and move towards reproductive justice.

Moving Forward: A Call to Action

The contributions to this volume demonstrate just how vigorous and rich the study of abortion history and politics in Canada has become. Nevertheless, much remains to be examined and accomplished in regard to women's equality and reproductive choices. Our historical understanding of the reproductive lives of Indigenous peoples in what is now called Canada is incomplete. The same can be said for racialized, immigrant, and refugee women – as well as trans-identified people – all of whom have faced different challenges in their efforts to achieve reproductive control and autonomy and whose stories remain relatively unexamined within Canadian reproductive historiography. There is much work to be done to include settler colonialism and critical race theory into the study of abortion and women's reproductive lives. As Salamanca reminds us, "We have only just begun to grapple academically with processes of migration and adjustment, and the ways in which they may complicate women's reproductive lives." The adoption of a reproductive justice framework offers researchers the ability to contextualize abortion into women's reproductive lives more fully. As well, although contributions in the collection begin to complicate our understandings of the anti-abortion movement both historically and at present, further work needs to be done. While Saurette and Gordon ask us to reconsider the dominant messages and discursive strategies of the leaders of these groups, we must also continue to work towards a better understanding of the core membership of such groups and their motivations. Thinking historically, there is much to be considered and reconsidered in the existing abortion historiography. While emerging scholars are re-examining the decades of the 1960s and 1970s, our understandings of abortion in the 1950s and earlier remains incomplete and examination of abortion politics in the 1980s also requires further reconsideration

This collection has been driven by a need to evaluate abortion politics and the study of abortion in a post-*Morgentaler* era. The downfall of focusing on the success of the 1988 Supreme Court decision is that it has allowed the majority of Canadians to believe that the struggle for abortion access is over. Many, for example, view the closing of the sole abortion clinic that took place in New Brunswick following Morgentaler's death as an aberration instead of business as usual. At the federal level, largely unbeknownst to most Canadians, there have been no fewer than forty-two attempts to introduce anti-abortion bills in the House of Commons since 1988.[4] Instead of attacking women's right to access abortion specifically, many anti-abortion politicians, activists, and organizations have, as Gordon and Saurette illustrate, shifted their tactics away from fetal rights and instead framed the issue around the protection of women more generally. In the provinces and territories, access to abortion remains tenuous at best, especially in rural and northern regions.[5]

Responses to access challenges in PEI and New Brunswick, however, give us hope as they show that there is a new and social media savvy generation of abortion rights activists that are entering the scene, building on more than a decade of Internet activism by many pro-choice organizations in Canada.[6] Many of these activists are enthusiastically adopting the reproductive justice framework in Canada, inspired by the activism and leadership of people like Jessica Danforth and the Native Youth Sexual Health Network.[7] Social media has opened new avenues for discussion and connection between abortion advocates, as well as new methods to shape the terrain of Canadian politics and elections, as we saw in New Brunswick in 2014 when online activism not only made abortion an issue in the fall provincial election, but also saw fundraising of more than $100,000 towards reopening the province's sole abortion clinic.[8] Unfortunately, what this has also shown is that women continue to have to stand at the barricades to protect abortion and this limits our ability to make broader and deeper economic, social, and political changes in women's lives that demonstrably improve the well-being of families and communities. The

October 19, 2015 federal election saw a majority win for Justin Trudeau's Liberal Party. During Trudeau's campaign, he indicated that it was necessary for all Liberal candidates to be pro-choice and he has, since becoming prime minister, repeatedly referred to himself as a feminist. Whether his political stance and self-identification will be operationalized into ensuring that women not only have unfettered access to abortion, but also the resources to make meaningful choices, remains to be seen. But as of late 2017, two years into Trudeau's mandate, the status of access – and of women more generally – remains largely unchanged.

Notes

1 Anne Collins, *The Big Evasion: Abortion, the Issue That Won't Go Away* (Toronto: Lester and Orpen Dennys, 1985).

2 Shelley A.M. Gavigan, "On 'Bringing on the Menses': The Criminal Liability of Women and the Therapeutic Exception in Canadian Abortion Law," *Canadian Journal of Women and the Law* 1, 2 (1986): 284.

3 *Report of the Royal Commission on the Status of Women in Canada* (Ottawa: Information Canada, 1970), 286.

4 Abortion Rights Coalition of Canada, "Position Paper #51: Free Votes, Private Members' Bills, and Abortion," accessed June 12, 2015, http://www.arcc-cdac.ca/politics.html.

5 Christabelle Sethna and Marion Doull, "Spatial Disparities and Travel to Freestanding Abortion Clinics in Canada," *Women's Studies International Forum* 38 (2013): 52–62.

6 Lianne McTavish, "Virtual Activism and the Pro-choice Movement in Canada," *Canadian Woman Studies* 25, 3 (2006): 121–26.

7 Jessica Yee, "Reproductive Justice – For Real, For Me, For You, For Now," http://www.nativeyouthsexualhealth.com/reproductivejustice.pdf.

8 Jane Taber, "Incoming New Brunswick Premier Moves to Remove Barriers to Abortion" *Globe and Mail,* September 24, 2014, http://www.theglobeandmail.com/news/politics/incoming-new-brunswick-premier-moves-to-remove-barriers-to-abortion/article20781406/.

Contributors

Katrina Ackerman is a SSHRC postdoctoral fellow at the University of Regina. She completed her PhD at the University of Waterloo and has published articles on abortion and reproductive rights activism in several peer-reviewed journals. Her broader research project investigates the emergence and longevity of social movement organizations and their impact on abortion barriers that continue to shape access to the procedure in Atlantic Canada.

Rebecca Beausaert is an adjunct professor in the Department of History at the University of Guelph. Her research interests include food, leisure, and gender in late nineteenth- and early twentieth-century rural and small-town Ontario. Her doctoral dissertation, which examined the importance and proliferation of leisure activities for women in three small Ontario communities between the years 1870 and 1914, is currently being prepared for publication.

Lori Brown is a professor at the Syracuse University School of Architecture. Her work is grounded in the belief that architecture can participate in and impact people's everyday lives.

Kristin Burnett is an associate professor in the Department of Indigenous Learning and the graduate coordinator of the Social Justice Studies program at Lakehead University.

Frances E. Chapman is an associate professor in the Bora Laskin Faculty of Law at Lakehead University. Her areas of interest are in criminal law and defences, including brainwashing, automatism, duress, necessity, and mental disorder. She focuses particularly on false confessions, wrongful convictions, violence against women, and domestic violence.

Marion Doull has a PhD in population health. Her research focuses on adolescent sexual health, particularly the ways in which sex/gender, equity, and power intersect to affect sexual health outcomes. She is also a founding member of the Sex/Gender Methods Group, part of the Cochrane and Campbell Equity Methods Group, which focuses on the application of sex/gender analysis to systematic reviews.

Erika Dyck is Canada Research Chair in History of Medicine and a professor in the Department of History at the University of Saskatchewan. Her books include *Psychedelic Psychiatry: LSD on the Canadian Prairies*; *Facing Eugenics: Reproduction, Sterilization, and the Politics of Choice*; and *Managing Madness: Weyburn Mental Hospital and the Transformation of Psychiatric Care in Canada*.

J. Shoshanna Ehrlich is a professor in the Women's and Gender Studies Department at the University of Massachusetts Boston. Her interdisciplinary scholarship focuses on the sexual and reproductive rights of young women and abortion law. Her books include *Who Decides? The Abortion Rights of Minors*; *Regulating Desire: From the Virtuous Maiden to the Purity Princess*; a family law textbook; and a forthcoming co-authored monograph on current attacks on abortion rights in the name of protecting women from regret.

Kelly Gordon is an assistant professor in the Political Science Department at McGill University. Her research focuses on the anti-abortion movements in Canada and the United States and their organizational structure, discourse, and strategies of persuasion and activism. Her work also examines the role of gender in Canadian politics more largely, particularly in conservative movements across Canada.

Travis Hay is a doctoral candidate in the Department of History at York University. His research focuses on the colonial function of science in Canadian history as well as changes and continuities in federal Indian policy.

Rachael Johnstone is an assistant professor at the Bader International Studies Centre, Queen's University. She specializes in political studies and gender studies, with a particularly strong interest in the intersection of politics, law, and health care as they relate to gendered bodies. She has written extensively on the politics of abortion in Canada and her book, *After Morgentaler: The Politics of Abortion in Canada,* explores the regulation of abortion in Canada following *R v Morgentaler* (1988), the Supreme Court case that decriminalized the procedure in Canada.

Colleen MacQuarrie, an associate professor in and chair of the Department of Psychology at the University of Prince Edward Island, is an academic activist and developmental health researcher who has been working in feminist community organizations for more than twenty years. Critical perspectives on social justice are central to her research, teaching, and community actions.

Evelyne Morrissette has a master's degree in sociology from the University of Ottawa, where she studied social movements and the politics surrounding abortion. She is currently working at the federal government in policies and research.

Beth Palmer has a PhD in history from York University. Her research explores pro-choice activism in Canada from the 1969 omnibus bill that began decriminalizing abortion to the 1988 *Morgentaler* decision. Her work has been published in the *Canadian Historical Review* and *Labour/Le Travail.* She has worked in federal politics and in policy and advocacy for universities.

Tracy Penny Light is an associate professor of history at Thompson Rivers University. Her research explores how gender and sexuality are represented in and constructed by the medical profession and the media in nineteenth- and twentieth-century North America.

Jen Rinaldi is an assistant professor in the Legal Studies program at the University of Ontario Institute of Technology. She earned a doctoral degree in critical disability studies at York University, where she researched how disability diagnostic technologies affect reproductive decision making. Her current research employs narrative and arts-based methodologies to deconstruct eating disorder recovery and to reimagine recovery in relation to queer community. She also works in collaboration with Recounting Huronia, a SSHRC-funded arts-based collective that explores and stories traumatic histories of institutionalization.

Laura Salamanca is a community organizer and sexual health counsellor at a busy Toronto clinic. She has a master's degree in medical anthropology from the University of Toronto and is working on a holistic reproductive health practitioner designation. Laura contributes regularly to Action Canada for Sexual Health and Rights and MUJER, an advocacy organization for Latin American communities in Toronto.

Paul Saurette is an associate professor in the School of Political Studies at the University of Ottawa. His research focuses on the communication and organizational strategies of political movements, contemporary ideology, the role of emotion in politics, conservative and progressive movements, and international politics.

Caitlin Scott is a PhD candidate and SSHRC doctoral fellow at the University of Waterloo in the School of Environment, Resources and Sustainability. Her research explores the challenges of governing for sustainable diets, focusing on ideational debates and power. In addition to her research, Caitlin is the student coordinator for the Waterloo Food Issues Group, the administrator and treasurer for the Canadian Association of Food Studies, and a volunteer program analyst for the Regional Sustainability Initiative at Sustainable Waterloo Region.

Christabelle Sethna is a historian and full professor at the Institute of Feminist and Gender Studies. She researches and publishes in the history of sex education, contraception, and abortion. She received SSHRC funding for investigating Canadian women's travel to free-standing abortion clinics and, most recently, a five-year SSHRC grant to investigate women's international travel to access abortion services.

Shannon Stettner teaches in the Women's Studies Department at the University of Waterloo. Her research examines women's abortion rights activism and public opinion about abortion in Canada. She is the editor of *Without Apology: Writings on Abortion in Canada* and co-editor of *Transcending Borders: Abortion in the Past and Present.*

Sarah Marie Wiebe grew up on Coast Salish territory in British Columbia and now lives in Honolulu. She is an assistant professor in the Department of Political Science at the University of Hawai'i, Mānoa, where she focuses on environmental sustainability. Her book, *Everyday Exposure: Indigenous Mobilization and Environmental Justice in Canada's Chemical Valley*, won the Charles Taylor Book Award and examines policy responses to the impact of pollution on the Aamjiwnaang First Nation's environmental health. Alongside Jennifer Lawrence (Virginia Tech), she is the co-editor of *Biopolitical Disaster*. As a community-engaged researcher and filmmaker, she is currently collaborating with artists from Attawapiskat on a project titled "Reimagining Attawapiskat."

Index